ILLUSIONS OF CHOICE

Late in the program, [Defense officials] thought they could still control events. . . . They sustained the illusion that they could still choose.
—Air Force R&D official commenting on the F-111 program

ROBERT F. COULAM

Illusions of Choice

The F-111 and the Problem of Weapons
Acquisition Reform

PRINCETON UNIVERSITY PRESS

PRINCETON, NEW JERSEY

FOR
Wendy

CONTENTS

LIST OF FIGURES AND TABLES

AMC	Air Materiel Command, USAF
ARDC	Air Research and Development Command, USAF
Bu Weps	Bureau of Naval Weapons, USN
DOD	Department of Defense
DDR&E	Director of Defense Research and Engineering
FX	Fighter, Experimental
ICBM	Intercontinental Ballistic Missile
IRBM	Intermediate-Range Ballistic Missile
MRBM	Medium-Range Ballistic Missile
Mil-Specs	Standard Military Specifications
NACA	National Advisory Committee on Aeronautics
NASA	National Aeronautics and Space Administration
NASC	Naval Air Systems Command, USN
OSD	Office of the Secretary of Defense
RDT&E	Research, Development, Testing, and Evaluation contract
SAC	Strategic Air Command, USAF
SOR-183	Specific Operational Requirement Number 183
SACEUR	Supreme Allied Commander in Europe
SWIP	Super Weight Improvement Program
SPO	System Program Office, USAF
TAC	Tactical Air Command, USAF
TFX	Tactical Fighter, Experimental
USAF	United States Air Force
USN	United States Navy
VAX	Attack Aircraft, Experimental
VFAX	Fighter-Attack Aircraft, Experimental
VFX	Fighter Aircraft, Experimental
WIP	Weight Improvement Program

ACKNOWLEDGMENTS

This essay is the product of an effort which spanned four years. During this time, I have enjoyed the assistance and support of many individuals and organizations. I am pleased to have this opportunity to acknowledge their contributions.

My research was generously funded by the Research Seminar of the Institute of Politics at Harvard University. I have particularly appreciated the Institute's sustained support through what proved to be a prolonged period of writing. The Harvard-MIT Program on Science and International Affairs provided helpful support during one stage of revising the study. I want to thank Susan Ackerman and Jayne Berry, who edited successive versions of the manuscript, and Arlene Agree, Judy Randolph, and Suzanne Wire, who cheerfully translated my drafts into typed copy. In its Winter 1975 issue (Vol. 23, pp. 1–38), *Public Policy*, the quarterly journal, published an essay of the author's drawn from Chapter III. The journal has kindly granted permission for the use of that material in the present study.

I was aided in my research by the substantive contributions of two organizations. The General Dynamics Corporation—prime contractor for the F-111 program—offered me both hospitality and candor during my visit to the company's Fort Worth, Texas, facility. The Permanent Subcommittee on Investigations of the Senate Committee on Government Operations proved equally accommodating, as it gave me access to the extensive files of its investigation of the F-111 program. I owe these organizations a special thanks.

Many direct participants in the F-111 program were kind enough to grant me interviews. These individuals must unfortunately remain anonymous, as anonymity was a necessary ground rule for the interviews. These individuals are identified by their institutional role in the reference section of this book (see page 393). I am very much in their debt.

Robert Art, William Capron, Barry Carter, Philip Heymann, Arnold Kanter, Joseph Kruzel, James Kurth, Benjamin Lambeth, Mark Moore, James Reece, Anne Simon, Gregory Treverton, and John Weiss favored me with comments on earlier drafts of the study, as did Ernest May, former director of the Institute of Politics. Friends and summers' colleagues at the Rand Corporation—Arthur Alexander, Edmund Dews, Alvin Harman, Nancy Nimitz, and Robert Perry—have also favored me with comments on the essay. Francis Bator, David Mundel, and Harry Rowen made valuable comments on an earlier version of Chapter III. Roland Cole and Thomas Garwin were especially helpful in the comments they made and the good-humored encouragement they offered. John Crecine and Morton Halperin provided important criticisms of the essay's final drafts. Sanford Thatcher and Lewis Bateman of Princeton University Press have been very helpful, and great pleasures to work with, in bringing the manuscript to publication.

Frederic Morris provided substantive comments and much-needed moral support through each draft of the essay. Richard Neustadt has been more helpful than he knows in his advice and encouragement from the early days of this effort. Richard Smoke has been generous with his time and rigorous in his criticisms, far beyond what the author could reasonably have asked of him. His advice and encouragement have been crucial factors in the development of the argument that follows. Graham Allison, on whose work the study repeatedly draws, was of great assistance in the refinement of the conceptual argument. He has been an unfailing supporter and a particularly valued critic throughout the writing of this essay.

My greatest debt, however, is to John Steinbruner, who has been my kind teacher for many years. His teaching and writing inspired this study, and his insight lies behind any strengths it might have. Without his understanding and support, its completion would not have been possible.

Having been so fortunate in the assistance I received in preparing this study, I am realistically responsible for any failings in it that remain.

R.F.C.

Cambridge, Massachusetts
September 1975

ILLUSIONS OF CHOICE

The F-111A: The Original Air Force Version of the F-111 (Courtesy of the General Dynamics Corporation).

The world of defense procurement stretches across some 10 percent of U.S. production and whole hemispheres of geography, but its fortunes rise and fall with the moves and moods of its single customer in Washington. It has only begun to feel the impact of an epochal defense contract awarded four months ago, the first step in a $7 billion outlay for design and production of a fighter plane known as the TFX, or Tactical Fighter Experimental [later designated the F-111]. Nine airframe companies and three engine manufacturers were initially involved in the battle over this joint Air Force-Navy plane. . . . When it was over, General Dynamics-Grumman had won the airframe part of the contract (expected to reach $4.2 billion by 1970), Pratt & Whitney had run away with a potential billion-dollar order for the engines, and Defense Secretary Robert Strange McNamara had wrought a profound shift in what might be called the realpolitik, the working strategy, of U.S. weapon procurement.

—*Fortune*, March 1963[1]

In February 1961, after barely three weeks in office, Robert McNamara directed the Navy and Air Force to combine their separate plans for new tactical aircraft. *One* tactical fighter was to be developed to serve the needs of *both* services into the 1970s. It was a move without precedent. Never before had the services jointly developed a major weapon system. To no one's surprise, the services fought this attempt. But McNamara persevered. Ultimately, he succeeded in obtaining service acceptance of a joint devel-

[1] Richard Austin Smith, "The $7 Billion Contract That Changed the Rules," Part I, *Fortune*, Vol. 67 (March 1963), p. 96.

opment program for a common aircraft. As the F-111 program began, it was the symbol of a new order in defense management.

Yet many years later, as it drew to completion, the F-111 program was a symbol for the failures of that order. The Navy never procured or deployed its version of the aircraft, as the Navy version was cancelled in 1968, and the Navy was then allowed to develop its own tactical fighter, the F-14. The Air Force ultimately procured only one-third as many F-111s as originally planned and did so at twice the originally expected costs.[2] It, too, was soon allowed to develop its own tactical fighter, the F-15. By the end of the decade, then, the effort to achieve bi-service use of a single aircraft—to achieve "commonality"—had failed; and even for the Air Force, the service that did procure the plane, the F-111 was not the exclusive tactical fighter for the 1970s. What happened? Between the promise of the decisions in the early 1960s and the indications of failure at the end of the decade, what went wrong?

PURPOSE OF THE STUDY

This study attempts to explain the troubling results of the F-111 program. In it, we will examine the central development problems of the Air Force and Navy versions of the F-111 and will explore the reasons for cancellation of the

[2] Alvin J. Harman, assisted by Susan Henrichsen, *A Methodology For Cost Factor Comparison and Prediction*, Rand Memorandum No. RM-6269-ARPA (August 1970), pp. 53–56. This estimate of F-111 cost growth represents "real" growth. Calculated using widely acknowledged Rand estimation techniques, it adjusts nominal cost figures to account for price changes (inflation) and procurement quantity changes, among other things. In nominal terms, actual F-111 production costs were approximately three times original estimates, and actual R&D costs were four times original estimates. For estimates of nominal R&D and production expense, planned and actual, see U.S. Senate, Committee on Government Operations, Permanent Subcommittee on Investigations, *TFX Contract Investigation*, Report, 91st Cong., 1st Sess. (1970), p. 81 (this report hereafter cited as *TFX Report*).

Navy version. In this endeavor, we will reopen questions that were in the past a source of great controversy—to the Defense Department, to the Congress, and to the public. Our study will detail that controversy. More important, however, it will advance an argument that the passage of time appears to have confirmed: namely, that the very real problems of the F-111 development were essentially typical of the problems that have long plagued American weapon system programs. The TFX decisions of 1961 were thought to portend a revolution in weapons acquisition management. We will argue that in fact the 1960s were a time of striking continuity in major features of structure and behavior in the weapons acquisition process. The bi-service character of the F-111 program was unique and affected development efforts in ways our study will describe. Yet we also will attempt to show how central phenomena of the F-111 experience parallel the experience in other system developments of the postwar era. Indeed, we will argue that processes common to most Air Force developments of the postwar era were responsible for the unfortunate, though not unusual, results of the F-111 program.

Our study will reveal how McNamara and his associates in the F-111 program failed to understand and to anticipate the influence of these processes. While a bi-service program may have appeared desirable in terms of straightforward economic analysis, it was freighted with severe implementation difficulties. A far-flung bureaucratic network would exert substantial control over the actual development of the F-111. The calculations and procedures of this variegated network would importantly distort the bi-service option that McNamara and his associates conceived. The hopes invested in a bi-service program were ultimately overwhelmed by these influences—influences which McNamara and his associates could not realistically have prevented, but which they could broadly have foreseen. Had their conception of the defense management problem recognized the significance of such implementation problems, they might well have made different choices in the early years of the program. They might well have chosen more wisely.

Implementation problems have received increasing attention in the theoretical literature on organizations.[3] This literature provides a wealth of clues on what to look for and what to expect in analyzing complex organizational activities, like the F-111 program. It is a central proposition of this literature that the basic assumptions underlying most policy analyses conform to intuitive notions of rationality or purposive behavior.[4] The intellectual dominance of theories of rational choice, it is contended, importantly limits our understanding of complex decision processes. An alternative paradigm of the decision process has been formulated that departs from the logic of rational choice. This alternative paradigm—the *cybernetic paradigm*—emphasizes the routine pursuit of unintegrated, and often conflicting, goals by a highly fragmented decision process. The paradigm itself will be described in detail in Chapter I. It will provide us with a valuable framework of assumptions for understanding the implementation problems that McNamara and his associates failed to foresee. Indeed, we will argue that a full understanding of the implementation difficulties of the F-111 program requires the explicit adoption of the cybernetic paradigm as a supplemental framework for analysis. There is an analytically important similarity between the insights evoked by the cybernetic paradigm and the organizational characteristics ignored by McNamara and his associates. In this similarity, we will contend, lies an important foundation for a refined understanding of the weapons acquisition process.

[3] Graham T. Allison, *Essence of Decision: Explaining the Cuban Missile Crisis* (Boston: Little, Brown, 1971), chaps. 3, 4, and 7; and John D. Steinbruner, *The Cybernetic Theory of Decision: New Dimensions of Political Analysis* (Princeton: Princeton University Press, 1974), chaps. 1, 3, 4, and 10.

[4] Allison, *Essence of Decision*, Introduction and chap. 1; and Steinbruner, *Cybernetic Theory*, chaps. 1 and 2.

ORGANIZATION OF THE STUDY

The study begins in Chapter I with a summary statement of the theoretical premises that will guide our analysis of the F-111 program. This summary statement should prove sufficient to make our theoretical argument intelligible to the reader unfamiliar with the relevant theoretical literature. Our study is designed to be self-contained. Given the summary in Chapter I, the reader will find it unnecessary to detour into the theoretical literature in order to follow parts of our discussion (though that detour is a journey we highly recommend).

Chapter II provides an overview of the origins, development, and production of the F-111. It should give the reader a general background on the F-111 program, a substantive frame of reference for the far more detailed analytical chapters to follow.

The subsequent three chapters focus on the substantive puzzles raised by the overview in Chapter II. Chapter III focuses on the operational purposes—the missions—contemplated for the F-111 when McNamara instituted the program. McNamara arrived at the Pentagon hoping to redirect American force capabilities away from the heavy reliance on nuclear weapons which had characterized defense planning in the 1950s. He hoped greatly to expand America's non-nuclear capabilities. The F-111 was to be a major step in that direction, a true multi-purpose aircraft. Yet, in fact, the F-111's design emphasized demanding profiles for the delivery of nuclear weapons. The plane was, as a consequence, disappointingly limited in the range of capabilities it provided. The satisfaction of Navy goals in the program was made far more difficult. Our examination of this puzzle will reveal some of the critical relationships between the generation of new weapons requirements by the services and attempts at doctrinal innovation by the Secretary of Defense.

Chapter IV will then consider a major technical difficulty of the program: the problem of mating the F-111's engines to the F-111 airframe. The F-111's engines incorporated certain important new technologies. Only after a long series of unanticipated remedial efforts were the new engines able to achieve more or less normal operation in the F-111. Our examination of these remedial efforts will reveal much about how the development process responds to unanticipated technical problems. It will, moreover, demonstrate the unique organizational difficulties of integrating technically interdependent hardware when the interdependent components (in this case, the engine and the airframe) are developed by separate organizations (Pratt & Whitney and General Dynamics, respectively).

Chapter V will focus on the most widely recognized issue of the entire F-111 program: the controversial development and cancellation of the Navy version of the F-111, the F-111B. In its attempt to get the Navy and the Air Force jointly to develop a major weapon system, the F-111 program was virtually without precedent. Our examination of the failure of this attempt will provide a useful vehicle for understanding powerful constraints on the initiative of the Secretary of Defense.

While we will concentrate on the issues described above, we will touch upon many other development problems at various points in our study. Through our analysis of all of these issues, using the theoretical approach to be sketched in Chapter I, we hope to illumine "what went wrong" in the F-111 program. Chapter VI, our final chapter, will provide a summary and more general understanding of these problems. It will bring into focus the image of the weapons acquisition process that our theoretical approach provides. From that image, it will draw a series of conclusions on the F-111 program, the postwar acquisition experience, and the possibilities for weapons acquisition reform.

We should emphasize here two tasks we will not attempt to accomplish in this study. First, we will not attempt to provide a complete history of the F-111 development, even for the issues at the center of our analysis. Though we will detail these issues at length, we will concentrate on the evolving interaction between the results of lower-level development processes and the attempts of high-level officials to combat these results. High-level officials decisively structured the program at its inception and participated in the management details of the program to an extraordinary degree. They were the ones attempting to change the dominant defense doctrines and procurement practices, and our study will focus on their efforts to implement these concerns in the F-111 program.[5]

Second, we will not attempt to explore in detail the extraordinary political controversies of the program—most notably, the controversy surrounding the award of the development contract to General Dynamics. These issues have been treated, though not resolved, elsewhere.[6] Our study will focus on the influence of bureaucratic phenomena on the F-111 development and will attempt to demonstrate the value of the cybernetic paradigm for evoking, and giving

[5] Moreover, as Steinbruner observes, the higher levels of the organization are the likely locus of the integrating calculations presupposed under established analytic assumptions. Hence, the clear presence of cybernetic behavior at these levels will provide an important indication of the explanatory power of this alternative to analytic logic. See Steinbruner, *Cybernetic Theory,* p. 72.

[6] Thomas Alexander, "McNamara's Expensive Economy Plane," *Fortune,* Vol. 75 (April 1967), pp. 89–91, 184–187; Robert J. Art, *The TFX Decision: McNamara and the Military* (Boston: Little, Brown, 1968); Richard Austin Smith, "The $7 Billion Contract That Changed the Rules," *Fortune,* Vol. 67, Part I (March 1963), pp. 96–101, 182–188, and Part II (April 1963), pp. 110–111, 191–200; I. F. Stone, "In the Bowels of the Behemoth," *New York Review of Books,* Vol. xviii (March 11, 1971), pp. 29–37; U.S. Senate, Committee on Government Operations, Permanent Subcommittee on Investigations, *TFX Contract Investigation,* Hearings, 88th Cong., 1st Sess. (1963), Parts 1–10 (these hearings hereafter cited as *TFX Hearings— First Series*); U.S. Senate, Committee on Government Operations, Permanent Subcommittee on Investigations, *TFX Contract Investigation (Second Series),* Hearings, 91st Cong., 2d Sess. (1970), Parts 1–3 (these hearings hereafter cited as *TFX Hearings—Second Series*); and *TFX Report.*

logical coherence to, these phenomena. While the politics of an unusually controversial program may at first seem neglected, we hope to demonstrate that this alternative conception of the decision process powerfully augments our understanding of the role of politics in the program. Indeed, we hope to demonstrate that, in spite of its uniqueness, the F-111 program was decisively shaped by processes of considerable generality and that a study of this program can offer new insights into the troubling results of modern weapon system developments.

CHAPTER I

Paradigms of the Decision Process

The main theoretical argument of our study is that key characteristics of behavior in the F-111 program are best understood within a particular framework of non-purposive assumptions, the cybernetic paradigm. To clarify what the cybernetic paradigm is, and to provide readers unfamiliar with the theoretical literature a sufficient background for the analysis to follow, it will be worthwhile here to summarize our theoretical premises and to suggest their implications for our study.[1]

A paradigm of the decision process is a basic set of working assumptions on how decisions are made in large organizations. These assumptions provide a coherent intellectual framework for the analysis of decision making in large organizations, as they define which problems receive intellectual attention, identify what data are most pertinent to the understanding of these problems, and provide logically consistent explanations for the phenomena of central interest in the decision process. The assumptions of the paradigm are not generally held open to question, but rather provide the basis for defining the issues that are debated.[2]

The assumptions of a paradigm form the underlying logic for a broad range of diverse formulations, from the precise axioms of formal models to the largely implicit assumptions of casual observers.[3] Across this diversity of forms the paradigm provides a common set of basic assumptions. We

---

[1] Readers familiar with the theoretical literature are urged to skim this chapter.

[2] John D. Steinbruner, *The Cybernetic Theory of Decision: New Dimensions of Political Analysis* (Princeton: Princeton University Press, 1974), pp. 8–12. See also Thomas Kuhn, *The Structure of Scientific Revolutions* (Chicago: University of Chicago Press, 1963).

[3] Steinbruner, *Cybernetic Theory*, p. 25.

shall employ two different paradigms of the decision process in this study: the analytic paradigm and the cybernetic paradigm.

THE ANALYTIC PARADIGM

For decision making in large organizations, assumptions of rational choice have served as the dominant, while largely implicit, paradigm of analysis. These assumptions have structured the on-going research, the theorizing, and the practical analysis of those seeking to explain complex organizational activities. After a long period of development, these assumptions now provide "both sophisticated and more casual analysts with the necessary means for focusing their attention and for drawing inferences about inherently ambiguous events."[4]

One formal articulation of a paradigm of rational choice is provided by Steinbruner. His formulation is a set of *positive* assumptions which purport to explain how actual, empirical decision processes work. To avoid the normative connotations commonly associated with the word "rational," Steinbruner has labeled this paradigm the *analytic paradigm*, a label that fittingly evokes the spirit of this view of the decision process. We shall adopt Steinbruner's formulation here.[5]

The analytic paradigm formalizes a widely held, intuitively appealing image of the decision maker: that of the purposeful calculator, who seeks out and selects those courses of action that best promise to fulfill his intended purposes. This is the image of the profit-maximizing entrepreneur, the calculating bureaucrat, and the shrewd President. When for example, we observe in a given instance that "the President sought to mollify his right-wing critics without alienating his moderate support," or that "the Secretary of Defense is attempting to achieve a force

---

[4] Ibid., pp. 11–12. [5] Ibid., pp. 26–27.

posture that maintains our armed strength within the tight defense budgets expected for the future," we are expressing this image of the decision process and are partaking, albeit casually, in the intellectual tradition articulated in the analytic paradigm.

Formal discussions of analytic decisions generally begin with a single decision maker whose values have been aggregated to form a set of preferences regarding alternative states of the world. The decision maker has absolute discretion to define his values, and the only requirement is that his preferences be transitive in some sense (normally meaning that, if A is preferred to B and B is preferred to C, then A is preferred to C).[6] The major postulate of the analytic paradigm (and of derivative constructs) is that decisions will be taken which maximize the decision maker's values, given the constraints of the situation. In the complex environment where most decisions in the real world take place, the achievement of one objective will commonly conflict with the achievement of another objective (more "guns" usually means less "butter" or, at a lower order of aggregation, procurement of one type of aircraft with one set of capabilities means procurement of fewer aircraft with alternative capabilities). The analytic paradigm holds that these competing, directly pertinent objectives will be deliberately balanced or "traded-off" by the decision maker as an integral part of his reaching a decision.

Of course, in the real world, the decision maker necessarily will be uncertain of the range of possible outcomes that might result from any given choice. Moreover, he will have difficulty estimating the likelihood even of the outcomes that he foresees.[7] The analytic paradigm posits that a decision maker will be sensitive to these facts: that events may not follow a single course and that the possible courses of events may differ in their desirability. Above all, the

[6] Ibid., p. 28.
[7] This is a condition that Steinbruner terms "structural uncertainty." See Ibid., p. 18.

13

paradigm anticipates that the decision maker will engage in *outcome calculations*, a direct attempt to predict the consequences of alternative courses of action. In the same spirit, the paradigm holds that a decision maker will pay attention to information pertinent to the alternatives under consideration and that he will adjust his outcome calculations under the impact of the new information. Steinbruner observes:

> Time brings accumulating experience and changes in the environment, both of which by the assumptions of the paradigm should produce adjustments in decision calculations. Perhaps the central characteristic of the analytic decision maker is the construction of careful, explicit, disaggregated calculations of the possible results of his actions. By the assumptions of the paradigm, the analytic decision maker constructs a model of the causal forces controlling the environment in which he acts. As new information becomes available over time, it should be integrated into the working model and the critical causal assumptions of the model should be adjusted whenever the weight of evidence requires it. That is, the assumptions of alternative outcome calculations and sensitivity to pertinent information require a *causal learning* process in which new information is integrated into explicit causal inferences.[8]

The assumptions of the analytic paradigm have been worked out at the level of the individual decision maker. Yet any useful paradigm must give some account of collective decision processes—that is, of situations where power to make the decision is dispersed over a number of individuals and/or organization subunits. Unfortunately, there are formidable logical barriers to extending the analysis of individual decision makers to the collective level. Steinbruner summarizes the problem: "Logical conceptions

[8] Ibid., pp. 40–41.

14

of utility which are now available do not provide for the comparison of utility values across individuals, and this effectively prevents a process of aggregating the separate calculations of analytic actors under trade-off conditions. Accordingly, there is a logical gap between the individual level and the collective level of decision making which is decidedly problematic to rigorous analytic models."[9]

Despite these formal logical barriers, understanding of public decisions based on the analytic paradigm cannot and does not remain trapped solely at the individual level of explanation. If the activities of the government are to be comprehended at all, some conception of the collective decision process, however tacit, must be adduced, and this obviously has been done. There are in fact conceptions of the collective decision process in general use by political analysts, and the most prominent and widely used of these conceptions are based on the logic of the analytic paradigm.[10]

The most common resolution of the problem of collective decision is to assume that the decision making entity, whether a small bureau or the entire government, acts as if it were a single person, as if it could assert objectives and calculate strategies to achieve those objectives with the intellectual coherence of a single mind. (Popular language reflects this approach: such phrases as "the administration thinks," "the British feel," and "the Air Force argues" pervade political discourse of all kinds.) When employed too casually, this device risks tautology. The assumed individual does not exist to be observed, yet calculations conforming to the paradigm are imputed to him. The applicability of the paradigm itself is assumed from the outset and not held open to challenge by any evidence adduced.

[9] Ibid., pp. 36–37. See also Richard M. Cyert and James G. March, *A Behavioral Theory of the Firm* (Englewood Cliffs: Prentice-Hall, 1963), chap. 3; and William J. Baumol, *Welfare Economics and the Theory of the State* (London: Longmans, Green and Company, 1952).

[10] Steinbruner, *Cybernetic Theory*, p. 37. For an excellent overview of this literature, see Allison, *Essence of Decision*, pp. 10–28.

15

This difficulty can be resolved by requiring that calculations fitting the assumptions of the paradigm be relatively explicit and observable and that they have a direct effect on decisions made and actions taken:

> A reasonable approximation of this requirement can be achieved if the public objectives at stake are clearly identified, if their trade-offs are explicitly considered, if some model of the problem allowing estimates of possible outcomes is explicitly worked out, and if the numerous actors involved accept, or at least are constrained by, the estimates. This posits a collective decision process working by consensus in which the multiple actors attempt to evolve by debate and mutual effort a set of calculations which meet the criteria of analytic logic. If a dominant decision emerges from the explicit, shared analysis, then according to the paradigm that should be the one taken. If clear dominance of one alternative does not emerge, then the decision taken should at least be within the range defined by the common calculations if the decision is held to be the result of an analytic process.[11]

This formulation leaves some residual vagueness, to be sure; however, it does capture the spirit of the paradigm and provides enough specificity for testing the applicability of the paradigm to specific government activities.

To summarize: the analytic paradigm assumes that, subject to the constraints of the situation, decisions will be made that maximize the given goals of an individual or an organization. For a particular decision problem the analytic paradigm posits that a number of alternatives will be conceived, with consideration given to the probable outcome of each; that relevant goals will be integrated as an *intrinsic* part of the decision process; that the process will seek out and respond to new information; and finally, that the alternative

[11] Steinbruner, *Cybernetic Theory*, p. 38.

16

chosen will be the one with the highest probable net payoff in terms of the decision maker's goals. For a collective decision problem, it requires that calculations fitting these assumptions be explicit and observable and that the calculations be shared (in the sense defined earlier) by the actors involved.

THE CYBERNETIC PARADIGM

The analytic paradigm has received broad empirical support and cultural ratification. We need not digress into the literature to make the point. However, we question whether the analytic paradigm (and its formal and informal derivatives) can account for all the observed phenomena of decision making. Critics have long noted that paradigms of rational choice assume such sophisticated processing of information that it strains credulity to impute such procedures to real decision makers.[12] From studies of the way human beings process information, a logic of decision distinct from analytic logic has emerged. Steinbruner has isolated a set of propositions which characterize this alternative logic. He labels these propositions the cybernetic paradigm. We shall adopt his label here and use it throughout our study.[13]

Cybernetic Decision Processes and Cognitive Theory

The conception of the decision process articulated by the cybernetic paradigm is that of decision makers acting routinely on the basis of simplified images of complex prob-

[12] Ibid., pp. 12–13.
[13] Ibid., chaps. 3–4. The term "cybernetic paradigm" will be used throughout this study to refer to Steinbruner's expansion of basic cybernetic principles to incorporate cognitive theory (as will become clear later in the text). This label is, it should be noted, slightly at variance with that adopted by Steinbruner, who for presentational purposes terms this expanded version of cybernetic principles the "cognitive paradigm." For our purposes, the term "cybernetic" better evokes the underlying logic of the paradigm and better distinguishes these notions from the contrasting analytic logic.

17

lems, oblivious to the results of their efforts except insofar as the simplifications themselves are implicated. This conception builds upon a key metaphor: the servomechanism. Servomechanisms are exceedingly simple decision making devices. The favorite example of a servomechanism is the common thermostat; but other examples are readily available, ranging from airplane autopilots and heat-seeking missiles to biological equivalents in the navigation of honeybees and DNA operations in chromosomes.[14] These mechanisms perform no output calculations. Instead, they merely track a few feedback variables and react solely to the variations in this select information. In all other respects, they are essentially blind to the environment. They have a repertory of operations which they perform in sequence while monitoring the few feedback variables. (In the thermostat case, the device opens and closes a circuit as temperature respectively rises and falls past a critical level.) They produce an outcome as a result of completing the sequence, *but the outcome is not conceptualized in advance.* Degrees of complexity in the environment are of no concern within the servomechanism itself, and the burden of calculation that the analytic paradigm seems to impose is not a problem.[15]

[14] Ibid., pp. 48–56.

[15] The committed analytic theorist is likely to assert that this structure is itself a product of rational design and that any cybernetic decision maker operating within that structure is actually fulfilling intended purposes. (In this connection, think of the role of the designer of the thermostat.) Steinbruner notes, however, that this argument fails because, in the extremely complex environments characteristic of policy problems, it is difficult to point to the designer or even to conceive of him. Moreover, even where a designer can be found whose decisions might be discovered, the decision making system he sets up for a complicated problem will produce results that could not be foreseen—that is, it will produce solutions not inherent in the design alone. The analogy to heuristic computer programs is apt on this point. (See Ibid., pp. 57–58.) Hence, one risks tautological application of the analytic paradigm in imputing conscious purpose to the structures in which cybernetic mechanisms operate on complex problems. By the logic of the cybernetic paradigm, we would expect these structures ultimately to be grounded in the cognitive operations de-

As the mechanical and biological examples cited above suggest, simple cybernetic mechanisms can produce strikingly adaptive outcomes. However, the success of a cybernetic mechanism clearly depends a great deal on the character of the surrounding environment. If variation in the environment is too great along certain dimensions, the mechanisms will be unable to adapt.

Herbert Simon has confronted this issue most directly.[16] He argues that, in a number of physical and biological systems which contain a great deal of variety, there is a hierarchical organization which imposes structure on complexity. Complex environments are everywhere in nature and in human affairs divided into subsystems down through many levels of organization. (For example, the human body is divided into systems, which are divided into major and minor organs, which are composed of basic parts and tissues, and so on, down to the elements of individual cells.) Within such hierarchically organized systems, the interactions and interrelationships among elements of the same subsystem are generally greater than interaction among elements of separate subsystems—a property which renders complex systems "nearly decomposable" in Simon's terms.

In a decomposable environment, there are hierarchically arranged channels of variation that at an abstract level already provide the conditions for successful adaptation by cybernetic mechanisms of decision. The mechanism can operate within a particular subsystem of such an environment and encounter variation that is a great deal more regular

---

scribed in the text and, accordingly, to lack the integrated purposes imputed by the analytic theorist. For example, we might expect these structures to be the result of unexplained (and often outmoded) tradition or "normal practice," or to be an accumulation of minor changes over many years that have aggregated to a major change which no one contemplated or considered optimal.

[16] Herbert A. Simon, "The Architecture of Complexity," in Herbert A. Simon, *The Sciences of the Artificial* (Cambridge: MIT Press, 1968), pp. 84–118. See also Steinbruner, *Cybernetic Theory*, pp. 56–62.

than in the environment as a whole and certainly more regular than would be the case were hierarchical organization not present: "The cybernetic paradigm, in positing a decision mechanism based on selective feedback and programmed operations . . . is building upon the notion of hierarchically organized environments. The adaptive capacity of cybernetic decision mechanisms occurs when the decision maker is operating within a stable environmental subsystem. There may be great complexity in hierarchical levels above and/or below this subsystem, and the consequences of actions taken in these other areas of the environmental hierarchy may be considerable. However, whatever the consequence in the larger environment, decisions according to the paradigm are controlled by events within the subsystems."[17] Hence, when there is a fair amount of natural structure and stability in the environment, cybernetic decision makers can be remarkably adaptive. On the other hand, when the environment is not naturally structured or stable, and when there is significant interaction among levels of hierarchy, there is a clear potential for trouble.

For complex policy problems, where uncertainty is high, there is likely to be little immanent structure or stability in the environment and a great deal of interaction among levels of hierarchy. In such environments, it is difficult to imagine how simple, cybernetic decision processes could operate. Steinbruner has formulated a solution to this puzzle. He asserts that the decision process in a highly complex and interactive environment becomes structured in a relatively stable and general way that reflects the patterns of cognitive inference of the individual decision maker.[18] By understanding certain systematic features of cognitive operations, Steinbruner suggests, we can understand the stable structures of belief within which cybernetic mechanisms of decision operate in complex environments.

[17] Steinbruner, *Cybernetic Theory*, p. 61.
[18] Ibid., chap. 4.

The basic principles of cognitive psychology to which Steinbruner refers are widely held assumptions within the field. They have received considerable experimental study and verification (but whether that renders them "proven" is, of course, another question). They are asserted to hold across idiosyncrasies of personality and culture. Even as they provide a basis for the operation of cybernetic decision processes, we should note, they present a sharp contrast to the conception of the decision maker implicit in the analytic paradigm.

There is a consensus within cognitive theory that a great deal of information processing is conducted apparently prior to and certainly independent of conscious direction. In this activity, the mind routinely performs logical operations of considerable power. The regularities of these logical operations indicate that the mind is a mechanism which craves certainty. In situations where uncertainty is high, the mind will impose non-probabilistic, categorical beliefs on the situation and will manipulate information to maintain those beliefs *independent of the weight of objective evidence.*

What is important here is the structure of beliefs; that is, the way in which the relationships between beliefs are organized in the mind and the manner in which information is processed in reference to existing beliefs. It is known that memory is inferential. The mind imposes structural relationships—hierarchical and lateral—on the information in memory. Thus, if a person is asked to recall the Munich conference, he is very likely to think first of the notion of appeasement and then gradually bring back subordinate details (such as the specific issue of Czechoslovakia, the participants, the actual date). Lateral associations between this and other hierarchically organized concepts are likely to include, say, a negative or positive association between the issue of Czechoslovakia and the issue of Vietnam. Hence, "in obviously important, if imperfectly understood ways, the components of memory are related, and the mental process

21

of drawing inferences is affected by these relationships once they are established."[19]

The mind is not unconstrained in imposing these relationships on the information it possesses. Specifically, it operates in such a way as to keep internal belief relationships (lateral and hierarchical) consistent with one another. This constraint affects both the organization of memory and the processing of new information. If new information challenges the structure of beliefs in memory, cognitive processing mechanisms work unconsciously to restore the disturbed consistency. Furthermore, the inference mechanisms of the mind are constrained by what Freud termed the reality principle. The human mind is in contact with its environment, and stable, important features of the environment impose themselves quite reliably on the mind. However it happens, many features of the environment are *clearly enough presented* that virtually any given individual will perceive them in substantially the same way. Finally, the mind, while it maintains a complicated, interacting set of beliefs and while it is constrained by external reality and internal consistency, is clearly in need of principles of economy:

> The world—"reality"—is enormously varied and constantly in a process of change. If everything in it were recorded and if the abstractions of cognitive operations were kept perfectly consistent, the burden of information processing would far exceed even the remarkable capacities of the mind. As it is, we know that the mind is highly selective about the information to which it attends and that which it uses. The mind remembers some things of importance but forgets a great deal and never even attends to most of the information it physically receives.[20]

Cognitive theory offers two principles that govern the process of selection: simplicity and stability. The principle

---

[19] Ibid., p. 97.   [20] Ibid., p. 101.

of simplicity asserts that cognitive inference mechanisms work to keep the structure of belief as simple as possible. The principle of stability asserts that cognitive inference mechanisms resist change in the core structure of beliefs. Because of extensive lateral and hierarchical relationships within a system of beliefs—each of which must be held to some level of consistency—a major restructuring of beliefs is likely to set off a chain reaction, imposing severe burdens on the information processing system. Economy thus requires a bias against change in major components of belief structure once they have been established.

The five general features of cognitive operations—inferential memory, consistency, reality, simplicity, and stability—provide a sufficient basis for an independent conception of the decision maker. This conception can perhaps best be understood by contrast to the conception of the decision maker contained in the analytic paradigm. The analytic paradigm postulates that a decision maker acting on two objectives which conflict with each other will integrate the two objectives in reaching a decision (i.e., he will seek the optimum feasible trade-off between the two objectives in terms of his own preference ordering). Cognitive research suggests that value integration is not the only pattern of human inference in trade-off situations. Integration tends not to occur under conditions of intense uncertainty:

> For the two-value trade-off problems, the cognitive structure required to make the trade-off explicit violates the principle of consistency. Under the assumptions of cognitive theory, the information-processing mechanisms of the mind operate to deny the trade-off relationship unless compelled to recognize it by a highly structured external situation (the reality constraint). Under uncertainty, the reality constraint is weakened, and the cognitive criterion of consistency forces a mental dissolution of the trade-off. Cognitive principles thus suggest the contrary *assumption of value separation*. According to this assumption, the

two values of a complex problem will not be related to one another in the mind of the decision maker. . . . The information-processing operations of the human mind strain to set up single-value decision problems.[21]

Hence, when uncertainty is high enough to permit some interpretive latitude, the decision maker will suppress trade-offs by conceptualizing his world in such a way that the values do not seem in conflict. For example, he will conceive the values not to be in conflict and will pursue them separately, as if they were independent considerations. Or he will view the two values as actually being consonant, serviceable by the same policy.[22]

Once these beliefs are established, the mind will work to impute certainty to them:

> The cognitive theorist expects, according to the consistency principle, that in the processing of information favorable outcomes will be inferred for preferred alternatives and that unfavorable outcomes will be projected for alternatives the decision maker intends to reject. Quite generally, the inferential structures which cognitive operations impose on inherently uncertain situations tend to be simple and coherently organized to present a single-valued problem and a single-preferred alternative to which the decision maker is committed from the outset of the decision process. Under complexity, the mind, in this view, does not match the uncertain structure of the environment in which events might take a number of alternative courses. Rather, it imposes an image and works

21 Ibid., p. 108.

22 An example of the latter would be an international crisis situation, where values of peace and national power might conflict. A cybernetic decision maker might dissolve this trade-off by imputing a belief that war now actually serves the long-run interests of peace. He thereby renders the conflicting values consonant: peace *requires* war, by this inference. Jack L. Snyder, "Rationality at the Brink: Uncertainty and the Cognitive Dynamics of a Two-Value Game" (unpublished paper, Department of Political Science, Columbia University, 1974), pp. 13–22.

to preserve that image. A single course of events is projected; evidence for alternatives outcomes is manipulated to preserve the expectations. We might call this, then, the *assumption of a single outcome calculation*.[23]

In this view, the behavior of the decision maker is fundamentally driven by the need to manage uncertainty. Pertinent information may enter the decision process or it may be screened out, depending on how it relates to the existing pattern of belief. A certainty will be imputed to events that is unwarranted by the weight of objective evidence. The decision maker will not be very sensitive to new information—his learning process will be highly constrained. New information and new decision problems will be fit into established conceptual structures without causing any general adjustment of the structure. The belief system will not be static, as new ideas, information, and perceptions will be formed at low levels of generality. However, the basic structure of conceptualization will remain stable and partial (partial, that is, in relation to the complexity of the environment), even over very extended periods. *A fuller awareness of the complexity of the environment and the trade-offs it imposes is unlikely, unless the trade-offs are unavoidably and unambiguously self-evident; that is, unless the reality principle is strong.*

This conception of the decision maker suggests a source of the stable structure required for cybernetic mechanisms of decision to operate in complex environments. As noted earlier in our discussion, cybernetic decision makers screen out information which the established set of responses are not programmed to accept. They generate decisions and outcomes, but psychologically they are not engaged in the pursuit of an explicitly designed result. Similarly, when uncertainty is high and the reality principle is weak—as in complex, interacting environments, where Simon's near decomposability does not obtain—cognitive processes of the

[23] Steinbruner, *Cybernetic Theory*, p. 123.

mind work unconsciously to screen out information that does not correspond to existing patterns of belief, to project a single course of events, and to manipulate evidence to preserve expectations. In spite of the objective complexity and variability of the environment, these structures of belief nonetheless will possess the necessary stability and simplicity to allow cybernetic processes of decision to proceed quite smoothly.

Of course, an actual decision maker is unlikely to confront the environment alone and simply to impose his own inferences—he will generally be part of a large organization. Large organizations provide a major simplification of the environment for cybernetic mechanisms: "Under conditions of complexity, decision-making organizations arise which attempt to match the complexity of their environment by means of an internal complexity which is *not* the property of a single decision maker, but rather of the collective. This is the natural cybernetic explanation for the rise of mass bureaucracy. According to the cybernetic paradigm, each individual decision maker of such an organization will be a cybernetic operator, a fact which might be expected to yield systematic characteristics of the behavior of the organization as a whole."[24]

Having examined in detail the assumptions of the cybernetic paradigm for the individual decision maker, we now may inquire into the systematic characteristics of cybernetic decisions at the collective level.

Organization Behavior

How does the cybernetic decision maker operate in a large organization? Picture such an individual being hired into an organization. He will bring to his new job a set of career experiences, professional identifications, and other attributes that comprise his existing structure of beliefs.

[24] Ibid., p. 69.

The organization will act powerfully to modify that belief structure, to make it conform, more or less, to the prevailing belief structures in the organization (and in the organization subunit of which he is more specifically a part). The new employee will "learn the ropes." From the training and policy manuals he reads to the cumulating experience he acquires, the new employee will gradually come to share approximately the same simplifications and focused sensitivities that his colleagues with greater seniority possess.[25]

In other words, by the assumptions of the cybernetic paradigm, the organization regiments the belief structures of the individuals who comprise it. While the organization as a whole is a coalition of separate individuals with diverse goals, these individuals will be located in subunits which coordinate individual behaviors and produce a coherent set of products as a result of the collective individual efforts. At the level of the smallest subunit, these individuals attend to a small piece of the organization's task. It is readily understood how individuals in these subunits could share a common structure of beliefs. But how are the efforts of these subunits aggregated? The diversity of the subunits would seem to make focused sensitivity and stable problem simplifications impossible for higher-level decision makers.

Fortunately, considerable attention has been devoted to cybernetic accounts of organizational behavior; and, from these efforts, a solution to the problem of aggregation over levels of hierarchy emerges. In particular, March and Simon[26] and Cyert and March[27] have supplied well-articu-

[25] This is a direct implication of the cognitive principles discussed earlier. It suggests one reason organizations hire individuals with certain backgrounds and training. An individual with a sufficiently strong professional identification at variance with the operative simplifications of the organization could find the required adjustment of his belief structures too extreme. He would not likely remain with the organization very long. On the more general point, see Ibid., pp. 124–125.

[26] James G. March and Herbert A. Simon, *Organizations* (New York: Wiley, 1968).

[27] Cyert and March, *A Behavioral Theory of the Firm.*

27

lated arguments as to how cybernetic mechanisms determine organizational decision making.

Organization subunits, the argument runs, produce a coherent set of products. It is assumed (and is virtually always the case) that the organization subunits are hierarchically related so that subunits performing one set of activities are subjected to managerial oversight by subunits whose area of responsibility includes a more diverse set of activities. The process of decision, according to Cyert and March, is one in which decisions peculiar to individual subunits are held separate. Top management, in their view, focuses in sequential order on the decision issues raised by the separate subunits and does not integrate across subunits in its deliberations. Decisions are made wholly within the context of the subunit raising the issue. Complex problems are thus fragmented by organizations into separate components corresponding to subunit organization, and the decision process at the highest levels preserves this fragmentation. Such a process is labeled "sequential attention to goals," a major hypothesis of the Cyert and March theory.[28] Thus, "as with uncertainty, the model holds that the problem of aggregating across different individuals who are involved in the decision process is solved by avoiding it."[29]

In the Cyert and March formulation, the decision process for each subunit proceeds as described by the cybernetic paradigm. The decision makers avoid uncertainty and do not attempt to calculate outcomes. While they generally will believe that they are receiving broad information about the environment, they actually will monitor relatively few feedback channels and discover the effects of their actions only insofar as they register on feedback variables. By this logic, decision problems result from unacceptable variations in feedback.[30] When unacceptable feedback is received, the

[28] Ibid., chap. 6. See also, Allison, *Essence of Decision*, pp. 76–77; and Steinbruner, *Cybernetic Theory*, pp. 71–78.

[29] Steinbruner, *Cybernetic Theory*, p. 72.

[30] The determination of the acceptability of feedback is achieved by what Cyert and March label "acceptable-level objectives" (a con-

subunit will start a relatively restricted search process—the "problemistic search"—which reveals options first in the area of marginal adjustments to the alternative in use, then in the area of the next, pre-programmed item in the response repertory.[31] As these options are applied, new feedback information will be generated. Once the new information represents a return to acceptable levels, the search process will end. There is, in short, a relatively closed cycle of categorical and short-range responses to unfavorable feedback variation, with little higher-order calculation to be expected. By contrast with the analytic paradigm, the cybernetic paradigm assumes the decision process will be neither speculative nor forward-looking. Even when problems are foreshadowed by considerable information, a subunit will not necessarily act to forestall them. It will act only when this information registers on feedback variables to which it is attuned.

Together with our earlier discussion of the individual cybernetic decision maker, these propositions of cybernetic behavior at the organizational level provide a relatively

---

cept derived from Simon's satisficing model). Organizations establish measures of performance and act to hold these measures at levels deemed appropriate. These levels of acceptability may derive from traditional practices, coordinating requirements among subunits, political expectations, and other sources. Once established, they tend to endure, as part of the simplified structure imposed on a complex problem. As time passes, if acceptable levels become relatively easy to achieve, aspirations in the organization and related levels of acceptability are likely to rise. Conversely, if acceptable levels become difficult to achieve, aspirations and levels of acceptability are likely to decline. But if acceptable levels are being achieved with normal difficulty, aspirations and levels of acceptability are likely to remain unchanged. The organization will in that event proceed routinely, with subunits performing their programmed activities without intervention. See Allison, *Essence of Decision*, pp. 76–77, 82; Cyert and March, *A Behavioral Theory of the Firm*, pp. 117–118; Herbert A. Simon, "A Behavioral Model of Rational Choice," in Herbert A. Simon, *Models of Man: Social and Rational* (New York: Wiley, 1957), pp. 241–260; and Steinbruner, *Cybernetic Theory*, pp. 62–63, 74.

[31] Cyert and March, *A Behavioral Theory of the Firm*, p. 74. See also Steinbruner, *Cybernetic Theory*, pp. 74–75.

complete and coherent paradigm of the decision process. The paradigm represents the common underlying logic in a diverse set of formulations—from casual notions of "organizational momentum" and "bureaucratic tunnel vision" to the precisely formulated propositions of rigorous behavioral models, such as Cyert and March's behavioral theory of the firm and Allison's derivative Model II.[32] Through all these formulations runs a common vision of organization subunits operating routinely on factored pieces of larger problems. While the paradigm offers no normative sanction for such behavior, it renders the behavior understandable—a considerable gain, as we hope to demonstrate in this study.

POLITICS AND THE ROLE OF THE PARADIGMS

Our summary of the logic of the cybernetic and analytic paradigms necessarily leaves many residual ambiguities. Application of the paradigms to the case material will provide the needed clarification. However, we can at this point cite major summary differences between the two paradigms. The analytic paradigm posits value maximization, value integration, broad outcome calculations, and a sensitivity to pertinent information—all, of course, subject to the constraints of the situation. By contrast, the cybernetic paradigm posits acceptable-level objectives, value separation, and only the narrowest sensitivity to outcomes and new information. In much of the theoretical work to date, these cybernetic assumptions have been assimilated into the basic framework of a theory of rational choice. This approach is notably apparent in some of the pathbreaking work of Herbert Simon and the Carnegie School.[33] For the present study, however, we will keep the cybernetic paradigm sep-

[32] Allison, *Essence of Decision*, chap. 3; Cyert and March, *A Behavioral Theory of the Firm*, chaps. 1–6.
[33] See, for example, Simon, "A Behavioral Model of Rational Choice."

arate and distinct from analytic assumptions. We do so for a reason: we hope to demonstrate that the cybernetic paradigm is especially useful for understanding the peculiar difficulties of implementation in established organizations, difficulties of the kind that were decisive in the F-111 program.

The careful reader will have noted that, while our ultimate purpose is to understand the behavior of large public institutions on a major weapons program, we have nowhere mentioned in our theoretical discussions a widely recognized feature of such programs: politics. The literature describing the political character of the decision process is unusually rich.[34] The point of departure in this literature is the existence of a number of actors, each with some power to affect the other actors and thus the ultimate decision. The actors are assumed (or found) to be in disagreement on the issues being explained and, more important, to stand in quite general competition with one another over a much

[34] For the general subject area of concern in the present study, prominent examples include Michael H. Armacost, *The Politics of Weapons Innovation: The Thor-Jupiter Controversy* (New York: Columbia University Press, 1969); Art, *The TFX Decision*; Morton H. Halperin, *Bureaucratic Politics and Foreign Policy* (Washington: Brookings Institution, 1974); Paul Y. Hammond, *Super Carriers and B-36 Bombers: Appropriations, Strategy and Politics*, Interuniversity Case Program No. 97 (New York: Bobbs-Merrill, 1963); Roger Hilsman, *To Move a Nation* (New York: Doubleday, 1967); Samuel P. Huntington, *The Common Defense: Strategic Programs in National Politics* (New York: Columbia University Press, 1961); Richard E. Neustadt, *Alliance Politics* (New York: Columbia University Press, 1970); Richard E. Neustadt, *Presidential Power* (New York: Wiley, 1960); Harvey M. Sapolsky, *The Polaris System Development: Bureaucratic and Programmatic Success in Government* (Cambridge: Harvard University Press, 1972); and Warner R. Schilling, Paul Y. Hammond, and Glenn H. Snyder, *Strategy, Politics, and Budgets* (New York: Columbia University Press, 1952). Charles E. Lindblom has articulated the theory behind a political view of the decision process in *The Intelligence of Democracy* (New York: The Free Press, 1965). Finally, as a means of explaining policy outcomes, Graham Allison has aggregated this literature by specifying its assumptions and major propositions, in *Essence of Decision*, chaps. 5 and 6.

31

broader range of issues. They are seen to engage in a variety of bargaining and coercive maneuvers to exert their will, and the "pulling and hauling" which results is seen as the essential characteristic of the decision process. In this view, outcomes occur as consequences of an elaborate bargaining game which spins them out, as often as not, as a by-product of action taken in the course of play. What happens is rarely intended and even more rarely preferred by any one of the actors individually. The stakes of the game are high, and the play is commensurately rough. It generates the "heat" which is a common attribute of struggles over policy issues.[35]

What emerges from this conception of the decision process is a perspective which supplements the analytic and cybernetic paradigms. The maneuvers whereby political actors seek to convince, bargain with, cajole, and coerce each other are inherent features of major public issues. In order to address themselves to complex policy problems, our decision paradigms must operate within such a setting. Politics is thus a critical element of the context of a decision, but the basic conception of the *decision maker* is still provided by either the analytic or cybernetic paradigms. Steinbruner notes that "the fact that theories of bargaining concern themselves with the overall effects of a number of partially powerful actors immediately establishes such analysis on the collective level of explanation, and hence the political analysis is clearly open to any set of assumptions about [the] particular decision process in which each of the actors is engaged."[36] The most developed body of theory assumes that the individual actors operate in accord with the analytic paradigm.[37] However, we can readily imagine cybernetic actors operating in a political context. For example:

[35] Steinbruner, *Cybernetic Theory*, pp. 140–141.
[36] Ibid., pp. 142–143.
[37] See Anthony Downs, *Inside Bureaucracy* (Boston: Little, Brown, 1967); and Steinbruner, *Cybernetic Theory*, pp. 143–146.

If [cybernetic] actors are engaged in politics, the natural presumption is that the role of bargaining as traditionally understood will be sharply diminished. Bargaining implies a willingness and capacity on the part of actors to adjust their conflicting objectives in a process of reaching an accommodation—a clear form of value integration. It is natural to suppose, by contrast, that [cybernetic] actors will not display the same degree of deliberate accommodation, will act more independently, and will by-pass bargains which under analytic assumptions would appear to be obvious. The limited outcome calculations, the single-value focus, and the dependence on selected feedback channels should all retard the process of accommodation. If, because of the peculiarities of a given decision problem, conflict among the separate actors is relatively intense, then the overall decision process should display less coherence than that produced by mutual accommodations among analytic actors.[38]

With these propositions in mind, we will conceive politics as a critical part of the environment in which decision makers—analytic or cybernetic—operate.

Clearly, the present study will rely heavily on the cybernetic paradigm as a source of insight into the problems of the F-111 program—otherwise, why draw the distinctions that that paradigm asserts? Yet, in this effort, we may proceed with some confidence, as cybernetic logic has demonstrated already its usefulness as a tool for understanding empirical problems. For example, the formulation developed by Cyert and March has been applied usefully to a variety of decision problems, from department store pricing to defense budgeting.[39] In his pathbreaking study of the

[38] Steinbruner, *Cybernetic Theory*, p. 147.

[39] John P. Crecine and Gregory Fischer, *On Resource Allocation Processes in the U.S. Department of Defense*, Institute of Public Policy Studies, University of Michigan, Discussion Paper No. 31 (1971); and Cyert and March, *A Behavioral Theory of the Firm*, chap. 7.

Cuban missile crisis, Allison has demonstrated the utility of applying his formulation to a complex policy problem. He has developed a set of concepts and propositions to guide the student and the practitioner of public policy to an understanding of how organizational routines powerfully affect organizational outcomes. His analysis of the Cuban missile crisis demonstrates that this form of analysis yields a very different understanding of events than that which emerges from traditional, analytic-based approaches.[40] Steinbruner has articulated the paradigm logic by synthesizing a diverse set of propositions from information theory, cognitive psychology, economics, and other fields. He has applied these formulations to the issue of sharing the control of nuclear weapons among members of the North Atlantic Treaty Organization (NATO).[41] In the present study, we will be following the lead of Cyert and March, Allison, Steinbruner, and others as we apply alternative paradigms of the decision process to the F-111 development. Compared to these earlier works, a study of the F-111 development provides a greater opportunity to examine an extended period of implementation on a complex policy problem. In this examination, we will employ the alternative paradigms as highly general frameworks for analysis. The paradigms will remain largely in the background throughout the study, structuring the exposition without unduly intruding into it. We hope to show that, even at this level of generality, the two paradigms provide us with critical leverage for understanding the complex problems of the F-111 program.

[40] Allison, *Essence of Decision*, chaps. 3, 4, and 7.
[41] Steinbruner, *Cybernetic Theory*, chaps. 6–9.

CHAPTER II

Overview and Central Issues

This chapter will establish a set of central questions as the focal point for our analysis of the F-111 program. The chapter begins with an overview of the origins, development, and production of the aircraft. From this overview, it formulates key questions on the conduct and results of the program. Subsequent chapters will attempt to answer these questions.

AN OVERVIEW OF THE F-III PROGRAM

In the years following World War II, dramatic technical advances in military hardware occurred. The most captivating and publicized of these advances were in the area of strategic weaponry. The postwar development of thermonuclear weapons and ballistic missile delivery systems portended an age of "push-button" warfare and instant destruction that naturally captured the public's imagination. Yet in these years dramatic developments in tactical weapons occurred as well. In the postwar years, the jet engine replaced the propeller on new tactical aircraft of the Air Force and Navy. Experimental aircraft broke the sound barrier in the late 1940s. Thereafter, the military services developed a succession of operational fighters capable of supersonic speed. By the late 1950s, operational fighters were attaining maximum speeds in excess of twice the speed of sound. At the same time, nuclear weapons were rapidly shrinking in size, to the point that these weapons could be carried on the relatively small tactical fighters of the Air Force and Navy.[1]

---

[1] These nuclear weapons were called "tactical" nuclear weapons. The label refers more accurately to the tactical commands using the weapons than to the explosive power of the weapons themselves.

Increasingly in the 1950s, and especially for the Air Force, the performance of tactical aircraft was keyed to specialized scenarios for delivering nuclear weapons.

Against this background of great technical progress and an increasing emphasis on nuclear weapons, the story of the F-111 unfolds.

The Genesis of Requirements

The F-111 had its origins in requirements separately conceived by the Navy and the Air Force.[2] In 1959, the Air Force's Tactical Air Command (TAC) was attempting to define its needs for a follow-on to its F-105 fighter-bomber. The F-105 was designed primarily for the high performance delivery of tactical nuclear weapons at low altitudes, although it did possess an ancillary capability for aerial combat and the delivery of conventional ordnance.[3] With

[2] Except as noted, the narrative on the origins of the TFX and the decisions leading to common development is drawn from Robert J. Art, *The TFX Decision: McNamara and the Military* (Boston: Little, Brown, 1968), chaps. 1, 2. For an interesting alternative explanation of the origins of weapon systems, see James R. Kurth, "A Widening Gyre: The Logic of American Weapons Procurement," *Public Policy*, Vol. 19 (Summer 1971), pp. 385–392. Kurth's explanation focuses on the political factors influencing the timing and character of service weapon choices. By his argument, new weapon programs are generated partially in response to political pressures from key aerospace contractors who need new business to maintain their production lines in operation. Note that, to document Kurth's proposition for the F-111 program, we would have to succeed where even an intensive Congressional investigation failed—that is, we would have to be able to document political influences on the TFX contract award. (The Congressional investigation itself will be described later in the present chapter.) For a critique of Kurth's thesis and an examination of the problems of empirical verification it presents, see Arnold J. Kanter and Stuart J. Thorson, *The Weapons Procurement Process: Choosing Among Competing Theories*, Institute of Public Policy Studies, University of Michigan, Discussion Paper No. 41 (1972).

[3] Leon H. Dulberger, "Advanced Fighter-Attack Aircraft," *Space/ Aeronautics*, Vol. 45 (April 1966), pp. 80–81; George Weiss, "The F-111: The Swing-Wing May Surprise You Yet," *Armed Forces Journal*, Vol. 108 (July 19, 1971), p. 23; and Interview 21 (the reader is directed to the list of interviews on p. 393 for all references

its emphasis on nuclear weapons delivery, the F-105 fully reflected the doctrine of Massive Retaliation, the established defense doctrine of the time. However, the priority accorded to strategic nuclear weapons under this doctrine had placed tactical aircraft in a subordinate and threatened position.[4] As a partial result, TAC was having some difficulty specifying the requirements for a successor to the F-105.

The tentative requirements that TAC envisioned were an incremental extension of the F-105's capabilities. TAC wanted a fighter able: (1) to carry a compact weapons load (tactical nuclear weapons) internally; (2) to fly across the Atlantic Ocean without refueling; (3) to operate from dispersed, semi-prepared fields in Europe; (4) to reach a maximum speed of Mach 2.5 (2.5 times the speed of sound) for high-altitude engagements with enemy fighters; and (5) to travel at *high subsonic* speeds at low altitude (below an enemy's radar) for an extended range.[5] The actual mission

---

to interviews by the author). See also Jacob Stockfisch, *Plowshares Into Swords: Managing the American Defense Establishment* (New York: Mason & Lipscomb, 1973), p. 145.

[4] Art, *The TFX Decision*, p. 16; and Richard G. Head, "Decision-Making on the A-7 Attack Aircraft Program" (unpublished Ph.D. dissertation, Syracuse University, 1970), pp. 86–91.

[5] Art, *The TFX Decision*, pp. 15–18; Robert L. Perry, *Innovation and Military Requirements: A Comparative Study*, Rand Memorandum No. RM-5182-PR (August 1967), pp. 68–69; Richard Austin Smith, "The $7 Billion Contract That Changed the Rules," Part I, *Fortune*, Vol. 67 (March 1963), pp. 97–99; and Interview 22. In the public record of the program (including the sources cited above), the Air Force is described as wanting a *supersonic* speed (Mach 1.2, or 1.2 times the speed of sound) for the sea-level dash from the very beginning of its program deliberations. However, according to an internal government report made available to the author (a report hereafter cited as Government Report I), the Air Force initially specified *high subsonic* speed for the sea-level dash. As will be discussed in the text, the Air Force raised the dash requirement to Mach 1.2 at a later point in its deliberations.

The reason that this dash was to be performed at a low altitude is fairly simple. Radar systems of the late 1950s could only see in a straight line. (For example, at a 50-foot altitude, most radar could see only 60 to 80 miles to the horizon.) Hence, the lower the altitude of a plane's penetration to the target, the longer would be the time

that TAC had in mind was a so-called Low-Low-High mission, a label referring to the altitude sequences contained in the mission (see Figure I). This mission profile would be difficult for an enemy to defend against, since penetra-

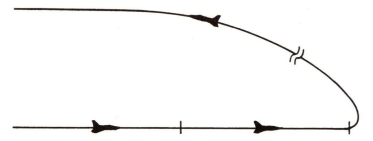

Figure I. Proposed Mission Profile for the TFX.

(1) Low—Low altitude cruise at subsonic speed. (2) Low—Low altitude dash to the target at high-subsonic speed. (3) High—High altitude, long-range cruise back to a friendly base at subsonic speeds.

tion to the target would be at an altitude below the line of sight of the enemy's radar. At the same time, the plane's high top speed would allow it to engage enemy interceptors. Unfortunately, aerospace contractors predicted that an aircraft meeting most of these requirements would weigh in excess of fifty tons, too heavy for operation from semi-prepared fields. The central problem was that TAC's requirements were aerodynamically contradictory. The TAC desire for transoceanic range, as well as its need for short take-off and landing capability from semi-prepared fields, required a relatively long, unswept wing for the proposed aircraft. However, its desire for high speed dictated a relatively short, sharply swept wing.

---

before the plane was detected by enemy radar. On the desirability of this sea-level capability, see Larry Booda, "Soviet Gains Blunt U.S. Bomber Potential," *Aviation Week and Space Technology*, Vol. 75 (August 14, 1961), pp. 26–27.

TAC nonetheless did not wish to compromise its requirements. With matters at this impasse, TAC was approached in 1959 by John Stack of the National Aeronautics and Space Administration (NASA). Through extensive wind tunnel tests, Stack and his associates had developed stable, variable-sweep wing configurations.[6] These tests promised a reconciliation of TAC's theretofore contradictory requirements. A single, fighter-sized aircraft could now have a large or small wing area simply by varying the sweep angle of the wings in flight (see Figure II). Moreover, new developments in jet propulsion—principally, the development of "turbo-fan" engines sized for military aircraft—promised important increases in fuel economy.[7] An aircraft with variable-sweep wings and turbo-fan engines could meet the TAC requirements at a reasonable gross weight.

The commander of TAC, General F. F. Everest, was persuaded by Stack's presentation, and he and Stack formulated a set of specific requirements for the proposed aircraft. These requirements included: (1) an unrefueled ferry range of 3,300 miles; (2) a "Low-Low-High" mission radius of 800 miles; (3) within that radius, a sea-level dash range of 400 miles at high subsonic speed; and (4) a capability to operate from short, unprepared grass airstrips.[8] The only specific ordnance requirement they established was that the

---

[6] Art, *The TFX Decision*, pp. 20–24; Perry, *Innovation and Military Requirements*; Staff Report, "TFX: Mission and Design," *Space/Aeronautics*, Vol. 29 (June 1963), pp. 76–78; W. T. Gunston, "TFX: A Next Generation Military Aeroplane," *Flight International*, Vol. 81 (February 8, 1962), p. 208; and *TFX Hearings—First Series*, Part 1, pp. 11–38.

[7] Turbo-fan engines differ from straight turbo-jets mainly in terms of the airflow through the engine. In a straight turbo-jet, all air entering the fan-type compressor goes through the "core" of the engine—that is, through the gas generator or combustion chamber. In a turbo-fan engine, the airflow is split between the core engine and a by-pass duct. This by-passed air itself provides thrust for the aircraft. The principal benefit of the turbo-fan is lower specific fuel consumption (i.e., fuel economy) at cruise speeds, for a given total thrust.

[8] *TFX Report*, pp. 5–6; and Government Report I.

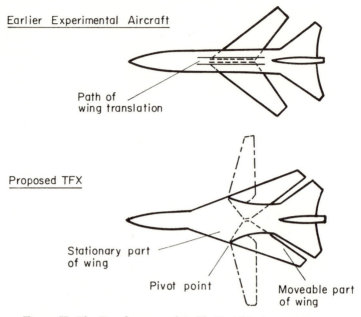

Figure II. The Development of Stable Variable-Sweep Wing Configurations.

To change the angle of sweep in earlier experimental aircraft, it was necessary to move the entire wing structure fore and aft, because the pivot point for the wing had been placed inside the fuselage at the wing root. Sweeping the entire wing upset the longitudinal stability of these planes by moving their center of gravity and center of lift. The centers of gravity and lift differed with each angle of sweep; however, these two centers had to maintain a stable relationship if the aircraft were to remain stable in flight. As a result, these earlier experimental planes were unstable in flight. The NASA breakthrough placed the pivot point on the wing and hence outside of the fuselage. (In this way, only part of the wing would move, with the rest remaining stationary.) This stabilized the variable-sweep design, since, as the angle of wing sweep grew sharper, the *proportion* of total lift provided by the *stationary* part of the wing increased considerably—thus counteracting the rearward shift in the center of lift brought on by rotating the outer section of the wing. Indeed, the researchers discovered that, by juggling the proportion of moveable wing to stationary wing, they could actually reverse the direction in which the center of lift moved with increasing sweep. Art, *The TFX Decision*, pp. 21–23; and Perry, *Innovation*, p. 66.

plane be capable of carrying a tactical nuclear weapon internally.[9] Internal carriage of this compact nuclear weapons load was necessary to minimize the aerodynamic drag of the aircraft for its high-speed, low-altitude dash under the enemy's radar. The plane was to be capable of carrying conventional bombs, but the amount of such bombs to be carried went unspecified. (A conventional mission would, in any event, require a higher tonnage payload and the external mounting of bombs.) Similarly, no mission profile or scenario was established for the conventional mission.[10]

Following the establishment of these requirements, General Everest began the process of inducing Air Force headquarters to ratify the formal requirements that TAC had composed. He succeeded in February 1960, when the System Development Requirement was approved. The System Development Requirement was followed, in July 1960, by the issuance of Specific Operational Requirement Number 183 (SOR-183), which officially committed the Air Force to what was now being called the TFX project.[11] The most important aspect of this ratification process, other than the fact that it formally committed the Air Force to a successor to the F-105, was that *the required speed for the 400-mile, sea-level dash had been increased from Mach 0.9 to Mach 1.2*.[12] This increase in dash speed is not described or defended in the public record. (The public record suggests that the dash speed requirement was set at Mach 1.2 from the beginning of Air Force deliberations.) The increase was

[9] Larry Booda, "Rift May Affect TFX Role, Configuration," *Aviation Week and Space Technology*, Vol. 79 (September 1963), p. 26; *TFX Hearings—First Series*, Part 3, p. 720; and *TFX Report*, pp. 5–6.

[10] That is, none of the performance specifications articulated a specific scenario for delivering conventional bombs. Any conventional mission performed by the plane would employ the de facto conventional capabilities provided by the nuclear mission requirements. See Notes of the Icarus meeting, September 10, 1966, in *TFX Hearings—Second Series*, Part 3, p. 548. See also the discussion in Part 1, pp. 183–198, of the hearings.

[11] Perry, *Innovation and Military Requirements*, p. 70; and *TFX Hearings—First Series*, Part 1, pp. 13–14.

[12] Government Report I.

apparently the result of TAC's need to differentiate the TFX from the F-105 in order to sell the proposed plane to Air Force superiors. The F-105 had a subsonic dash speed for an extended range at sea level. The promise of a supersonic dash speed on the TFX would thus provide an intuitively compelling indication of improved performance over the F-105.

But when this dash *speed* requirement was increased, NASA informed the Air Force that the dash *range* requirement was impossible to meet without a great increase in aircraft size and weight. Subsequently, the Air Force's own, in-house studies basically confirmed NASA's judgment.[13] Nonetheless, TAC insisted on proceeding.

This modification of the requirement for the sea-level dash was critical, for it placed unique burdens on the design of the aircraft, burdens reflected in the NASA warnings. Supersonic speed is a critical threshold in aircraft design. Because of the unique flow properties of air at supersonic speeds, aircraft design for such speeds is significantly more costly than for subsonic speeds. This would be especially true at the low altitude the Air Force specified for the supersonic dash. The air at low altitudes is both dense and turbulent. In such a medium the aerodynamic drag and structural stresses on an aircraft are particularly high, requiring a more rigid and aerodynamically refined structure for the aircraft. Because of the higher drag, fuel consumption is greater, requiring a larger volume in the aircraft for fuel storage. Indeed, this fuel requirement would dictate the size of the aircraft. And in addition to these penalties in terms of design difficulty, aircraft weight, and program cost, a supersonic speed capability on the low-level dash might not have promised major survivability benefits.[14] In

[13] Ibid. The Air Force studies were performed at Wright Air Development Division, Air Research and Development Command, the Air Force command that at that time supervised system developments and performed advisory studies on new requirements.

[14] The survivability advantages of a low altitude dash are primarily a function of the low altitude, with changes in speed at that altitude

any event, this capability was usable only on a mission for which ordnance was stored internally—that is, only on a nuclear mission. (A higher tonnage, conventional mission, for which bombs would have to be hung from the wings, would generate too much drag for the plane to have sufficient range at supersonic speeds.)[15] Nonetheless, TAC was committed to a supersonic speed capability on the low-level dash for delivering nuclear weapons. This capability would provide TAC with an airplane having unique penetration characteristics, an airplane seemingly able to "compete with the missiles" in the delivery of nuclear weapons.[16]

At the time the Air Force was establishing SOR-183, the Navy also was in the process of formulating requirements for a new tactical aircraft. The Navy in part wanted a plane capable of providing close support for friendly troops in land battle. However, the service saw an even more pressing need at this time to improve the defense of the surface fleet from air attack. It feared that future enemy aircraft would be able to fire air-to-sea missiles at the fleet from unusually long ranges. To counter this threat, the Navy needed a new fighter that could identify the enemy planes and shoot them down at an extended range—that is, shoot them down before they fired their missiles at Navy ships.

The Navy was divided on how best to meet these broad requirements. Clearly, a long-range air-to-air missile and a sophisticated fire-control system were required; but the characteristics of the aircraft—the "missile platform"—were

---

—between high-subsonic and Mach 1.2—altering survivability very little. This issue will be discussed in greater detail in Chapter III.

[15] Booda, "Rift May Affect TFX Role," p. 26; *TFX Hearings—Second Series*, Part 1, pp. 189–190; and Interview 16.

[16] Art, *The TFX Decision*, pp. 16–18, 45; Booda, "Rift May Affect TFX Role," p. 26; Alain C. Enthoven and K. Wayne Smith, *How Much Is Enough? Shaping the Defense Program, 1961–1969* (New York: Harper and Row, 1971), pp. 262–266; I. F. Stone, "In the Bowels of the Behemoth," *New York Review of Books*, Vol. XVIII (March 11, 1971), pp. 34–35; and Eugene Zuckert, "The Service Secretary: Has He A Useful Role?" *Foreign Affairs*, Vol. 44 (April 1966), p. 471.

a matter of considerable debate. Some in the Navy air arm felt that, without a supersonic capability, the proposed aircraft would be obsolete when it was deployed.[17] Others felt that, since the actual interception was to be performed by the long-range, high-speed missile, and since Navy close support aircraft were universally subsonic, it was unnecessary "to bore supersonic holes in the sky" with the aircraft. Moreover, they argued that the Navy did not have a pressing need for a supersonic fighter, since the new, supersonic F-4 Phantom was then entering service.[18]

In the end, the advocates of a simpler, subsonic aircraft emerged victorious. This decision to accept subsonic capability on the aircraft was apparently the result of austerity moves imposed by the Eisenhower Administration in its Fiscal Year 1960 budget.[19] A subsonic aircraft would be cheaper and would free sufficient funds for the anticipated expense of the long-range missile and avionics (aircraft electronics) system.

The Navy program was approved. The Navy then awarded a design contract to the Douglas Aircraft Company to develop the aircraft (to be called the F-6D Missileer). Meanwhile, the Bendix Corporation continued work it had earlier begun on the missile and avionics (the Eagle missile system).[20]

[17] Testimony of the Assistant Secretary of the Navy for Research and Development, Dr. James H. Wakelin, in *TFX Hearings—First Series*, Part 6, pp. 1476, 1533–1534.

[18] Art, *The TFX Decision*, pp. 25–27; Cecil Brownlow, "Navy Stresses Simplicity, Reliability to Ease Budget Pinch," *Aviation Week and Space Technology*, Vol. 70 (March 9, 1959), p. 79; U.S. Senate, Committee on Armed Services, *Military Procurement Authorization: Fiscal Year 1962*, Hearings, 87th Cong., 1st Sess. (1961), p. 20; and Interview 19.

[19] Brownlow, "Navy Stresses Simplicity," p. 78.

[20] Art, *The TFX Decision*, pp. 25–26; Cecil Brownlow, "Douglas Wins Contract for Missileer Design," *Aviation Week and Space Technology*, Vol. 73 (August 1, 1960), p. 33. As initial work on the Missileer began, the Soviet threat to Navy ships appeared to intensify. Previously, the main threat was presented by subsonic Badger bombers, modified to launch air-to-sea, standoff missiles. However, in the

It was now late 1960. The Navy at last was proceeding with the development of its new aircraft for fleet defense. The Air Force had formalized its requirements for a successor to the F-105 and was ready to inaugurate a competition among aerospace contractors to determine which company would develop the aircraft. At this point, however, the out-going Eisenhower Administration intruded, as it did not want to commit the new administration to any major weapons programs. It halted further development of the Missileer and prevented the Air Force from inaugurating a source selection competition.[21] Moreover, it instructed the Director of Defense Research and Engineering (DDR&E) to begin efforts to coordinate the requirements of the services into a single, multi-service fighter.[22] This coordinating effort would be long and difficult. However, with Robert McNamara soon to enter the Defense Department, the effort would shortly acquire an unusually determined sponsor.

Two Become One: McNamara Enters the Pentagon

It has been said of Robert McNamara that he was the first Secretary of Defense to read the description of his job and to take it seriously. McNamara brought to his new assignment a well-known set of ideas and managerial con-

---

late 1950s, the first prototypes of the new Tu-22 Blinder bomber began flying. The improved performance of this new bomber presented a more serious threat to Navy ships.

[21] Art, *The TFX Decision*, pp. 26–27; *TFX Hearings—First Series*, 6, p. 1385; and U.S. Senate, Committee on Armed Services, *Military Procurement Authorization: Fiscal Year 1962* (1961), p. 20.

[22] Government Report I. DDR&E was established in 1958 as a component of the Office of the Secretary of Defense, to serve as primary advisor to the Secretary on technical matters. It directed an interdepartmental advisory group on weapons procurement, the Weapon System Evaluation Group (WSEG), which was to be the vehicle for coordinating the multiple requirements of the services into a single, multi-service requirement. For information on the establishment of DDR&E and the function of WSEG, see C. W. Borklund, *The Department of Defense* (New York: Praeger, 1968), pp. 74–75, 83–84.

cepts, as well as a unique determination to put them into practice.[23] Moreover, he enjoyed the full backing of the new President, a President whose campaign had stressed the need for changes in the doctrine and management of the Defense Department.

Two areas of change advocated by the incoming administration are particularly relevant to our concerns. First, both Kennedy and McNamara were determined at the outset to end the needless duplication of weapon systems that plagued defense planners in the 1950s. The Eisenhower years had seen duplication in the development and procurement of many different types of weapons. As observed in 1957 in a much-quoted report of the House Appropriations Committee: "Each service, it would seem, is striving to acquire an arsenal of weapons complete in itself to carry out any and all possible missions. It is the firm belief of this committee that this matter of rivalry is getting completely out of control."[24] Prominent examples of this rivalry included the

[23] There are many good accounts of the innovations McNamara and his associates brought to defense management. See, particularly, Enthoven and Smith, *How Much Is Enough?* See also Charles J. Hitch, *Decision-Making for Defense* (Berkeley: University of California Press, 1965); William H. Kaufmann, *The McNamara Strategy* (New York: Harper and Row, 1964); Robert S. McNamara, *The Essence of Security: Reflections in Office* (New York: Harper and Row, 1968); and a good, short account, David Novick, "Decision-Making in the Department of Defense," in Edwin Mansfield (ed.), *Defense, Science, and Public Policy* (New York: Norton, 1968), pp. 44–61. For a critical evaluation, see Stone, "In the Bowels of the Behemoth." For an ingenious statistical study of the impact of the McNamara innovations on resource allocation in the Defense Department, see John P. Crecine and Gregory Fischer, *On Resource Allocation Processes in the U.S. Department of Defense*, Institute of Public Policy Studies, University of Michigan, Discussion Paper No. 31 (1971).

[24] Reproduced in Charles H. Donnelly, *United States Defense Policies in 1957*, House Document No. 436, 85th Cong., 2d Sess. (1958), p. 83. Another of many examples is a Senate report of 1957, which contended that the duplication of weapon systems was retarding force modernization efforts. See U.S. Senate, Committee on Armed Services, Subcommittee on the Air Force, *Airpower*, Report, 85th Cong., 1st Sess. (1957).

46

Army's Jupiter and the Air Force's Thor intermediate-range ballistic missiles (IRBMs), the Air Force's Snark and the Navy's Regulus cruise missiles, and the Army's Nike-Hercules and the Air Force's Bomarc anti-aircraft missiles. However, some of the rivalry and duplication even occurred within the services, as, for example, in the Air Force's F-105 and F-107 aircraft programs, and the Navy's F-4 and F-8 aircraft programs.[25] While some saw the duplication in positive terms—as being a sensible pursuit of multiple approaches to highly uncertain development tasks—the new administration saw the duplication as needless. Because of the frequency and cost of weapons duplication in the 1950s, Kennedy and McNamara (as well as the Congress) considered this an area where defense management needed to improve. The subject even warranted mention in Kennedy's first State of the Union address.[26]

The second area of agreement between the new President and the Secretary of Defense was their concern for reviving the "conventional option" in the United States' force posture. In the Eisenhower years, Massive Retaliation had emerged as the dominant doctrine for American defense capabilities. This doctrine—and its budgetary counterparts, the New Look and the New New Look—placed a heavy reliance on nuclear weapons to deter limited and full-scale Soviet aggression. Indeed, in 1957, Eisenhower's Secretary of Defense stated that "the smaller atomic weapons, the tactical weapons, in a sense have now become the conventional weapons."[27] Referring to a National Security Council

[25] Michael H. Armacost, *The Politics of Weapons Innovation: The Thor-Jupiter Controversy* (New York: Columbia University Press, 1969); Enthoven and Smith, *How Much Is Enough?*, pp. 15, 22, 169; Kaufmann, *The McNamara Strategy*, p. 30; and *TFX Hearings—First Series*, Part 9, pp. 2272–2273.

[26] "State of the Union Message," in *Congressional Quarterly Almanac*, Vol. 17, 87th Cong., 1st Sess. (1961), p. 859. See also Kaufmann, *The McNamara Strategy*, p. 47.

[27] U.S. House of Representatives, Committee on Appropriations, *Department of Defense Appropriations for 1958*, Hearings, 85th Cong., 1st Sess. (1957), Part 1, p. 36. For an excellent description

memorandum inherited by the Kennedy Administration, Sorensen notes that American planning at the time relied on nuclear retaliation for "any Communist action larger than a brush fire in general and [for] any serious Soviet military action whatsoever in Western Europe."[28] Both McNamara and Kennedy sought to modify this heavy reliance on nuclear weapons by providing greater flexibility in American defense capabilities.[29] While strategic nuclear forces were not themselves to be downgraded, conventional forces were to be expanded in number and strengthened in capability. Massive Retaliation was to be replaced by Flexible Response.

This new doctrine logically implied that defense decisions would begin to reflect the incoming administration's desire to strengthen the conventional option. True to his activist image, McNamara moved quickly in this direction. He commissioned a number of special task forces to study various aspects of the defense program. Within a month, these panels began submitting recommendations to him. For a few "most urgent and important problem areas," there were recommendations for immediate adjustments in the Fiscal Year 1962 budget already formulated by the Eisenhower Administration.[30] Among the several recommendations was a proposal for the modification of early models of the Air Force's F-105 fighter-bomber.[31] In April 1961, barely three months after assuming office, McNamara described the need for these F-105 modifications: "[We] recommend . . . the

---

of the formation of defense doctrine in the 1950s, see Samuel P. Huntington, *The Common Defense: Strategic Programs in National Politics* (New York: Columbia University Press, 1961), pp. 64–113.

[28] Theodore Sorensen, *Kennedy* (New York: Bantam, 1965), p. 703.

[29] Their concern was reinforced by Soviet Premier Khrushchev's speech of January 6, 1961, which endorsed "wars of national liberation," while it rejected more general wars. Ibid., p. 705; and Kaufmann, *The McNamara Strategy*, p. 60.

[30] U.S. Senate, Committee on Armed Services, *Military Procurement Authorization: Fiscal Year 1962*, p. 2.

[31] Ibid., p. 17.

modification of the earlier models of the F-105 tactical fighter to improve their performance and their capability to handle conventionally armed ordnance. . . . [The F-105's] conventional weapons potential is really quite limited, and in order to give it the power and to provide for the carrying of the additional weight necessary to use conventional weapons effectively, the pylons [and the installation of larger engines] must be undertaken."[32] The F-105 had been designed to deliver a low-tonnage payload—nuclear weapons—at very low altitudes and at very high speeds. The early models of the plane had not even incorporated provisions for carrying conventional ordnance.[33] The new doctrine of Flexible Response, however, revalued this earlier trade-off of conventional capability on the plane. The early F-105s would now be modified to perform the broader spectrum of missions that McNamara envisioned.

Later that year, in November, McNamara cancelled the F-105 program entirely, replacing it with the Navy's F-4 Phantom. Systems analysts in the Office of the Secretary of Defense (OSD) had been attempting all year to get the Air Force to buy the F-4 instead of the F-105. They saw the F-4 as a non-nuclear strike aircraft, possessing greater operational flexibility than the F-105. McNamara agreed with their position, and the Air Force ultimately acquiesced.[34] Clearly, in 1961 McNamara and his staff had acquired a detailed analytical grasp of the F-105's characteristics. Their concern for achieving greater flexibility in American tactical forces led them to discontinue a plane keyed to the nuclear mission emphasis of Massive Retaliation. In the case of the F-105, then, the operational implications of the new doctrine of Flexible Response were effectively articulated and implemented.

[32] Ibid., pp. 19, 83.
[33] Ibid. See also McNamara, *The Essence of Security*, pp. 77–79.
[34] Enthoven and Smith, *How Much Is Enough?*, p. 263; Head, "Decision-Making on the A-7 Attack Aircraft Program," pp. 155–170; and Kaufmann, *The McNamara Strategy*, p. 247.

The Air Force's proposed TFX was, of course, planned as a follow-on to the F-105, and the TFX requirements formulated by the Air Force were an extension of the basic operational emphases in the F-105's design. McNamara's intention to shift these operational emphases, as convincingly demonstrated in the modification and cancellation of the F-105, thus implied a repudiation of the basic operational doctrine behind the Air Force's proposed TFX. Consequently, one might plausibly have expected McNamara to modify the TFX requirements, to bring the requirements into conformity with the new defense doctrine. As a trade magazine speculated at the time, "enough has been said by President Kennedy and McNamara on the subject of the delivery of conventional weapons rather than nuclear weapons that another aircraft designed to deliver nuclear weapons [the proposed TFX] may not be well received."[35]

But the Air Force requirement was well received. In February 1961, the limited war panel (one of the special task forces McNamara had commissioned) reported to McNamara with a recommendation that the United States undertake the development of a multi-service fighter-bomber for use in the limited war environment. At the time he received this recommendation, McNamara had been considering the extant plans of the Navy and the Air Force for new tactical aircraft. At the apparent urging of DDR&E, which was already attempting to coordinate the requirements of the services, McNamara had begun to see the swing-wing, turbo-fan aircraft contemplated by the Air Force as providing the requisite operational flexibility to implement the new defense doctrine and to meet both services' requirements in a single aircraft.[36] The subsonic, trans-

[35] Larry Booda, "USAF and Navy Unable to Agree on Joint Tactical Fighter Project," *Aviation Week and Space Technology*, Vol. 75 (August 21, 1961), p. 27.

[36] Art, *The TFX Decision*, pp. 33–34; and *TFX Hearings—First Series*, Part 6, p. 1385. These sources refer to McNamara's increasing conviction that the Air Force's TFX requirement could be the basis for a joint development. The suggestion that DDR&E urged him in

oceanic range of the plane envisioned by the Air Force would provide the necessary subsonic loiter time for the Navy's fleet defense mission. It would also provide the capability for the subsidiary requirement contemplated by the Navy—the provision of close support to friendly troops in land battle, a mission which required long, subsonic loiter time over the battlefield. The high top speed of the plane envisioned by the Air Force would provide the desired capability for engaging enemy fighters. And the plane would have the ability to perform aerial interdiction with conventional or nuclear explosives.[37] Thus, when McNamara received the recommendation of the limited war panel, he felt that he had in hand the appropriate technical approach to avoid multiple service developments:

A new tactical fighter will be required eventually to supplement and replace the Air Force's F-105 and the Navy's F-4H. New developments in engine performance

that direction is the author's own surmise, based upon: (1) the fact that DDR&E had been studying the possibility of combining the Air Force and Navy requirements since the final months of the Eisenhower Administration; and (2) the publicly reported observation that DDR&E was always a strong supporter of a bi-service development. (See, for example, "Navy Facing Dilemma Over Decision on Fighter Plane," *Congressional Quarterly Weekly Report*, Vol. XXVI [February 16, 1968], p. 284.) As primary technical advisor to the Secretary of Defense, DDR&E would have given McNamara advice on all extant service requirements for new weapons when McNamara entered office. Since DDR&E had been attempting earlier to combine the Air Force and Navy fighter requirements, and since DDR&E is widely recognized as having been the strongest advocate in OSD of a bi-service development, it is likely that DDR&E suggested the combination of the requirements. In other words, the idea of applying commonality to these requirements probably originated in DDR&E and certain highly tentative decisions made during the final months of the Eisenhower Administration. The idea apparently was not McNamara's own. McNamara was responsible for making the concept bureaucratically viable, by imposing it on the Air Force and Navy.

[37] Art, *The TFX Decision*, pp. 33–34; Smith, "The $7 Billion Contract," Part I, p. 98; and written statement by Secretary of Defense Robert McNamara, *TFX Hearings—First Series*, Part 2, p. 376.

and aerodynamics, particularly the variable geometry wing concept evolved by NASA, now make it possible to develop a tactical fighter which can operate from aircraft carriers as well as from much shorter and cruder runways, and yet can carry the heavy conventional ordnance loads needed in limited war.

In general, what we are striving for is one fighter to fill the needs of all the services—a fighter which could operate from the large number of existing smaller airfields all over the world and yet fly without refueling across the ocean, thus greatly increasing its value for limited war purposes.[38]

McNamara saw the proposed multi-service fighter as primarily a means to increase American limited war capability. He thus accepted the recommendation of the limited war study group. Under McNamara's direction, Herbert F. York, Director of Defense Research and Engineering, on February 14 ordered the Navy and the Air Force to study the development of a joint tactical fighter. They were instructed to base their studies on the tactical fighter then under consideration by the Air Force. Following these joint studies, the services were to prepare a single specific operational requirement and technical development plan for York's approval.[39]

The Navy quickly reacted to McNamara's proposal for a multi-service development. The initial Navy reaction, in March 1961, depicted the planned Air Force plane as "having little or no application to meet Navy or Marine missions." Those Navy planes in existence or in planning stages were seen to offer superior capabilities. The proposed TFX was described as a "large, complex, expensive aircraft basically unsuited for limited war missions" and as a "useful

[38] U.S. Senate, Committee on Armed Services, *Military Procurement Authorization: Fiscal Year 1962*, p. 19.

[39] Art, *The TFX Decision*, p. 34; and written statement by Secretary of the Navy Fred Korth, *TFX Hearings—First Series*, Part 6, p. 1385.

aircraft for nuclear weapon visual attacks and, to a lesser degree, for all-weather nuclear attacks."[40]

Negotiations between the services proceeded nonetheless, under the auspices of DDR&E. By May, all parties recognized that the Navy-Marine close support requirement could not be reconciled with the other Navy and Air Force missions. Hence, they separated this requirement from the TFX negotiations and established a separate Navy program to meet it.[41] (This program was designated VAX—attack aircraft, experimental—and ultimately led to the A-7 attack aircraft.)

After this separation of the close support requirement, the Navy concurred in the need to develop a bi-service TFX—the Missileer had been cancelled by OSD in April, apparently in anticipation of the forthcoming joint program of the Air Force and Navy. With the Missileer's cancellation, the Navy no longer had a program of its own for a fleet defense aircraft, and the proposed joint program provided the only viable alternative.[42] In its concurrence on the joint program, however, the Navy proposed an alternative TFX design concept and contended that the Navy should manage the joint program. The Navy's proposed design would meet virtually all Air Force requirements except the Mach 1.2 sea-level dash speed—the Navy proposed a dash speed of Mach 0.9—and at the same time would, the Navy argued, be smaller and better suited to the carrier environment.[43] By

[40] Memorandum for the Director of Defense Research and Engineering, from Assistant Secretary of the Navy for Research and Development James H. Wakelin, Jr., dated March 9, 1961, re Aircraft for close support, interdiction, air superiority, and reconnaissance, printed in *TFX Hearings—First Series*, Part 6, pp. 1462–1463.

[41] Art, *The TFX Decision*, p. 38; and prepared statement of Secretary of the Navy Korth, *TFX Hearings—First Series*, Part 6, p. 1387.

[42] Art, *The TFX Decision*, p. 47; James C. Fahey, *The Ships and Aircraft of the U.S. Fleet* (Annapolis: U.S. Naval Institute, 1965), p. 29; and *TFX Hearings—First Series*, Part 6, p. 1476.

[43] Interview 19. Allusions to this alternative TFX can be found in Memorandum for the Secretary of Defense, from Secretary of the Navy John E. Connally, dated May 31, 1961, re Project 34 (the name for the 1961 project that was responsible for reviewing and

contrast, the proposed Air Force TFX was described as "too large and expensive" because of the supersonic, sea-level dash mission: "This is the critical mission that increases aircraft size and weight; it is a nuclear mission and not a limited war mission."[44]

McNamara, however, decided to keep the Air Force TFX as the basis for the joint program. In June he instructed Air Force Secretary Zuckert to make another attempt to obtain the Navy's concurrence on the specifications that the Air Force had drawn up for its follow-on to the F-105.[45] Negotiations between the Air Force and the Navy continued through that summer, reaching a final impasse late in August. The Navy then argued for termination of the plans for bi-service development and the initiation of separate service programs.[46] At this point, with his bi-service program in jeopardy, McNamara entered more forcefully into the picture. He resolved the stalemate virtually by fiat, through his so-called "Memorandum of September 1," which took the form of an addendum to the Air Force's original specific operational requirement (SOR-183 of July 1960). This addendum specified additional criteria of performance and physical dimension that the proposed plane was to satisfy,

---

coordinating the various service requirements), printed in *TFX Hearings—First Series*, Part 6, pp. 1387–1391. Recall in this context that the early Air Force requirement had itself specified a high-subsonic dash speed. The Navy's proposed design was essentially an exhumed design study the Navy had performed back in 1959, when it was still considering a supersonic aircraft for fleet defense and was conferring with NASA on possible employment of variable-sweep wings. (This latter information from a government report provided to the author, cited hereafter as Government Report II.)

[44] Memorandum for the Secretary of Defense, from Secretary of the Navy John B. Connally, dated May 31, 1961, re Project 34, printed in *TFX Hearings—First Series*, Part 6, pp. 1388–1389.

[45] Art, *The TFX Decision*, p. 39; and *TFX Hearings—First Series*, Part 6, p. 1391.

[46] Art, *The TFX Decision*, pp. 48–49; and Memorandum for the Secretary of Defense, from Acting Secretary of the Navy Paul P. Fay, Jr., dated August 22, 1961, re TFX, printed in *TFX Hearings—First Series*, Part 6, pp. 1464–1465.

beyond the SOR-183 requirements. It also specified the management arrangements for the joint program. Finally, it mandated that compromises of Air Force requirements to meet Navy requirements were to be held to a minimum in the course of the development.[47]

Thus, what had been two separate requirements when McNamara arrived had now become one requirement. In the process, McNamara had demonstrated his determination to end duplication in weapon system developments. But he had strangely neglected his larger goal of shifting American defense doctrine. The proposed bi-service aircraft was intended to possess a broad spectrum of capability for the limited war environment. But like the F-105, the bi-service TFX would be keyed to the high-speed, low-level delivery of an internal payload of nuclear weapons—a capability of narrow application to the limited war environment. If the cancellation of the F-105 was justified in light of the new defense doctrine, the character of the TFX requirements was not. The Air Force's nuclear mission requirements would structure the fundamental design choices on the proposed aircraft. As a result, the plane would not possess the broad spectrum of capabilities anticipated for it. It would be a specialized interdiction aircraft, a true Massive Retaliation fighter plane, not a multi-purpose fighter for limited war. Moreover, with the weight and cost burdens implicit in the dominant Air Force requirements, the achievement of Navy objectives would be more difficult.[48]

[47] Memorandum for the Secretary of the Air Force and the Secretary of the Navy, from Secretary of Defense Robert S. McNamara, dated September 1, 1961, re TFX, printed in *TFX Hearings—First Series*, Part 6, pp. 1513–1514. Many specifications were deleted from this printing of the memorandum due to security classifications in effect at the time of the first series of hearings on the TFX. For these specifications, see *TFX Report*, pp. 5–9.

[48] This difficulty would be compounded by the so-called growth factor, a factor which relates an increment of component weight to an increment in gross take-off weight. The growth factor is expressed as a multiple of the original increment of weight. When an increment of weight is added to an aircraft—for example, to strengthen a por-

Ultimately, McNamara's only recognition of the F-105 experience was his stipulation in the Memorandum of September 1 that the plane be capable of carrying 10,000 pounds of ordnance. In essence, this was a stipulation that "hardpoints" for bomb attachment be incorporated on the wings. The original performance requirements were unaffected.[49]

Nonetheless, for both McNamara and the services, the big question now was whether or not industry could design a satisfactory plane to meet the painfully established requirements. A source selection competition among aerospace companies thus began, a competition that proved as extended and difficult as the earlier establishment of requirements.

The Source Selection Competition

To prepare for the source selection competition, the services jointly formulated a "Work Statement" for the proposed aircraft. This document took the approved parameters of the

---

tion of the fuselage—it sets in motion an iterative cycle of further increases in fuel, engine power, structural strength, and so on, necessary to accommodate the original weight increment without a decrease in capabilities. (In high-density fighter aircraft, the growth factor has been estimated to be between 7 and 10.) This phenomenon meant that, in the bi-service TFX program, where significant commonality between versions was maintained, the unique requirements of each service would impose on the other service's aircraft a *multiple* of the weight needed strictly to meet the unique requirement. The dash mission of the Air Force, for example, would have a large growth-factor impact on the Navy version's weight, and the Navy was, of course, highly sensitive to the aircraft's weight.

The burden imposed by the nuclear mission requirements threatened McNamara's own objectives as well. A bi-service development could be justified mainly in terms of the money it could save. Yet if each service's version of the aircraft carried too much weight generated by the *other* service's unique requirements, the savings of a common development would be wiped out, since added weight in the aircraft would translate into added cost. See Leo Celniker and E. R. Schuberth, "Synthesizing Aircraft Design," *Space/Aeronautics*, Vol. 51 (April 1969), p. 60.

[49] *TFX Report*, pp. 5–9.

original SOR-183 and addendum and expanded them into far more detailed specifications and requirements.[50] While the SOR-183 and addendum were three or four pages long, the Work Statement was 250 pages long. The preparation of the Work Statement involved using the Air Force's original, 1960 Work Statement as a baseline, then adding Navy inputs in light of McNamara's September 1 addendum.[51] On October 1, the services issued their Request for Proposal to the aircraft industry, accompanied by the Work Statement. The source selection process began.

The source selection process ran one year, lasting an unprecedented four rounds. The first two rounds of the competition (October 1961 to May 1962) reduced the field of competitors from six to two: Boeing and General Dynamics. At that point, the combined Navy-Air Force Source Selection Board judged the proposals of both remaining contractors to be unacceptable. Two further rounds of competition (June 1962 through November 1962) produced acceptable proposals from both contractors. The Navy-Air Force Source Selection Board unanimously recommended the selection of Boeing, since Boeing's design promised greater attention to individual service requirements (through less commonality between Air Force and Navy

[50] Smith, "The $7 Billion Contract," Part I, pp. 182–184. See *TFX Hearings—First Series*, Part 6, pp. 1374–1377, for a description of the process of translating the Specific Operational Requirement into the more detailed Work Statement.

[51] *TFX Hearings—First Series*, Part 1, p. 50, and Part 6, pp. 1374–1375. The Department of Defense describes a Work Statement in the following terms: "The work statement must describe the application which the various areas of science and technology have in the work to be done. It must also reflect total engineering and development requirements, including laboratory work and tests. It must cover tooling concepts. Support equipment needs must be envisioned. Training requirements both personnel and devices must be covered. Testing programs—static testing and flight testing in the case of aircraft and missiles—must be developed. And, above all, the performance goals which the new weapon system is to achieve must be clearly identified." See U.S. Senate, Committee on Armed Services, *Procurement Study*, Hearings, 86th Cong., 2d Sess. (1960), Part I, p. 101, cited in Art, *The TFX Decision*, p. 24.

versions) and also proposed certain technical innovations the services found attractive. But McNamara overruled the Source Selection Board. He contended that the General Dynamics proposal was less risky in technical terms, more realistic on costs, and more productive of a truly common aircraft than the Boeing proposal. For him, these factors allegedly were decisive and, in any event, the services had judged the proposals of both contractors to be acceptable.[52]

[52] For a description of the source selection process and the contract award, see, especially, Art, *The TFX Decision*, chaps. 3–6; and Richard Austin Smith, "The $7 Billion Contract that Changed the Rules," Part II, *Fortune*, Vol. 67 (April 1963), pp. 110–111, 191–194, 199–200. Note that, while General Dynamics' cost estimates ultimately proved inaccurate, that fact does not by itself challenge the wisdom of McNamara's 1962 judgment about the superior *relative* accuracy of General Dynamics' estimates. It does not imply that Boeing's estimates were "actually" more accurate than General Dynamics' estimates. (Cf. *TFX Report*, pp. 78–82.) Indeed, a 1969 Defense Department study made available to the author (hereafter cited as Government Report III) tends to confirm McNamara's summary judgment that General Dynamics' cost estimates were the more reliable. The study is a detailed parametric analysis of fighter aircraft acquisition costs. It suggests that Boeing would have had to achieve major cost efficiencies over General Dynamics (and over aerospace industry norms) for its proposal estimates to have been more accurate than those of General Dynamics. Of course, whether or not Boeing could have achieved these major efficiencies is an open question, since a Boeing F-111 was never built. But this DOD study at least suggests one of the proper questions to ask to determine the correctness of McNamara's 1962 judgments on the relative accuracy of the two contractors' estimates: would Boeing's performance of the contract have been far more efficient than General Dynamics', to the point of validating Boeing's greater optimism in cost estimation? Obviously, as he judged the relative accuracy of Boeing's proposal estimates, a Secretary of Defense could not easily rely on Boeing's promises of atypically efficient performance.

In Boeing's possible favor, note one additional factor: if a Boeing F-111 would have included an ultimately successful Navy version, an F-111B procured in volume, then its cost estimates could be viewed as more accurate than General Dynamics' estimates, because the latter, *as it happened*, did not include a successful F-111B. While the lesser commonality of the Boeing planes may have provided greater technical promise of satisfying Navy requirements, and while McNamara's overruling of the Navy (and Air Force) preference for Boeing may have reduced the F-111B's prospects by further inflaming Navy antipathy to the joint program, it is still very difficult to assert with any confidence that a Boeing F-111B would have been success-

McNamara's decision to award the contract to General Dynamics touched off a heated public controversy, which will be discussed shortly. But certain aspects of the source selection competition and the contract award should be noted here. First, as Robert Art has recounted, the Navy resisted selecting a source until the completion of the fourth round of competition. In the first two stages of the competition, the Navy attempted to terminate the bi-service program in light of the unsatisfactory contractor proposals. Then, after McNamara indicated to the Navy that the only fleet defense aircraft it could get would be in this bi-service program, the Navy attempted to use its hesitancy to commit itself as a means of creating leverage for design compromises in its favor—the Air Force and OSD were, after all, anxious for the development program to begin.[53] This latter Navy tactic apparently succeeded in convincing McNamara to take its requirements more seriously, since requirements of commonality were relaxed for the fourth round of competition.

A second point to note is that in 1962 McNamara had a still-secret study of the program performed by private consultants. The study indicated that commonality would probably save as much money as McNamara anticipated, but would produce a serious weight problem on the Navy version.[54] Thus, McNamara was apprised of a potentially seri-

---

ful where a General Dynamics' F-111B was not (and thus to assert that Boeing's cost estimates were, in this indirect sense, more accurate than General Dynamics' estimates). Based on what McNamara could have known at the time, his judgments on the relative accuracy of the contractors' cost estimates seem reasonable. For a discussion of the general problem of estimating weapon costs, see J. Ronald Fox, *Arming America: How the U.S. Buys Weapons* (Boston: Harvard Business School, 1974), pp. 153–168.

[53] Art, *The TFX Decision*, pp. 68–71, 151–152.

[54] Interview 2. For information on the original expectation of savings from commonality, see *TFX Hearings—First Series*, Part 5, pp. 1190–1191. The conclusions on the Navy weight problem came as no surprise to some civilians under McNamara. These individuals had expected a weight problem even before the predictions of this study, as the variable-sweep wing promised unique weight penalties. On a

ous weight problem *before* the development actually commenced. Moreover, contrary to the public record, at least this one analysis of the F-111 specifications was performed before the contract award. McNamara did not simply acquiesce in the specification parameters that the services had sent out to the industry in October 1961.[55]

In any event, the outcome of the source selection process was the award in December 1962 of a Research, Development, Testing and Evaluation (RDT&E) contract to General Dynamics, in spite of the unanimous preference of the military hierarchy for Boeing.[56] The unique development program that was about to begin—the first bi-service development of a major weapon system—required unusual organizational arrangements for its management. The program was to be managed through the regular Air Force

---

fixed-wing aircraft, wing stresses are transmitted not only to the basic wing structure, but also to the general fuselage structure and aircraft skin. This is the so-called monocoque construction. On a variable-sweep wing aircraft, however, all wing stresses concentrate in the area of the wing pivot, requiring an extraordinarily heavy wing mounting. See A. Ernest Fitzgerald, *The High Priests of Waste* (New York: Norton, 1972), pp. 132–133.

[55] Cf. Enthoven and Smith, *How Much Is Enough?*, p. 262. See also Enthoven's testimony in U.S. Senate, Committee on Government Operations, Subcommittee on National Security and International Operations, *Planning, Programming, Budgeting*, Hearings, 90th Cong., 1st Sess. (1967), pp. 235–241. The assertion here is simply that some formal analysis was applied to the specifications before the contract award. This analysis was not, however, applied by Enthoven's fledgling systems analysis group in the comptroller's office.

[56] Though the TFX contract award was certainly the most publicized major award in McNamara's early years, it was not the first time under McNamara that OSD had overruled the unanimous contract choice of military source selection officials. In June 1962, five months *before* the TFX award, Pentagon civilians overruled the Bureau of Naval Weapons in awarding the contract for a vertical and short take-off and landing (V/STOL) aircraft to Bell Aircraft instead of Douglas. One year later, four months after the McClellan hearings on the TFX award began, Senator John Stennis' Preparedness Investigating Subcommittee began hearings on the V/STOL award. See U.S. Senate, Committee on Armed Services, Preparedness Investigating Subcommittee, *Award of X-22 (VTOL) Research and Development Contract*, Hearings, 88th Cong., 1st Sess. (1963).

development organization.[57] A small number of Navy personnel would be added to the Air Force F-111 System Program Office (SPO) in Ohio. These Navy program officials were to be subordinate to the Air Force command in the SPO. They were, however, to cooperate with the Air Force on common concerns in the development program and to maintain liaison with Navy technical bureaus in Washington.

All funds for the development of the F-111 airframe (both versions) and for the development of the TF-30 engines powering it would be budgeted by the Air Force. The Navy, for its part, would budget for and supervise the development of the Phoenix air-to-air missile—its fleet defense missile—and would supervise (though not budget for) the development of the TF-30 engines. The Navy would, in addition, budget for the production of its own version of the aircraft.[58] (This arrangement of program funding meant

[57] For the F-111 program, the regular Air Force development organization included an F-111 System Program Office (SPO) at Wright-Patterson Air Force Base in Ohio, which office was in turn part of the Aeronautical Systems Division of the Air Force Systems Command. The commander of Air Force Systems Command reports to the Chief of Staff of the Air Force, the highest ranking officer in the Air Force organization.

[58] Memorandum to the Secretary of the Navy, from the Chief of the Bureau of Naval Weapons, dated March 20, 1963, re Navy participation in management of F-111 (TFX) program, printed in *TFX Hearings—First Series*, Part 7, pp. 1817–1822. As the program began, the Navy planned to procure 235 F-111s, while the Air Force planned to procure 1,491 F-111s. For a point of reference on these figures (and on the volume figures to be cited throughout our study), note the following evolution of procurement plans from the early years of the program to the present:

| | Total Planned Procurement | | |
Date	Air Force	Navy	Total
October 1961	641	235	876
July 1962	1,491	235	1,726
March 1964	1,706	705	2,411
December 1964	1,017	355	1,372
November 1968	785	8	793
January 1976	557	8	565

These figures include the few R&D prototypes each service planned to procure (18 Air Force and, ultimately, 8 Navy prototypes). Also,

61

that the Navy's expenditures on the program would be relatively low until its version of the aircraft entered production.)[59]

Even the contractor arrangements for the program were unusual. General Dynamics had won the competition in partnership with the Grumman Corporation. Grumman had built more naval aircraft than any other American company. Consequently, it had considerable expertise in designing carrier aircraft and enjoyed a close working relationship with the Navy. By contrast, General Dynamics (Convair) had been almost exclusively a builder of Air Force aircraft since World War II: the F-102, F-106, and B-58. General Dynamics entered the partnership both to secure design expertise on carrier aircraft and to reassure the Navy that its needs were being taken seriously. Grumman was to be a major subcontractor for the development and production of both Air Force and Navy versions of the plane and was scheduled to perform the actual assembly of the Navy version.

With these arrangements established, the long-delayed TFX (now designated the F-111) development began. As full-scale development proceeded in 1963, the program became surrounded by a major controversy.

The 1963 McClellan Hearings

The controversy that enveloped the program was created by Senate hearings on the contract award.[60] The hearings were held by the Senate's Permanent Subcommittee on

---

the listed Air Force volumes include: (1) 24 Australian F-111s after 1962; and (2) 2 British F-111s and varying numbers of SAC FB-111s after 1964. For historical planning volumes in the program, see U.S. House of Representatives, Committee on Armed Services, *Hearings on Military Posture,* Hearings, 91st Cong., 1st Sess. (1969), p. 3202.

[59] The significance of this unusual timing of major Navy expenditures will be discussed in Chapter v.

[60] See Bert Z. Goodwin, "The TFX Hearings: A Study in Controversy Creation" (unpublished M.Sc. thesis, Massachusetts Institute of Technology, 1970), for a sophisticated critique of the McClellan hearings.

Investigations of the Committee on Government Operations, under the chairmanship of Senator John McClellan (Democrat of Arkansas). The hearings were initiated in response to Congressional suspicions that the contract award to General Dynamics had been politically motivated.[61] The losing Boeing proposal was thought to be both lower in cost and superior in performance to the General Dynamics proposal. And there was circumstantial evidence that political considerations had been decisive in the F-111 contract award. General Dynamics was in serious financial trouble in 1962, and its Fort Worth, Texas, facility—where the F-111 would be developed and produced—would likely have shut down had it not received the F-111 contract award.[62] Vice President Lyndon B. Johnson was, of course, from Texas and was thought to have exerted pressure in General Dynamics' favor. President Kennedy himself was suspected to have been involved, as he was considered potentially vulnerable to claims from campaign donors who had a large interest in financially troubled General Dynamics.

But for all these prior suggestions of impropriety, the hearings failed to provide any documentation of political influence on the contract award.[63] As they failed in that line

[61] Ibid.; Art, *The TFX Decision*, pp. 3–4; and *TFX Report*, p. 1.

[62] See Richard Austin Smith, "How a Great Corporation Got Out of Control," Part II, *Fortune*, Vol. 65 (February 1962), p. 188. General Dynamics' precarious financial position was primarily the result of: (1) a disastrous corporate venture into the commercial jet transport market; and (2) an impending termination of its B-58 strategic bomber program for the Air Force. The corporate loss on its jet transport venture was 425 million dollars, then the largest project loss by one corporation in commercial history.

[63] Art, *The TFX Decision*, pp. 6–7; Stone, "In the Bowels of the Behemoth," pp. 29–37; and *TFX Report*. The hearings did document that Roswell Gilpatric, Deputy Secretary of Defense, had performed extensive legal services for General Dynamics prior to his appointment, but only minor services for Boeing. However, Gilpatric's role in the decision was relatively minor, and no one demonstrated any direct influence by Gilpatric on the award. At the same time, the more general allegations of political influence cannot be disproved. A large number of skeptics remain unconvinced. The present study can offer no new evidence on the matter.

of inquiry, the hearings devolved into a consideration of whether the decision on the contract award had been mistaken on its merits. If the award was shown to be mistaken on its merits, political suspicions would have been indirectly validated, for politics would then be the sole remaining premise for the award to General Dynamics.[64] But this line of inquiry also proved inconclusive, except as it demonstrated that any decision on the contract award was reasonably a matter of judgment. Some factors favored Boeing, others favored General Dynamics, and the contractor one considered superior depended on the factors one considered most important.[65] Accordingly, the Committee could not prove politics to be the only conceivable premise of the award.

While the hearings were inconclusive on the substantive issues of the contract award, they had an important impact on the program itself. They certainly cast public doubt on the wisdom of McNamara's decision to award the contract to General Dynamics. In the process, they forced McNa-

[64] Goodwin, "The TFX Hearings," pp. 68–69.
[65] Ibid., pp. 73–78; Art, *The TFX Decision*, chap. 5; Smith, "The $7 Billion Contract," Part II, pp. 192–194, 199–200. For more critical views of the contract award, see Stone, "In the Bowels of the Behemoth," pp. 29–37; and *TFX Report*, pp. 10–51, 90. As noted earlier in the text, Boeing's design was superior in subsonic performance, in the technical features proposed in its airframe design, and in the greater possibility it offered for meeting each service's unique requirements through lesser commonality. The General Dynamics design was superior in supersonic performance, in what McNamara considered to be its greater realism in cost estimates and schedules, in its greater commonality between versions, and in its less risky design features. For the military officials of the Source Selection Board, the performance and technical features of the Boeing design were most important. For McNamara and his colleagues, however, the cost and schedule realism and the technical conservatism of the General Dynamics design allegedly were most important. They argued that the military's preference represented a parochial military emphasis on performance that needed to be broadened to include considerations of technical risk and cost. Their argument was itself reasonable, although critics of the contract award saw the argument as mere "window-dressing."

mara into a strong public defense of his decision and enlarged his stakes in the program. Because of the controversy that had been generated by the hearings, only a successful development program could vindicate McNamara's judgment. Beyond increasing McNamara's stakes in the program, the hearings created the basis for a political alliance between Senator McClellan and the Navy. In the hearings, Senator McClellan repeatedly contended or inferred that McNamara had been wrong to award the contract to General Dynamics. The Senator was sure to consider any subsequent deficiencies in the General Dynamics F-111 to be a vindication of this position. The Navy was also sure to be sensitive to any deficiencies in the F-111. Since the early program debates, the Navy had contended that the Air Force F-111 was not suited to Navy missions. While the Navy ultimately acquiesced in the joint program, it remained skeptical of the program's ultimate prospects for success. Deficiencies in the Navy F-111 would vindicate this early skepticism. The Navy's interests in the program were thus allied with those of Senator McClellan. Later in the program, this alliance would have fateful implications for the Navy version of the F-111.

The hearings were suspended in November 1963, following the assassination of President Kennedy. The President's death made further investigation of the politics of the contract award unseemly. Moreover, the debate had by that time shifted to the merits of the decision on its own terms, a debate that could better be resolved by the success or failure of the actual development than by abstract debate.

Although the hearings were suspended, the efforts of Senator McClellan continued to present a latent challenge to the program. The hearings were planned "to resume at a later date"; and, in any event, the controversy generated by the hearings had placed the development effort in a "goldfish bowl." According to one high-level Air Force official, trade-offs by the contractor and the government were very difficult to make because of the program visibility created by the hearings.[66] But with suspension of the hearings, the public controversy, at least, had subsided.

The Development Program and Its Outcomes

The full-scale development process for the F-111 commenced in December 1962 and proceeded during the time of the McClellan hearings. A large contractor design team (varying between 4,000 and 6,000 persons in the course of the program) performed the engineering effort. A much smaller Air Force System Program Office (SPO, ultimately composed of over 200 persons) monitored the contractor effort through a vast array of required reports and a less formal network of personal contacts.[67]

Fairly early in this effort, major development problems had to be addressed. Drag problems with the aircraft's configuration were discovered in the first year of the development by NASA scientists. Drag increases represented a particular problem for the Air Force, since the sea-level dash of the nuclear mission demanded an extremely "clean" aerodynamic configuration. In the dense air at sea level, high aerodynamic drag would drastically reduce the range of the supersonic dash.

In early 1964, Dr. Alexander Flax, Assistant Secretary of the Air Force for Research and Development, was apprised of these problems by NASA and advised to halt development pending reconfiguration of the aircraft. He was presented with a real dilemma, for General Dynamics had performed its own tests elsewhere and had had optimistic results. Dr. Flax chose not to halt the development because he had known that the F-111A (the Air Force version of the plane) would have a higher drag count than General

[66] Interview 13.

[67] See Fox, *Arming America*, chaps. 9–10, 20–24; Robert L. Perry et al., *System Acquisition Strategies*, Rand Memorandum No. R-733-PR/ARPA (June 1971), pp. 28–29; and *TFX Hearings—First Series*, Part 4, p. 1144.

Dynamics had anticipated. The NASA revelations did not surprise him. Moreover, the wind tunnel tests on which the opposing data were based were only simulations. Though Dr. Flax knew the General Dynamics figures were optimistic, the contradictory NASA figures were not necessarily accurate either. The real question was what could be done to refine the drag estimates and to reduce the drag levels of the aircraft. Hence, Dr. Flax decided to continue development, but to provide NASA with a more sophisticated wind tunnel model for further tests. In addition, existing models were to be tested in multiple tunnels.[68]

In late 1963, a second major problem appeared in the development: General Dynamics completed a new weight estimate, which projected an 8,000-pound weight increase in the F-111B, the Navy version of the aircraft. The Navy argued with McNamara for a halt in development and a redesign of the F-111B, at a February 1964 management review of the program. George Spangenberg, an aeronautical engineer for the Navy, later said that this appeal for redesign, and others that were to follow, were really ploys to achieve a separate Navy program.[69] McNamara decided instead to continue common development and to initiate a concentrated weight control and improvement program (dubbed the Super Weight Improvement Program, or SWIP). In addition, he approved the development of "fallback" design studies of the Navy version, in the event that the weight savings programs failed.

Later that year, in a July review of F-111B progress and of the fall-back redesigns, McNamara was confronted with optimistic Air Force and General Dynamics estimates—and pessimistic Navy estimates—of the F-111B's weight and performance. McNamara decided again to continue development, while reaffirming the focus of management atten-

[68] Interviews 12 and 13. For a general discussion of the drag problem and the decisions made to resolve it, see *TFX Hearings—Second Series*, Part 2, pp. 339–365. Note that NASA did not receive the more sophisticated model for six months.

[69] *TFX Hearings—Second Series*, Part 2, p. 408.

tion on the weight problem and suggesting the need to wait for "hard data" on the aircraft's weight and performance. Meanwhile, as the development continued, the configuration of the aircraft was "hardening." A prototype would fly in a few months, and major configuration changes to rectify any problems would become even more difficult to make.

The first F-111 prototype, an F-111A, flew in December 1964. Initial tests of this aircraft were run by General Dynamics, which, by virtue of a mistake in the preparation of the program contracts, was not legally obligated to provide information on them to the Government.[70] The first F-111B was delivered in May 1965. Flight testing proceeded through the summer, culminating in a formal Navy evaluation in October 1965. These tests gave Pentagon officials the hard data they had been awaiting. And this data, along with that of subsequent test flights in 1966 and 1967, seemed to prove the pessimists right. Both the Air Force and the Navy versions of the F-111 were judged "underpowered" and "sluggish." Moreover, problems of compatibility between the engine and airframe were obstructing the progress of the flight test program, initially preventing the plane from even attempting supersonic speeds.[71] The flow of air to the plane's engines was turbulent, and the engines were overly sensitive to this turbulence. As a result, the engines were repeatedly "stalling" (losing power or shutting down completely) in flight. The main positive factor in the flight tests was the successful performance of the variable-sweep wings, which were, ironically, the primary technical advance in the airframe design.

[70] *TFX Hearings—Second Series*, Part 3, pp. 498, 501–503. This mistake apparently was the result of pure inadvertence. The Air Force was trying out a new data reporting system in the F-111 program. In constructing this complicated new system (which became a part of the contract), the Air Force accidentally omitted coverage of *contractor* flight test data. Interview 19.

[71] *TFX Hearings—Second Series*, Part 1, pp. 205–207, and Part 3, pp. 498–499.

Meanwhile, in April 1965, the Defense Department made a formal commitment to production of the F-111 by signing a *letter contract* with General Dynamics. This important commitment was made by the government *before it had any rigorous flight test data of its own on either the F-111A or F-111B*.[72] Later that year, immediately following the initial Navy and Air Force flight tests of the F-111, Mc-Namara announced the decision to produce a strategic version of the F-111A (the FB-111A), which was to have altered avionics and extended wingtips (as on the Navy version).[73] It was intended to replace the Strategic Air Command's (SAC's) aging B-52C through F models, which were to be phased out.[74]

[72] A *letter contract* formally authorizes development or production to begin, but it does so only by specifying general obligations and parameters for the authorized effort. A letter contract is used to expedite development or production by avoiding the delays of contract negotiations. These negotiations proceed concurrently with the actual development or production that they are to cover. The detailed contract that results from these negotiations is a *definitized contract*. (The fact that the government confidently signed the letter contract for F-111 production before receiving detailed flight test information, except as General Dynamics chose to give it, is of major interest in terms of cybernetic assumptions, as we shall see in later chapters.) *TFX Hearings—Second Series*, Part 3, pp. 498, 501–503, 580–581; and Interview 19.

[73] According to a summary of NASA support efforts in the F-111 development, wind tunnel tests on a Strategic Air Command (SAC) version of the F-111 were underway as early as September 1964. See Staff of the NASA Research Centers, *Summary of NASA Support of the F-111 Development Program: Part I—December, 1962-December, 1965*, Langley Working Paper 246 (Langley Station, Virginia, undated), p. 17 (from the files of the Permanent Subcommittee on Investigations, Committee on Government Operations, U.S. Senate, Exhibit 13 of the *TFX Hearings—Second Series*).

[74] *TFX Hearings—Second Series*, Part 3, pp. 501–504; and U.S. Senate, Committee on Armed Services, *Supplemental Military Procurement and Construction Authorizations: Fiscal Year 1967*, Hearings, 90th Cong., 1st Sess. (1967), p. 424. Some considered this program for a strategic F-111 to be a means of sweeping tactical F-111 R&D expense "under the rug," as well as being a means for Mc-Namara to finesse Air Force pressures for a new SAC bomber as the older B-52's were phased out. See Thomas Alexander, "McNamara's Expensive Economy Plane," *Fortune*, Vol. 75 (April 1967), p. 184;

By mid-1966, improvements in inlet performance had been obtained, but stalls were still considered a problem.[75] Moreover, it had become clear to the Secretaries that the performance of both versions of the F-111 was significantly less than that specified in the contract.[76] At this point, with aircraft coming down the production line, McNamara entered more forcefully into the picture, commencing weekly (later bi-weekly) meetings with his Secretarial associates and high-level General Dynamics and Pratt & Whitney officials. These meetings later became commonly known as "Project Icarus."[77]

The Icarus meetings were dominated by problems with the performance of the F-111A and with the weight and

J. S. Butz, "FB-111: Second Look at the Third Version," *Air Force and Space Digest*, Vol. 49 (February 1966), pp. 37–38; Captain William R. Liggett, USAF, "FB-111 Pilot Report," *Air Force Magazine*, Vol. 56 (March 1973), pp. 31–37; George C. Wilson, "AMSA Goal Limits F-111 Bomber Design," *Aviation Week and Space Technology*, Vol. 83 (December 20, 1965), pp. 21–22; and Claude Witze, "FB-111: Answer to Our Strategic Needs?" *Air Force and Space Digest*, Vol. 49 (January 1966), pp. 18, 21–22.

[75] Interview 16; *TFX Hearings—Second Series*, Part 3, pp. 518–519; and, for example, "Abstract, Navy Evaluation of the Production F-111B High-Lift Devices: Final Report," dated November 23, 1966 (from the files of the Permanent Subcommittee on Investigations, Committee on Government Operations, U.S. Senate, Exhibit 22B of the *TFX Hearings—Second Series*). This latter document, dealing with Navy flight tests of the F-111B in May 1966, notes that "Navy evaluation of the SWIP F-111B airplane in the high-lift configuration should not be conducted until . . . the airplane has been adequately cleared for stalls."

[76] See Telegram to Pratt & Whitney and General Dynamics, from the USAF System Program Office, dated July 21, 1966, re Performance of the F-111A and F-111B, printed in *TFX Hearings—Second Series*, Part 3, p. 510. The pessimistic performance estimates were presented to the Secretaries in a July 20, 1966, executive management review. The telegram requested General Dynamics and Pratt & Whitney to develop a detailed plan for achieving contract specifications.

[77] *TFX Hearings—Second Series*, Part 3, p. 540. An Air Force officer was responsible for the "Icarus" label. Icarus was the figure from Greek mythology who used wings of wax and feathers to escape from the island of Crete. However, he flew too close to the sun, his wings melted, and he fell into the sea.

performance of the F-111B. McNamara and his associates considered the central performance problem on the F-111A to be its performance on conventional missions.[78] As Mc-Namara commented in September 1966, " 'The failure to have [the conventional mission] specified from the outset was a DOD error and was a fall-out from the day when emphasis was almost exclusively on tactical nuclear missions.' "[79] Remedies for the poor conventional mission performance were being sought at that time, and further remedies were to be initiated over the following two years. In June 1966, against the wishes of the Air Force, McNamara moved to enhance the F-111A's avionics capabilities for the conventional mission by inaugurating the development of the extremely sophisticated Mark II avionics package.[80] In the course of the later Icarus meetings, the Secretaries took another step to improve the F-111A's conventional capabilities, a step reminiscent of the F-105 modification program McNamara had approved in 1961:

[78] Interviews 10, 11, 12, and 20; and *TFX Hearings—Second Series*, Part 3, p. 548.

[79] *TFX Hearings—Second Series*, Part 3, p. 548. On the lack of specification for the conventional mission, see Part 1, pp. 193–198 of the same series of hearings.

[80] This new avionics package provided greater navigational accuracy for all missions, including nuclear interdiction, but most of its new features (e.g., the ability to track moving targets on the ground at night and in bad weather) were quite specifically addressed to the conventional mission. McNamara approved the program for its offering of additional conventional capabilities. (The latter information from Interviews 11, 20, and 22.) More general information on the Mark II avionics in "U.S. Air Force Selected Acquisition Report on the F-111A/D/E/F," dated December 31, 1969, p. 16 (from the files of the Permanent Subcommittee on Investigations, Committee on Government Operations, U.S. Senate, Exhibit 10 of the *TFX Hearings—Second Series*); U.S. Congress, Joint Economic Committee, Subcommittee on Economy in Government, *The Military Budget and National Economic Priorities*, Hearings, 91st Cong., 1st Sess. (1969), pp. 794–818; U.S. Senate, Committee on Armed Services, *Fiscal Year 1972 Authorization for Military Procurement*, Hearings, 92d Cong., 1st Sess. (1971), pp. 1564–1565, 3885–3887; and Claude Witze, "The F-111's Mark II Avionics System—Weapons Effectiveness or Electronic Gadget?" *Air Force and Space Digest*, Vol. 52 (August 1969), pp. 62–65.

they commenced a program to develop larger engines to give the F-111 the additional power needed for conventional missions.[81]

However, both the engine and avionics improvements came too late to be incorporated in 235 of the 437 tactical F-111s that are ultimately to be produced.[82] At the same time, the F-111's sea-level supersonic dash capability was limited to only 30 miles within the specified nuclear mission radius of 800 miles (or, alternatively, to 200 miles within a mission radius of 540 miles). The aerodynamic drag of the airframe and the fuel consumption of the engines exceeded expectations and limited the range of the dash.[83] With these range limitations, much of the dash on a nuclear mission would be performed at subsonic speeds. Similarly, as was apparent from the outset of the program, all of the dash on a conventional mission would be performed at subsonic speeds. Yet a broad spectrum of design choices had been keyed to a *supersonic* dash for the nuclear mission. If a *subsonic* dash had been sought from the outset, a smaller

---

[81] The so-called P-100 engine (TF-30-P-100) resulted from this program, an engine whose increased performance was specifically directed toward the conventional mission. This was an expensive program: as of 1969, the R&D cost for the P-100 engine was estimated to be 83 million dollars. The cost of retro-fitting the P-100 engine in the 190 F-111s already produced that could accept the engine was estimated at two million dollars *per plane*, or 380 million dollars in total. See *TFX Hearings—Second Series*, Part 1, pp. 206, 211–213, and 244; and Part 2, pp. 323–326.

[82] *TFX Hearings—Second Series*, Part 1, p. 191.

[83] *TFX Hearings—Second Series*, Part 1, p. 59; "U.S. Air Force Selected Acquisition Report on the F-111A/D/E/F," dated December 31, 1969, p. 3 (from the files of the Permanent Subcommittee on Investigations, Committee on Government Operations, U.S. Senate, Exhibit 10 of the *TFX Hearings—Second Series*); and U.S. Senate, Committee on Appropriations, *Department of Defense Appropriations: Fiscal Year 1973*, 92d Cong., 2d Sess. (1972), Part 4, p. 781. For the specified nuclear mission, the 30-mile dash range noted in the text applies only to those F-111s with the original production inlet—that is, for the 141 F-111As with the "Triple Plow I" inlet. As will be discussed momentarily in the text, the other F-111s have a higher-drag inlet. For most of these remaining F-111s, the dash range is less than 30 miles.

and lighter plane would have been possible, a plane more in keeping with McNamara's doctrinal concerns and, at the same time, less inflammatory to the Navy.[84] But because the plane was heavy (the heaviest tactical fighter in operation), lacking in relative power (the lowest engine thrust relative to aircraft weight of any supersonic American fighter), and lacking in relative wing area (the highest ratio of aircraft weight to wing area of any operational American fighter), the F-111A lacked the acceleration and maneuverability necessary for flexible, multi-purpose capability.[85] Such a plane could not be the only Air Force fighter into the 1970s. To be sure, the F-111 did possess unique and valuable capabilities. It could "fly blind" at low altitudes for operation at night or in bad weather. Compared to other fighter aircraft, it could carry a larger payload for a longer distance at a faster low-altitude speed. But in spite of these capabilities, it remained more bomber than fighter—a far more expensive and specialized aircraft than anyone intended, a plane that could not provide the broad spectrum

[84] Interviews 6, 9, 12, 19, and 22. See Celniker and Schuberth, "Synthesizing Aircraft Design," pp. 60–66; Leon H. Dulberger, "Advanced Strategic Bombers," *Space/Aeronautics*, Vol. 45 (June 1966), pp. 62, 74; William K. Greathouse, "Blending Propulsion With Airframe," *Space/Aeronautics*, Vol. 50 (November 1968), p. 62; *TFX Hearings—First Series*, Part 5, pp. 1197–1199; U.S. Senate, Committee on Appropriations, *Department of Defense Appropriations for Fiscal Year 1969*, Hearings, 90th Cong., 2d Sess. (1968), p. 328; and U.S. House of Representatives, Committee on Armed Services, *Hearings on Military Posture* (1969), p. 2631.

[85] "Aerospace in Perspective: Strategic Warfare," *Space/Aeronautics*, Vol. 51 (January 1969), p. 89; "Aerospace in Perspective: Tactical Warfare," *Space/Aeronautics*, Vol. 51 (January 1969), p. 98; and *TFX Hearings—Second Series*, Part 1, pp. 199–200, 204. For brief discussions of the relative importance of these crude but suggestive measures, see Stuart M. Levin, "F-15: The Teething of a Dogfighter," *Space/Aeronautics*, Vol. 52 (December 1969), pp. 38–39; Michael P. London, "Tactical Air Superiority," *Space/Aeronautics*, Vol. 49 (March 1968), pp. 63–70; and Michael P. London, "VFX—The Navy's Choice," *Space/Aeronautics*, Vol. 50 (November 1968), pp. 51–52. For a comparison with Soviet fighters on these measures, see Robert D. Archer, "The Soviet Fighters," *Space/Aeronautics*, Vol. 50 (July 1968), pp. 67–71.

of capability envisioned for it in the early 1960s.[86] As a partial result, the Air Force began in the mid-1960s to develop plans for a new fighter (the FX, or fighter experimental) that would, among other things, fill the gap in aerial combat capability created by the deficient and, in many respects, disappointing F-111 performance.[87] In short, while the nuclear mission performance of the F-111 was itself deficient, the attempt to obtain supersonic performance for that stringent mission had subsumed broader aircraft capabilities.

In any event, during the time of the Icarus meetings, the stall problem continued to plague the F-111s. The resolution of this problem continually required the Secretaries' attention. Until early 1968, a number of minor modifications of

[86] For a description of the F-111's unique characteristics, see C. M. Plattner, "F-111 Shows Unique Interdiction Capability," *Aviation Week and Space Technology*, Vol. 90 (February 3, 1969), pp. 42–44, 49–51; U.S. House of Representatives, Committee on Armed Services, *Hearings on Military Posture* (1969), pp. 3207–3209; U.S. House of Representatives, Committee on Armed Services, *Hearings on Military Posture*, Hearings, 91st Cong., 2d Sess. (1970), pp. 7538–7540. (It should be cautioned that, in the 1969 hearings cited, the version whose effectiveness is being described is the F-111D. The 96 F-111Ds are the only F-111s with the extremely sophisticated Mark II avionics.) For a description of the F-111's 1968 operational experience in Southeast Asia, see the 1970 House hearings cited above, pp. 7541–7542. For favorable descriptions of its 1972–1973 combat experience, see Cecil Brownlow, "F-111 Shows Bombing Support Strength in Indochina," *Aviation Week and Space Technology*, Vol. 98 (April 30, 1973), pp. 88–93; "F-111's Prove Worth in Southeast Asia," *Armed Forces Journal*, Vol. 110 (March 1973), pp. 22–23; Wayne Thomis, "Whispering Death: The F-111 in SEA," *Air Force Magazine*, Vol. 56 (June 1973), pp. 22–27; and U.S. House of Representatives, Committee on Armed Services, *Hearings on Cost Escalation in Defense Procurement Contracts and Military Posture*, Hearings, 93d Cong., 1st Sess. (1973), pp. 1538–1568. There is a problem in interpreting these reports, since they may contain important biases that are hidden to the reader. For example, the Air Force's favorable reports of the F-111A's 1968 combat effectiveness in Southeast Asia may have been drawn from a selective, 40 percent sample of the actual missions flown (Interview 22).

[87] See "The TFX Verdict," *Aviation Week and Space Technology*, Vol. 94 (January 4, 1971), p. 7; *TFX Hearings—Second Series*, Part 1, pp. 188–189; and *TFX Report*, pp. 75–76.

the existing inlet were attempted. But in February of that year the Secretaries approved a major change in inlet design. This change increased the drag of the inlet, but it effectively removed the stall problem and, at the same time, provided the increased air intake capacity necessary for the larger engines then being envisioned. However, 141 F-111s were already beyond the point in the production line where this larger, more stall-resistant intake could be economically incorporated.[88]

The F-111B was inevitably a source of particular concern to the Secretaries, for in its prospects for success lay the prospects of vindicating McNamara's original judgments in the program, from his decree of common development to his choice of General Dynamics as the program contractor. The F-111B's problems were considered primarily a result of the plane's growth in weight. Since earlier weight reduction programs had removed all the airframe weight that it was safe to remove, the Secretaries concerned themselves with compensating technical remedies, such as slightly larger engines and higher-lift wings.

These efforts on the F-111B continued through 1967. However, in October 1967 the Grumman Corporation submitted an "unsolicited" redesign proposal for the F-111B, and the Navy secured approval to study this alternative.[89] In early November, high-level Navy officials, including the Chief of Naval Operations, moved to have the F-111B cancelled. Later that month, McNamara announced his resignation, to be effective in February 1968.[90]

The Navy ultimately succeeded in its cancellation move, for in March 1968 the Navy and the Defense Department

[88] Minutes of the Icarus meeting, February 16, 1968, excerpted in *TFX Hearings—Second Series*, Part 3, p. 565; *TFX Hearings—Second Series*, Part 1, p. 244, and Part 3, pp. 518–519; and Interview 16.

[89] Interview 18.

[90] *New York Times* (November 4, 1967), p. 1; *New York Times* (November 28, 1967), p. 1; and *New York Times* (November 30, 1967), p. 1. McNamara's resignation was for reasons unrelated to the F-111 program.

apparently worked out an agreement to cancel the F-111B quietly following the presidential elections later that year. The agreement provided for a reduction in initial production commitments that year—from 30 units down to 8 units —and an acceleration of the development of a successor aircraft, then in the planning stages. High-level Defense Department officials approached the Senate Armed Services Committee to arrange the deal. But the Committee wanted to cancel the F-111B outright and had only been awaiting word that the Navy could afford a delay in the deployment of a new fleet air defense capability. The deal proposed by Defense Department officials was taken by the Committee to indicate that a delay could be afforded.[91] Thereupon, the Committee formally recommended cancellation of the F-111B. In the end both houses of Congress agreed. The Defense Department terminated the F-111B program on July 10, 1968.[92]

The F-111A program continued, as the inlet, engine, and avionics changes already described were phased into production. The program was to face other problems, including, most importantly, fatigue and stress cracks in the plane's wing box. An expensive redesign and modification program for the wing box was required to correct the problem.[93]

[91] "New Plane Seen More Costly, Little Better Than F-111," Congressional Quarterly Weekly Report, Vol. xxvi (May 3, 1968), pp. 1007–1009. This article is reprinted in U.S. Senate, Committee on Armed Services, Preparedness Investigating Subcommittee, U.S. Tactical Air Power Program, Hearing, 90th Cong., 2d Sess. (1968), pp. 27–31. Notably, in a Navy rebuttal to the article in the hearings (pp. 31–32 of the hearings), the Navy does not refute the alleged deal.

[92] See John W. Finney, "Senate Unit Bars Navy F-111B Jets," New York Times (March 29, 1968), p. 13; "House Unit Backs End to the F-111B: Action on Funds Viewed as Plane's Death Sentence," New York Times (July 3, 1968), p. 14; and Harold Gal, "Pentagon Halts Navy F-111 Work," New York Times (July 11, 1968), p. 17.

[93] The wing box provides the structural "shoulders" of the aircraft, to which the pivoting wings are attached. For a description of the F-111's wing box problem and of the measures taken to resolve it, see TFX Hearings—Second Series, Part 2, pp. 259–270, 289–293,

But the main outcomes of the program were already clear. Through Fiscal Year 1975, as the program neared completion, the Air Force had procured 141 F-111As, with relatively restrictive and stall-prone inlets that prevented the retrofit of more powerful engines; 96 F-111Ds, with the extremely sophisticated Mark II avionics, a slightly more powerful engine, and the enlarged, more stall-tolerant inlet; 94 F-111Es, with the enlarged inlet, but the same engine and avionics as the F-111A; 106 F-111Fs, with the enlarged inlet and a substantially more powerful engine, as well as a sophisticated avionics system that is less expensive than the Mark II system; and, finally, 76 FB-111As, with the same basic inlet as the F-111D, but with different avionics, the Navy's extended wing tips, and a slightly more powerful engine.[94] For most of the tactical F-111s, performance results were disappointing. Note in Table I the F-111A results.[95]

---

and Part 3, p. 658; U.S. House of Representatives, Committee on Armed Services, *Hearings on Cost Escalation* (1973), pp. 1559–1560; and U.S. Senate, Committee on Armed Services, *Fiscal Year 1972 Authorization for Military Procurement*, pp. 1297–1298.

[94] For a decription of the various F-111 versions and the number of each to be produced, see *Jane's All the World's Aircraft, 1975–76* (New York: McGraw-Hill, 1975). The figures listed in the text exclude an additional 18 Air Force R&D prototypes (all basically F-111As), 5 Navy R&D prototypes, 2 Navy production aircraft (actually 2 additional R&D prototypes covered under the production contract), 24 F-111Cs (F-111s purchased by Australia, which are basically F-111As), and 2 F-111Ks (R&D prototypes, basically F-111As, intended for Great Britain until that country terminated its involvement in the program in January 1968, just after McNamara's resignation). Later, in the mid-1970s, 40 of the F-111As were to be converted to a specialized configuration for electronic warfare. These converted F-111As were to be designated EF-111As.

[95] The percentage deficiencies listed for takeoff weight, acceleration time, takeoff distance, and landing distance are actually percentages over requirement (lower values are more desirable on these measures). For all other performance measures, higher values are more desirable, and the deficiency percentages represent shortfalls from specifications. All of these performance figures should be considered illustrative only, since there may have been slight improvements in the

Table I. F-111A: Specified Performance Versus Actual Capability.

Category	Specified Performance	Actual Performance	Deficiency (Percent)
Take-off Weight	69,122 lbs.	82,500 lbs.	20
Maximum Speed			
—High Altitude	2.5 Mach	2.2 Mach	12
—Sea Level	1.2 Mach	1.2 Mach	0
Cruise Speed, High Altitude	2.2 Mach	2.2 Mach	0
Combat Ceiling	62,300 ft.	58,000 ft.	7
Acceleration Time (Mach 0.9 to Mach 2.2)	1.45 min.	4.0 min.	275
Take-off Distance	2,780 ft.	3,550 ft.	28
Landing Distance	2,250 ft.	2,320 ft.	3
Nuclear Mission (Dash/Radius, in nautical miles)	210 n.m./ 800 n.m.	30 n.m./ 800 n.m., or 200 n.m./ 540 n.m.	85/0 5/37
Ferry Range (nautical miles)	4,180 n.m.	2,750 n.m.	34
Avionics		Met or exceeded all major requirements	
Maximum Payload		Nearly double the original requirement	

performance of the plane in recent years. However, the content of the chart is fairly representative, and the order of magnitude of each deficiency should be accurate. While the performance cited applies specifically to the F-111A, the performance of the F-111E is nearly identical. The performance of the F-111D is only a slight improvement over the F-111A, except in avionics equipment. The F-111D's Mark II avionics enjoy a significant improvement in navigation and weapons delivery features over the F-111A's Mark I avionics, yet they suffer from markedly inferior reliability (and, we should add, dramatically higher costs). Finally, the performance of the F-111F is still classified, but is known to be a major improvement over the performance of the F-111A. If all the F-111s were F-111Fs, there would doubtless have been fewer criticisms of F-111 performance. As it is, only 24 percent of the tactical F-111s are F-111Fs. Performance data are taken from *TFX Hearings—Second Series*, Part 1, p. 59; "U.S. Air Force Selected Acquisition Report on the F-111A/D/E/F," dated December 31, 1969 (from the files of the Permanent Subcommittee on Investigations, Committee on Government Operations, U.S. Senate, Exhibit 10 of the *TFX Hearings—Second Series*); U.S. Senate, Committee on Appropriations, *Department of Defense Appropriations: Fiscal Year 1973*, Part 4, pp. 781–784; and Interview 16.

For these capabilities, the government paid twice as much in real terms as it had originally estimated.[96] And, while initial production commitments and aircraft deliveries were made on schedule, problems in the aircraft's structure and in the F-111D's Mark II avionics delayed operational availability of the various F-111 versions by two years (a time overrun of perhaps 30 to 40 percent).[97]

These results were certainly unfortunate, but they were not really unusual. On the average, Air Force programs of the 1950s exceeded their target costs by 100 to 200 percent and their planned development times (to operational availability) by 36 to 50 percent. Achievement of specified performance was common—on the average, specifications were fully achieved—but there was significant variation from program to program.[98]

In this light, the F-111 program appears far more typical in its results than the critics of the program would admit.[99]

[96] Alvin J. Harman, assisted by Susan Henrichsen, *A Methodology for Cost Factor Comparison and Prediction*, Rand Memorandum No. RM-6269-ARPA (August 1970), pp. 30–47, 53–56. For a brief discussion of the F-111 cost growth, see p. 58n of the present study.

[97] *TFX Hearings—Second Series*, Part 2, pp. 259–270, and Part 3, pp. 654–659; U.S. House of Representatives, Committee on Armed Services, *Hearings on Cost Escalation* (1973), pp. 1559–1560; and Interview 16. The fact that early production proceeded as scheduled, in spite of all the problems we have noted, is an interesting phenomenon, especially from the perspective of cybernetic assumptions. Subsequent chapters will examine this issue in detail.

[98] See A. W. Marshall and W. H. Meckling, "Predictability of the Costs, Time and Success of Development," in Richard Nelson (ed.), *The Rate and Direction of Inventive Activity* (Princeton: Princeton University Press, 1962), chap. 5; Merton J. Peck and Frederick M. Scherer, *The Weapons Acquisition Process: An Economic Analysis* (Boston: Harvard Business School, 1962), chaps. 2 and 16; and Robert Summers, *Cost Estimates as Predictors of Actual Weapons Costs: A Study of Major Hardware Articles*, Rand Memorandum No. RM-3061-PR (March 1965).

[99] For example, note the observation of Perry et al. in a 1969 Rand study: "The [cost growth factor] of the F-111 program is not quite as good as the mean of fighter aircraft programs [for the 1950s], but it is certainly closer to the mean of these programs than to the high range of the dispersion." See Robert L. Perry et al., *System Acqui-*

79

Indeed, the program seems to represent continuity, not deterioration, in the results of Air Force acquisition programs. As our analysis proceeds, we will observe in much greater detail how typical the problems and results of the F-111 program were.

What were the problems of the F-111 development, behind the typical summary results in cost, development time, and performance? This chapter provides us with a fairly specific appraisal. As the program drew to a close, the Navy version had been cancelled altogether. In spite of persistent evidence of engine-inlet compatibility problems dating from the first F-111 flight, 141 F-111As had been produced with relatively restrictive air inlets and a permanent susceptibility to engine stalls. And all F-111s had been burdened by the dominant requirement for performing a stringent nuclear mission, a mission that imposed high costs and offered debatable benefits, even as it differed from McNamara's original purposes for the plane.[100] For all this, the government paid more than nine billion dollars.[101]

---

sition Experience, Rand Memorandum No. RM-6072-PR (November 1969), p. 38.

[100] Of course, there were other persistent problems in the program, including most importantly the cost, time, and performance troubles with the Mark II avionics and the structural weaknesses in the F-111's wing box (both noted earlier in the text). The Mark II avionics will be discussed in conjunction with nuclear mission issues, in Chapter III. The wing box deficiencies will be discussed in conjunction with the engine-inlet compatibility problems, in Chapter IV.

[101] This figure represents a rough estimate of total acquisition costs for the program. Operation and maintenance expenditures are excluded. Over the operating life of the planes, these expenditures normally equal or exceed original acquisition costs. Since a detailed final accounting has not been released, the final cost figure for the program is not known with precision. (For the same reason, the final "cost overrun" factor for the program is not known.) For basic cost detail on the program, see *TFX Hearings—Second Series*, Part 3, pp. 587, 666. The cost estimates in the *TFX Hearings* should be adjusted to include approximately 500 million dollars in additional Mark II avionics expenditures and 720 million dollars in additional acquisition expenditures for 48 more F-111Fs. For these additional costs, see U.S. Senate, Committee on Armed Services, *Fiscal Year 1973*

CENTRAL ISSUES

For analytical convenience, we can separate the problems of the F-111 program between the two versions of the aircraft. The engine-inlet compatibility problems affected both Air Force and Navy versions, but they were primarily an Air Force problem—that is, the Navy could and did rely on the Air Force to resolve them. By contrast, the Navy took vigorous action on the weight problem, since the Air Force had a lesser concern for weight. The Navy could not rely upon altruistic efforts by the Air Force to cure the F-111B's weight problem.[102] That said, the following questions appear to be the most critical puzzles for our analysis to resolve:

Authorization for Military Procurement, pp. 1190–1191. Apparently, one cost savings anticipated for the bi-service program—a reduction in the Air Force's characteristic excess of spare parts inventories for its planes—was never realized, thus contributing to high operating costs of the plane. In 1963, McNamara hoped that bi-service deployment of the F-111 would, through a joint Air Force-Navy supply program, reduce the Air Force's excess inventories: "The disadvantages of operating many different weapon systems can be observed in the Navy and the Air Force today. The Navy currently has a rate of aircraft out of operation for lack of parts which is altogether too high. The Air Force is maintaining a better operational rate, but at a cost of excessive spare parts inventories. With the present rapid rate of technological change, the Air Force has acquired a $2.2 billion inventory of spare parts that are already obsolete and practically worthless." However, in 1972, the General Accounting Office charged (and the Air Force basically agreed) that spare parts inventories were more than 162 million dolllars excessive for the F-111. The demise of the F-111B had been paralleled by the demise of anticipated changes in Air Force routines for ordering spare parts. See Richard Witkin, "Air Force Waste on Parts Charged," _New York Times_ (February 22, 1972), pp. 1, 11; and _TFX Hearings—First Series_, Part 2, p. 276.

[102] On the Navy's relative lack of concern with the inlet problem, see U.S. House of Representatives, Committee on Armed Services, _Hearings on Military Posture_, 90th Cong., 2d Sess. (1968), p. 8765. On the Air Force's relative acceptance of the weight growth, see the testimony of Harold Brown, then Secretary of the Air Force, in U.S. Senate, Committee on Armed Services, _Military Procurement Authorizations, Fiscal Year 1966_, Hearings, 89th Cong., 1st Sess. (1965), pp. 476, 489.

Air Force Version

1. Why was a nuclear bomber developed to fulfill limited war missions? Why was this initial commitment to the Air Force's specifications sustained throughout the development?

2. Why were 141 F-111s produced with relatively restrictive air inlets and a permanent susceptibility to engine stalls?

Navy Version

1. Why did the aircraft gain weight in the course of development?

2. Why were the Navy pleas for redesign never accepted?

3. Why was the Navy version cancelled?

A closer look at each of these puzzles begins in the next chapter, where the problems of the Air Force's design and mission are examined. Subsequent chapters will analyze the engine-inlet compatibility problems and the Navy version problems. In each of these chapters, competing paradigms of decision will be used to reveal a set of factors in the development process to which McNamara and his colleagues were insufficiently sensitive—factors which help to explain the otherwise puzzling outcomes of this controversial program.

CHAPTER III

Why a Nuclear Bomber?

Although there is no indication what decision Secretary Mc-Namara will make when presented with the impasse, enough has been said by President Kennedy and McNamara on the subject of delivery of conventional weapons rather than nuclear weapons that another aircraft designed to deliver nuclear weapons may not be well received.

—Aviation Week and Space Technology, August 1961[1]

In the heated debates surrounding the F-111 program, there was one issue on which all participants reached agreement: the formal performance requirements of the Air Force and Navy were impossible to meet within the technical state of the art of the 1960s. Sources as disparate as Navy admirals, Air Force generals, Senator McClellan, Alain Enthoven, NASA, I. F. Stone, and General Dynamics shared this conclusion.[2]

Why were such ambitious requirements established? They embodied a demanding nuclear mission at odds with the multi-purpose capabilities McNamara envisioned for the

[1] Larry Booda, "USAF and Navy Unable to Agree on Joint Tactical Fighter Project," *Aviation Week and Space Technology,* Vol. 75 (August 21, 1961), p. 27.

[2] Alain C. Enthoven and K. Wayne Smith, *How Much Is Enough? Shaping The Defense Program, 1961–1969* (New York: Harper and Row, 1971), pp. 262–266; the 1968 testimony of Rear Admiral Thomas F. Connolly, then Deputy Chief of Naval Operations for Air (the head of naval aviation), in U.S. House of Representatives, Committee on Armed Services, *Hearings on Military Posture,* 90th Cong., 2d Sess. (1968), pp. 9360–9388; I. F. Stone, "In the Bowels of the Behemoth," *New York Review of Books,* Vol. xvi (March 11, 1971), pp. 29, 34–37; *TFX Hearings—Second Series,* pp. 187–188; *TFX Report,* pp. 7–9, 74–76, 90; and Interview 16.

plane. They imposed a significant design burden on the aircraft, a burden that certainly made the simultaneous fulfillment of Navy requirements a task beyond the state of the art.[3] Moreover, McNamara's acceptance of these requirements as the foundation for a joint development represented a paradoxical lack of awareness on his part. At the time that the joint requirement for the F-111 was being established, McNamara was acting on the advice of his systems analysts to cancel the F-105, a plane tailored to the delivery of nuclear weapons. In the case of the F-105, McNamara and his colleagues demonstrated a fairly sophisticated understanding of the weapon characteristics implied by the new doctrine of Flexible Response. This understanding was notably absent in the F-111 deliberations.

In attempting to explain why these requirements were sustained throughout the program, this chapter will address two issues of more general significance in defense affairs. First, it will demonstrate how design flexibility is lost at the outset of weapons developments. It will show the importance of establishing analytical coherence between doctrine, mission, and requirements *before* the development of a weapon begins, particularly if it is to be a bi-service weapon, the development of which involves sufficient management difficulties to warrant minimizing problems of attaining specified performance. Second, this chapter will reveal some of the difficulties a Defense Secretary faces in implementing a new doctrine. Especially when a new doctrine involves modifying rather than merely augmenting existing capabilities, it can imply substantial disruption in the plans and operations of important suborganizations like TAC. These suborganizations will resist the disruption. Moreover, they will often have rather subtle influence over the process of implementing the new doctrine: they exert substantial control over the agenda of new requirements and directly supervise the actual development efforts for any approved program. When he forced the Air Force and

[3] Interviews 11, 16, 19, and 22.

the Navy into a common development program in 1961, Mc-
Namara failed to appreciate the influence TAC and the Air
Force exerted over the character of new weapon systems.
An advocate of Flexible Response, McNamara inaugurated
the development of the consummate Massive Retaliation
fighter plane.

F-III MISSION AND DESIGN

The propositions sketched above will emerge gradually in
our examination of the problems of mission and design in
the F-111 program. The argument we will present is straightforward. The original TFX requirements were a routine extension of TAC's assumptions and experience under the
doctrine of Massive Retaliation. These requirements and
those of the Navy constituted the range of available options
when McNamara entered office. With little close analysis,
he simply chose the most nearly appropriate of the options
—the ostensibly flexible aircraft that TAC planned—as the
basis for a joint program. The design process worked
quickly to translate the nuclear mission emphases of the
joint requirement into design emphases in the actual hardware, in a manner relatively impervious to qualitative considerations outside the formal requirements. When McNamara became fully aware of the nuclear mission emphasis
in 1966, it was too late to modify the aircraft in any substantial way.

The Selective Incrementalism of the Requirements
Process: Establishing SOR-183

[Organizations] avoid uncertainty. By arranging a negotiated environment, *organizations regularize the reactions of
other actors with whom they have to deal. . . . Where the
international environment cannot be negotiated, organizations deal with remaining uncertainties by establishing a set*

85

of standard scenarios *that constitute the contingencies for which they prepare.*

—Graham T. Allison[4]

Tactical aircraft are weapons of extraordinary complexity. The possible combinations of engines, aerodynamic features, avionics, armament, and other components that can be incorporated in a tactical aircraft are virtually infinite. The number of possible missions or scenarios for which a tactical aircraft may have to be prepared is also vast, as it includes (within certain outer limits) an enormous array of possible altitude, speed, load, maneuverability, and other sequences. Any attempt to match means to ends—that is, in practice, to match capabilities to missions—runs up against high uncertainty as to which missions and capabilities are the most important. Moreover, it runs up against physical realities that impose stringent trade-offs among capabilities, and hence among missions for which the plane can be optimized.

In the abstract, then, the formulation of requirements for a new fighter aircraft is a problem of great complexity and uncertainty. In practice, however, the organization avoids confronting much of this complexity and uncertainty, concentrating instead on a few "standard scenarios" or missions that simplify the problem. The organization usually establishes one of the missions as the dominant operational contingency of the organization. This central mission will emphasize a small subset of the wide array of possible performance capabilities. (For example, it might require a particular ferry range, top speed, and maximum payload capability.) Capability for the remaining missions will be achieved as a *de facto* by-product—it will "fall out"—of the capabilities required for the dominant mission.

The dominant mission and the performance parameters it

[4] Graham T. Allison, *Essence of Decision: Explaining the Cuban Missile Crisis* (Boston: Little, Brown, 1971), p. 84. Emphasis in the original.

emphasizes evolve over time in response to operational experiences, perceived technological opportunities, budgetary emphases, interservice rivalries, and other factors. In the Air Force, for example, TAC is charged with three basic missions: (1) *close air support*—air cover for friendly ground troops; (2) *air superiority*—control of the skies over the combat zone; and (3) *air interdiction*—reduction of enemy supply and mobility capability through aerial bombardment.[5] At any point in time, certain performance requirements of one mission may be seen as more important than the requirements of the other missions. The select requirements of the more important mission will be placed at the center of technical efforts to develop a new aircraft or to improve an existing one. The determination of which mission and performance characteristics are the most important occasionally will be a matter of great debate within TAC, particularly when there is pressure for change from within the organization (such as, following unfavorable combat experiences) or from external sources (such as, shifting budget emphases). The central mission itself will be replaced or substantially modified. At other times, the pressure for change is minimal, and the central mission is undisturbed. Requirements for new aircraft will then be routinely derived as improvements over old aircraft along the dimensions of performance emphasized in the old aircraft. In this latter case, the fighter in use will be the bench mark for the formulation of a new requirement, as it embodies design emphases commensurate with the organization's simplified view, its "standard scenario," of the tactical environment.

The process can be observed in the evolution of Air Force fighter-bombers since World War II. For the Air Force, the central design lesson of World War II, a lesson later rein-

---

[5] Richard G. Head, "Decision-Making on the A-7 Attack Aircraft Program" (unpublished doctoral dissertation, Syracuse University, 1970), pp. 97–99. The argument that follows in this section of the text owes a considerable debt to extended discussions with Thomas Garwin and Frederic Morris.

forced by the Korean War, was the importance of speed for reducing combat losses.[6] Since the air-superiority mission required the highest speed to engage enemy aircraft, the Air Force commonly designed fighter aircraft to achieve high speed and then accepted whatever bomb-carrying capability was available as a by-product. The postwar evolution of fighter aircraft designs is witness to this doctrine: from the F-86 to the F-111, each generation fighter-bomber possessed a top-speed increase over the prior generation.[7]

[6] Ibid., pp. 105, 115–116; Pierre Grasset, "Dogfighting Makes a Comeback," *Interavia*, Vol. 29 (December 1974), pp. 1188–1191; and Frederic A. Morris, "Perspectives on the Air Force Lightweight Fighter Program" (unpublished paper, Harvard University Program on Science and International Affairs, 1975), p. 5. The actual, objective value of high speed may have been overestimated by the Air Force. The Air Force F-86, the fighter that appeared to demonstrate the importance of high top speed, achieved 65 percent of its victories as a result of making the first firing pass, an achievement based more on relative pilot abilities than on the speed of the aircraft. Nonetheless, the Air Force saw in the Korean combat a validation of the top-speed lesson.

[7] After the Korean War, as top speeds increased beyond the speed of sound, fighter aircraft placed increasing emphasis on sophisticated air-to-air missiles and avionics for air superiority. In the "new era of extreme speeds," the close-range, visually targeted "dogfight" between aircraft armed with machine guns was thought obsolete. Strictly in terms of their aerial combat capability, the fighter designs of the era—in particular, the F-4, F-104, F-105, and F-106, as well as the F-111 that was to follow—were basically very fast radar and missile platforms. The high top speeds of these planes would allow them to move quickly to the optimal point for firing infrared or radar-guided missiles at enemy planes that had been electronically detected (often detected beyond visual range or under conditions of darkness or bad weather). The high top speed was also thought to be useful for penetration of an enemy's airspace for deep interdiction. Because the air-to-air missiles would, as it were, do the dogfighting for the plane, *the issue of maneuverability in these (increasingly large and heavy) aircraft did not have to be confronted.* As we shall discuss later in our study (p. 136n), this conception of the air superiority mission was subsequently modified in response to the unfavorable aerial combat experience in Vietnam: visual identification rules predominated in that conflict, close-range dogfighting proved important, and the sophisticated air-to-air missiles proved less useful than had been anticipated. Indeed, some pilots and observers thought the sophisticated missiles to be less useful than the "old fashioned" machine gun or cannon. Among other things, the *new* lesson of combat

In the 1950s, the rise of the Massive Retaliation doctrine led to a de-emphasis of the air-superiority mission *per se* and a greater emphasis on the interdiction mission, particularly nuclear interdiction.[8] This emphasis first became apparent in the F-100, a plane developed in the early 1950s. Like the F-86 before it, the F-100A was designed closely to the speed requirement of the air-superiority mission—it was, after all, the first operational aircraft to be capable of combat maneuverability and sustained flight at supersonic speeds.[9] However, under the influence of the Massive Retaliation doctrine, the plane later evolved into a fighter-bomber (in its C, D, and F versions) through changes in its electronic subsystems and modifications of its provisions for external stores. In the end, the Air Force procured ten times as many of the fighter-bomber versions as of the original air-superiority version.[10]

---

experience was the importance of maneuverability, a capability that had been more or less ignored over the years under the influence of the top speed assumption. Now, from the vantage point of the mid-1970s, the top speed assumption seems to be a gross simplification of the demands of the air superiority mission. However, with an eye to our theoretical argument, we should emphasize that, in its day, the top speed assumption was as much the conventional wisdom on air superiority as, today, the maneuverability emphasis is. An excellent discussion of these air superiority issues, on which this note relies, is Morris, "Perspectives." See also Grasset, "Dogfighting," pp. 1188–1191; Head, "Decision-Making on the A-7 Attack Aircraft Program," pp. 115–116; Stuart M. Levin, "F-15: The Teething of a Dogfighter," *Space/Aeronautics*, Vol. 52 (December 1969), p. 40; and Thomas Marschak, "The Role of Project Histories in the Study of R&D," in Thomas Marschak, Thomas K. Glennan, Jr., and Robert Summers (eds.), *Strategy for R&D: Studies in the Microeconomics of Development* (New York: Springer-Verlag, 1967), pp. 98–99.

[8] Head, "Decision-Making on the A-7 Attack Aircraft Program," pp. 90, 114–116.

[9] Marschak, "The Role of Project Histories," p. 92. This is a fairly clear example of a routine follow-on. The F-100 design was actually based on the configuration of the F-86, a plane which saw extensive combat action in Korea. North American Aviation was prime contractor for both aircraft.

[10] Ibid., pp. 95–96; and Head, "Decision-Making on the A-7 Attack Aircraft Program," pp. 114–116.

The follow-on to the F-100 was the F-105, a plane "designed from radome to afterburner eyelids as a TAC nuclear weapons delivery airplane."[11] Head has commented on the F-105, "This emphasis on the design of fighters to carry tactical nuclear weapons exemplified the trend of the Air Force in the 1950's, to have the Tactical Air Command participate in the strategy of Massive Retaliation."[12] Defense budgets were emphasizing the delivery of nuclear weapons. To avoid budget famine, TAC needed strong capabilities in this area. It was a time when "the smaller atomic weapons, the tactical weapons, in a sense [had] become the conventional weapons."[13]

The F-105 first flew in 1955 and provided top speed, low-altitude speed, range, and other improvements over the F-100.[14] It was particularly designed for the high-performance delivery of nuclear weapons at low altitudes.[15] As we noted in Chapter II, the first version of the F-105 did not even have adequate provisions for *carrying* conventional ordnance. The main provision for ordnance carrying was the internal bomb bay—the first to be incorporated in a fighter-bomber—that would allow a compact weapons load (tactical nuclear weapons) to be carried internally, to reduce aerodynamic drag for low-altitude operation.[16] The resulting mission profile would permit nuclear weapons

[11] Interview 21.
[12] Head, "Decision-Making on the A-7 Attack Aircraft Program," p. 90.
[13] Congressional testimony of Defense Secretary Charles Wilson, in U.S. House of Representatives, Committee on Appropriations, *Department of Defense Appropriations for 1958*, Hearings, 85th Cong. 1st Sess. (1957), Part I, p. 36.
[14] *Jane's All the World's Aircraft, 1961–62* (New York: McGraw-Hill, 1961), pp. 296–297; and *Jane's All the World's Aircraft, 1970–71* (New York: McGraw-Hill, 1970), pp. 339–340.
[15] Leon H. Dulberger, "Advanced Fighter-Attack Aircraft," *Space/Aeronautics*, Vol. 45 (April 1966), p. 81; Head, "Decision-Making on the A-7 Attack Aircraft Program," p. 90; George Weiss, "The F-111: The Swing-Wing May Surprise You Yet," *Armed Forces Journal*, Vol. 108 (July 19, 1971), p. 23; and Interview 21.
[16] Head, "Decision-Making on the A-7 Attack Aircraft Program," p. 90; and *TFX Hearings—First Series*, Part 1, p. 19.

delivery at a low-altitude, high-speed combination that enemy interceptors would have difficulty matching.[17] Nuclear interdiction at low altitudes and high speeds had emerged as the dominant TAC scenario, as the budget environment shaped the organization's perception of the combat environment.

Even with this shift in the focus of TAC doctrine and capabilities, the organization had entered a period of major force reductions. During and after the Korean war, the number of TAC aircraft wings (each comprised of approximately 54 aircraft) had risen from 19 to a high of 34 in 1957. After 1957 dramatic reductions occurred: to 26 wings in 1958 and to 18 wings in 1959. A further reduction of 3 wings was contemplated for the early 1960s.[18]

At the same time, more fundamental threats to the viability of manned strike aircraft were emerging. Shortly after the first flights of the F-105, the nation's attention was riveted upon the awesome new capabilities provided by nuclear-tipped ballistic missiles. The Soviet Union had just launched its first Sputnik, and the American reaction was intense. American missile programs were accelerated. The increasingly prominent role foreseen for missiles seemed to portend the obsolescence of manned aircraft in the strike role.

These threats to the role of tactical aircraft were explicit. In 1958, General Lauris Norstad, Supreme Allied Commander in Europe (SACEUR), who held ultimate operational command over Air Force tactical aircraft in Europe, argued that tactical aircraft in Europe had become too vulnerable and ought to be replaced with medium-range ballistic missiles (MRBMs).[19] His suggestion hardly could

[17] Weiss, "The F-111," p. 23.
[18] Head, "Decision-Making on the A-7 Attack Aircraft Program," pp. 122–123, 165–169. See also William D. White, *U.S. Tactical Air Power: Missions, Forces, and Costs* (Washington: Brookings Institution, 1974), p. 15n.
[19] William H. Kaufmann, *The McNamara Strategy* (New York: Harper and Row, 1964), p. 38.

have been more ominous to TAC, since Europe was the most likely theater of engagement for the tactical nuclear capability of TAC. The tactical aircraft in Europe were considered vulnerable because of the ever-growing length of visible concrete runway which they required for take-offs and landings. While the F-100 had required 9,000 feet of runway for take-offs and landings, the F-105 required 10,500 feet.[20] An English writer observed:

> With full external load, the modern tactical aeroplane needs up to two miles of high-strength concrete. *This is a crippling handicap, which would never have been accepted had it not come about in gradual increments over a period of years.* In many parts of the world it is physically impossible for such a runway to be constructed; and when an operating platform to this standard has been built . . . it becomes an immovable and unconcealable target which would almost certainly be destroyed within a few minutes of the start of a "hot" war.[21]

The "gradual increments" of concrete runways could no longer be tolerated. Enemy missiles made such runways vulnerable, and American missiles could conceivably perform the mission of the aircraft which needed the vulnerable runways. Needless to say, TAC's control of the nuclear interdiction mission was in jeopardy.

In this context, General Everest of TAC set out in the late 1950s to establish the requirements for a successor to the F-105. This was in many respects to be a routine follow-on to the F-105. Nuclear interdiction at low altitudes and high speeds remained the dominant TAC mission. The aircraft that General Everest initially envisioned would extend the F-105s' capabilities for that mission.[22] The new aircraft

[20] W. T. Gunston, "TFX: A Next Generation Military Aeroplane," *Flight International*, Vol. 81 (February 8, 1962), p. 208. The runway lengths noted in the text are approximations for the normal operations of both aircraft, when fully loaded with fuel and ordnance.

[21] Ibid. Emphasis added.

[22] Refer to Chapter II for a description of the mission profile Everest envisioned.

would be capable of a low-altitude dash at high-subsonic speed for an unusually long range: 400 miles. The Mach 2.5 top speed for the new aircraft—considered necessary for performing the air superiority mission as a by-product capability—would be a marginal improvement over the Mach 2.15 top speed of what were then the fastest F-105s, the F-105Ds.[23] However, in one respect, more than incremental improvement over the F-105 was required: "[The F-105 was] regarded by the USAF as its most versatile equipment for fighting any kind of war, but General Everest did not welcome its need of a 10,500 ft. runway. He formulated the view that the correct TAC aeroplane should fly similar missions from a 3,000 ft. field, without any previous preparation of the surface."[24] Everest also specified an unrefueled transoceanic range for the prospective aircraft. Taken together, the range and semi-prepared field capabilities would remove the vulnerability problem for tactical aircraft in the European theater. The proposed aircraft could be based in the United States and fly to an unprepared (and hence, an unpredictable) field at the outset of hostilities. Given the alleged unpredictability of these field locations, the runways for TAC aircraft could not easily be destroyed in a pre-emptive attack. The transoceanic range and semi-prepared field requirements did add a critical new dimension to the design of the proposed aircraft, however. If these capabilities had been omitted, the plane could have been designed as a turbo-jet aircraft, embodying only evolutionary refinements in the airframe and propulsion areas.[25] The inclusion of these capabilities meant that variable-sweep wings and turbo-fan engines would have to be incorporated in the new aircraft. Nonetheless, these capabilities were necessary to

[23] Robert J. Art, *The TFX Decision: McNamara and the Military* (Boston: Little, Brown, 1968), p. 18; Head, "Decision-Making on the A-7 Attack Aircraft Program," p. 105; and *Jane's All the World's Aircraft, 1961–1962*, p. 311.

[24] Gunston, "TFX," p. 208.

[25] Interview 22; and U.S. Senate, Committee on Armed Services, *Authorization for Military Procurement, Research and Development, Fiscal Year 1971, and Reserve Strength*, Hearings, 91st Cong., 2d Sess. (1970), p. 1011.

counter the claims of aircraft vulnerability then being raised. Not surprisingly, Everest campaigned for a crash program on the proposed new aircraft, since it was needed to remedy "a serious deficiency in his command"—and a serious threat to the Air Force's tactical mission.[26]

This initial formulation of the TFX requirements was modified during General Everest's efforts to obtain the approval of Air Force headquarters for the new program. Sometime in the process of ratification, the proposed speed of the long-range dash "on the deck" was increased from high subsonic to Mach 1.2. Subsequently, NASA and the Air Force's in-house technical staff predicted that this increase would cause important size and weight problems in the new aircraft.

The Air Force was not diverted by these warnings. Its persistence in spite of strong warnings is puzzling, since the supersonic dash, a critical threshold in terms of design difficulty and cost, may not have offered major performance or survivability benefits. Indeed, a supersonic dash may actually have portended a decrease in probable aircraft survivability. The survivability benefits of a low-level dash are primarily a function of the low altitude. Changes in speed at that altitude, between high subsonic and Mach 1.2, alter survivability very little.[27] At the same time, a plane capable

[26] Art, *The TFX Decision*, pp. 16–18, 44–45; and Gunston, "TFX," p. 208.

[27] For an aircraft to avoid flying into the ground, it must generally perform a supersonic dash at a higher altitude than a subsonic dash. Moreover, an aircraft capable of performing a supersonic dash must be especially large and heavy. Accordingly, *against ground-based, anti-aircraft defenses* having a given line of "sight" in all directions, the times of exposure and the probabilities of being hit will be nearly the same for subsonic-dash and supersonic-dash aircraft. *Against intercepting aircraft*, which themselves have a given "cone" of intercept capability (picture a cone with a horizontal axis emanating from the interceptor), the supersonic-dash aircraft will spend somewhat less time in this cone of vulnerability, but will, because of its lesser agility, be less able to take evasive action once intercepted. See W. T. Gunston, *Attack Aircraft of the West* (New York: Charles Scribner's

of performing a supersonic dash for extended ranges must be especially large and strong, with minimal drag and wing area. Other things being equal, it will be much heavier, less agile, and more costly than a supersonic plane capable of only a subsonic dash for long ranges at low altitude. Thus, while a supersonic dash would not promise major survivability benefits, it would exact major penalties in aircraft performance and cost. For any given acquisition budget, fewer of the supersonic-dash planes could be procured, and those planes that were procured would possess a narrower spectrum of performance capabilities than could be obtained from subsonic-dash designs.

It is difficult, then, to describe the Air Force's specification of the supersonic dash as being the result of sophisticated trade-off calculations. The increase in dash speed from high subsonic to Mach 1.2 has the appearance of a relatively simple-minded extension of intuitive, "common-sense" notions of performance. The F-105 had a subsonic dash on the deck. The F-111 would promise a supersonic dash on the deck. This increase was especially appealing to the Air Force, as that service had long held the belief (an almost mystical belief, in the opinion of some observers) that supersonic speed was desirable to insure aircraft survivability in combat environments.[28] Such an appeal was ideally suited to the kind of process in which it was induced: the process

---

Sons, 1974), pp. 174–175, 236; interview with Russell Murray II, a tactical aircraft specialist on the systems analysis staff under Dr. Alain Enthoven, in Head, "Decision-Making on the A-7 Attack Aircraft Program," pp. 190–191; Michael P. London, "B-1: The Last Bomber?" *Space/Aeronautics*, Vol. 53 (April 1970), p. 30; Memorandum for the Secretary of Defense, from Secretary of the Navy John B. Connally, dated May 31, 1969, re Project 34 (the name for the 1961 project that was responsible for coordinating the various service requirements), printed in *TFX Hearings—First Series*, Part 6, p. 1388; and testimony of USAF Brigadier General Alfred L. Esposito, *TFX Hearings—Second Series*, Part 2, p. 285.

[28] Head, "Decision-Making on the A-7 Attack Program," pp. 152–158, 252–255.

of ratification by Air Force headquarters, during which General Everest was an advocate trying to "sell" his (theretofore subsonic dash) requirement.

As compared to the F-105, then, the proposed TFX promised range *and speed* increases on the low-level dash of the dominant mission of nuclear interdiction—these, in addition to the plane's higher top speed at high altitudes for enhanced air superiority performance and its unique transoceanic range and semi-prepared field capabilities for neutralizing claims of airfield vulnerability.

Air Force headquarters approved this formidable operational requirement in July 1960, with the issuance of Air Force SOR-183. NASA and Air Force technical studies continued to indicate important size and weight penalties for the proposed aircraft. Back in 1959, before the adoption of variable-sweep wings, when TAC expected to use a fixed-wing aircraft for what was then a subsonic-dash mission, similar warnings of size and weight penalties caused TAC to continue deliberations on its new requirement. However, such warnings were now to little effect. Unlike the earlier period of deliberation, TAC now had a definite requirement formally approved by Air Force headquarters. TAC had made a major commitment to that requirement and insisted on moving ahead vigorously with the new program.

Of course, the outgoing Eisenhower Administration upset these plans and suspended the TFX program, pending review by a new administration. Moreover, it directed DDR&E to begin coordinating the various requirements of the services into a single aircraft. McNamara's later intervention was to delay the program further. Before we examine his initial impact on the program, it will be useful to reflect briefly on the evolution of tactical aircraft sketched in this section.

Overall, this process can best be characterized by its *highly selective incrementalism.* In all four cases (the F-86, F-100, F-105, and F-111), the planes were designed primarily to the most demanding requirements of a central mission: the speed requirement of the air-superiority mission for the F-86 and F-100; and the low-altitude, high-speed delivery requirement of the nuclear interdiction mission for the F-105 and F-111. In the F-111 case at least, these requirements were pressed beyond technical frontiers by the pressure to promise increased performance along a conspicuous performance dimension of the prior aircraft, the F-105. In all four cases, capabilities for subordinate missions were provided as a by-product from the central mission's requirements. The central mission itself changed over time under the influence of the increasing doctrinal and budgetary emphasis on Massive Retaliation in the 1950s. This evolution was reflected in the shift from an initial air superiority emphasis in the F-100A, to the greater emphasis placed upon interdiction in the F-100C/D/F and in the F-105 and F-111. In spite of the increasing decisiveness of the interdiction mission for these aircraft, it was maintained for both the F-105 and the planned F-111 that their high top speeds would provide the performance necessary for engagements with enemy fighters. Finally, a critical challenge to the aircraft interdiction role occurred in the late 1950s, as a consequence of the emergence of ballistic missiles and the rather sudden vulnerability of concrete runways. This challenge was met by the inclusion of transoceanic range and semi-prepared field capability in the requirements for the proposed TFX. But the basic scenario for nuclear interdiction remained intact in the new requirement, as all other TFX performance specifications were tailored to that mission.

The mission doctrines were thus relatively stable over time and were structured at each point in time by the characteristics of the fighter in use. They changed primarily in response to threats to the organization's position, first in the form of threats to the organization's budget (under Massive Retaliation, which reduced funds for maintaining conventional capabilities), and later in the form of threats to the organization's operational role (from ballistic missiles in the late 1950s).[29] Standard scenarios of this sort serve an important function in the organization. They become the organization's map of critical relationships in the operational environment. They provide a set of basic concepts which give purpose and focus to the organization's operational capabilities. As such, they give meaning to the design emphases in its weapons. For the formulation of new requirements, they possess a stability and structure that simplifies the choice of weapon characteristics from the bewildering range of possible combinations.

The TFX requirements were a product of this selective incrementalism and would await McNamara when he became Secretary of Defense. Although these requirements reflected a doctrine McNamara sought to change, he did little to alter them.

Establishing the Joint Requirement

The menu of alternatives defined by organizations in sufficient detail to be live options is severely limited in both number and character. The short list of alternatives reflects not only the cost of alternative generation but, more important, each organization's interest in controlling, rather than presenting, choices. . . .

—Graham T. Allison[30]

When McNamara entered the Pentagon, he was sensitive to the need for changes in two particular areas of defense management. He saw the operational need to rehabilitate the conventional option within the force posture and the economic need to end duplication in military procurement. The President supported him in both endeavors.

McNamara was not long in confronting the opportunity

[29] Other threats to the organization's operational role can be readily imagined. A particularly important example which we shall encounter later in the chapter is unfavorable combat experience.

[30] Allison, *Essence of Decision*, p. 90.

to demonstrate these concerns to the Pentagon bureaucracy. In February 1961, the limited war panel, a study group appointed by McNamara,[31] reported to him with the recommendation that a multi-service aircraft be developed for limited war use. At that time, McNamara had been reviewing the requirements of the Navy and Air Force for new tactical aircraft and apparently had been receiving DDR&E recommendations that he combine the two requirements. (As noted earlier, DDR&E had been directing a study of the possibility of combining the Air Force and Navy requirements and, in the process, had become an advocate of a joint program.)

McNamara was thus being encouraged to develop a multi-service fighter for limited war use (by the study panel) and being presented with ostensible means to do so (by DDR&E), even as he was being pressured by the services for a go-ahead on their separate programs. After a mere three weeks in office, McNamara was being forced to make a major decision that conceivably would influence the tactical force posture for a decade or more. In this burden of decision, however, lay a significant opportunity. McNamara was determined to seize the initiative in the Department. The recommendations of the limited war panel and DDR&E provided a seemingly ideal method of doing so. If McNamara could force the Air Force and Navy into a joint development for a limited war aircraft, there would be little doubt in the defense bureaucracy that he meant business.

McNamara thus concluded that a multi-service fighter could be developed. Through DDR&E, he directed the Navy and Air Force to formulate a coordinated operational requirement and development plan for a single tactical fighter to fulfill all missions (air-superiority, interdiction, and close support) for the 1970s. The services were further directed to base their deliberations on the tactical fighter

[31] This was one of the earlier-noted panels McNamara commissioned following his appointment by President-elect Kennedy. See Kaufmann, *The McNamara Strategy*, p. 48.

then contemplated by the Air Force. In acting upon the recommendations of DDR&E and the limited war panel, McNamara had simply selected one of the two options with which he was presented and made it the basis for achieving other requirements. The seemingly flexible aircraft envisioned in the Air Force requirement was taken to be an appropriate foundation for the joint development and for his limited-war purposes.

The services responded to McNamara's directive with harsh criticisms. To reconcile the differences between the services, Herbert York, Director of Defense Research and Engineering, convened a Committee on Tactical Aircraft. In the course of the Committee's deliberations, the close support requirement of the Navy presented the most difficult problem of reconciliation. This problem was to be expected, for the close support mission was one explicitly articulated in Navy doctrine. The Navy had long held that its close support (attack) aircraft should be subsonic in performance and low in relative cost.[32] The Navy's close support requirement thus presented a clear conventional mission profile (of a special type, to be sure) that conflicted with the detailed nuclear mission profile of the original Air Force requirement. To incorporate the close support capability would have required full integration of performance requirements to obtain a joint development. Instead, the close support mission was split off from the TFX negotiations in May. With the separation of this clearly defined conventional mission, the pressure for full integration of performance capabilities in the TFX was removed.[33] The SOR-183 remained firmly on track.

[32] Head, "Decision-Making on the A-7 Attack Aircraft Program," pp. 124–134; and *TFX Hearings—Second Series*, Part 3, p. 483.

[33] This observation is not a summary judgment that the close support requirement *should* have been kept within the multi-service project. All that is being suggested is that the inclusion of the conflicting close support requirement would have compelled a sophisticated integration of the various service requirements, if a single requirements statement for a joint development was to be achieved. For example, it would have constrained the Air Force to confront

McNamara ratified the conclusions of the Committee on Tactical Aircraft and instructed Air Force Secretary Zuckert to make another attempt to obtain Navy concurrence on the original Air Force specifications. Deliberations between the services continued through the summer, only to reach an impasse in August.

McNamara's reaction to this impasse was swift. He instructed DDR&E to establish the joint requirements for the development. Working with representatives of the Navy and the Air Force, DDR&E negotiated the basic constraints to be placed on the Air Force specific operational requirement (SOR-183).[34] These constraints were then formally established in McNamara's "Memorandum of September 1," an addendum to SOR-183. The constraints McNamara added were as follows:

1. The ability to accommodate a radar dish 36 inches in diameter, for the Navy's missile system;
2. A maximum length on the Air Force version of 73 feet;
3. A maximum Air Force version weight of 60,000 pounds, with internal fuel and 2,000 pounds of internal stores;

---

and to acknowledge the costs and benefits of the capabilities it sought, something the Air Force never really did at any time in the program. That the close-support requirement was separated from the negotiations thus suggests something about the character of the negotiations themselves: their inability to perform the difficult trade-offs necessary to reconcile the various service requirements into a coherent statement of more or less attainable performance objectives. As we shall observe momentarily in the text, the negotiations later failed to integrate the remaining requirements of the Air Force and Navy, especially with reference to McNamara's objectives.

[34] These negotiations proceeded within a fairly narrow scope. The task for DDR&E was not to perform high-order trade-offs among performance requirements, but rather to reconcile the physical characteristics (such as length and fuselage diameter) of the separate aircraft specified by the Navy and the Air Force. To obtain an idea of how these constraints were negotiated, observe that the ultimate length constraint of 73 feet was exactly half-way between the length for which the Navy had argued (56 feet) and the ideal length that the Air Force had sought (90 feet). For the length data, see Art, *The TFX Decision*, p. 40. Information on the negotiations from Interview 25.

4. The ability to carry 10,000 pounds of conventional ordnance;

5. The ability to carry two, 1,000 pound, air-to-air missiles internally or semi-submerged;

6. The ability to withstand carrier operations;

7. The ability in the Navy version to carry six, 1,000 pound missiles for 3.5 hours at 150 miles from a carrier; and

8. A take-off gross weight for the Navy mission of 55,000 pounds.[35]

This stipulation of requirements did not replace any of the SOR-183 *performance* requirements for the Air Force version (although it obviously reduced the possibility of attaining them). The addendum placed physical constraints upon the aircraft itself—to provide the Navy minimal assurance of the aircraft's carrier compatibility—and then simply added the Navy's performance requirements. The requirement was a "joint" requirement in the sense that Navy and Air Force requirements now formally coexisted on paper. Any actual integration of performance requirements was to be a *de facto* product of contractor design efforts, as recounted by Fred Korth, the Navy Secretary at that time: ". . . when we discovered [in the summer of 1961] that our divergence of requirements was so wide it was suggested by Admiral Burke [Chief of Naval Operations] that the way to resolve this question was to submit the proposals and the requirements of each service to industry, and let them determine realistically what they could provide to the Air Force and what they could provide to the Navy in versions of the TFX . . . . This is what in fact we did, in the fall of 1961."[36] Since the Air Force and Navy refused to rank their performance requirements—individually or collectively—in

[35] Memorandum for the Secretary of the Air Force and the Secretary of the Navy, from Secretary of Defense Robert McNamara, dated September 1, 1961, re TFX, printed in *TFX Hearings—First Series*, Part 6, pp. 1513–1514. See *TFX Report*, p. 8, for the data in the memo classified at the time of the first series of TFX hearings.

[36] *TFX Hearings—First Series*, Part 6, p. 1477.

the source selection competition that ensued, the reconciliation of these requirements was indeed left to the contractors.[37]

Beyond this lack of integration of performance requirements, the most notable aspect of the joint requirement is the extent to which the assumptions behind the original Air Force plans went unexamined in the decision process. Although the Navy raised questions as to the appropriateness of the SOR-183 requirements for limited (versus nuclear) war, SOR-183 remained the baseline for joint consideration. There is no evidence that these basic performance requirements received detailed scrutiny by McNamara and his associates in light of the limited war purposes for which they intended the plane—a somewhat puzzling omission, given the relatively close scrutiny and sophisticated judgments being made during these same months on a plane with a similar mission emphasis, the F-105. In 1961, McNamara initiated a program to modify early F-105s, so that these planes could carry conventional ordnance loads. Later that year, he canceled production of the most recent F-105s, so that the Air Force would procure the more flexible capability of the Navy F-4. Yet, during this same period, he uncritically accepted the Air Force's TFX requirements, which embodied the same nuclear mission scenario as the F-105 and indeed extended that scenario to new extremes of range and speed. McNamara did add the stipulation that the plane be capable of carrying 10,000 pounds of conventional ordnance, a requirement perhaps reflecting his prior experience in having had to modify the early F-105s to carry conventional ordnance. But this surely missed the larger lesson of his experience with the F-105. At most, it merely required "hard points" on the wings of a plane otherwise designed to meet nuclear mission requirements for the Air Force.[38]

[37] Interview 13.

[38] It was not even a very demanding "hard point" (and wing strengthening) requirement. Note, for example, that F-4 versions available in 1961 could carry as much as 16,000 pounds of conventional bombs.

103

The key to this extraordinary difference between the F-105 and TFX decisions of 1961 lies in the character of the options McNamara confronted when he entered the Defense Department. When he assumed office, anxious to expand limited war capabilities, McNamara was not presented with a wide range of options, covering the whole variety of possible approaches to the tactical air mission. Instead, he received only two options: those of the Navy and the Air Force. These options represented years of effort by each of the services and hundreds of agreements among interested parties within each service. These options were not static, hypothetical abstractions. They were firmly on track, difficult to modify or to stop, and drew upon powerful forces for persuasion with a whole array of organization resources behind them, generating enough information and "heat" to overwhelm the consideration of imagined alternatives lacking organizational sponsorship. Of critical importance, one of these options—the Air Force requirement—possessed the powerful backing of DDR&E, the highest ranking suborganization in OSD and the only suborganization in OSD actively involved in the early program decisions.

To understand the constraints operating on McNamara's vision, a brief survey of the organizations involved in these early decisions will be useful. The Air Force was of course a strong supporter of its own requirement, SOR-183. It was aware of McNamara's intent to strengthen conventional forces, but it remained committed to a central role for nuclear weapons in the force posture, for it had been a beneficiary of this emphasis in the defense budgets of the 1950s.[39] In early 1961, when Air Force Secretary Zuckert had been "not thirty days" on the job, the Air Force leaked a memorandum to McNamara from Dean Rusk, the new Secretary of State, recommending an increase in non-nuclear capabili-

[39] See Kaufmann, *The McNamara Strategy*, pp. 22–23; and Table 6 in Harvey M. Sapolsky, *The Polaris System Development: Bureaucratic and Programmatic Success in Government* (Cambridge: Harvard University Press, 1972), p. 172. According to Sapolsky's data, the Air Force budget share grew from 33 percent to 43 percent of the total defense budget, between fiscal years 1954 and 1961.

ties. The Air Force leak was intended to precipitate a Congressional and European response that would block this shift in emphasis before it got started.[40]

More generally, the Air Force was "emotionally opposed" to the non-nuclear option. It did not believe the non-nuclear option to be as important as the nuclear option, and it doubted McNamara's staying power.[41] Prior to McNamara, Secretaries of Defense had averaged only two years in office, with the longest tenure being only four years.[42] The Air Force could thus expect in 1961 that McNamara would be gone when the TFX became operational six years later. Why, then, should it compromise the requirements it sought? Even in 1962, after the F-4 had been substituted for the F-105, the Air Force remained committed to the nuclear option: "The Air Force wanted to start with a very slow procurement program [on the F-4]. . . . In part, this was the old strategic versus tactical fight that [sic] the less money spent for TAC the better, and particularly if TAC was not going to be a nuclear force. Because the F-105 was built as a nuclear delivery airplane."[43] And although the Air Force later became enthusiastic about the F-4—the F-4's performance was certain to delight TAC fighter pilots —OSD had great difficulties inducing the Air Force to procure enough conventional ordnance to take advantage of the F-4's conventional capability.[44] The position of the Air Force in 1961 is thus reasonably clear. Systems analysts in OSD had begun efforts to cancel the F-105 by mid-1961.[45]

[40] Eugene M. Zuckert, "The Service Secretary: Has He A Useful Role?" *Foreign Affairs*, Vol. 44 (April 1966), p. 467.
[41] Enthoven and Smith, *How Much Is Enough?*, p. 266; Jacob Stockfisch, *Plowshares Into Swords: Managing The American Defense Establishment* (New York: Mason & Lipscomb, 1973), p. 145; and Interviews 10, 12, and 24.
[42] C. W. Borklund, *The Department of Defense* (New York: Praeger, 1968), pp. 312–313.
[43] Interview with Victor Heyman, a systems analyst in OSD, in Head, "Decision-Making on the A-7 Attack Aircraft Program," p. 164.
[44] Stockfisch, *Plowshares Into Swords*, p. 145.
[45] Head, "Decision-Making on the A-7 Attack Aircraft Program," pp. 156–165.

As this pressure to cancel the F-105 mounted, the proposed TFX increasingly became the Air Force's major means to a strong nuclear interdiction capability in the future. Under these circumstances, and given McNamara's obvious predisposition on the matter, the Air Force was itself unlikely to draw attention to the nuclear mission emphasis of its TFX requirements.

Instead, the Air Force emphasized the flexibility that its proposed aircraft would provide. Although "not one bolt" had changed in the requirement since it was formulated for the Low-Low-High mission, the Air Force began selling the conventional mission capabilities of its proposed aircraft.[46] McNamara apparently agreed with their position in 1961:

> New developments in engine performance and in aerodynamics, particularly the variable geometry wing concept evolved by NASA, now make it possible to develop a tactical fighter which can operate from aircraft carriers as well as from much shorter and cruder runways, and yet can carry the heavy conventional ordnance loads needed in limited war.
>
> In general, what we are striving for is one fighter which could operate from the large number of existing smaller air fields all over the world, and yet fly without refueling across the ocean, thus greatly increasing its value for limited war purposes.[47]

Notably, the transoceanic range and semi-prepared field capabilities of the TFX, which were initially intended to reduce the vulnerability of TAC's nuclear strike aircraft in

---

[46] The Air Force was aided in its advocacy by the fact that it planned to procure twice as many TFXs as did the Navy in 1961. In this quantitative sense, the Air Force was to be the major user and its opinions had to be taken seriously. The Navy and Air Force procurement plans for the TFX are noted in U.S. House of Representatives, Committee on Armed Services, *Hearings on Military Posture,* 91st Cong., 1st Sess. (1969), p. 3202.

[47] U.S. Senate, Committee on Armed Services, *Military Procurement Authorization: Fiscal Year 1962,* Hearings, 87th Cong., 1st Sess. (1961), p. 19.

Europe, are depicted here (for the first time) as being useful for flexible deployment in limited war. Little was said about the plane's performance once it *was* deployed, other than that it would be able to carry heavy ordnance loads. The nuclear mission scenario, as embodied in the F-105, remained the dominant design requirement for the TFX.

But there was a critical difference between McNamara's choices on F-105 and the TFX. The modification and cancellation of the F-105 resulted from aggressive efforts of systems analysts in OSD to expand the conventional capabilities of the Air Force. These analysts performed the role of advocating alternatives to the options advanced by the Air Force. In that role, these analysts were served by the existence of a *proven* alternative, the Navy's F-4, a plane which promised to provide the more flexible, non-nuclear capabilities that OSD sought. They were not advocating a hypothetical "paper" airplane for the Air Force to develop and deploy in the future. The inevitably high uncertainty of such an alternative would have allowed wide latitude for Air Force counter-formulations and counter-moves, conditions for a bureaucratic battle the analysts would find difficult to win. Instead, they had in hand (by luck, to be sure) a high confidence alternative with demonstrated attributes of performance and cost, an alternative which at the same time was attractive to a critical Air Force constituency—the fighter pilots—and consistent with the new doctrine the analysts hoped to implement. This was a battle that the analysts could hope to win and, with considerable effort, did win.[48]

[48] Alain Enthoven later recalled: "There was a certain amount of criticism in the Air Force of the F-4, and for a time they fought very hard to keep the F-105. [But] a number of Air Force officers told us privately that they really believed we were on the right track in going for the F-4, that it was just a lot better plane. So we did press that to . . . a successful conclusion in stopping the F-105 and buying the F-4 . . ." Or, as Jacob Stockfisch, a Rand consultant, has observed: "[The] Navy's F-4 was acquired by the Air Force, but only with mixed feelings on the part of the Air Staff. . . . But since an airplane like the F-4 evokes enthusiasm among pilots, the mixed feelings rap-

However, during the early decisions on the TFX, no firm alternatives were available. The early TFX decisions amounted to a choice on which "paper" airplane to develop and produce. Given the high uncertainty of the alternatives, the Air Force could successfully claim that its requirement embodied the flexible capabilities McNamara desired. Its claims went relatively unchallenged within OSD, since systems analysts remained aloof from the early TFX decisions. The group itself was quite small at the beginning of Mc-Namara's tenure (though not too small, we should note, to challenge the Air Force's F-105 procurement within a few months). Moreover, some observers have plausibly argued that Alain Enthoven, then Deputy Comptroller in OSD, made a conscious decision to keep his analysts out of the TFX debates because the proposed program was too controversial for the embryonic analytical group.[49] It could not afford so difficult a battle so early in its bureaucratic life. As noted by *Congressional Quarterly*:

> Pressure within the Defense Department for a single, sophisticated, multimission aircraft came from the Office of Defense Research and Engineering. . . . Although the concept was opposed by the young systems analysts that Defense Secretary Robert S. McNamara had brought with him to the Pentagon, they were not then in a position to conduct a running battle with [the Director of Defense Research and Engineering] Brown. At the time, the Office of Systems Analysis was subordinate to the Pentagon Comptroller which was one level below Brown.[50]

---

idly faded away." See the interview with Dr. Enthoven in Head, "Decision-Making on the A-7 Attack Aircraft Program," p. 163; and Stockfisch, *Plowshares Into Swords*, p. 145.

[49] Stone, "In the Bowels of the Behemoth," p. 35; and Interview 22.

[50] "New Plane Seen More Costly, Little Better Than F-111," *Congressional Quarterly Weekly Report*, Vol. xxvi (May 3, 1968), p. 1007–1009 (reprinted, with Navy rebuttal, in U.S. Senate, Committee on Armed Services, Preparedness Investigating Subcommittee, *U.S. Tactical Air Power Program*, Hearings, 90th Cong., 2d Sess. [1968], pp. 27–31).

Moreover, after McNamara made his early commitment to a joint program based on the Air Force requirement, any analysis by this group would have been as much a threat to the Defense Secretary as to the Air Force and Navy. It is fair to surmise that the systems analysts would be far less inclined to scrutinize the Defense Secretary's own commitments than the commitments of the military services.[51]

With systems analysts out of the picture, for whatever reason, McNamara's primary source of advice on the program within OSD was DDR&E, which had been studying means to combine requirements before McNamara arrived and had become a strong advocate of a joint program based on the Air Force requirements. Unfortunately, through the mid-1960s, this office was dominated by specialists in the technologies of Massive Retaliation, especially ballistic missile technologies such as nuclear physics and guidance electronics. It did not share the intense concern of the systems analysts for modifying detailed operational capabilities to strengthen forces for conventional operations. To DDR&E officials involved in the early program decisions, "The requirements didn't matter—what was important was to sit down with reasonable people to convince them that this [joint program] was in their interest."[52] The problem,

[51] James Schlesinger has framed this issue in provocative terms: "Will the decisionmaker tolerate analysis—even when it is his own hobby horses which are under scrutiny? . . . Dr. Enthoven has quite properly objected to the canard that analysis is somehow responsible for what are regarded as the mishaps of the TFX decisions, pointing out that the new procedures were only tangentially involved. A more penetrating question, it seems to me, is: why did the analysts steer away from the issue? How many hobby horses are there? Are they off limits to the analysts?" See James R. Schlesinger, "Uses and Abuses of Analysis," printed in U.S. Senate, Committee on Government Operations, Subcommittee on National Security and International Operations, *Planning, Programming, and Budgeting*, Hearings, 90th Cong., 1st Sess. (1967), pp. 127–128.

[52] Interview 25. By this argument, DDR&E succeeded in achieving an acceptable foundation for a joint program. The real problem, in this view, was McNamara's later rationalization of a political decision (to award the contract to General Dynamics) on technical grounds. McNamara's defense of the contract award is alleged to have discredited the program in the Navy's eyes and to have undermined the

then, was to reconcile the Navy to the program without losing Air Force support, rather than to fine-tune the requirement to meet McNamara's doctrinal objectives and to minimize the possibility of politically crippling deficiencies on the Navy version. The uncertainty of the options at this stage of the program provided wide interpretive latitude for DDR&E to conceive its task in these simplified terms.

Hence, in the earliest weeks of his tenure when he was still uncommitted on the matter, McNamara received only favorable OSD evaluations of the Air Force requirements. Instead of having his options refined and expanded by OSD organizations, McNamara faced a restricted set of options reinforced by them. He had entered the Defense Department wanting to expand capabilities for limited war and to end duplication of weapon systems. The limited war panel suggested that a multi-service aircraft was one way to begin this effort, and DDR&E handed McNamara a ready program with which to begin it. Lacking any internal challenge to the Air Force requirement, and being otherwise new to his job and intensely busy with a whole variety of major decisions, McNamara understandably assimilated DDR&E's simplified view of the problem. The intense debates that fol-

---

delicate compromise DDR&E had worked out. A Boeing F-111, it is surmised, would have had satisfactory multi-purpose capability.

The argument we are presenting in the text critically differs from this DDR&E interpretation. While not denying the importance of the contract award and the subsequent Congressional investigation for stiffening Navy resistance, we would argue that Navy resistance pre-dated the contract award. This argument will be presented in detail in Chapter v. For now, against the DDR&E position, let us only note the observation of a high-level Navy officer (Interview 26): the Navy knew its interests would not be served in a bi-service program when the joint requirement statement itself, the compromise negotiated by DDR&E, increased the specified empty weight of the proposed Navy F-111 to 55,000 pounds, an increase of 5,000 pounds over the maximum empty weight the Navy had said it could accept.

In any event, as was argued in Chapter ii and as will be further detailed in the present chapter, the requirements did indeed matter in determining the suitability of the Air Force version for limited war missions and the acceptability of the Navy version in the Navy's own terms.

lowed doubtless confirmed the central tenet of that view in McNamara's mind: namely, that the opposition to a joint development was parochial, and that the main problem in establishing a joint development was convincing the services that it was in their interest to reach agreement—agreement, in effect, to accept the new order of things in the Defense Department.

In his subsequent struggle to implement that option over the opposition of the services, McNamara and his associates could claim some success: a bi-service requirement for the TFX development finally was established, an unprecedented accomplishment for so major a program. Yet McNamara and his associates on this issue remained committed to the Air Force requirement throughout this process and *never once really demonstrated an awareness of the complicated long-term problems that a bi-service development inevitably portended.* Their simplified view of the problem is strikingly asserted in the Memorandum of September 1, which resolved by virtual fiat the hiatus in negotiations between the services. In that memorandum, McNamara directs that "Changes to the Air Force tactical version of the basic aircraft to achieve the Navy mission shall be held to a minimum."[53] These are not words of balance or skepticism from OSD.

On this basis, the source selection process began. The design proposals of the contractors were to achieve some of the integration that protracted negotiations had failed to achieve. The services still were not convinced that a single aircraft could meet their requirements. But a joint requirement had at least been established.

The Source Selection Competition

The joint requirement and accompanying Work Statement became the basis for the source selection competition

---

[53] See the "Memorandum of September 1," in *TFX Hearings—First Series*, Part 6, pp. 1513–1514. Notably, this document was composed by DDR&E for McNamara's signature.

that extended through most of 1962. As an inherent part of such a competition, the requirements were fixed throughout. The services, on their part, refused to establish any priorities among their requirements.[54]

But the contractors had to sort out the various requirements and develop design proposals to meet them. According to the winning contractor, it was known that all the requirements could not be met.[55] If, as NASA had earlier determined, the Air Force requirement could not be met within the original Air Force weight constraint, it surely could not be met at the lesser weight and length requirements of the joint program.[56] Hence, since contractors were given no guidance on priorities within each service's requirements, they were required to determine where the compromises in performance would be made.

From the point of view of the Defense Department, then, choice would be possible only between the proposals that the contractors presented. As compared to the joint requirement and the Work Statement, these design proposals were articulated in far greater detail and were based upon more extensive engineering calculations and wind tunnel tests. In other words, more information, although still information of a highly speculative variety, would now be available. A second difference was that the Defense Department altered these proposals in a way that it could not alter the requirements in 1961. In the fourth round of the source selection competition (July 1 through September 11, 1962), source selection officials worked with each contractor as if that contractor had "won" the competition, pointing out weaknesses

[54] Interview 13.
[55] Interview 16.
[56] This can be seen by contrasting the "ideal" and the actual length-diameter ratios for the F-111A. The length-diameter (or "fineness") ratio, though a crude measure, is an approximate indicator of aerodynamic efficiency for supersonic flight. The optimum length-diameter ratio for supersonic flight is between 11 and 14. On the F-111, due to the Navy length constraint, this ratio was between 8 and 10. See Staff Report, "TFX: Mission and Design," *Space/Aeronautics*, Vol. 39 (June 1963), p. 76.

in the contractor's design proposal and suggesting revisions.[57]

But the basic formulation of design proposals remained in the contractor's hands. The Air Force, on its part, continued to pursue the maximum performance on the sea-level, supersonic mission. The Navy attempted to enhance the carrier compatibility and loiter performance of the proposals. Consequently, the source selection competition sustained the thrust of the joint requirement, with the contractors left to bring coherence to the statement.

In the end, of course, General Dynamics won the competition. As compared to the Boeing design, the General Dynamics design emphasized the supersonic performance of the aircraft.[58] McNamara selected General Dynamics because the General Dynamics proposal was acceptable to both the Air Force and the Navy, even as (he thought) it possessed greater commonality, less development risk, and more realistic cost estimates than the Boeing proposal.[59] Mission emphasis was apparently not a factor in the selection, just as it has not been in the earlier establishment of a joint requirement. This was to be expected, since OSD's primary concern now was to obtain a design that both services judged acceptable.

The development program commenced with the emphasis of the Air Force mission intact. General Dynamics' proposal had been evaluated to provide approximately 135 miles of supersonic, sea-level dash, but General Dynamics held out the promise of achieving over 200 miles.[60] The Air Force moved at the outset of the development program to obtain this higher capability. Hence, the source selection competition had done little to alter the decisive specifications built into the joint requirement.

[57] Art, *The TFX Decision*, p. 75; and Memorandum to the Chairman of the Source Selection Board, from Secretary of the Air Force Eugene Zuckert, dated June 29, 1962, re TFX Program, printed in *TFX Hearings—First Series*, Part 1, p. 65.

[58] *TFX Hearings—First Series*, Part 3, p. 665, and Part 4, p. 1066.

[59] Art, *The TFX Decision*, chap. 5.

[60] Interviews 13 and 19.

Formal Requirements and the Decomposition of the Design Problem

In both the establishment of the joint requirement and the selection of a prime contractor, there was little examination of the Air Force emphasis on a nuclear mission. This section will consider how the development process translated the requirements into actual designs. The focus will be on the way in which formal requirements serve as a baseline for successive design iterations down to the level of design detail. Through this focus, we will get an idea of how quickly design flexibility vanished—that is, how quickly the basic tactical nuclear aircraft became the configuration within which any F-111 mission would be performed. The two previous sections have shown the lack of critical analysis in the early stages of the program. This section will serve to demonstrate the importance of these early stages to the design that ultimately emerged.

By the time of the contract award, the broad performance criteria of the initial operational requirement had evolved through the more detailed design specifications of the Work Statement and, finally, into a proposed configuration for the actual aircraft. The aircraft was still purely a "paper" design at this stage, but the basic aerodynamic configuration had been proposed; the layout of all essential subsystems had been established (such as the relative location of avionics, fuel tanks, bomb bay, crew capsule, and landing gear); the approximate technical qualities of the proposed aircraft had been determined (such as its probable weight and structural strength); and the likely performance of the aircraft had been estimated. For these latter determinations, standard engineering calculations, as well as empirical data derived primarily from wind tunnel models, were used to document the estimates.[61]

[61] Interview 16. Unless otherwise indicated, the information on the design process that follows in the text is from Interview 16.

The full-scale development process for the F-111 commenced in December 1962.[62] Though the essential outlines of the aerodynamic configuration of the aircraft were fairly firm at this point, extensive wind tunnel tests were under way by both the contractor and NASA to refine this basic design.[63] With the internal layout of the aircraft already specified, design efforts extended to more detailed problems, even to the level of individual parts. Paralleling this extension of design was an extension by the government of specification detail covering the aircraft. The 1961 Work Statement contained relatively general specifications. This second specification effort can be viewed as an attempt by the government to set requirements for the design to meet at each successive level of detail.[64]

By August 1963, the design was fully detailed, and the scheduled "mock-up" inspection (Development Engineering Inspection) commenced. This is a government inspection of a full-scale model of the aircraft. It allows the inspection of such features as cockpit layout and maintenance access in a way difficult to provide with paper designs.[65]

[62] *TFX Hearings—First Series*, Part 4, p. 1144.

[63] See *TFX Hearings—Second Series*, Part 2, pp. 324–343, for a description of how NASA normally aids in aircraft developments. In the 1963 to 1964 period, NASA ran 14,179 hours of wind tunnel tests at its Langley, Ames, and Lewis research centers. From Staff of the NASA Research Centers, *Summary of NASA Support of the F-111 Development Program: Part I—December, 1962–December, 1965*, Langley Working Paper 246 (Langley Station, Virginia, undated), p. 2 (from the files of the Permanent Subcommittee on Investigations, Committee on Government Operations, U.S. Senate, Exhibit 13 of the *TFX Hearings—Second Series*).

[64] Subcontract arrangements required the contractor, in turn, to establish specifications for parts or subsystems whose development was being subcontracted. For an idea of the magnitude of this effort, note that approximately two-thirds of the dollar volume of the development contract (1.2 billion dollars out of 1.8 billion dollars in total) was passed on to subcontractors. A better measure of this subcontracting specification effort, the proportion of subcontracted parts out of the total number of parts, is not known.

[65] One participant described it to the author as "getting one hundred different opinions on how to build an airplane."

115

It is also a legal requirement, scheduled in the contract. Until the design has passed the mock-up inspection by incorporating all formally proposed changes, no engineering drawings can legally be released for the fabrication of actual hardware.

The F-111 completed mock-up inspection in September 1963. In October, the first drawings were released for the fabrication of parts. (By early January 1964, 20 percent of the drawings had been released; by early June 1964, 90 percent of the drawings had been released.)[66] Meanwhile, in late November 1963, the first actual part had been fabricated for the first R&D prototype.

Major assembly of this first aircraft began in June 1964, and the first aircraft itself rolled out the following October, on schedule. Since all prototypes were constructed on production tooling, any later design changes would be extraordinarily costly. After December 1964, design efforts would be directed at marginal refinements, since the plane's configuration would then be firm.[67]

Yet to depict the issue in this way—that is, to imply that a "point" is reached at which the design was basically irreversible—is to distort the nature of the development process. It assumes that, prior to December 1964, the process was open to alternative requirements and design approaches. But this kind of flexibility and broad sensitivity is notably absent from the development process.

Retracing our steps for a moment, we know that the contractors took the Work Statement of October 1961 and developed initial design proposals. In this *initial* process, a

---

[66] Memorandum, by Keith Dentel, Bureau of Naval Weapons weight engineer, dated January 14, 1964, re Model F-111B Weight and Contractor's Weight Control Program; and Memorandum, by John Brick, staff member of the Permanent Subcommittee on Investigations, Committee on Government Operations, U.S. Senate, dated June 17, 1964, re Staff Briefing at SPO (both memoranda from the files of the Permanent Subcommittee on Investigations, Committee on Government Operations, U.S. Senate, Exhibits 15 and 26-W4 of the *TFX Hearings—Second Series*).

[67] Interview 16.

broad range of alternatives was developed and considered.[68] Engine choices had to be made, and they were. Overall design strategies—whether to please McNamara by maximizing commonality, or to please the services by maximizing performance—had to be chosen, and they were. A final design configuration had to be established and tested.[69]

But once a proposal was finally accepted, the design process quickly became narrowly focused. The winning design proposal was decomposed and elaborated as development efforts proceeded. The proposal set the basic shape of the ultimate design and, through a process of progressive disaggregation, the shape of component designs as well. For engineers, each successive level of design was a parameter for the following, greater-detailed level. The government led the way through this effort by establishing specifications against which the successive levels of design were to be developed. This devolution to lower design levels sometimes led to alteration of the higher level specification parameters,

[68] Within the time limits of the source selection competition, test procedures were a major constraint on the number of options that could be generated. Design proposals had to be documented by test data, such as from wind tunnel models. Until the fourth round of the F-111 source selection competition, it took six weeks to build a wind tunnel model, a time period which required a relatively early foreclosure on major changes in proposed configurations (i.e., foreclosure more than six weeks before the due date for proposals). For the fourth round of the F-111 competition, General Dynamics developed a method for making test models in one week. This allowed General Dynamics to test a much larger number of configurations and to make great improvements in its design. See Art, *The TFX Decision*, pp. 76–77. The importance of this constraint is that it suggests how arbitrary the level of design refinement might be when development begins—that is, when the rigidities of the design process take hold. For another example of this phenomenon, see J. W. Devanney III, "The DX Competition," *United States Naval Institute: Proceedings*, Vol. 101 (August 1975), pp. 18–29.

[69] For a comparison of corporate design strategies, and a description of how General Dynamics emphasized commonality while Boeing emphasized performance in the design competition, see Art, *The TFX Decision*, pp. 115–132 and 149–155. See also pp. 62–67, for a description of how General Dynamics and Boeing selected engines at the outset of the source selection competition.

but such alteration was not judged by the contractor to have happened often. Instead, the aircraft design was disaggregated progressively in the course of the engineering effort, with fairly stable parameters established around each level.[70] This decomposition of the design proposal was reflected in the structure of the contractor's engineering teams, as well as in those of the Air Force. The contractor's engineering staff was functionally divided by category of design. For example, the airframe engineering unit was broken down into wing, fuselage, empennage ("tail"), alighting gear, environmental control, and other groups. The Air Force engineering groups at the Wright-Patterson System Program Office (SPO) were organized in a parallel fashion, with horizontal communications quite extensive between counterpart contractor and Air Force civilian engineers.[71] James Reece observes:

> New weapon systems . . . are broken down into subsystems (e.g., propulsion, fuselage, avionics, etc.), and again into still smaller subsystems, until 'pieces' of manageable size can be assigned to individual engineers. This process takes place both in the contractor organization . . . and in the smaller Government organization . . . where the engineering effort is monitored. Thus, at some level in the hardware breakdown, there are counterpart engineers: i.e., an engineer in each of the two organizations responsible for the design and performance of the same piece of hardware.[72]

Since in general both of these men were civilians and had similar professional training, communications between them

[70] As noted by Celniker and Schuberth, the airframe configuration is the primary baseline for design efforts, since it has the broadest interface with the various disciplines to be synthesized into an aircraft design. Leo Celniker and E. R. Schuberth, "Synthesizing Aircraft Design," *Space Aeronautics*, Vol. 51 (April 1969), pp. 63–64.

[71] James S. Reece, "The Effects of Contract Changes on the Control of a Major Defense Weapon System Program" (unpublished D.B.A. dissertation, Harvard Business School, 1970), chap. 2, p. 23, and chap. 5, pp. 8–10.

[72] Ibid., chap. 2, p. 23.

were technically fluent and easily understood.[73] Moreover, their definition of what constituted "acceptable" results in design efforts was determined by the elaborate unfolding of initial requirements and specifications. The extensive reporting and monitoring procedures employed by the government enforced attention to these specifications.[74]

The effect of these relationships was a narrow vision of "design problems" within contractor and government organizations. Since a nuclear mission requirement structured the levels of acceptability in the highly disaggregated design efforts, performance on limited war missions did not emerge as an issue during the development period of the program. During that period, what was seen as an "issue"— by engineers, by Air Force officials, and by high-level Pentagon officials—was determined by disparities versus specifications relating to the nuclear mission decomposition. Development problems threatening to nuclear mission performance, such as aerodynamic drag increases projected in 1964, were the subject of intense development efforts. NASA, for example, spent more wind tunnel time on the F-111 development than on any fighter development in its history.[75] Problems threatening to multi-purpose capabili-

[73] Ibid., chap. 2, pp. 23–24.

[74] J. Ronald Fox, *Arming America: How The U.S. Buys Weapons* (Boston: Harvard Business School, 1974), chaps. 20–23; and U.S. Senate Committee on Armed Services, *Weapons System Acquisition Process*, Hearings, 92d Cong., 2d Sess. (1972), pp. 1–43.

[75] Staff of the NASA Research Centers, *Summary of NASA Support of the F-111 Development Program: Part I–December 1962–December, 1965*, p. 2. By the end of 1968, a total of 30,000 hours of occupancy time in NASA wind tunnels had been devoted to F-111 development support. Of this total, 22,000 hours occurred at NASA's Langley Research Center in Virginia. By way of comparison, Langley provided approximately 5,000 hours of wind tunnel occupancy for the F-105 program. This large support effort for the F-111 was in part a result of the multiple versions, missions, and wing-sweep positions of the plane, which required multiple test runs to ascertain specific characteristics of the aircraft. However, much of the effort was a result of problems identified with the General Dynamics design. In particular, because of the critical effect of transonic drag on the performance of the low-level supersonic mission, extensive efforts were devoted to reducing the F-111's transonic drag levels. See the

ties, such as the F-111A's declining thrust-to-weight ratio, were not aggressively pursued. Indeed, significant thrust improvements, which were not really important for nuclear mission performance, were not sought until 1969, following necessarily influential *combat* reports of the F-111A's lack of power.[76] For most of the program, performance on the conventional mission was a qualitative consideration outside the quantitative decomposition of design efforts.[77]

In other words, since the requirements process had focused on a dominant mission and ignored the rest, the development process did likewise. There was little opportunity for "learning" in the development process, for performing trade-offs among desired capabilities. Since broad, multi-mission performance was a by-product capability insufficiently captured in the nuclear mission specifications, the multi-purpose capabilities McNamara anticipated for the plane were neglected by design efforts. Broad design flexibility was therefore lost when development efforts began. The F-111 that emerged from this process was too heavy, lacking in relative power, and lacking in relative wing area to provide the acceleration and maneuverability necessary for multi-purpose capability.[78] Although these attributes of the F-111 bore out NASA's predictions of 1960 and could, in any event, have been fully ascertained by October 1964 (when the first actual prototype rolled off the

discussion of NASA development efforts by Edward C. Polhamus, a NASA aeronautical engineer, in *TFX Hearings—Second Series*, Part 2, pp. 339–363.

[76] On the importance of the thrust-to-weight ratio for conventional and nuclear missions, see *TFX Hearings—Second Series*, Part 1, p. 210. On the major thrust improvement, see Minutes of the Secretary of Defense F-111 Meeting, December 12, 1968, excerpted in *TFX Hearings—Second Series*, Part 1, p. 206; and U.S. House of Representatives, Committee on Armed Services, *Hearings on Military Posture* (1969), pp. 2631–2632.

[77] *TFX Hearings—Second Series*, Part 1, pp. 193–198, and Part 3, p. 548.

[78] See, for example, Gunston's discussion in *Attack Aircraft*, pp. 175–176.

assembly line), no one really paid much attention to the problem until late 1966. At that time, routine Air Force flight tests were performed carrying conventional ordnance.[79] These tests revealed that the problems for the conventional mission were severe. It was then that McNamara realized that " 'The failure to have [the conventional mission] specified from the outset was a DOD error . . . a fall-out from the day when emphasis was almost exclusively on tactical nuclear missions.' "[80]

Hard Data: Vietnam, Flight Tests, and Adaptations to Conventional Missions

As the government flight tests began in late 1965, the United States was in the midst of its dramatic intensification of the air war over Indochina. Together, the tests and the war experience were to have an important impact on the way in which military and civilian officials alike perceived the F-111 program. In effect, the long-avoided conventional missions were imposed on the program deliberations.

The Vietnam experience emphasized the unique characteristics of the conventional interdiction mission: "Exposure to conventional ground fire of a multimillion-dollar aircraft carrying gravity bombs never did make economic sense, but our previous strategy left us with nuclear weapons platforms while the need is for conventional weapons delivery."[81] Or, as James Schlesinger, himself later to become Secretary of Defense, suggested at the time:

> For many years the selecting of equipment and the training of personnel in the Air Force have presupposed the use of nuclear weapons in major conflict conditions. . . . Aircraft were expensive and designed for nuclear deliv-

[79] Interview 20.
[80] Notes of the Icarus meeting, September 10, 1966, excerpted in *TFX Hearings—Second Series*, Part 3, p. 548.
[81] "Aerospace in Perspective: Tactical Warfare," *Space/Aeronautics*, Vol. 49 (January 1968), p. 112.

ery. . . . On the other hand, the DOD has repeatedly signalled its intention to keep wars conventional if possible. Nonetheless, the aircraft inventory permitted was adjusted to a war different from the one being fought in Vietnam. Expensive and vulnerable aircraft are flying repeated sorties against heavy ground fire. The cumulative attrition is high. Not only are costs far higher than they would be with more appropriate aircraft, but the attrition in this peripheral war is draining the inventory at an unanticipated rate.[82]

A conventional mission was now being enacted on a massive scale. The TAC organization, of course, had a major part in the Vietnam air war, as did SAC with its B-52 strategic bomber.[83] Throughout the history of the Air Force, combat experience has taught "lessons" that served as the cornerstone of subsequent service doctrine on aircraft design.[84] Thus, given the professional attitudes of the Air Force, the Vietnam combat experience plausibly represented the most important information that the service could receive. The message emphasized the importance of conventional bombing and the vulnerability of some of the nuclear mission aircraft.[85] In OSD there was a greater

[82] James R. Schlesinger, "Organizational Structures and Planning," in Roland McKean (ed.), *Issues in Defense Economics* (New York: National Bureau of Economic Research, 1967), pp. 202–203.

[83] See comments by Schlesinger on B-52 use in Southeast Asia, in Ibid., p. 202n.

[84] See Head, "Decision-Making on the A-7 Attack Aircraft Program," pp. 85–154, for a discussion of the importance of combat experience in the formation of service doctrines.

[85] For example, since the F-105 design was tailored to the high-performance delivery of nuclear weapons "on the deck" and not for conventional dive-bombing, it was not well suited to absorb even moderate punishment from ground fire. Through 1968, at least, the F-105 was flying most of the TAC interdiction missions for the Air Force. The F-105's vulnerability, however, led the Air Force to begin escorting the F-105s with F-4s on bombing runs, a step strikingly at odds with prior Air Force doctrine on fighter-bomber capabilities. The Air Force had earlier maintained that its tactical bombers were self-sufficient and did not require fighter escorts. See Ibid., pp. 106–116; and Michael P. London, "Tactical Air Superiority," *Space/Aeronautics*, Vol. 49 (March 1968), pp. 62–63.

awareness of the need for simpler, less expensive aircraft adapted to the conventional air-to-ground mission.[86] Enthoven and Smith, two central figures in the systems analysis group in OSD, later commented that there was a real shift in doctrine by 1967 away from the nuclear mission emphasis of the original F-111 requirements.[87]

The problems of the F-111 program were addressed in the context of this growing awareness of the Vietnam experience. Flight tests of tactical aircraft are routinely performed using nearly every compatible form of bomb and munition. These tests necessarily reveal the performance of the plane for missions outside formal requirements. By-product capabilities are no longer so implicit, since data are generated that measure in fairly precise terms what these by-product capabilities actually are. For the F-111, routine flight tests revealed critical information about the by-product conventional capability: the F-111A was discovered to be severely underpowered in the high-drag, high-tonnage payload configuration of the conventional interdiction mission.[88] This lack of power was most critical in "military power" (that is, without afterburner), which is the key to conventional mission performance.[89] Initially, improvements in the installed performance of the F-111A's TF-30 engines were sought. Marginal improvements were ultimately achieved, as the original P-1 version of the TF-30 engine was upgraded to the P-3 version. There was, however, no *thrust* increase on the P-3 engines, which were installed in

[86] Interviews 10, 11, 12, 22, and 24.

[87] Enthoven and Smith, *How Much Is Enough?*, pp. 262–265.

[88] See the flight test survey, with Air Force comments, in *TFX Hearings—Second Series*, Part 1, pp. 205–206. The awareness at this time of conventional mission problem was also noted in Interviews 11, 12, and 20.

[89] The afterburner is an additional "combustion chamber" at the aft end of the core engine. In the afterburner, fuel is sprayed into the hot exhaust gases expelled from the core engine, thereby providing a significant augmentation in thrust (particularly on a turbo-fan engine). The afterburner consumes fuel much less efficiently than the core engine, however. It cannot be used extensively without incurring severe range penalties—hence the importance of military power performance for conventional missions.

123

the 96 F-111Es as well as in the 141 F-111As. For 94 F-111Ds (the F-111Es with the Mark II avionics), an engine with 6 percent more power, the P-9, was developed.[90] Later, eight months of operational experience with the F-111A in Southeast Asia (March 1968 through November 1968) made clear the desirability of large increases in thrust for any conventional interdiction. In December 1968, immediately after the return of the F-111As from combat, the Air Force indicated to Secretary of Defense Clifford the need for additional power: "In the F-111 development program there has been an increasing need for additional engine thrust. Early experience in the operational use of the F-111 has revealed this need for additional thrust in military power ratings as well as afterburning thrust."[91] Or, as the President of General Dynamics noted at the same meeting: "The airplane is underpowered for the conventional mission. It was designed for the nuclear mission. This badly needs to be attended to. The P-100 [the advanced engine then envisioned] would solve the situation."[92]

While necessary to improve the F-111's conventional mission performance, the larger-thrust engines were not really needed for the nuclear mission.[93] But by this time, the importance of conventional capabilities had become clear to all parties, the Air Force as well as OSD.[94] Gone were the days of an exclusive emphasis on nuclear interdiction in the Air Force. The P-100 engine development was approved in early 1969. At a cost of approximately 100 million dollars,

[90] *TFX Hearings—Second Series*, Part 1, pp. 203–208. In military power, the P-9 engine provided a 12 percent increase in thrust over the P-3 engine.

[91] Air Force presentation to Secretary of Defense F-111 Meeting, December 12, 1968, excerpted in *TFX Hearings—Second Series*, Part 1, p. 206.

[92] Minutes of Secretary of Defense F-111 Meeting, December 12, 1968, re Discussion of an Advanced Engine Called P-100 for the F-111, excerpted in *TFX Hearings—Second Series*, Part 1, p. 206.

[93] *TFX Hearings—Second Series*, Part 1, p. 210.

[94] U.S. House of Representatives, Committee on Armed Services, *Hearings on Military Posture* (1969), pp. 2631–2632, 3203, and 3208.

the P-100 program obtained a 35 percent increase in the military power and the maximum thrust of the TF-30 engine. The P-100 version was developed in time to be incorporated into the 106 F-111Fs.[95]

Though the available evidence on F-111 engine improvements is not extensive, the pattern of these improvements is fairly clear. The Vietnam experience created a vivid awareness of the significance of conventional capabilities, particularly in the Air Force, which until that time had maintained its emphasis on nuclear capabilities. In reaction to the initial test reports of a severely underpowered aircraft for the conventional mission, marginal improvements were attempted within the alternative then in use (the P-1 engine), which led to the P-3 engine. This was done even though the 20 percent weight growth and the unexpectedly high drag of the F-111A meant that substantial thrust improvements would be necessary to obtain performance approximating original expectations.[96] Predictably, reports of the need for greater power in the conventional mission persisted, leading to further marginal thrust improvements with the P-9 engine. Actual F-111 combat experience followed and finally created sufficient pressures for the dramatic thrust improvements of the P-100 engine.

How can we characterize this process? The weight, power, and approximate drag levels of the F-111A—and hence the plane's relative power—could have been ascertained with some confidence in early 1964, when the first

[95] No public announcement of the approval of the P-100 program was discovered by the author. However, as indicated in footnotes 91 and 92 above, discussions on the new engine were being held in December 1968, immediately after the conclusion of the Southeast Asian deployment of the aircraft. By March 1969, the P-100 program had been approved (ibid., pp. 2631–2632). Hence, the program was approved sometime between late December of 1968 and mid-March of 1969. For more data on the P-100, see *TFX Hearings—Second Series*, Part 1, pp. 191, 203–212; and U.S. Senate, Committee on Armed Services, *Fiscal Year 1975 Authorization for Military Procurement*, 93d Cong., 2d Sess. (1974), p. 4355.

[96] *TFX Hearings—Second Series*, Part 1, p. 59, and Part 2, pp. 339–365; and Interview 12.

actual prototype was assembled. The plane's relative power could have been ascertained with precision after January 1966, when test flight reports of a severely underpowered aircraft began accumulating.[97] Yet the P-100 program was not approved until three years after the first test flights and nearly five years after the first prototype was assembled. Meanwhile, throughout this period, production continued substantially as had been planned at the outset of the program, which meant that the P-100 engine would not be available until 331 F-111s had already been produced.[98] Engine-inlet compatibility problems (to be described in the next chapter) account for part of the delay, since these problems necessarily preoccupied General Dynamics and Pratt & Whitney engineers during the first two or three years of flight tests. Still, especially in light of the continued production of the aircraft throughout this period, it is obvious that the F-111 thrust improvements were not characterized by a speculative, forward-looking decision process, a process sensitive to new information and continually updating its approaches and plans in response to technical surprises. Instead, the process was marked by a sustained adherence to initial schedules and technical formulations. The prospect of an underpowered aircraft in 1964 did nothing to dislodge the process from its initial plans, and persistently unfavorable test reports on aircraft power led only to marginal reorientations of technical approach. Even after three years of unfavorable reports, it took criticisms of the F-111's power *in combat* to induce the fresh approaches required to resolve the problem. By that time, a fresh ap-

[97] See *TFX Hearings—Second Series*, Part 1, pp. 205–206.
[98] That is, until 141 F-111As, 96 F-111Ds, and 94 F-111Es had been produced. That this result was not a product of conscious trade-off calculations by McNamara and his associates will become clear in the next chapter. As detailed in that chapter, McNamara and his associates did not realize until 1967 that they were in full-scale production, although they had committed the government to production in April 1965 and would ultimately have to accept those aircraft already produced. The skeptical reader is urged to suspend judgment on the issue until the discussion in Chapter iv.

proach could benefit only the final quarter of the F-111 production run, the 106 F-111Fs.

Of course, there were other responses to improve conventional mission performance, most notably the Mark II avionics program. This program commenced formally on July 1, 1966. It grew out of analyses made by groups outside the uniformed Air Force: the President's Scientific Advisory Board, the Air Force Scientific Advisory Board, and DDR&E.[99] These groups believed that a dramatic improvement in delivery accuracy for conventional weapons was possible with more sophisticated avionics.[100] Moreover, they saw the need to provide greater air-to-air avionics capability for the F-111, since it had a greater unrefueled range than any possible fighter escort.

The Air Force itself, particularly its program management personnel, strongly opposed the program. It considered the Mark I avionics, specified as a part of the original F-111 Work Statement, to be a reliable, highly accurate, fully sufficient system. The proposed Mark II program threatened to increase F-111 costs and to reduce avionics reliability, all to achieve an additional capability that the Air Force considered unnecessary.[101] Notably, this additional capability applied mainly to conventional missions—

[99] Claude Witze, "The F-111's Mark II Avionics System—Weapons Effectiveness or Electronic Gadget?" *Air Force and Space Digest*, Vol. 52 (August 1969), p. 65; and Interview 23.

[100] The far greater explosive power of tactical nuclear weapons made increased accuracy for the delivery of these weapons a less pressing issue.

[101] Interviews 16, 20, and 22. The relative success of the Mark I system was in part the result of avionics problems that General Dynamics and TAC's General Everest experienced just prior to the F-111 program. In the B-58 program of the 1950s, a program to produce a new, medium-range bomber for the Air Force, General Dynamics (the prime contractor) had experienced severe difficulties with the plane's complicated avionics. During this same period, General Everest was close to some of the major Air Force developments and was impressed by the avionics problems that those programs encountered. Reportedly, he paid great attention to the F-111's avionics specifications and was ruthless in resisting any proposals that would push the Mark I system beyond technical frontiers.

both conventional interdiction and air-to-air combat—
which were relatively undervalued by the Air Force at
that time.[102]

However, the Air Force program managers lost control
of events. DDR&E pushed hard for the new avionics program and was, by most accounts, the organization primarily
responsible for approval of the program. As noted earlier,
this organization was dominated by men with backgrounds
in the technologies of guided missiles and electronics.[103] As
an organization, DDR&E had had its formative experiences
in the dramatic ICBM programs of the late 1950s. There
was little aeronautical engineering expertise in DDR&E in
the mid-1960s. By numerous accounts, DDR&E treated
aircraft as vehicles for avionics. It had criticized the "austerity" of the Mark I avionics.[104]

DDR&E took the advisory board recommendations and
its own studies and began pushing for the new avionics
package. For obvious reasons, electronics contractors were
strong supporters of the proposed program. With DDR&E,
they described the program as an evolutionary, "state of
the art" development task, which promised to provide
superb conventional bombing capabilities for the F-111, a
claim to which McNamara was responsive.[105] By contrast,
DDR&E described the Mark I avionics as being primarily

[102] *TFX Hearings—Second Series*, Part 1, pp. 215–217; U.S. Senate, Committee on Armed Services, *Fiscal Year 1972 Authorization
for Military Procurement*, 92d Cong., 1st Sess. (1971), pp. 3885–
3888, 3920–3921; Witze, "The F-111's Mark II Avionics," pp. 63–65;
and Interviews 11 and 22.

[103] Interviews 10 and 11.

[104] Interviews 11, 16, 20, and 22.

[105] U.S. Congress, Joint Economic Committee, Subcommittee on
Economy in Government, *The Military Budget and National Economic
Priorities*, Hearings, 91st Cong., 1st Sess. (1969), p. 796; and Interviews 20 and 22. For some perspective on the initial claims that the
Mark II system was "state of the art," the reader should note the
following experience: in his five years in the Defense Department, an
assistant secretary for one of the services had *never* received a development proposal acknowledged to be beyond the "state of the art"
in any way. Of course, many of the proposals he received had in fact
envisioned performance far beyond technical frontiers (Interview 4).

useful for the nuclear mission and incapable of giving the F-111 the true multi-purpose capability McNamara sought in the plane.[106] McNamara was thus easily sold on the program. Air Force program officials continued to resist, but they were fighting a losing battle and they knew it. Realizing that they were "eating up their own lead time," they acquiesced in February 1966. The requirements were formalized, and DDR&E performed the source selection.[107]

The Mark II program had built up a momentum that, when it reached the Air Force program officials, was impossible to stop. The logical OSD agency to have thwarted the pressure of DDR&E was the Office of Systems Analysis, whose economic emphasis could have counterbalanced DDR&E's drive for high technology. (Systems Analysis was generally skeptical of sophisticated avionics.[108]) However, sometime prior to 1965, DDR&E and Systems Analysis had worked out a "treaty," which assigned DDR&E the responsibility for supervising the development phase of weapons acquisition for OSD, while Systems Analysis supervised the procurement phase.[109] This treaty was established to reduce the recurrent conflict which the two groups had earlier experienced. Its net effect, however, was to leave the field relatively free to DDR&E for such development decisions as Mark II.

[106] Interview 22.

[107] Interviews 20 and 22.

[108] For a description of the prevailing values of the systems analysis group in OSD, particularly as compared to those of DDR&E, see Head, "Decision-Making on the A-7 Attack Aircraft Program," pp. 53–66, 386–391, 409, 444–446, 559, 570–576.

[109] Stockfisch, *Plowshares Into Swords*, p. 147; and Interview 22. This treaty was reportedly worked out between Alain Enthoven, head of the systems analysis group in OSD from 1961 to 1968, and Harold Brown, Director of Defense Research and Engineering from 1961 to 1965. This treaty is of obvious significance in light of the enormous "leverage" that R&D decisions have on procurement expenditures. In the development of the options to be available for procurement, the technology bias of the scientists in DDR&E would not be mitigated by the greater cost consciousness of the economists in Dr. Enthoven's group.

In the Mark II program, then, the long-standing pressure of DDR&E for more sophisticated F-111 avionics bore fruit. The advisory board studies were the catalyst for this DDR&E success, as they offered prestigious corroboration for the argument DDR&E had been making all along. Mc-Namara was responsive to the promise of the Mark II program, since according to DDR&E it would give the aircraft a true multi-purpose capability. The Vietnam build-up, as well as the results of early F-111 test flights, made McNamara sensitive to this need.

The Mark II program is a classic example of what is generally termed "goldplating," the selective pursuit of the single value of technical sophistication. (Notably, in this case the pressures for goldplating came from OSD—not from the military services, the organizations normally assumed responsible for goldplating requirements.[110]) DDR&E's pursuit of this value was a carry-over from its formative experiences in the ballistic missile field. The treaty between DDR&E and Systems Analysis insured that there would be little opposition within OSD to the Mark II program. While Systems Analysis did provide analyses of the F-111 program beginning in 1965, these analyses dealt with procurement issues and, it should be added, generally recommended cutbacks in planned production buys.[111]

Ultimately, the Mark II program cost four times original estimates, or approximately one billion dollars. The program's schedules slipped by two years, and the system itself proved to be 15 percent as reliable as anticipated at the program's outset.[112] The trouble-plagued, Mark II-

110 Later, however, the Air Force staunchly defended the program, as the service's management competence was called into question by the cost and performance problems which plagued the program. See the submissions of A. Ernest Fitzgerald, in U.S. Congress, Joint Economic Committee, Subcommittee on Economy in Government, *The Military Budget and National Economic Priorities*, pp. 976–818.

111 Enthoven and Smith, *How Much Is Enough?*, pp. 262–265.

112 U.S. Senate, Committee on Armed Services, *Fiscal Year 1972 Authorization for Military Procurement*, pp. 3888, 3920. In these hearings, the Air Force estimated total Mark II-IIB expenditures (including initial spares and non-recurring items) to be approximately

equipped F-111Ds were not to be operational until 1973.[113] Moreover, because of the expense and the delay on the Mark II avionics, a stripped-down Mark II system (the Mark IIB), suffering only marginal performance reductions, was developed for the F-111Fs (and, with further modifications, for the SAC FB-111s). The Mark IIB system lacks the Mark II's ability to track moving targets on the ground, has nine percent less accuracy for weapons delivery, less air-to-air radar capability, and less sophisticated cockpit display systems (the latter being a prime source of cost growth on the Mark II system). For these concessions, per-unit savings of 50 to 75 percent over the Mark II system were obtained—a clear indication that, for the original Mark II avionics, the marginal dollar bought very little additional performance.[114] However, the Mark II schedules were high-

---

940 million dollars. To this figure should be added 60 million dollars to cover the approximate production expense for avionics in the 48 F-111Fs which were authorized and procured after this Air Force estimate was prepared. (The estimate provides for only 58 F-111Fs, while 106 F-111Fs were ultimately authorized.) For additional information on the Mark II-IIB cost problems, see Cecil Brownlow, "Mk. 2 Hits Severe Cost Problems," *Aviation Week and Space Technology*, Vol. 90 (March 3, 1969), pp. 16–17; U.S. Congress, Joint Economic Committee, Subcommittee on Economy in Government, *The Military Budget and National Economic Priorities*, pp. 796–818.

[113] U.S. Congress, Committee on Armed Services, *Fiscal Year 1973 Authorization for Military Procurement*, Hearings, 92d Cong., 2d Sess. (1972), pp. 1190, 3501.

[114] For cost, performance, and schedule data on the two avionics systems, see "Defense Digest: F-111 Avionics Cost Sliced," *Armed Forces Management*, Vol. 16 (November 1969), p. 64; *TFX Hearings—Second Series*, Part 1, pp. 168, 215, 246; U.S. Senate, Committee on Armed Services, *Fiscal Year 1972 Authorization for Military Procurement*, pp. 3888, 3920–3923; and U.S. Senate, Committee on Armed Services, *Fiscal Year 1973 Authorization for Military Procurement*, p. 1190. Note that the Mark II's lack of reliability apparently reflects a general phenomenon that plagues follow-on avionics systems. Characteristically, new avionics for a given weapon system are less reliable than the initial avionics for that system. See Bernard Nossiter, "Weapons Systems: A Story of Failure," *Washington Post* (January 26, 1969), printed in U.S. Congress, Joint Economic Committee, Subcommittee on Economy in Government, *The Military Budget and National Priorities*, pp. 95–99; and Richard A. Stubbing, "Improving the Acquisition Process for High-Risk Electronics Systems," printed in

ly compressed and the system moved into production as scheduled, before testing was completed. By the time the problems with the Mark II were revealed and the need to substitute the Mark IIB finally acknowledged, an ongoing production process had foreclosed a decision on the first production lots of the Mark II system. As with the engine improvements and the nuclear mission design itself, an awareness of the Mark II's technical problems, of the critical interdependencies among its requirements, came too late in a production process which proceeded according to foreordained schedules.[115] The reduction of key technical uncertainties lagged behind the enactment, on schedule, of irretrievable program commitments.

Overall, the mission adaptations of the F-111 program were a delayed response to important but restricted dimensions of the mission-design problem. The engine improvements derived from a categorical cycle of improvements in performance and reports of power inadequacy. The Mark II avionics program grew from DDR&E's single-valued advocacy of more sophisticated avionics. In neither case was the response balanced against the composition of the F-111 force which was being established *de facto* by the continuing production of the aircraft. The adaptations to the conventional mission were costly, and they came too late to achieve the integration of capabilities that had been avoided many years earlier.

PARADIGMS OF THE DECISION PROCESS BEHIND THE EXPLANATION

Our discussion of why the F-111 was a nuclear bomber has been a chronicle of how high-level officials failed to understand the character of the original Air Force requirement

---

Congressional Record—Senate, Vol. 115, 91st Cong., 1st Sess. (February 7, 1969) pp. 3171–3176.

[115] The next chapter will discuss the production process in greater detail.

and of the actual development process. The original TFX requirement was in essence a routine extension of the Air Force's doctrinal emphasis on nuclear missions in the 1950s. McNamara hoped to change this doctrine when he entered office. However, with the recommendations of the limited war panel and the urgings of DDR&E, he accepted the Air Force requirement as the basis for a joint program. The development process routinely decomposed the actual design along the lines of the nuclear mission emphasized in the requirement. Problems were perceived in terms of deficiencies against nuclear mission specifications. Only Air Force flight tests and combat experience revealed the severity of the problems for multi-mission performance. In spite of these revelations, production continued more or less as planned, through the late 1960s. Engine improvements were pursued in an evolving cycle of reports on power inadequacy and attempts at performance improvement. Avionics improvements were pursued without any timely understanding of critical interdependencies among technical requirements. Throughout this period, there was little recognition of the F-111 force composition being established by the continuation of production.

Although the central purpose of this study is to examine the main questions of the F-111 development, its secondary purpose is to demonstrate the usefulness of employing alternative paradigms of the decision process to obtain satisfactory explanation. It is therefore important that the role of these paradigms in our examination of the F-111 mission puzzle be made explicit. In the sections that follow, each major point in the explanation of the F-111 mission puzzle will be subjected to a brief, critical review, framed by the competing paradigms of the decision process.

The Origins of the Air Force Requirement

The observed evolution of tactical aircraft requirements provides a good illustration of the assumptions of the cybernetic paradigm. The prospective combat environment is highly uncertain. Even when we know enemy capabilities in some detail, we cannot predict with great confidence what capabilities will prove to be best for fighting (or deterring) an enemy. In other words, the enemy threat provides no clear-cut or self-evident criteria for use in choosing which weapons, among the infinitude of technically feasible weapons, we should develop and deploy. There inevitably exists wide interpretive latitude on these matters. In a complicated and uncertain environment of this sort, the cybernetic paradigm posits that the decision maker will tend to conceptualize the environment so as to avoid recognizing trade-offs. While, objectively, any course of action implies critical trade-offs among important dimensions of value, the decision maker will suppress these trade-offs by conceptualizing his world in such a way that the values do not seem in conflict. Once these simplified conceptualizations are established, the mind of the decision maker will impute unwarranted correctness to them and will work actively to preserve them, in a process strikingly insensitive to the weight of objective evidence. Information will be unconsciously manipulated to affirm the existing structure of beliefs. Non-probabilistic, categorical inferences (for example, inferences of complete certainty or impossibility) will be attached to alternatives that are actually problematic or uncertain, in a manner which confirms the structure of beliefs. When new information reveals inconsistencies in beliefs, simple inferences will be irrepressibly generated which restore consistency with a minimum amount of restructuring. Only when the threats to consistency are unavoidable and unambiguous—that is, only when uncertainty is low and the "reality principle" is strong—will the mind sustain a major restructuring of beliefs and confront those trade-offs it normally and unconsciously avoids.[116]

[116] John D. Steinbruner, *The Cybernetic Theory of Decision: New Dimensions of Political Analysis* (Princeton: Princeton University Press, 1974), chaps. 3–5. A well-written summary and interesting discussion of the theory is Jack L. Snyder, "Rationality at the Brink:

This paradigm of the decision maker, and the derivative paradigms of organization behavior sketched in Chapter I, accord reasonably well with the observed evolution of Air Force requirements. In the formulation of a new requirement, decision makers focused on the select parameters of a central mission: the air-superiority mission for the F-86 and F-100, and the low-altitude, high-speed delivery of nuclear weapons for the F-105 and F-111. The central mission profile represented an objectively biased and simplified model of the environment. But it greatly reduced the problem of conceptualizing a requirement for a new aircraft (and a role for old aircraft). It allowed decision makers to monitor a few variables of aircraft performance related to the combat environment and thus to avoid the uncertainty and complexity that otherwise would be confronted. The general criterion for a new requirement was that it provide for incremental improvements on the variables of performance being monitored. Hence, from the F-86 to the F-111, top speed, low-altitude speed, and maximum range capabilities improved for each new generation of aircraft. Performance parameters outside the few parameters of the central mission often did not. For example, approximate measures of acceleration and maneuverability critical to the air superiority mission—the thrust-to-weight ratio and wing loading—were inferior on the F-111 as compared to the F-105, yet the costs of this inferiority were unacknowledged.[117]

Uncertainty and the Cognitive Dynamics of a Two-Value Game" (unpublished paper, Department of Political Science, Columbia University, 1974).

[117] The thrust-to-weight ratio is the ratio of engine thrust to aircraft mission weight. The wing loading is the ratio of aircraft gross weight to wing area. Other things being equal, a higher thrust-to-weight ratio provides greater excess thrust for acceleration and maneuvers, and a lower wing loading provides greater maneuverability. See "Aerospace in Perspective: Tactical Warfare," *Space/Aeronautics*, Vol. 51 (January 1969), p. 98; *Jane's All the World's Aircraft, 1961–62*, p. 297; *Jane's All the World's Aircraft, 1970–71*, p. 350; and *TFX Hearings—Second Series*, Part 1, pp. 59, 200 and 204.

A recognition of the actual trade-offs among missions—such as among the central nuclear interdiction mission and the conventional interdiction, close support, and air superiority missions—was avoided. A simple inference—the assumption that capabilities for secondary missions would "fall out" of the central mission's requirements—enabled Air Force officials to perceive the conflicting missions as "actually" being consonant: the Air Force firmly believed that excellent by-product capabilities for secondary missions would be provided by the pursuit of the central scenario's requirements. Given the high level of uncertainty as to the actual performance that a future conflict would demand and that a specific development program could provide, the belief in "fall out" capabilities normally could be maintained. In an example given above, F-111 maneuverability and acceleration performance for the air-superiority mission were observed to have suffered under the burden of the central nuclear interdiction mission. Yet back in 1960, the Air Force believed that its planned 35-ton, 90-foot-long plane would be able to "fly high altitude air superiority missions" simply because of the plane's high top speed: Mach 2.5 at high altitude.[118] Reflecting Air Force doctrine

[118] Larry Booda, "USAF and Navy Unable to Agree on Joint Tactical Fighter Project," *Aviation Week and Space Technology*, Vol. 75 (August 21, 1961), p. 27. The assumption that top speed was the decisive criterion for air superiority was a routine extension of the World War II and Korean War experience in *subsonic* aerial combat. (See p. 88n for a description of air superiority doctrine before the F-111.) The routine extension of the top-speed lesson drawn from subsonic experience became increasingly inappropriate as aircraft speeds moved higher in the supersonic regime, notwithstanding the increased reliance on sophisticated air-to-air missiles and avionics, which were thought to reduce the importance of aircraft performance for the air superiority mission. The day of the aerial "dogfight" proved not to be over, as the Air Force (and Navy) had more or less assumed in the 1950s. Aerial combat between supersonic fighters normally takes place at subsonic speeds and medium-to-low altitudes. Combat at high altitudes and supersonic speeds is rare in part because the energy loss is great in sharp turns at high altitudes. Moreover, the turning radius is so large at high altitudes and supersonic speeds that multiple-pass, close-in aerial combat is impractical. The continuing

since World War II, this assumption dissolved the trade-off between the air-superiority mission and a stringent nuclear-interdiction mission and facilitated the exclusive focus on the nuclear mission.

Later, it would become clear that the F-111 had no real aerial-combat capability, as the nuclear-mission burden made the plane too deficient in acceleration and maneuverability for it to engage in aerial combat. These deficiencies were ascertainable early in the program, but they were

---

Air Force focus on high top speed into the Mach 2 region penalized maneuverability and acceleration in the transonic regime (Mach 0.8 to Mach 1.5) where most aerial combat would actually take place. For example, wing area was minimized to obtain high speeds, with the result that transonic maneuverability suffered. However, as is understandable in cybernetic terms, the Air Force avoided fully acknowledging these penalties, as it assumed that high speed plus sophisticated missiles and avionics would satisfy air superiority requirements. This assumption implicitly avoided disrupting the increasingly demanding interdiction scenarios evolving at the time. The Air Force maintained the "top speed" assumption until it was presented with the sharp operational reality of the Vietnam air war—specifically, under the visual identification rules of that conflict, the reality of unprecedentedly high exchange rates of American planes for North Vietnamese planes in air-to-air combat. When these rates reached their most unfavorable levels, in the June 1967 to October 1968 period—a time when more F-4s were lost to MIG-21s than vice versa—the Air Force began to acknowledge the need for greater maneuverability and acceleration in its fighter aircraft and for more innovative tactics in fighter operations. This change in thinking led, among other things, to the acceleration and maneuverability emphases in the Air Force's subsequent fighter developments, the F-15 and F-16. See Dulberger, "Advanced Fighter-Attack Aircraft," p. 36; Michael Getler, "The MIG and the Phantom," *Space/Aeronautics*, Vol. 51 (May 1969), p. 83; Grasset, "Dogfighting," pp. 1188–1191; Head, "Decision-Making on the A-7 Attack Aircraft Program," pp. 113–116; Levin, "F-15," pp. 36, 43; Levin, "Why the Swing-Wing?," *Space/Aeronautics*, Vol. 50 (November 1968), p. 71; Michael P. London, "VFX—the Navy's Choice," *Space/Aeronautics*, Vol. 50 (November 1968), p. 51; Craig Powell, "FX: Designed to Control the Skies," *Armed Forces Management*, Vol. 15 (November 1968), pp. 38–40; Robert C. Seamans, Jr., "Tac Air: A Look at the Late '70s," *Air Force Magazine*, Vol. 56 (January 1973), p. 33; *TFX Hearings—Second Series*, Part 1, p. 29; and U.S. Senate, Committee on Armed Services, *Fiscal Year 1974 Authorization for Military Procurement, Hearings*, 93d Cong., 1st Sess. (1973), pp. 4076–4088, 4390–4408.

muted or camouflaged by simplifying assumptions. The exclusiveness of the nuclear mission to the detriment of the other missions in the F-111 requirement is a strong indication of the power of cognitive simplifications and focused attention to a few feedback variables to screen out critical relationships in the environment. As Allison observes, when organizations cannot "negotiate" their environment—when they cannot establish a fixed set of relationships with the environment, as the Air Force surely cannot with the future combat environment—they deal with uncertainty and variability by establishing a set of missions or standard scenarios that constitute the contingencies for which the organization prepares.[119] Within the organization, the scenarios are firmly believed to be objective maps of critical relationships in the environment. In fact, however, they are selective simplifications of the environment that preserve the basic structures of belief within the organization. They will be reflected in the plans, training, doctrine, informal expectations, and hardware of the organization and will be highly resistant to contradictory evidence. They will be extremely difficult to modify or redirect, as McNamara discovered in all of his attempts to move TAC away from nuclear weapons.

The central mission did change over time, however, in response to information from routine channels to which service decision makers were attentive, such as the shift of funds away from tactical aircraft under the Massive Retaliation doctrine of the 1950s. By the logic of the cybernetic paradigm, substantial revision of the central mission conception would be highly disruptive. This conception provides a widely held simplification of the requirements problem that achieves the status of a service doctrine.[120] It gives meaning to the design emphases in an aircraft and to the operational expectations of the organization. As such,

[119] Allison, *Essence of Decision*, p. 84.
[120] Head, "Decision-Making on the A-7 Attack Aircraft Program," pp. 83–142.

it is not generally amenable to rapid shifts. Hence, the shift from an air superiority to a nuclear-interdiction emphasis in the 1950s occurred over two generations of aircraft and did not in any event displace the importance of high top speeds. Later, when the nuclear interdiction mission became critically challenged by other information to which TAC was also attentive—namely, the fundamental challenge to tactical aircraft from ballistic missiles in the late 1950s—the response was a conservative, low-order neutralization of the threat. Requirements were added for the TFX which freed the aircraft from long, vulnerable concrete runways. But the only mission profile articulated in the requirements remained the nuclear-interdiction mission, as evolved from the F-105. The mission conception itself was basically undisrupted, and no broad sensitivity to the trade-off among missions was demonstrated.

This observed evolution of fighter-bomber requirements is at odds with the outcome calculations, the broad search for alternatives, and the integration of conflicting values presupposed by the *analytic* paradigm. The major difficulty of an analytic explanation lies in the exclusiveness of the central missions that the service contemplates. Such a simplification imposes costs on the performance of other missions, yet the service tends to avoid confronting these mission trade-offs by imputing by-product capabilities where the cautious analyst would find grounds for skepticism. We have seen what these assumptions meant for the multimission capabilities on the F-111. In a world of fixed physical laws, it was impossible for so demanding an interdiction mission to have provided sufficient capabilities for demanding by-product missions. The general problem has perhaps best been described by James Schlesinger, in a Rand study which examined force optimization in the Air Force. Schlesinger concludes:

> [I]nsufficient attention has been given to examining the implications for force composition of the wide range of

conflicts in which the United States might become engaged. Implicitly, it is accepted that forces optimized for one kind of war will be suitable for other kinds of war; that forces designed for a major struggle (for example, an all-out Soviet assault in Europe) will prove quite adaptable for lower-order conflicts. As between types of conflict, the relevance of optimization seems to disappear, because it is assumed that lower-order capabilities are automatically provided as spillovers from capabilities for major conflicts. In short, forces are viewed as highly complementary for certain major conflicts, but the same forces are seen as highly substitutable in different conflicts. For a specific conflict, optimization is crucial, but among conflicts it is insignificant. . . . The ultimate effect of any such line of thought, it should be noted, is that optimization of forces is achieved by contemplating a single type of conflict—and ignoring the rest.[121]

This is an apt characterization of the genesis of the original TFX requirements. The Air Force believed that capabilities for lower order, conventional conflicts would be by-products (or, in Schlesinger's words, "spillovers") from capabilities for a nuclear exchange. Unfortunately, when McNamara confronted the Air Force requirements, he too assumed that broad capabilities were adequately provided.

Commonality and the Establishment of the Joint Requirement: 1961

When McNamara entered the Defense Department, he was sensitive to the need to strengthen the conventional option in the force posture and to end the duplicative procurement of weapon systems. The limited war panel soon recommended that a multi-service fighter be developed for

[121] Schlesinger, "Organizational Structures and Planning," pp. 199–201.

140

limited war missions. Shortly thereafter, DDR&E proposed that this program could be based on the aircraft contemplated by the Air Force. McNamara responded favorably. He sought a bi-service development of a plane that would be the sole tactical fighter in the American inventory through the 1970s. The joint requirement that ultimately was established was essentially the original Air Force statement (SOR-183) with Navy requirements added to it. The disparate performance demands of the services went unintegrated. Moreover, the nuclear emphasis of the Air Force requirement was not altered. A 10,000-pound payload specification for conventional bombs was added; but nothing was said about the performance of the plane when carrying this payload, nor about its broad utility in the limited war environment.

Under the assumptions of the analytic paradigm, McNamara can perhaps be seen to have made optimizing decisions under a critical handicap: the absence of critical advice from systems analysts in OSD. The efforts and advice of systems analysts had been decisive in the F-105/F-4 case, but were absent in the F-111 case. Consequently, McNamara was in a position to make less penetrating and sophisticated judgments on the Air Force and Navy plans with which he was presented when he entered office. The Air Force and DDR&E both spoke optimistically of the ability of the proposed TFX to meet the demands of the limited war environment and to satisfy the needs of the Navy. Lacking countervailing advice from systems analysts in OSD, McNamara was susceptible to their claims, for the variable-sweep, turbo-fan TFX that the Air Force envisioned appeared to be flexible.

He thus established the Air Force's SOR-183 as the basis for inter-service negotiations on a joint development. The subsequent negotiations were characterized by intense bargaining among the participants, as each jockeyed for maximum advantage. In this heated adversary process, McNamara could not easily have modified his initial commitments. However, there is no evidence that he ever wanted to do so. Throughout, he clearly believed in the Air Force requirement and fought hard to obtain a bi-service development based upon it. To insure some conventional mission capabilities, he forced the addition of a 10,000-pound payload specification to it. Moreover, he succeeded in inducing the Navy to enter the joint program by cancelling the Missileer early in the year, thus leaving the Navy with no alternative to the joint program. While he added Navy specifications to the basic Air Force requirement, he stipulated that changes in the Air Force version to meet Navy's performance goals were to be held to a minimum—a position consistent with his understanding of the Air Force requirement. The Navy, after all, was planning to buy only one-half as many planes as the Air Force, and the services were being (in McNamara's eyes) self-interested and parochial in their unwillingness to agree. By this logic, McNamara won in the end, as a bi-service development was finally instituted, an unprecedented accomplishment for a program of this magnitude. Although one might have wished for a better integration of Navy requirements and conventional capabilities, the absence of systems analysts early in the process made greater analytic sophistication in the requirements unlikely.

The main substantive assumption behind this analytic explanation is that McNamara was seeking, above all, to secure a joint program. From that assumption, the rest of the explanation follows. But this assumption obscures an important aspect of the process of instituting a joint program. If it is assumed that McNamara focused his efforts primarily upon the achievement of a joint requirement, then it is implicitly assumed that he operated with reference to a near-term goal—that is, with reference to a 1961 goal of inaugurating a joint program rather than to a 1967 goal of achieving a successful, money-saving deployment of a common aircraft for the Navy and Air Force. As the development program made clear, these two goals were not synonymous.

Indeed, in view of the controversy surrounding the negotiations of 1961, any presumption that the two were synonymous represented a gross simplification of the complex political, technical, and managerial task they had initiated. A successful program could not mean the development of a fighter-bomber designed to a stringent nuclear mission of debatable value. It could not mean building an aircraft so lacking in air-superiority capability as to require the early initiation of plans for a new air-superiority fighter a few years later. And it could not mean placing the services' joint performance goals beyond the state of the art, which led to deficiencies relative to specifications on the F-111B, a major cause of the F-111B's cancellation. All of these problems were a result of the relatively unintegrated requirements that McNamara never seriously questioned.

An argument framed by the assumptions of the cybernetic paradigm can offer important insights into these weak points in our analytic argument. McNamara's focus on the single, near-term goal of achieving a joint program can be seen to reflect the lack of outcome calculation and the focused pursuit of a single value assumed in the cybernetic paradigm. Within OSD, McNamara's primary advisor and agent for the early program decisions was DDR&E. Because DDR&E did not share McNamara's doctrinal concerns, it conceived the problem mainly in terms of securing the acquiescence of the services, not in terms of fine-tuning the requirements themselves. All of the services' specifications had one point in common: the need for long subsonic range.[122] In other respects, such as size, cost, weight, and speed, they were substantially different. But the single dimension of similarity among them evoked an image of their basic compatibility for a joint program. Lacking any internal OSD challenge to the Air Force's proposed TFX, and being otherwise preoccupied with a number of major deci-

[122] At that time, there were three requirements: (1) the Air Force's TFX requirement; (2) the Navy's fleet defense (Missileer) requirement; and (3) the Navy's close support requirement.

143

sions, McNamara understandably was drawn to DDR&E's simplified conception of the problem of establishing a bi-service program. Like DDR&E, he failed to recognize major complexities in the task he had proposed. He acted on a greatly simplified image of the proposed program, an image that presented a single-valued problem—achieving a joint program—and a single-preferred alternative—the Air Force's SOR-183—which he maintained throughout the deliberations. Information threatening to this simplified image, such as Navy protests that the proposed TFX was a nuclear bomber and not a limited war fighter-bomber, was ignored. Information that supported the image, such as Air Force claims that the Navy had used aircraft of the size and weight of the proposed TFX, was taken to heart and viewed as confirmation of the image's validity. Steinbruner generalizes this pattern of behavior in his formulation of the cybernetic paradigm:

> [The cybernetic paradigm posits] that in the processing of information favorable outcomes will be inferred for preferred alternatives and that unfavorable outcomes will be projected for alternatives the decision maker intends to reject. Quite generally, the inferential structures which cognitive operations impose on inherently uncertain situations tend to be simple and coherently organized to present a single-valued problem and a single-preferred alternative to which the decision maker is committed from the outset of the decision process. Under complexity, the mind, in this view, does not match the uncertain structure of the environment in which events might take a number of alternative courses. Rather, it imposes an image and works to preserve that image. A single course of events is projected; evidence for alternative outcomes is manipulated to preserve the expectations.[123]

As this logic would suggest, the fitness of the Air Force requirement for providing multi-purpose capabilities and

[123] Steinbruner, *Cybernetic Theory*, p. 123.

for satisfying Navy needs went unexamined. The simplified conception of the problem shared by McNamara and DDR&E directed their attention elsewhere.

In the negotiations that followed McNamara's proposal for a multi-service fighter development, the VAX requirement was split off from the negotiations. This requirement presented a definite scenario for the conventional mission, as a matter of long-standing Navy doctrine. Its separation from the negotiations thus relieved the pressure for integrating the services' demands across multiple dimensions of performance, since this firmly detailed close-support mission conflicted with the succinct nuclear mission profile of the Air Force's proposed TFX and would have necessitated full integration of performance goals to obtain a joint development. But as it happened, the two fully articulated strike missions (conventional VAX and nuclear TFX) were separated and independently pursued. The joint requirement that was later imposed on the services further avoided any real integration of performance goals. It appended Navy performance requirements along the single dimension of range ("loiter") and added physical constraints on the aircraft that were at odds with the basic, unaltered Air Force performance requirements. The results of these negotiations tend to confirm Steinbruner's hypothesis that a bargaining process among cybernetic actors will produce less coherent results and much coarser bargains than are to be expected from mutual accommodations among analytic actors.[124]

The establishment of the joint requirement thus presents a mixed explanation in terms of our paradigms of decision. The analytic explanation emphasizes McNamara's shrewdness in obtaining a joint requirement and an "acceptable" source selection. The cybernetic explanation emphasizes McNamara's single-valued, short-range conception of what was in reality an extraordinarily complex, long-range problem. The absence of independent advice from the systems analysis group in OSD is important to both explanations.

[124] Ibid., p. 147.

145

In the analytic explanation, the lack of this advice (particularly in the first weeks of McNamara's tenure) is an essential handicap under which McNamara's optimizing decisions were made. In the cybernetic explanation, the lack of such critical advice possibly encouraged McNamara to proceed on the basis of the simplified image of the problem that he drew from DDR&E.

Both explanations are helpful to an understanding of how McNamara and his associates shaped the program at this early stage. The analytic paradigm evokes an explanation of how they achieved a joint development, an accomplishment that deserves emphasis. The cybernetic paradigm evokes an explanation of why they accepted the anomalous requirements as the basis of the joint development. This, too, deserves emphasis. As most participants later agreed, these requirements had a fateful impact on the development program that followed.

The Development Program: 1962–1965

The actual design of the aircraft began with the formulation of a design proposal. The contractors' design proposals were based on the joint requirement and the accompanying Work Statement. Since this basic documentation provided little guidance as to service priorities, the contractors were on their own in bringing coherence to the package of service demands.[125]

This initial process of formulating design proposals conforms well to the assumptions of the analytic paradigm. The proposals were formulated in an environment of intense competition. This was expected to be one of the last major aircraft contracts of the 1960s. The contractor that won the

---

[125] Air Force requirements were, of course, emphasized in the joint requirement, as changes to the Air Force version to meet Navy requirements were "to be held to a minimum." However, the contractors knew that the Navy would have to be satisfied with the carrier compatibility and loiter performance of the proposals. Navy demands could not be ignored.

competition could expect a decade of relative financial health: 6.5 billion dollars were to be spent on the program through 1970.[126] The contractors that lost the competition could look forward to a decade of major financial uncertainty (and possible bankruptcy, in the special case of General Dynamics).[127] The prospect of so unambiguous a success or failure was coercive to the contractors. Certainly, this was no time for business as usual.

In this environment, each contractor developed a conscious strategy for meeting the demands of the joint requirement. Boeing chose to focus on meeting the individual demands of each service. Commonality between Boeing's Air Force and Navy designs suffered somewhat: they were evaluated to be virtually "two separate airplanes" in structural terms. However, Boeing believed that, as had been the norm in source selections of the 1950s, the most important criterion for this source selection would be the potential of its designs for meeting the performance goals of the services. General Dynamics, on the other hand, took McNamara at his word and emphasized the degree of commonality between the Air Force and Navy versions it proposed.[128]

The actual formulation of design proposals involved the selection of engines and other subsystems, the development

[126] Art, *The TFX Decision*, p. 2; and "Defense Plans to Spend $6.5 Billion Through 1970 for Tactical Fighter," *Aviation Week and Space Technology*, Vol. 75 (October 9, 1961), p. 24.

[127] Art, *The TFX Decision*, pp. 2–3; and Richard Austin Smith, "How a Great Corporation Got Out of Control," Part II, *Fortune*, Vol. 65 (February 1962), p. 188. The prospects of financial difficulty were naturally reduced for those companies that had other major contracts in hand at the time. Note that, notwithstanding any political advantage that General Dynamics might have enjoyed in the contract competition, the company faced major inducements to excel in the source selection evaluations. To the degree General Dynamics' proposal proved inferior to other proposals, the Kennedy Administration would find it politically difficult to award the contract to that company—in a perfectly fair source selection, or in a politically predetermined source selection.

[128] Art, *The TFX Decision*, chap. 5, especially pp. 149–155; and Richard Austin Smith, "The $7 Billion Contract That Changed the Rules," Part I, *Fortune*, Vol. 67 (March 1963).

147

and consideration of a broad range of alternative airframe configurations, and the final choice of a particular design package for submission to the government. The winning General Dynamics proposal offered an elegant resolution of the conflicting demands of the services. To achieve the loiter requirement of the Navy, General Dynamics provided longer, "bolt-on" wing tips for the Navy version, which gave that version a greater wing span for better subsonic loiter performance. At the same time, the Air Force design was not compromised by the added drag of a longer wing. General Dynamics also gave the Navy version a shorter nose section than the Air Force version, which improved clearances for carrier handling of the Navy aircraft. These design approaches—technically conservative and sensitive to individual service needs, while, at the same time, productive of a truly common aircraft—were important reasons given for the decision to award the contract to General Dynamics.[129] Further to strengthen its position, General Dynamics, which theretofore had almost exclusively produced planes for the Air Force, proposed to have a close prime contractor-subcontractor relationship in the program with Grumman Corporation, which had produced more naval aircraft than any other company in the world.[130] Navy fears of its concerns being neglected by an "Air Force contractor" were thus to be mollified.

General Dynamics technical and managerial proposals, formulated under the intense competitive pressure of the source selection process, reflected a fairly sophisticated integration of the complex demands of the bi-service program. As the analytic paradigm posits, there was a demonstrated generation of alternatives, an integration of relevant values, and a reasonably clear set of choices made with reference to desired outcomes.

[129] Art, *The TFX Decision*, chap. 5.
[130] See testimony of Roger M. Lewis, President of General Dynamics Corporation, *TFX Hearings—First Series*, Part 4, pp. 1057–1058, 1074.

But once this proposal was accepted, the competitive pressures diminished, and the extensive program management routines of the government took hold. The design process became far more rigid and focused in its sensitivities to problems. General Dynamics began to elaborate its design into ever greater detail. This was a process of progressive decomposition, where engineers took each successive level of design as a parameter for the following, greater-detailed level. As described earlier in this chapter, the government led the way through this effort by establishing specifications against which successive levels of design were to be developed. This devolution to lower levels rarely led to alteration of the higher-level specifications and design parameters. Instead, the parameters were fairly stable, as the engineering effort progressively disaggregated the design.

Overall, this process strongly suggests the hierarchical decomposition central to the cybernetic paradigm. This paradigm provides that, in an environment of great variety and uncertainty, the decision problem will be factored into more manageable "pieces" for which feedback variation is relatively stable. The focus of efforts on these smaller pieces of the problem will lie in developing component designs for which relevant performance and engineering measures fall within specification (or specification-implied) parameters. Initially, specified engineering and performance measures will define acceptable levels of achievement on the component designs. However, as the perceived likelihood of achieving specified measures increases or decreases over time, the operative levels of acceptability will evolve to some increment or decrement from specified measures. Engineers will proceed routinely in their design efforts as long as feedback information along specification parameters falls within the levels of acceptable performance. When the variation moves outside this range, design efforts will focus on the category of the unfavorable variation, in an attempt to return the measures to acceptable levels. (This process can be observed in the evolution of General Dynamics' expectations on supersonic dash range for the nuclear mission between 1964 and 1969—from 210 miles, to 196 miles, to 128 miles, and finally to 30 miles.)[131]

A design "problem," then, is in essence an unfavorable variation in feedback information. In turn, the measures for whether or not feedback information is favorable for the performance of the aircraft derive from the elaborate hierarchical structure of specification and design detail. And this structure represents a progressive decomposition from the original requirements and the design proposal. The original Air Force requirement, as well as the joint requirement, articulated performance for a nuclear mission. The broad performance capabilities McNamara hoped to achieve were not adequately captured within the hierarchy of specification detail.[132] Accordingly, deficient performance on these missions was not perceived as a design deficiency within the development process. The basic value integration of the process took place in the formulation of initial design proposals. Thereafter, the design effort was decisively structured by the shape and layout of the approved design proposal and the elaborate unfolding of initial specification parameters. Broad trade-offs among capabilities, substantial shifts in basic technical approaches, and major alteration of physical design layouts would be disruptive. They would disturb the elaborate, highly interdependent structure of specified interfaces within the design and would threaten

[131] Notes of the Icarus meetings for August 25, 1966, and September 10, 1966, excerpted in *TFX Hearings—Second Series*, Part 3, pp. 544–545, and 548. See also Part 1, p. 59, of these hearings.

[132] There were, of course, requirements for a 10,000-pound payload capability and a Mach 2.5 top speed, and these would be operative in design efforts. However, these measures did not adequately capture the broader demands of multi-purpose capability, demands which conflicted with the nuclear mission TAC had specified. Accordingly, these broader demands went unrecognized. See, for example, discussions of the F-111A's acceleration, wing-loading, air-superiority, and conventional-mission performance in *TFX Hearings—Second Series*, Part 1, pp. 184, 188–190, 194–195, 199 and 208.

the underlying cognitive simplifications through which engineers perceived their design task and monitored its evolution.

The design process is, in other words, an extensively "negotiated" environment.[133] Rather than treat the environment as exogenous and to be predicted, it tends to reduce the perception of variety and uncertainty by imposing stable simplifications on the design problem, simplifications that focus the attention of contractor and government officials alike. The environment is negotiated laterally: as described earlier in this chapter, contractor and Air Force engineers are organized in parallel fashion, and their common definition of "acceptable" results in design efforts is determined by mutually recognized specification measures. The environment is also negotiated vertically: the hierarchical organization of the design layout (from the exterior shape of the plane, down to the shape and location of its subsystems, down to the shape and location of particular parts) and the hierarchical structure of specification detail, which establishes measures for the interfaces between and the performance of successive levels of design, allow each engineer to avoid uncertainty about the actions of other engineers in making his design decisions.

As a result, while technical "learning," the reduction of uncertainties, is a critical part of the task of formulating a concrete design, the learning in this process is highly constrained or channeled by the simplifying structure imposed on the design. For example, tests performed in the course of design efforts—an important source of feedback information on the "acceptability" of designs—will concentrate on the dimensions of performance embodied in this simplifying structure. Dimensions of performance not captured in that structure will be neglected. Even problems to which the process is sensitive, problems which register on monitored feedback variables, will not cause major, disruptive revi-

[133] See Richard M. Cyert and James G. March, *A Behavioral Theory of the Firm* (Englewood Cliffs: Prentice-Hall, 1963), pp. 119–120.

sions in this structure. Unfavorable results will be accepted (aspiration levels will, over time, adjust) before the need for substantial design changes is acknowledged. For example, the revelation of drag problems early in the F-111 development led to intense efforts to refine the plane's design, since these problems impacted on the prospects for achieving nuclear mission specifications. However, these extra efforts were devoted to conservative, low-order design changes (such as changes in minor external contours), not to changes in the shape and layout of the plane itself. Changes of the latter sort would have been required to achieve substantial reductions in drag.[134]

The result of this process was a long-delayed recognition of the design costs of the demanding Air Force mission. Early in the program, the Air Force had insisted on a long-range supersonic dash, in spite of NASA technical warnings, in spite of the questionable survivability value of a supersonic dash, and in spite of the necessity to perform conventional missions with a subsonic dash in any event. The Air Force's supersonic mission nonetheless became the basis for the joint requirement and, as already noted, determined most of the critical design parameters: the size, weight, and internal volume of the aircraft, its structural strength, its wing area, the optimization of its engines, the location and complexity of its inlet design, and other features. Yet even though the design was decisively structured by the dash mission, the supersonic dash range ultimately achieved was quite small: 30 nautical miles within the specified mission radius of 800 nautical miles. With so short a dash range, even a nuclear mission dash would be almost entirely subsonic, whatever the merits of supersonic speed. While the F-111 does possess unique low-level interdiction capabilities —conventional and nuclear—it falls far short of the multi-

[134] William K. Greathouse, "Blending Propulsion with Airframe," *Space/Aeronautics*, Vol. 50 (November 1968), p. 68; and Levin, "F-15," p. 42.

mission capabilities originally envisioned for it. Partially as a result, the Air Force and, for related reasons, the Navy commenced new fighter developments much earlier than had been anticipated. If a subsonic dash had been specified from the outset, the F-111 would reasonably have been smaller, lighter, cheaper, and more amenable to Navy wishes. It would conceivably have possessed a broader range of capabilities, while conceding little in the performance of the specialized interdiction missions at which the actual F-111 excels. But the inflexible, narrowly focused design process delayed a full understanding of this implicit trade-off until it was far too late to modify the critical early choice for a supersonic dash.

The next chapter will explore in greater detail why the development process resists acknowledging such costly choices as were made on the supersonic dash. At this point, note that this inflexibility in the design process has been a characteristic feature of American weapons programs in the postwar years.[135] In this country, the contractor design teams and government supervisory offices have been generally so large,[136] the designs produced have been characteristically so complex,[137] and the management style has been universally so reliant on formal documentation and elab-

[135] See Arthur Alexander, *Design to Price from the Perspective of the United States, France, and the Soviet Union*, Rand Memorandum No. P-4967 (February 1973); Alexander, *Weapons Acquisition in the Soviet Union, United States, and France*, Rand Memorandum No. P-4989 (March 1973); Burton H. Klein, "A Radical Proposal for Military R&D," *Fortune*, Vol. 57 (May 1958), pp. 122ff; and Marschak, "The Role of Project Histories," pp. 49–139.

[136] American design teams and government supervisory offices may each be as much as *ten times* as large as their European counterparts. For example, see development personnel totals for the French Mirage IV program and the F-111A program in Robert L. Perry et al., *System Acquisition Strategies*, Rand Memorandum No. R-733-PR/ARPA (June 1971), pp. 28–29. See also U.S. Senate, Committee on Armed Services, *Fiscal Year 1975 Authorization for Military Procurement*, p. 2988.

[137] Albert Shapero, "Life Styles of Engineering," *Space/Aeronautics*, Vol. 51 (March 1969), pp. 58–65.

orate plans[138] that rapid, informal communication and quick redirection of designer efforts have been impossible in most American weapons programs. Nonidiosyncratic regularities of behavior, as posited by the cybernetic paradigm, interact with the peculiarities of American development practices to produce striking rigidity in design efforts. Out of all the Air Force programs of the postwar years administered under standard acquisition practices, this author could discover only one mainline Air Force weapon system for which poor performance caused a major redesign in mid-development. This single example is the F-102, a supersonic interceptor developed by General Dynamics (Convair) in the early 1950s. In 1952, Air Force engineers concluded that severe drag problems would prevent the F-102 even from attaining

[138] Note, for example, that the B-58 strategic bomber program required the processing of 15,000 pages of formal documentation per month, and NASA's Apollo moon-landing program required the processing of 200,000 pages per month. The few development programs of comparable technical difficulty *administered outside standard acquisition organizations* (such as Lockheed's Mach 3 SR-71, or the more recent Air Force prototype programs, the AX and the Lightweight Fighter) have subsisted on as few as 35 pages of documentation per month. This represents strong evidence that the heavy documentation requirements typical of American programs are not dictated by the intrinsic qualities of the weapons themselves, but rather are the product of the peculiar acquisition practices this country has long employed in its standard programs. More will be said on this subject in later chapters. The documentation data cited above are from Clarence L. "Kelly" Johnson (former head of the Lockheed Skunkworks), "Prerequisites For a Successful Skunkworks," speech delivered before the Seminar on Prototyping, National Security Industrial Association, St. Louis, Missouri (February 23, 1972). On the general documentation problem, see Alexander, *Design to Cost*, pp. 6–8; Fox, *Arming America*, chapters 20–23; Robert L. Perry, *A Prototype Strategy for Aircraft Development*, Rand Memorandum No. RM-5597-1-PR (July 1972), pp. 21–26; and Harvey M. Sapolsky, "The Military/Industrial State in Comparative Perspective," unpublished paper, Conference on Comparative Defense Policy, United States Air Force Academy, Colorado Springs, Colorado (February 1973). See also Michael Getler, "David Packard: Presiding Over a Revolution," *Armed Forces Management*, Vol. 16 (March 1970), pp. 24–29; and William S. Hieronymus, "Packard Urges Defense Decentralization," *Aviation Week and Space Technology*, Vol. 93 (August 31, 1970), pp. 15–16.

supersonic speed. The drag estimates of the contractor were considered optimistic. It was not until 1953, however, that the F-102 was redesigned, and then in response to a new design rule—the "ideal body" area rule—developed by the National Advisory Committee on Aeronautics (NACA, the predecessor of NASA) in work unrelated to the F-102.[139] The F-102 was not redesigned until the appearance of this rule, even though the available evidence urged redesign. Program personnel resisted acknowledging the severity of the F-102's problems and implicitly resisted the disruption that redesign portended. Once the NACA theory appeared, however, a new standard design procedure was available, one that could simply be fed into the routines of the design process *without open-ended search and revision*. At that point, the F-102 was redesigned.[140]

[139] The area rule provided a method for minimizing the drag of a plane at transonic and supersonic speeds. According to this rule, the fuselage should be indented at its junction with the wing and increased in length to conform to a minimum acceptable ratio of length to cross-section area. The discovery of this rule led thereafter to the notable "Coke-bottle" shape of fuselages for supersonic aircraft. See C. V. Glines, "Will the First 'A' in NASA Be Given the Go-Signal?" *Armed Forces Management*, Vol. 16 (November 1969), pp. 35, 38; and Marschak, "The Role of Project Histories," p. 106.

[140] Marschak, "The Role of Project Histories," pp. 98–110; Burton H. Klein and William H. Meckling, "Application of Operations Research to Development Decisions," *Operations Research*, Vol. 6 (May-June 1958), p. 359; and Merton J. Peck and Friedrich M. Scherer, *The Weapons Acquisition Process: An Economic Analysis* (Boston: Harvard Business School, 1962), p. 6. Note the contrast between the F-111 and F-102 developments. As mentioned earlier in the text, an unacceptable growth in aerodynamic drag was revealed early in the F-111 program. At that time, NASA argued to Dr. Alexander Flax, Assistant Secretary of the Air Force for Research and Development, that the F-111 should be redesigned in certain ways to reduce the drag. Dr. Flax reportedly felt that a *new aerodynamic principle* would be necessary to achieve acceptable drag levels (Interview 12). By contrast with the F-102 development, such a decision rule was not forthcoming, and the F-111 was not redesigned. Instead, drag estimates were refined and "harder" data were awaited, while development proceeded without abatement. Of course, the continuation of the latter increasingly reduced the potential impact of the former. This response is characteristic: short of a new decision rule

With this conception of the design process, the results of the F-111 effort are not surprising. The program began with the formulation of a design proposal in a manner conforming naturally to the assumptions of the analytic paradigm. Optimizing, highly integrating calculations were made, but within the constraints of the services' performance demands. Hence, although analytic coherence had been brought to the joint requirement, the nuclear mission emphasis of the requirement was sustained. Technical uncertainties were still high, but the development process inflexibly decomposed along the dimensions of the nuclear mission embodied in the proposed design configuration and the increasingly detailed specifications. The process served to screen out problems for missions outside the central nuclear-interdiction mission and prevented the revision of design approaches as the severity of technical trade-offs became clearer.

An analytic process had thus established—at a time of

---

or an accidental discovery, the existing design—a *de facto* outcome of the development process—will be presumed to be an optimal synthesis of existing design technology.

That the existing design is frequently not an optimal synthesis is clear from the success of the "improvement" programs undertaken in many development programs when performance results are unfavorable. For example, as we will discuss in Chapter v, General Dynamics was able to reduce the F-111B's airframe weight by 16 percent, after early F-111B prototypes were determined to be too heavy for performing the specified Navy missions. It is also apparent from the many "accidental" performance improvements that have occurred in past weapons programs. For example, when McDonnell-Douglas added form-fitting fuel tanks to each side of the fuselage of the Air Force's F-15 fighter, fuselage drag was expected to increase, since the tanks made the fuselage wider and increased its surface area. However, for reasons McDonnell-Douglas engineers "have not yet explained to their satisfaction," the tanks actually reduced fuselage drag at speeds below Mach 0.85. What these examples suggest is that conventional engineering practices may camouflage opportunities for performance improvement, unless the design process is fortuitously directed toward them. This is a natural corollary to the inflexible, narrowly focused design process depicted in the text. On the F-15 experience, see Warren C. Wetmore, "Fuel Pallets Increase Range of F-15A," *Aviation Week and Space Technology*, Vol. 101 (September 9, 1974), p. 39.

great technical uncertainty, when problems could not be fully recognized—*the relatively rigid structures from which a cybernetic process ensued.* The relatively unexamined specifications of the joint requirement remained unexamined. The hard data emerging after 1964 from flight tests would provide new and compelling measures of performance, measures outside the narrow focus of earlier design efforts. However, these new measures came too late, and the design process remained too inflexible, fully to resolve the problems that were revealed.

Hard Data: Vietnam, Flight Tests, and Adaptations to Conventional Missions

The flight tests that began in late 1965 routinely examined the entire performance spectrum of the F-111. Higher-confidence measures of the actual performance of a flying aircraft now substituted for the earlier, more uncertain predictions of performance based on wind tunnel tests and engineering calculations. Accordingly, new and more accurate measures of acceptability were imposed on the design process. Multi-mission performance could no longer be assumed an adequate by-product capability, since flight tests clearly demonstrated that the by-product capabilities were disappointing. At the same time, the intensifying air war in Vietnam served to dramatize the seriousness of deficiencies that the flight tests revealed.

The improvements in engines and avionics that followed conform naturally to the assumptions of the cybernetic paradigm. The engine improvements derived from an evolving cycle of reports on power inadequacy and attempts at performance improvement. These efforts led first to the P-3 improvements in the alternative then in use (the P-1 engine); then, as reports of power inadequacy continued, to the marginal thrust improvements of the P-9 engine; and, finally, under the impetus of combat reports of power inadequacy, to the dramatic thrust improvements of the P-100

157

engine. Although the first reports of a severely underpowered aircraft were available in early 1966, and although the weight growth and higher-than-expected drag of the F-111A meant that dramatic thrust improvements would be necessary in any event to obtain original performance expectations, the P-100 program was not approved until 1969, and then following complaints evoked by combat experience with the P-3-equipped F-111As. This pattern of engine improvements—drawn out in time, reactive rather than forward-looking, restrictive in the options considered—is an excellent example of the problemistic search assumed in the cybernetic paradigm.

While this relatively narrow search process proceeded, production of the aircraft continued. As the next chapter will discuss, McNamara and his associates were not fully aware that they were in production until late 1967. Hence, F-111s continued to be produced in this period, with engine improvements incorporated as they were (slowly) developed. The composition of the F-111 force that resulted was not a matter of integrating calculations. Instead, it was a by-product of an on-going production process and a relatively unintegrated power improvement process, each proceeding along channels of its own.

The avionics improvements on the F-111, principally the Mark II avionics, represent a different kind of problem. By contrast with the conservatism we noted on the engine improvements, the Mark II program grew from specific pressures for change: DDR&E's long-standing advocacy of more sophisticated avionics for the F-111. This pursuit of the single value of avionics sophistication was a carryover from DDR&E's heavy involvement in ballistic missile electronics. A design mentality for one type of weapon—ballistic missiles—was being applied to a different type of weapon—a tactical fighter-bomber. The field was relatively free for this application, since the DDR&E/Systems Analysis treaty (literally a negotiated environment) kept systems analysts out of the decisions on Mark II, and since McNamara was receptive to the promised increase in the F-111's multi-purpose capabilities.

Once begun, the Mark II program repeated in the small the larger problem of the F-111 development: by the time the problems of the program were apparent, an early commitment to production had already foreclosed a revision of approach for the first production lots of the system. The Mark IIB system, which provided a dramatic cost reduction with marginal performance concessions, could not be substituted for the Mark II system until 96 units of the more expensive system had already been committed.

In the end, the Mark II-IIB acquisition program cost approximately one billion dollars and equipped 278 planes (the F-111Ds, F-111Fs, and FB-111s) with avionics. For illustrative purposes, note that those 278 planes could have been equipped with Mark I avionics, for approximately 300 million dollars.[141] From what was ultimately spent on the Mark II-IIB system, enough money would have been left to produce approximately 70 complete aircraft, an increment equivalent to 15 percent of the tactical F-111 force actually produced.[142] This represents a significant opportunity cost that the Air Force and DDR&E would not have been willing to pay, one surmises, if they had been presented with that kind of clear-cut choice. As it is, the development

[141] The production unit cost of the Mark I avionics was approximately 1.1 million dollars (a figure including the author's estimate of 0.2 million dollars per unit for an initial allocation of support equipment and spare parts). See *TFX Hearings—Second Series*, Part 1, p. 215.

[142] The calculation that 70 additional aircraft could have been produced assumes that the average production unit cost of the additional F-111s would have been approximately 10 million dollars. This is a reasonable cost estimate for the production of a Mark I-equipped tactical F-111 (with its associated support equipment and spare parts) in the late 1960s. However, we should emphasize that this cost figure is useful for illustrative purposes only. A more precise cost estimate would require detailed consideration of a number of issues: production timing, economic inflation, engine choice (e.g., between the P-100 used in the F-111F or the cheaper P-3 used in the F-111A), and so on. For cost data, see *TFX Hearings—Second Series*, Part 2, p. 307; and *TFX Report*, p. 81.

159

process, once started, gains a momentum of its own and inexorably forecloses such choices before they become clear-cut. Uncertainty is defied in the establishment of elaborate development and production plans: the concrete, detailed plans evince a certitude and exactness far beyond what can be known with confidence at this stage of the program. But the uncertainty is real; and, during development, when problems emerge to threaten pre-established schedules or specifications, that uncertainty leaves sufficient ambiguity around any unfavorable information to allow sustained adherence to original development plans. As in the larger results of the F-111 program, so too in the avionics improvements: the development process translated demanding requirements into irreversible choices, choices with unacceptable opportunity costs even to the sponsoring organizations.

This is really the worst of two worlds: the requirements for American acquisition programs characteristically demand the highest performance, yet the behavior of acquisition organizations prevents a later recognition of costly interdependencies among the demanding requirements. The technical learning of the Mark II-IIB program, too slow for the inflexible, narrowly focused design process in which it occurred, epitomizes this unfortunate combination.

Overall, then, the engine and avionics adaptations in the F-111 program accord reasonably well with the assumptions of the cybernetic paradigm. They depict a product improvement process of considerable magnitude and cost that proceeded along channels of its own, relatively divorced from a larger vision of the problems at issue and of the composition of the F-111 force being established. The cybernetic paradigm gives logical coherence to these otherwise puzzling efforts.

It would decidedly oversimplify these efforts, and others we have discussed in this chapter, to argue that our cybernetic explanations are the only conceivable explanations of the relevant facts, or that our explanations resolve every interesting question these efforts evoke. But it is apparent

160

that our cybernetic suppositions have led us to an intriguing understanding of why the F-111 was a nuclear bomber, an understanding that perhaps captures in a new way many of the rigidities and anomalies that we casually sense to be an important part of the weapons acquisition problem. In subsequent chapters we hope to build upon this understanding.

THE IMPORTANCE OF THE BEGINNING: TECHNICAL UNCERTAINTY, DOCTRINAL INNOVATION, AND THE F-III PROGRAM

[S]ince the wartime roles of the military chiefs dictated that at all times they be at or near the center of the military organization, giving them the main voice in determining military requirements had the effect of centralizing authority in the military service departments. . . .

—Paul Y. Hammond[143]

The weapon requirements process is service unilateral—the initiative for establishing new requirements lies almost wholly with the services. As the Defense Blue Ribbon Panel noted in 1970, "There is no opportunity for the Office of the Secretary of Defense (OSD) to review total requirements for priority, urgency or duplication before they are screened and filtered by the Services."[144]

This feature of the requirements process powerfully affected the results of the F-111 program. The Air Force's original specification of a supersonic dash mission was, as we have seen, a routine extension of that service's dominant scenario of nuclear interdiction at low altitudes. Supersonic speed did not promise major survivability benefits on the

143 Paul Y. Hammond, *Organizing for Defense* (Princeton: Princeton University Press, 1961), pp. 58–59.

144 U.S. Defense Blue Ribbon Panel, *Report to the President and the Secretary of Defense on the Department of Defense* (Washington: U.S. Government Printing Office, 1970), p. 68.

low altitude dash, it greatly increased the technical challenge of the proposed aircraft, and it emphasized the doctrine of Massive Retaliation explicitly rejected by the new Administration. Nonetheless, McNamara uncritically based the bi-service program on the Air Force's proposed TFX. The subordinate organizations on which he relied for assistance during the early program decisions conceived their task in ways that accommodated the Air Force requirement and avoided recognition of its disadvantages. From the outset, McNamara shared their conception of the problem. However, in accepting the Air Force requirement as the basis for a bi-service program, he unknowingly established a structure for development efforts that would filter out problems for multi-mission performance and would generate binding commitments before these problems could be known with confidence. When the deficiencies did become clear, costly ameliorative efforts proceeded incrementally, relatively divorced from an analytic vision of the larger problems at issue. In the end, the F-111 did not become the exclusive tactical fighter of the Air Force for the 1970s, nor was it the flexible, multi-purpose aircraft McNamara had envisioned. At the same time, the design burden of TAC's supersonic nuclear mission resulted in politically crippling deficiencies in the Navy F-111s, deficiencies which led to the cancellation of the F-111B. While far more capable than its critics would concede, the F-111 failed to fulfill McNamara's larger objectives for the program.

In the F-111 program, then, the requirements process served up an alternative that only partially addressed McNamara's objectives, while the nature of the development process made further refinement of that alternative unlikely. This experience suggests a set of key problems for managing the weapons acquisition process in the Department of Defense.

Of first importance, it suggests that the development process is not well suited to a major development task: making intelligent choices as uncertainties are reduced in the course of a program. To be sure, the process is suffused with analytics, but in important respects it is too narrowly focused and inflexible for the binding commitments it makes to be commensurate with the amount of learning or uncertainty reduction that has taken place. The F-111's supersonic dash requirement and its Mark II avionics program offer important evidence on this point. More is at issue here than the relative timing of overt program commitments, such as the timing of production commitments in relation to the timing of flight tests. As sketched in this chapter and as will be elaborated upon in subsequent chapters, implicit behavioral commitments to more or less fixed dimensions of the design problem occur early in the program. Indeed, these commitments begin to take hold at the very outset of development efforts.

Accordingly, the Secretary of Defense who expects to fine-tune development efforts is probably deceiving himself. He not only will find it difficult to redirect these efforts, he will find it difficult even *to know* to redirect them. Like the program people over whom he ultimately presides, he faces powerful cognitive pressures to avoid hard choices. With little conscious awareness of the distortions involved, he will conceptualize the program so as to make the costs of avoiding hard choices seem to disappear.[145]

Although the Secretary will find it difficult to redirect an on-going program under standard acquisition practices, he may have an opportunity to affect weapon characteristics at the beginning of a program, when the requirements—an important source of structure in design efforts—are established. To take advantage of this opportunity, the Secretary would clearly need the close assistance of analysts who shared his goals, assistance of the sort he did not have at the outset of the F-111 program. But even with appropriate

[145] While Chapter IV focuses on the engine-inlet compatibility problems of the F-111 development, it also will provide further detail on how McNamara and his associates avoided hard choices on F-111 performance issues.

163

staff assistance, the Secretary's flexibility is limited. The plans for new weapons are formulated in a process that is dominated by service initiative. They evolve incrementally over time in ways that it is difficult for a Secretary to influence or control. Proposals offered by the services are unlikely to be suitable for a Secretary seeking to *change* capabilities from what the services plan. Moreover, the beginning of a program, when performance requirements are approved, is the time of greatest uncertainty in program attributes. This uncertainty provides wide leeway for selective interpretations, counter-formulations, and counter-moves by services naturally resistant to doctrinal innovations emanating from the Secretary's office. Simultaneously, it provides broad interpretive latitude for the Secretary and his advisors to construe service proposals as being consonant with the Secretary's own objectives. In this environment, the dominant service initiative that characterizes the requirements process will be difficult for the Secretary to counter. Even if the Secretary and his advisors maintain a critical, independent conception of desirable program objectives, the bargaining power of the services—power deriving from their political position, their expertise, their delegated functions, and other sources—will impede any attempts to force service-opposed requirements onto the services' development agendas.

A Defense Secretary seeking to change force capabilities is thus critically constrained by the menu of alternatives presented by service organizations. Accordingly, the *de facto* composition of this menu may be the most significant indicator of the Secretary's probabilities for success in implementing a new doctrine.[146] Especially for a new De-

---

[146] Our discussion of McNamara's first year in office, and in particular of his decision to substitute the Navy F-4 for the F-105 in the Air Force's procurement plans, suggests a key indicator for evaluating the desirability of the options on this menu: the certainty of their attributes. In the F-4 decisions of 1961, McNamara not only enjoyed the aggressive assistance of analysts who shared his goals. As discussed earlier in the text (p. 107), he also benefitted from the character of

fense Secretary, who has not yet had time to make his mark on the Department, the presence of desirable options on this menu will be primarily a matter of luck, a fortuitous by-

---

the option he sought to impose: a "hard" option, one with fairly certain attributes of performance and cost. Note that in all four recent cases where OSD has succeeded in imposing a major procurement option on the Air Force—the F-4, FB-111, A-7, and the F-16 (with the A-10 a possible fifth supporting case)—it imposed a hard option, not a hypothetical requirement. By implication, the menu of extant hard options may provide the most significant clue to OSD's prospects for success in any attempts to reorient force capabilities. When a hard option is available, OSD can advance alternatives to service requirements with far more authority than is typically provided by "paper" designs and conjectural analysis. The open-ended vicissitudes of an entirely new development can be avoided. The services' normal ability to set the requirements agenda and structure the requirements debate can be vitiated.

How can OSD assure the presence of desirable hard options? A second service's programs may provide them, as the Air Force's F-4 and A-7 acquisitions suggest. (The importance of hard options for bi-service programs will be discussed in greater detail in the final section of Chapter v.) A second major source may be austere prototype programs, like the recent Lightweight Fighter Program that provided the hard option behind the Air Force's F-16 acquisition. Because these prototypes are not coupled to production processes and are not fully "missionized" (that is, are not fully outfitted with many expensive items, like fire control systems, that are required for any actual operational versions), they can be acquired relatively cheaply. The two pairs of Lightweight Fighter prototypes (the YF-16s and YF-17s) were acquired for 100 million dollars. By way of comparison, *miscellaneous design changes alone* cost 300 million dollars in the F-111 program. Due to the relative cheapness of the prototypes, elaborate doctrinal or operational justification is not necessary to institute them. The establishment of such a program does not require the kind of OSD-service agreement over doctrine and operational commitment that a normal program necessarily involves. (A normal program will consume hundreds of millions of dollars in a short period of time and cannot, therefore, be so casually instituted.) OSD may thus have unusual latitude in instituting prototype programs. Such programs may be a fertile source for hard options to compete with requirements proposed by the services. Prototype programs of the early 1970s have certainly been successful in this sense. It remains to be seen whether, because of this success, the services will fear the leverage that prototype programs provide and will resist the institution of such programs in the future. See *TFX Hearings—Second Series*, Part 3, p. 666; and U.S. Senate, Committee on Armed Services, *Fiscal Year 1975 Authorization for Military Procurement*, pp. 4233–4235.

165

product of the vast array of preceding requirements studies and development programs.

As McNamara began to implement the new doctrine of Flexible Response in 1961, he faced an array of alternatives that he inherited from the Eisenhower Administration. By chance, there was one alternative available that demonstrably aided the Secretary: the Navy-developed F-4, which possessed the broader range of capabilities McNamara sought to institute in the Air Force. However, for the early decisions on the F-111 program, desirable alternatives were not available, and McNamara conceived the program in the simplified terms that his advisory organizations had presented. In spite of all that he and Kennedy had said about expanding conventional capabilities, their first major weapons development would be a plane expensively tailored to the delivery of nuclear weapons.

CHAPTER IV

The Engine-Inlet Compatibility Problems

By most accounts, the engine-inlet compatibility problems of the F-111 program—the problems encountered in attaining smooth operation of the F-111's engines—represented "normal" development difficulties that were substantially resolved.[1] But the resolution of these problems was costly—over 100 million dollars[2]—and required an extraordinary amount of unforeseen technical effort, thereby disrupting flight test progress and delaying attention to other problem areas. Along with the Mark II avionics problems (discussed in the previous chapter), the Navy development problems (to be discussed in the next chapter), and aerodynamic drag and wing-box fatigue problems (to be touched upon in the present chapter), the engine-inlet compatibility problems were the most important technical difficulties of the F-111 program. Moreover, although the engine-inlet compatibility problems were substantially alleviated, some enduring performance penalties remained for the 141 F-111As. These planes have a greater susceptibility to engine compressor stalls (temporary power losses or complete shut-downs of the engines in flight), and they cannot be retrofitted with more powerful engines.

The present chapter will examine the sources of these problems and the response of the development process to their emergence. With some qualification, this examination will reveal a typical response of the development process to technical difficulties. It will extend and complement the previous chapter's consideration of the nature of the devel-

---

[1] For McNamara's view, see U.S. Senate, Committee on Armed Services, *Military Procurement Authorizations: Fiscal Year 1966*, Hearings, 89th Cong., 1st Sess. (1965), p. 308. Similar views were expressed in Interviews 6, 11, 12, 15, 16, and 20.

[2] Interview 16.

opment process and will provide some insight into the normal, yet costly, development difficulties that nearly every weapons program encounters. The discussion begins with explanations framed by the assumptions of the analytic paradigm.

AN ANALYTIC EXPLANATION

The production of 141 F-111As with a greater stall susceptibility and a more restrictive inlet could logically have been avoided if production of the plane had been halted when the engine-inlet compatibility problems appeared. As it was, production of the plane continued in spite of these problems. By the time a solution to the problems had been developed, 141 F-111As were too far down the production line for the solution to be incorporated.

The most compelling analytic explanation for this result is a relatively straightforward, economic explanation. It can be reasonably argued that the greater stall susceptibility of the F-111A is of restricted significance. The F-111A stall condition occurs in select performance regions—in maneuvering flight at speeds over Mach 2 and level flight at speeds over Mach 2.35.[3] Because of the allegedly "unlikely" occurrence in combat of these necessary conditions for stalls, it would have made little economic sense to incur the costs of slowing production to change the inlet.[4] A similar logic applies to the question of inlet restrictiveness. While the F-111As cannot be retrofitted with larger engines, it can be argued that these planes are still useful strike aircraft and that the benefits of having a larger inlet on the F-111As would have been offset by the costs of slowing or halting production.

[3] Interviews 4 and 16; *TFX Hearings—Second Series*, Part 1, p. 241; and "U.S. Air Force Selected Acquisition Report on the F-111A/D/E/F," dated December 31, 1969 (from the files of the Permanent Subcommittee on Investigations, Committee on Government Operations, U.S. Senate, Exhibit 10 of the *TFX Hearings—Second Series*).

[4] Interview 6.

Economic considerations—mainly, the costs of stopping or of slowing production—are thus essential to an analytic explanation of the inlet deficiencies on the F-111A. These costs are of two general kinds: General Dynamics' own, in-house costs; and the additional costs such a halt would generate through subcontracting arrangements.

General Dynamics' in-house costs are numerous and difficult to quantify, but it will be useful to provide some examples of these costs. Fixed and indirect costs are the most important in-house cost increment from a production slow-down. When production of a weapon system is slowed, fixed and indirect costs are borne over a longer period of time (or, alternatively, are absorbed by fewer production units for a given period of time). As a result, for a specific program volume, total program costs increase. If program volume is reduced to avoid growth in total program costs, the program cost per unit increases.[5] These fixed and indirect cost increases are reinforced by many direct cost increases. For example, when production is slowed, layoffs characteristically occur in the production work force. Because of union seniority rules, each layoff generates eight job changes within the plant, creating additional training, scheduling, and control costs.[6] The net consequence of all these potential cost increases is that decision makers are constrained in their choices on technical problems. Clearly, the production process within the prime contractor's plant is not amenable in the short run to drastic revisions in output plans.

Subcontracting arrangements are a second source of cost increases in a development or production stoppage. Subcontracts for research and development characteristically include options for production, since subcontractors need to know planning volumes to formulate bids for a subcontract.[7]

[5] Interview 6. For a brief discussion of the importance of fixed and indirect costs in weapons programs, see J. Ronald Fox, *Arming America: How the U.S. Buys Weapons* (Boston: Harvard Business School, 1974), pp. 325–330.

[6] Interview 16.

[7] U.S. House of Representatives, Committee on Armed Services,

These production options must be acted upon by a specified time in order to obtain prenegotiated prices. In the F-111 development, where approximately two-thirds of the 1.8 billion-dollar development prime contract was subcontracted, these clauses were a clear inducement to schedule adherence.[8] Hence, in April 1965, the government chose to sign the letter contract for production to allow General Dynamics to take advantage of these options.[9] To have slowed development before that time or to have avoided signing the production letter contract when it was signed would have been to lose these options and face much higher costs. Similarly, the *production* subcontracts contain clauses on delivery dates and prices. To slow or to halt production under these circumstances would have been to force renegotiations of prices and schedules. To use McNamara's words, " 'all hell would break loose on costs.' "[10]

In this view, then, the advantages of having the new, enlarged inlet on the F-111As would have been outweighed by the costs of slowing development and production to incorporate it. As one contractor official concluded, "It was not, on balance, a bad economic decision."[11] As an economic decision in this sense, it would conform to the most explicit and theoretically elaborate notions of analytic behavior.

This analytic explanation certainly is one aspect of the resolution of the engine-inlet compatibility problems. Contracts are necessary in weapons developments to define obligations among the contractors and between the contractors and the government. Contractual provisions become an

---

Hearings on Military Posture, 91st Cong., 1st Sess. (1969), p. 3214; and Interview 16.

[8] Interview 6.

[9] Memorandum for the Secretary of Defense, from Secretary of the Air Force Eugene Zuckert, dated April 13, 1965, re F-111 Program (from the files of the Permanent Subcommittee on Investigations, Committee on Government Operations, U.S. Senate, Exhibit 26-W51 of *TFX Hearings—Second Series*).

[10] From notes of preliminary Icarus meeting, April 27, 1967, quoted in *TFX Hearings—Second Series*, Part 3, p. 559. This interpretation of the subcontract constraint is from Interviews 6 and 16.

[11] Interview 6.

important constraint under which any optimizing decisions will be made. However, there are important questions left unanswered by this explanation. Of primary interest is the question of why the contract schedules were so highly compressed, leaving so little time and flexibility for resolving technical problems. If the schedules in the contracts were to be binding on the later program, why did they provide so little latitude for resolving any unanticipated problems that development efforts might reveal?

In addition, there is some fairly strong contradictory evidence for the analytic explanation. To begin with, the seriousness of the engine stall problem seems to have been considerably underestimated, particularly through 1965. There was a lull in wind tunnel testing of the inlet in 1965. As an Air Force official later observed, "Until late 1965, no one recognized how difficult the stall problem was."[12] Indeed, in his April 13, 1965, memorandum to the Secretary of Defense recommending a commitment to production, Secretary of the Air Force Zuckert did not even *mention* the stall problem, and the Defense Department proceeded to authorize production.[13] Yet by mid-1965, there had been 105 hours of test flights on the F-111, with repeated compressor stalls hampering the test effort.[14] Moreover, through the middle of 1967, Secretarial-level representatives at the Icarus meetings seemed unaware that the plane was in full-scale production, as it had been since early 1965.[15] Given the ear-

[12] Interview 14. Information on 1965 wind tunnel testing from Interview 12.

[13] Memorandum for the Secretary of Defense, from Secretary of the Air Force Eugene Zuckert, dated April 13, 1965, re F-111 Program (from the files of the Permanent Subcommittee on Investigations, Committee on Government Operations, U.S. Senate, Exhibit 26-W51 of the *TFX Hearings—Second Series*).

[14] General Dynamics, "GD F-111 Category I Flight Test Progress Report," dated 31 January 1965, FZM-12-988-1; and General Dynamics, "GD F-111 Category I Flight Test Progress Report," dated 30 June 1963, FZM-12-988-6 (from the files of the Permanent Subcommittee on Investigations, U.S. Senate, Exhibits 18A and 18F of the *TFX Hearings—Second Series*).

[15] Interview 15; and notes of the Icarus meetings, especially those of August 25, 1966, through April 29, 1967, excerpted in *TFX Hearings—Second Series*, Part 3, pp. 544–561.

lier lack of awareness of the gravity of the stall problem, and the later lack of awareness of options being foreclosed as production continued, it is difficult to envision how the Secretaries could have made the fairly sophisticated trade-offs described in our analytic explanation.

One might consider these objections to be based on unduly restrictive analytic assumptions. In particular, one might argue that unrealistic standards of awareness are being imposed on these very busy, high-level decision makers. This argument is partially justified, at least as it applies to the early ignorance of the stall problem. Government information on the problem was limited in 1965.[16] However, this objection would beg the question of why the Secretaries made the formal commitment to production in April 1965 if their information was so limited. As we shall see, the Secretaries were essentially unaware of their lack of information. Their commitment to production on the previously appointed date is more indicative of a simple conformity to schedules than of an analytic understanding of the problem. Moreover, their later unawareness that full-scale production had begun persisted in spite of contradictory information with which they were presented.[17]

Hence, although the analytic explanation offers insight into a very real difficulty facing the Secretaries as they addressed the stall problem, it leaves much unanswered. To extend the analytic explanation to these unanswered questions would require additional complexity in the explanation and a simultaneous qualification or loosening of the

[16] TFX Hearings—Second Series, Part 3, pp. 501–503. The Air Force was using a new data system on the F-111 program and neglected to provide contractual coverage for data submission on the first series of flight tests (Category I tests) which were run by the contractor (Interview 19). For a description of Air Force test procedures, see TFX Hearings—Second Series, Part 1, pp. 177–178.

[17] Notes of the Icarus meetings, September 10, 1966, November 4, 1966, January 14, 1966, and April 29, 1966, excerpted in TFX Hearings—Second Series, Part 3, pp. 548–552, 555–556; and Interview 12. This lack of awareness will be discussed in greater detail later in the chapter.

assumptions of the analytic paradigm. Both the complexity and the qualification are unnecessary, however. More fruitful is a change in our basic framework of analysis.

A CYBERNETIC EXPLANATION

The Secretaries' early lack of awareness of the extent of the stall problem, as well as their presumption in the face of contradictory evidence that they were not in full-scale production, suggests the selective focus on information and the rigidity of belief structures assumed in the cybernetic paradigm. Their conformity to pre-established schedules on the basis of this selective understanding similarly accords with the logic of the paradigm.

This section will develop a detailed explanation based on the cybernetic paradigm. It will first examine the evolution of the engine-inlet compatibility problems at the working level; then consider the source and the characteristics of the development and production schedules to which the program conformed, focusing on the impact of these schedules on the technical problems of engine-inlet compatibility; and finally discuss the way in which high-level civilians in DOD perceived these problems and responded to them.

The Engine-Inlet Compatibility Problems:
Timing and Source

Organizations do not attempt to estimate the probability distribution of future occurrences. Rather, organizations avoid uncertainty. . . . Where situations cannot be construed as standard, organizations engage in search. The style of search and its stopping point are largely determined by existing routines.

—Graham T. Allison[18]

---

[18] Graham T. Allison, *Essence of Decision: Explaining the Cuban Missile Crisis* (Boston: Little, Brown, 1971), p. 84.

Acquisition programs place a premium on the early recognition and resolution of technical problems. With the passage of time in these programs, development evolves into production: tools and machinery are acquired, elaborate production operations are organized, volume orders for parts and subsystems are placed, and an increasing number of aircraft units proceed to final assembly in the contractor's plant. The longer technical remedies are delayed, the more likely it is that these remedies will involve costly and disruptive changes—modifications of the production line, partial remanufacture of units on the production line, and retrofit programs for units already produced.

While the incentive to develop timely solutions was clear, the F-111 program suffered a number of critical delays in the resolution of engine integration difficulties. A recognition of these difficulties occurred only with the advent of flight tests in December 1964, a mere four months before an initial production commitment. Program schedules were highly compressed, creating a special urgency for remedial efforts. But these efforts were impeded by a sustained commitment to initial design approaches and by frictions between Pratt & Whitney and General Dynamics. High-level officials were slow to acknowledge these problems and to act to encourage solutions. Since the production buildup continued as scheduled in this period, the ultimate compatibility remedies were destined to be expensive and, in important respects, incomplete.

This section will examine why the compatibility problems were not recognized and addressed in an earlier stage of development. It will argue that the development process mounted technical efforts to resolve uncertainty only for those design problems that could not be construed as standard—that is, for those design problems whose decomposition was not a matter of accepted organizational routine. For non-standard problems—such as variable-sweep wings—intensive efforts were devoted to resolving the uncertainty through the generation of an acceptable structure

174

for the problems. But for the standard design problems—such as the integration of engines with airframe inlets—the development process proceeded routinely, using standard design approaches and resisting warnings of technical risks. The analytically important point will be that certain kinds of uncertainty are addressed and others are not, with the difference depending less on analytic anticipations of uncertainty (and on sequential "learning" to reduce that uncertainty) than on whether there exists an accepted design routine for the problem in question.[19] This interpretation will provide a graphic illustration of the importance of organization routines operating in a process where decision problems are factored among different organizations.

The Source of the Problem. Three different terms that describe airflow to the engine will be useful to keep in mind through the following discussion. The quality of air deliv-

[19] The analytic paradigm posits that, in an uncertain world, decision makers will choose options with the greatest expected net value in terms of the decision maker's preferences (including his preferences for risk). In situations of extreme uncertainty, the probability distribution of outcomes cannot be well known in advance. The appropriate analytic response under these conditions is for the decision maker to "learn" as development proceeds—that is, to reduce uncertainty by the acquisition of knowledge in the course of development. The probability distribution of outcomes (and the expected payoff to alternative courses of action) is sequentially updated, as new information is received.

The integration of turbo-fan engines into the F-111 was a problem of great uncertainty. Indeed, the use of turbo-fan engines on the F-111 was one of the two major innovations of the F-111 design (the other, of course, being the variable-sweep wings). Given this uncertainty, the response most natural to the assumptions of the analytic paradigm would be the allocation of research efforts to define the nature of the engine-inlet interface. However, as will be explored in detail in the text, efforts to define this interface were generally absent until actual test aircraft incurred severe stalls. Instead of concentrating on the definition of this interface, design efforts proceeded along paths marked by routine measures of engine-inlet integration. In other words, design efforts were keyed to the achievement of standard measures of engine-inlet compatibility rather than to analytic attention to the reduction of uncertainty associated with the new technology engines.

ered to the engine is expressed in terms of pressure recovery, distortion, and turbulence. *Pressure recovery* is the average of all total pressures across the face of the engine compressor. *Distortion* is the pressure recovery pattern and describes local peaks and valleys across the compressor face in terms of their location and magnitude. *Turbulence* is a dynamic characteristic indicating how certain areas of the distortion pattern are changing over time. Prior to the F-111 program, distortion had been the key measure of inlet performance.[20]

The compatibility of the engine with the air inlet and ducts of the airframe always was recognized as a potential problem in the F-111 development.[21] The F-111 was the first combat aircraft in the world to use an afterburning turbo-fan engine. Such engines were known to have different flow characteristics than turbo-jet engines and were also known to be particularly sensitive to airflow distortion. The airflow of a turbo-fan engine is split between the core engine and a by-pass duct to the afterburner, which allows a communication of backpressures from the afterburner into the inlet. Airflow to the engine would have to be more uniform than that required for a turbo-jet.[22] Moreover, the

[20] See William K. Greathouse, "Blending Propulsion With Airframe," *Space/Aeronautics*, Vol. 50 (November 1968), p. 60.

[21] Interviews 12 and 16. Unless otherwise noted, the information that follows in the text is from Interview 16.

[22] Greathouse, "Blending Propulsion With Airframe," p. 62; and Interview 16. The air inlet is the opening in the airframe that admits air (through internal ducts) to the engine. This air is then compressed in multi-stage, fan compressors at the front of the engine. In a turbo-fan engine, part of this compressed air is by-passed to the afterburner, and the rest enters the core of the engine: the combustion chamber (also called the gas generator) and the small turbines immediately following the combustion chamber. These latter turbines, in turn, use some of the engine thrust to drive the multi-stage compressors. The afterburner is essentially an additional combustion chamber at the rear of the engine, into which fuel can be sprayed to impart additional thrust to the hot exhaust gases leaving the engine.

A straight turbo-jet differs from a turbo-fan, in that all air entering the engine goes through the engine core—none of the air is by-passed. As a result, afterburner backpressures cannot be directly communicated to the compressors at the front of the turbo-jet engine.

wide range of operating conditions contemplated for the F-111—from the dense air at sea level for the supersonic dash to the rarefied air at high altitudes for high top-speed operations—meant that the inlet would have to handle a wide range of extremes in airflow. Given the sensitivity of the turbo-fan engines and the variations in inlet airflow, the design problem for the F-111 inlets was one of extraordinary complexity.[23]

General Dynamics' inlet design provided for quarter-round inlets located at the wing-fuselage juncture, or the "armpit" as it is called (see Figure III). This inlet design and location was dictated by the demanding supersonic

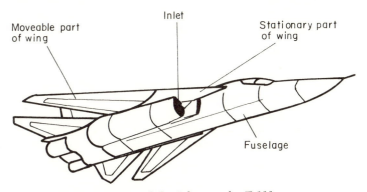

Figure III. Location of the Inlets on the F-111.

dash of the nuclear mission: "Normally, a smooth inlet air flow is provided by comparatively large area inlets having rounded cow lips. However, it was thought that this type of inlet would not be necessary on the F-111, because of the

[23] For a good general explanation of the problem of designing inlets for supersonic aircraft, see Staff Report, "Inlets for Supersonic Aircraft," *Space/Aeronautics*, Vol. 47 (May 1967), pp. 92–100. For information on F-111 inlet problems, see J. S. Butz, "FB-111: A Second Look at the Third Version," *Air Force and Space Digest*, Vol. 49 (February 1966), p. 38; Greathouse, "Blending Propulsion With Airframe," pp. 59–68; and Michael P. London, "VFX—The Navy's Choice," *Space/Aeronautics*, Vol. 50 (November 1968), pp. 54–55.

range penalties that would result at the very low altitudes and supersonic speeds required for the interdiction mission. The initial inlet design was tailored to the high speed low altitude requirement."[24] In the source selection briefings given to Secretarial officials by Air Force members, General Dynamics' inlet was expected to be superior for the sea-level dash mission, while providing an optimum flow of air to the engines (particularly at high angles of attack and at supersonic speeds).[25] There were technical risks to General Dynamics' approach, however. With the inlets close to the fuselage and under the wings, they would be in the proximity of airflow disturbances generated by the wing and fuselage at high speeds.[26] (By contrast, if the inlets were located away from the fuselage and in front of the wings, they would be outside most of this disturbed air—at a pen-

[24] See the prepared statement of General James Ferguson, Commander, Air Force Systems Command, in U.S. Senate, Committee on Armed Services, *Authorization for Military Procurement, Research and Development, Fiscal Year 1971, and Reserve Strength*, Hearings, 91st Cong., 2d Sess. (1970), p. 990.

[25] Notes of Albert Blackburn on source selection briefings by Air Force officials, in *TFX Hearings—First Series*, Part 5, pp. 1197–1199. The advantages of the General Dynamics inlet are described in Greathouse, "Blending Propulsion With Airframe," p. 62.

[26] Greathouse, "Blending Propulsion With Airframe," pp. 59–63; London, "VFX—The Navy's Choice," p. 54; and Staff Report, "Inlets for Supersonic Aircraft," pp. 92–100. These disturbances would be generated by shock waves and by boundary layer effects. Shock waves are generated by an aircraft traveling at supersonic speeds; unless the inlet design accommodates these waves (often in ways that actually put the shock waves to work to increase inlet efficiency), the waves can severely degrade the quality of airflow to the engines. Boundary layer effects derive from the fact that air closest to the aircraft's skin (the boundary layer air) moves more slowly than the air further away (the free-stream air), due to friction with the aircraft's skin. The difference in velocity between the boundary layer and free-stream air creates, among other things, airflow disturbances in the proximity of the aircraft's skin. This disturbed air must be diverted from the inlet if the quality of air flow to the engine is not to be degraded. The inlet design proposed by General Dynamics was particularly vulnerable to both shock waves and boundary layer disturbances, because the inlets were located next to the fuselage and beneath the wings.

178

alty of higher drag.) The formal Air Force evaluation of the winning General Dynamics design proposal offered a specific caution on this point: there was a danger that fuselage and wing disturbances of the airflow would be "ingested into the inlet," given the inlet's location under the wing and next to the fuselage.[27]

Nonetheless, no one at the Defense Department really paid much attention to the problem of defining what the engine's tolerance to airflow distortion should be (or, alternatively, the quality of airflow that the inlet should deliver to the engine).[28] Moreover, since afterburning, turbo-fan engines were an advance in the state of the art, there was little experience, experimental or in-flight, to guide the specification of precisely what the distortion tolerance should be. Because of this lack of knowledge and of direct attention—yet in spite of the technical risks of the new technology, turbo-fan engines—the so-called interface documents which delineated specification requirements between General Dynamics and Pratt & Whitney did not contain a definitive distortion index.[29]

General Dynamics had originally been experimenting with two variants of its basic inlet design, but opted for one of the two in late 1963.[30] In lieu of a definitive distor-

[27] "Excerpts from the Air Vehicle Section of the Technical Section of the 4th Evaluation Report Relating to the General Dynamics Aircraft, pages XXI A-30 to XXI A-50," in *TFX Hearings—First Series*, Part 9, p. 2268.

[28] Interviews 12 and 16.

[29] London, "VFX—The Navy's Choice," pp. 55–56; and Interview 12. Pratt & Whitney was an associate contractor to General Dynamics —the government itself bought the engines and furnished them to General Dynamics. The "interface documents" were necessary to define the mutual obligations of General Dynamics and Pratt & Whitney to each other, since neither contractor had contractual authority over the other.

[30] Interview 16. Note that this choice followed the mockup inspection of August 1963, after which inspection drawings could legally be released for the fabrication of parts. The design chosen by General Dynamics was a so-called external compression inlet, and the design rejected was a mixed (external-internal) compression inlet. (For an explanation of these terms, see Staff Report, "Inlets for Supersonic

tion index specification, General Dynamics in 1964 began supplying Pratt & Whitney with inlet distortion data derived from wind tunnel tests. At each successive stage, Pratt & Whitney approved the patterns that General Dynamics supplied. In July 1964, Pratt & Whitney provided the first distortion index for the General Dynamics inlet. This index was "area weighted" in that it weighted radial distortion equally at all distances from the center of the circular engine compressor. It was consistent with prior design approaches on turbo-jet (as opposed to turbo-fan) engines.[31] By November 1964, one month before the first flight test of the aircraft, Pratt & Whitney had performed engine tests with the distortion patterns that General Dynamics had furnished. Pratt & Whitney concluded that the distortion levels were acceptable and that, within their levels, stall-free operation would likely be obtained.[32]

The first flight test of the aircraft, as well as the flight tests that followed, showed the stall problem to be one of considerable severity. On the first flight, for example, the engine stalled on the ground.[33] An afterburner back-pressure

---

Aircraft," pp. 92–95.) The General Dynamics design incorporated two notable features. First, to cope with the problem of high performance at the variable altitudes demanded of the F-111, the inlet had a "spike" in it which could change shape and a cowl around it that could translate forward and backward. These automatically controlled variations would compensate for variations in air density. Second, to cope with the problem of boundary layer disturbances, the inlet was located two inches from the side of the fuselage and had a "splitter plate" extending forward from the side of the inlet face to divert the boundary layer air from the inlet face.

[31] Interview 16. For example, area-weighted indices were applied to the integration of the J-79 engine (in the B-58 and F-4) and the J-75 engine (in the F-105 and F-106).

[32] Interview 16. In other words, Pratt & Whitney concluded that the variation in pressure across the compressor face, or distortion, was acceptable, and that the weighted average of the pressures, or the pressure recovery, was acceptable. Pratt & Whitney had experienced some stalls with the TF-30 as early as October 1964, but these stalls were thought to be a consequence of the immaturity of the engine on which the tests were run.

[33] General Dynamics, "GD F-111 Category I Flight Test Progress Report," dated 31 January 1965.

problem, particularly in the throttle-transient state, was also apparent.[34]

The severity of the stall problem was to impede the entire aircraft test program, as normal supersonic flight was prevented.[35] To aid in the resolution of this problem, an F-111 prototype was fitted with inlet instrumentation in January 1965 to measure the distortion patterns, as well as to measure the dynamic change in the patterns (that is, to measure the turbulence).[36]

These tests showed that the flow distortion was slightly greater than that prescribed by Pratt & Whitney in July 1963, but that it was consistent with the distortion patterns General Dynamics supplied from its wind tunnel tests in early 1964. As a consequence of these tests, vortex generators were fitted in the air inlet and were flight tested. By April 1965, improvements were reported via this remedy.[37] The airflow being delivered to the engines was now within Pratt & Whitney's area-weighted distortion index of 1964.

But the stall problem remained severe. It had become clear that the engine was overly susceptible to stalls. In Navy altitude chamber tests, an early version of the TF-30 engine had encountered stalls during simulated steady-state flight at high altitudes when configured with a bell-shaped (zero distortion) inlet.[38] Since that time, engine

[34] Interviews 7 and 16; and General Dynamics "GD F-111 Category I Flight Test Progress Report," dated 30 June 1965.

[35] General Dynamics, "GD F-111 Category I Flight Test Progress Report," dated 30 June 1965.

[36] Ibid.

[37] Ibid.; and Staff of the Langley Research Center, *Summary of NASA Support of the F-111 Development Program: Part I—December 1962-December 1965*, Langley Working Paper 246 (Langley Station, Virginia, undated), pp. 23–24 (from the files of the Permanent Subcommittee on Investigations, Committee on Government Operations, U.S. Senate, Exhibit 13 of *TFX Hearings—Second Series*). Vortex generators are tiny vanes placed in the air stream which create a generalized turbulence that mixes the incoming air and equalizes pressure on the compressor face. The reader may recall seeing such tiny vanes on the top of the wings of Boeing 707s.

[38] Interview 16. One of the problems was apparently that the TF-30 engine had originally been designed for subsonic flight (in the Navy's

tolerance had improved, but instrumented flight tests revealed that the "compressor [was] sensitive to small deviations in relatively good distortion patterns, with the main difference being slight *changes* in the pressures near the engine hub."[39] The engine was thus most sensitive to dynamic changes in the distortion patterns—that is, to turbulence—near the hub of the compressor.

The peculiarities of inlet performance abetted the engine's sensitivity. Flight tests had revealed that the inlet could not accommodate the airflow disturbances created by the wing and fuselage, precisely as had been warned in the formal evaluation of the General Dynamics proposal back in 1962.[40] These disturbances were particularly acute at higher speeds and angles of attack. In these conditions, the airflow became turbulent, creating the kind of airflow disturbance to which the TF-30 engines were particularly susceptible.

Because of these problems, Pratt & Whitney soon disclaimed its area-weighted distortion index, contending that distortion patterns had to be looked at on a dynamic basis to define "a good yardstick for determining distortion levels."[41] Dynamic measurements of this sort had never before been required to integrate the propulsion with the

---

Missileer) and did not immediately adapt to supersonic flight. Interview 22.

[39] General Dynamics, "GD F-111 Category I Flight Test Progress Report," dated 30 June 1965, p. 10a (emphasis added). See also London, "VFX—The Navy's Choice," p. 54.

[40] Greathouse, "Blending Propulsion With Airframe," p. 62; London, "VFX—The Navy's Choice," p. 54; and Interview 16. This is not to suggest that General Dynamics and Pratt & Whitney should have foreseen the specific problem which flight tests ultimately revealed. It is only to suggest that the compatibility of engines and inlets was always known to be a problem of considerable uncertainty, yet development organizations proceeded to resolve it as if it were the same, standard compatibility problem they had grown familiar with, the problem of turbo-jet compatibility.

[41] Interview 16.

airframe on a supersonic jet aircraft.[42] Distortion had been assumed to be the key measure of compatibility, as on all prior aircraft. Consequently, turbulence indices had not been specified in the F-111 interface documents. Yet it was turbulence, not distortion, that was causing the stalls. Since legal responsibility for the stall problem could not be determined, each contractor blamed the other.[43] Pratt & Whitney blamed the turbulence in the airflow that the inlet provided.[44] General Dynamics, for its part, felt that the engine was overly sensitive to stalls, and that Pratt & Whitney should be tied down to certain obligations in reducing engine sensitivity. After all, the General Dynamics inlet had now met the Pratt & Whitney distortion criteria. Pratt & Whitney resisted the imposition of rigid obligations, and the Navy (the overseer of engine development) would not force such obligations on the contractor.[45]

[42] Stuart M. Levin, "F-15: The Teething of a Dogfighter," *Space/Aeronautics*, Vol. 52 (December 1969), p. 54; and London, "VFX—The Navy's Choice," p. 56.

[43] Interviews 12 and 19; and notes of the preliminary Icarus meeting, June 22, 1967, excerpted in *TFX Hearings—Second Series*, Part 3, p. 561.

[44] Pratt & Whitney could point to corroborating evidence: a Dassault-Mirage IIIF, a French fighter with inlets located next to the fuselage but ahead of the wings (that is, ahead and above the "armpit" location of the F-111 inlets), apparently experienced stall-free operation using the P-1 version of the TF-30 engine—the same version of the TF-30 engine which was stalling repeatedly in the F-111 R&D prototypes. See "Industry Observer," *Aviation Week and Space Technology*, Vol. 85 (August 1, 1966), p. 13.

[45] The reader might wonder why these associate contractor arrangements are pursued, if they are so prone to inter-contractor frictions and to difficulties in defining mutual obligations between the contractors. The answer apparently lies in three areas. First, the services like to develop an engine for a number of aircraft and, hence, like to control the optimizing decisions on the engine development. They could not exercise this direct control if the engine contractor were a subcontractor to the airframe contractor. Second, engines take longer to develop than airframes, so the government already will have started the engine development (in most cases) before airframe development begins. Finally, engines are supplied by the government because "that's the way it has always been done" (Interview 16). On more

General Dynamics required a resolution of the stall problem, since the Air Force demanded improvements and the flight test program was being delayed by the stalls.[46] In what has been called "integration by capitulation," General Dynamics moved to improve inlet airflow patterns beyond the earlier-specified levels. Pratt & Whitney moved to improve the stall tolerance of the engines. This dual effort was necessary, since the earlier, standard definition of responsibility in the contract (the distortion index) had been met by both contractors, while the stalls continued. A dimension of the interface not specified in the contract—turbulence— had to be addressed by both contractors if operational compatibility was to be achieved.

Inlet improvements proceeded in two stages. The first stage was the Triple Plow I inlet, a collection of minor modifications to the existing inlet (see Figure IV). These modifications were intended to reduce the turbulence created by fuselage and wing disturbances of incoming air at higher speeds. The TF-30 engines were also modified, to improve their performance and to reduce their stall sensitivity.[47] These changes were approved for production in early 1967 and were incorporated in all 141 F-111As. As noted earlier, the Triple Plow I inlet and the TF-30 engine improvements moved the stall zone of the aircraft out to Mach 2 in maneuvering flight and Mach 2.35 in level flight. General Dynamics was essentially satisfied with the Triple

---

recent aircraft developments (e.g., the F-15 and the B-1), there is evidence of greater attempts being made to specify the engine-airframe integration responsibility. See Michael Getler, "David Packard: Presiding Over a Revolution," *Armed Forces Management*, Vol. 16 (March 1970), p. 29; and U.S. Comptroller General, *Report to the Congress: Acquisition of Major Weapon Systems* (Washington: U.S. Government Printing Office, 1971), p. 37.

[46] *TFX Hearings—Second Series*, Part 3, p. 497.

[47] *TFX Hearings—Second Series*, Part 1, pp. 169–170; and Interviews 10 and 16. Pratt & Whitney modified the engine fan and compressor, the afterburner, and the controls for the engine, fuel system, and afterburner.

Plow I improvements.[48] Further improvements in stall tolerance would require structural changes in the aircraft. Since the aircraft was in full production, structural changes would be expensive, and General Dynamics was, of course, working under a fixed-price contract. With contractual responsibility for the stalls unclear, there was little incentive to the contractor to pursue further improvements.[49]

At this point, technical people in the Air Force's F-111 System Program Office (SPO) at Wright-Patterson became

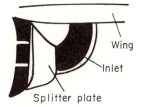 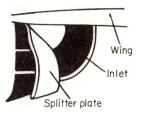

ORIGINAL INLET DESIGN   TRIPLE PLOW I DESIGN

Figure IV. The Change to Triple Plow I.

Turbulence in the air flow to the engines was the major cause of the compressor stalls. In turn, this turbulence was mainly the result of disturbances in the air flow generated by the fuselage and wings. Originally, it had been hoped that the "splitter plate" (see above) would divert this turbulent air away from the inlet. However, at higher speeds and angles of attack, this splitter plate could not handle all of the turbulent air. The Triple Plow I modifications managed to remove much of it, by curving the splitter plate outward four inches, thereby diverting more of the turbulent air; and by adding a notched side plate within the inlet, thereby bleeding additional turbulent air out of the inlet. The Triple Plow I modifications also included a slight thickening of the inlet lip and other minor changes in the original design.

[48] Interview 20; and author's impression gained from a visit to General Dynamics.

[49] For a discussion of this general problem, see Frederick M. Scherer, *The Weapons Acquisition Process: Economic Incentives* (Boston: Harvard Business School, 1964), pp. 155–156; and Richard Witkin, "Why the Flak Around the F-111?" *New York Times Magazine* (April 2, 1967), p. 47.

more involved in attempts to eliminate the stall problem. In effect, the SPO took over the responsibility for designing a solution more complete than the Triple Plow I. According to an Air Force officer, the Air Force engineers "saw an opportunity to shine" if they could design a solution to the stall problem.[50] The SPO's efforts led ultimately to the Triple Plow II inlet, a package of inlet modifications more radical than Triple Plow I. For Triple Plow II, the inlets and ducts were enlarged and moved outboard four additional inches from the aircraft's fuselage (see Figure V).[51]

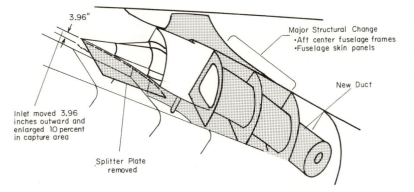

Figure V. The Change from Triple Plow I to Triple Plow II.

The basic changes in the Triple Plow II inlet over the Triple Plow I inlet are the enlargement of the inlet capture (cross-sectional) area by ten percent and the movement of the inlet and ducting outward by 3.96 inches. Because the ducting is routed through major fuselage frames, this enlargement and outward movement necessitated changes in fuselage side panels and major structural frames (shaded area in brackets, above). With the inlet further away from the fuselage, the splitter plate was no longer needed, so it was removed. (Source: Interview 16.)

These inlet changes required an alteration in the basic fuselage structure around the inlets and ducts. Coupled

[50] Interview 20.
[51] *TFX Hearings—Second Series*, Part 3, pp. 518–519; and Interview 16.

with improvements in the stall tolerance of the engines, the Triple Plow II inlet moved the stall region out beyond Mach 2.4, at high altitudes, and at high angles of attack or in sharp turns. The Triple Plow II improvements did, however, reduce the F-111's range for the sea-level supersonic dash of the nuclear mission. Moving the inlets outboard and enlarging their capture area had increased aerodynamic drag.[52]

For our concerns, the central characteristic of working-level behavior on engine-inlet compatibility problems is the response of the development process to technical uncertainty. We have described how the engine-inlet compatibility problems resulted from technical uncertainties with the new turbo-fan engines. General Dynamics' R&D prototype inlet, as improved, met the stall-tolerance index defined by Pratt & Whitney in 1964. However, that index, as we emphasized earlier, was simply the standard definition of acceptable design, drawn from a technically different design problem—the design of turbo-jet air inlets. It weighed distortion equally at all distances from the compressor's center, while turbo-fan engines proved to be more sensitive to pressure variation nearer to the compressor's center. Moreover, it relied upon the static measurement of distortion as the criterion of acceptability for design efforts, while turbo-fan engines proved to be particularly sensitive to dynamic changes (i.e., turbulence) in the distortion patterns. The index that allowed resolution of the problem specified different weights for the pressure variation at different distances from engine compressor's center, measured on a dynamic basis (see Figure VI).

The engine-inlet compatibility problems were thus a consequence of the application of old technical approaches to a new and critically different design problem. Only the

[52] "U.S. Air Force Selected Acquisition Report on the F-111A/D/E/F," dated December 31, 1969, p. 9 (from the files of the Permanent Subcommittee on Investigations, Committee on Government Operations, U.S. Senate, Exhibit 10 of the *TFX Hearings—Second Series*); and Interviews 6 and 16.

severity of the compressor stalls in flight induced the research that was necessary to adapt inlet and engine designs
to the exigencies of turbo-fan operation.

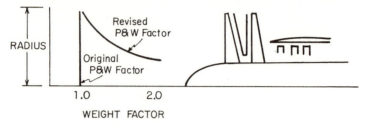

Figure VI. Weights for Inlet Pressure Variation.

*Paradigms of Decision and the Pattern of Technical Ef-
fort.* This experience with the engine-inlet compatibility
problem reflects a characteristic response of the development process to technical uncertainty. Returning to our
paradigms of decision, we noted earlier that the analytic
paradigm posits that uncertainty will be resolved through
a sequential learning process. This learning process is required because, for projects of considerable uncertainty like
the F-111, closed *initial* decisions will not in general lead
to optimal final outcomes—the probability distribution of
final outcomes for any initial decision cannot be well known
in advance. What is required, then, is "some strategy for
allocating and reallocating effort among different uncertainty reducing possibilities as development proceeds and
knowledge accumulates."[53] The development process should

---

[53] Thomas Marschak, "The Microeconomic Study of Development,"
in Thomas Marschak, Thomas K. Glennan, Jr., and Robert Summers
(eds.), *Strategy for R&D: Studies in the Microeconomics of Development* (New York: Springer-Verlag, 1967), p. 1. The main point here
is that a strategy of making fixed early commitments to specific design
approaches is not optimal, since uncertainty-reducing information can
be acquired at a relatively low cost. As long as no unusual constraints
are present, the optimal strategy will be to follow the kind of learning
process described in the text. On the implicit potential for acquiring
earlier information on engine-inlet compatibility, see "F-15 Engine-
Inlet Simulator Installed at AEDC [Arnold Engineering Development

aim to accumulate this knowledge, not to fulfill some pre-programmed approach that ignores the uncertainties involved. As this knowledge accumulates, probability distributions become firmer, and it becomes possible to make closed optimizing decisions—that is, optimal commitments to specific designs.

Only with difficulty can this analytic logic be used to describe the engine-inlet integration process for the F-111 program. Such learning as occurred before the first flight of the aircraft was highly constrained or "channeled" by the standard definition of acceptable design for engine-inlet compatibility: the distortion index. The role of turbulence was hidden by that index. Development efforts did not resolve uncertainties of engine-inlet integration; they proceeded as if the uncertainties had been resolved, meeting all preprogrammed schedules. After the first flight revealed the stall problem, the progress of technical efforts was poorly integrated with the rapid production buildup.

One may want to consider this suboptimizing behavior, that is, optimizing behavior with reference to values of an unfortunately low order, values that the organization had to take as given and controlling. Yet to do so is to eliminate by mere assumption a key part of the problem, as there is no evidence that anyone saw fit to contest the values that are pre-supposed to be binding. It is more informative to take this acquiescence as a clue, and to adopt a framework of analysis that postulates such acquiescence, the cybernetic paradigm.

The cybernetic paradigm posits that the decision process will avoid uncertainty and proceed routinely, finding technical problems only where fairly unambiguous, adverse in-

---

Center]," *Aviation Week and Space Technology*, Vol. 96 (February 28, 1972), pp. 44–45; W. T. Gunston, *Attack Aircraft of the West* (New York: Charles Scribner's Sons, 1974), pp. 186–188; and U.S. Senate, Committee on Armed Services, *Fiscal Year 1973 Authorization for Military Procurement*, 92d Cong., 2d Sess. (1972), pp. 3592–3595, 4030.

formation is received. It will respond to this information with narrow, short-range efforts. Such a process is not far-sighted, nor is it aggressive in acquiring and responding to new information on unanticipated dimensions of the problem. Instead, the process will work to satisfy standard measures and to preserve the projected future course of events. It routinely will make an initial commitment to a distortion index, generally will work to fulfill prepro-grammed schedules that ignore critical uncertainties, and will tend poorly to integrate problem-solving efforts with an on-going production process. As long as the basic de-composition of the problem is clear, a generalized awareness of technical uncertainties will count for little in this process.

The decomposition of the engine-inlet design problem was clear. Although there was a generalized awareness of turbo-fan sensitivity to variations in airflow, the design problem was structured as a standard one, as the routine measure of engine-inlet compatibility—the distortion index —was applied. This routine measure became the definition of acceptable performance in design efforts. To the airframe contractor, it defined the acceptable quality of airflow to be delivered by the inlet. To the engine contractor, it de-fined the acceptable resistance of the engine to airflow variations. Each contractor proceeded as if that single measure wholly embodied the engine-inlet integration problem, *as if satisfying that measure were equivalent to resolving integration uncertainties.* But while design efforts were keyed to the achievement of this standard measure of acceptability, the basic appropriateness of the measure itself went unexamined. As we would expect, in anticipation of the turbo-fan sensitivity, the distortion index that was ulti-mately used was slightly more demanding than the distor-tion indices used on earlier turbo-jet aircraft.[54] However, because the design problem had been construed as stand-ard, the organizations did not engage in a technical search process outside the areas indicated by standard measures.

[54] Interview 16.

Only with the advent of flight tests—and of stalls on the actual aircraft in flight—did the measure of acceptable performance change. In response to these stalls organizations commenced a search process to refine their understanding of the engine-inlet interface. As the contractor later concluded, the stall problem "sparked much needed propulsion research by government agencies which had been neglected up to this time"—research that anticipation of the problems had failed to spark.[55] In the late 1950s, beginning with the rise of its ballistic missile and space efforts, NASA had severely restricted its research efforts in aeronautics and propulsion-airframe integration.[56] In the early years of the TFX/F-111 program, no one moved to direct NASA efforts toward propulsion integration. The bulk of the NASA work in the course of the development was devoted to refining the configuration of the aircraft in an effort to reduce drag for the supersonic nuclear mission.[57] Propulsion integration received research emphasis only when feedback against a *new* measure of acceptable performance triggered a search process.

The search process was embodied in a characteristic insti-

[55] Interview 16.

[56] C. V. Glines, "Will the First 'A' in NASA Be Given the Go-Signal?" *Armed Forces Management*, Vol. 16 (November 1969), pp. 34–35, 38; Greathouse, "Blending Propulsion With Airframe," pp. 59–60; and B. Pinkel and J. R. Nelson, *A Critique of Turbine Engine Development Policy*, Rand Memorandum No. RM-6100/1-PR (April 1970), p. 12. This reduction in NASA research effort was particularly critical for propulsion integration, since the number of wind tunnel test points necessary to verify air induction systems increases exponentially with the top speed of the aircraft—from 1,000 test points at Mach 1.1, to 10,000 at Mach 2.2, to 100,000 test points at Mach 3.3. See Staff Report, "TFX: Mission and Design," *Space/Aeronautics*, Vol. 29 (June 1963), pp. 76–78.

[57] Staff of the Langley Research Center, *Summary of NASA Support of the F-111 Development Program: Part I—December 1962-December 1965*, passim; and Minutes of the Aerodynamics Consulting Group, meetings of July 31, 1963, October 2, 1963, January 14–16, 1964, and April 9–10, 1964 (from the files of the Permanent Subcommittee on Investigations, Committee on Government Operations, U.S. Senate, Exhibits 12A, B, C, D of the *TFX Hearings—Second Series*).

tutional mechanism for resolving technical problems: the ad hoc committee. As one frequent participant in these committees commented, "DOD hardly knows how to address problems without committees, and the DOD practice reflects down into the way the aerospace industry does business."[58] For minor problems, or for initial attempts at resolving more serious problems, these committees will be quickly assembled from personnel in the contractor's organization and the services' technical staffs.[59] More serious and enduring difficulties, such as the engine-inlet compatibility problems, become the object of advisory committees which include independent scientists, NASA personnel, and others without direct program responsibilities. These advisory committees are attempts to concentrate available expertise on a given difficulty, as well as to infuse the development process with fresh approaches to the problem (or, as one participant described it, "to get people who won't miss the forest for the trees").[60] These ad hoc committees avoid some of the rigidity of the official lines of authority and communication in the program.[61]

The inlet modifications of the F-111 program were the product of a number of ad hoc advisory committees formed between 1965 and 1967: the Sutton Committee, the Inlet-Engine Compatibility Group, the Supp Committee, the Rall Committee, the "Greasy Thumb" Working Group, and others.[62] Initially, the work of these committees (particularly of the Rall Committee and its wind tunnel tests) led to the Triple Plow I modifications. Though the contractor was satisfied with the results of Triple Plow I, a group of Air Force engineers at Wright-Patterson Air Force Base pur-

---

[58] Interview 16.

[59] These are nicknamed "tiger teams" at General Dynamics.

[60] Interview 16.

[61] See Englebert Kirchner, "The Project Manager," *Space/Aeronautics*, Vol. 43 (February 1967), pp. 59–60, for a discussion of the value of this sort of ad hoc flexibility in two space satellite programs.

[62] Memorandum to T. Keating, from F. T. Rall, dated May 11, 1967, re Summary Report of F-111 Inlet Status, printed in *TFX Hearings—Second Series*, Part 3, pp. 518–519; and Interviews 10 and 16.

sued a further resolution of the problem. They "pushed the specs to get the last ounce out of them."[63] In their efforts to improve on Triple Plow I, the Air Force engineers predicted improvements in stall tolerance, with only a slight degradation—or even an improvement—in sea-level, supersonic dash range. In fact, the improvements caused a significant decrease in dash range.[64]

Reece and Scherer have each described the way in which engineers pursue perfection and "technical elegance" in their work.[65] Engineers will keep trying to make something "work better," and will in this case do so for a service (the Air Force) particularly predisposed to obtaining the highest possible performance qualities in its aircraft.[66] They thus will keep on creating improvement options in a process receptive to their efforts, and the committees on which they sit often will be difficult to dissolve.[67] Especially as a problem persists and the receptivity to major modifications increases, such committees can provide a rich menu of options for resolving technical problems.

Hence, when a search process commences, it proceeds through a series of ad hoc committees that generate technical options that will provide alternatives for program personnel to adopt if feedback on technical performance remains negative. Initially, the options will represent marginal

[63] Interview 16.

[64] Interview 20; and "U.S. Air Force Selected Acquisition Report on the F-111A/D/E/F," dated December 31, 1969, p. 9.

[65] James S. Reece, "The Effects of Contract Changes on the Control of a Major Defense Weapon System Program" (unpublished D.B.A. dissertation, Harvard Business School, 1970), chap. 2, pp. 23–26; and Scherer, *The Weapons Acquisition Process: Economic Incentives*, p. 163.

[66] Merton J. Peck and Frederick M. Scherer, *The Weapons Acquisition Process: An Economic Analysis* (Boston: Harvard Business School, 1962), pp. 478–479.

[67] The committee assembled to resolve the problem with wing box fatigue (the Advisory Committee on D6AC Steel) made great strides in resolving the fatigue problem, but it resisted disbandment and soon became an action instrument, making decisions on a whole range of structural matters concerning the airframe. Interview 16.

changes of the alternative in use, reflecting a sustained belief in the validity of existing technical approaches. However, under the continuing pressure of negative feedback, this sustained belief will give way, and more radical options will be entertained and generated. This pattern of technical effort—the "problemistic search"—was apparent in our discussion of the F-111 engine improvements, in Chapter III. It seems to fit the inlet improvements as well. As a participating engineer described the efforts behind the inlet improvements, "We made minor change after minor change until Wright-Patterson [Air Force program management] said 'go ahead and make the big change,' which led to Triple Plow II."[68]

The pattern of technical effort on the engine-inlet compatibility problems provides an interesting complement to our discussion of the development process in Chapter III. As described in that chapter, the development process routinely decomposed and elaborated the contractor's design proposal into a complete design. The government led the way through this process, by establishing specifications against which successive levels of design were to be developed. One area where specifications had to be established was in engine-inlet integration, to define the mutual obligations of the airframe and engine contractors. Since the integration of turbo-fan engines was construed as standard, a distortion index routinely was established to measure these obligations. The narrow vision of the integration effort that followed was substantially similar to the insensitivity of the design process to broad mission-optimization problems. As the process generally ignored performance results outside those implied by the formal requirements, so too did it neglect dimensions of the integration problem outside those suggested by the distortion index. The aerodynamic drag measures of the aircraft, critical to the achievement of the specified supersonic dash, received great attention when

68 Interview 16.

194

tests revealed that these measures were above acceptable levels. The declining thrust-to-weight ratio did not. The distortion patterns of the F-111 inlet received much consideration through 1964, as the distortion index itself was refined. Non-standard dimensions of the integration problem did not.

The engine-inlet compatibility problems thus deepen our earlier discussion of the design process. The formal requirements will constrain the vision of the process in acting upon broad, mission-optimization problems. In the same manner, the carry-over of fine-grained development practices will constrain the vision of the process in acting upon important technical uncertainties.

Other Technical Problems and the Process of "Learning." An examination of other technical uncertainties that the process did and did not act upon at the outset of development will help to clarify our argument. It will also suggest one source of change in the extensive low-level practices that are carried over from development to development.

We may begin by examining the fatigue problem on the F-111 wing box. The wing box is a central structural member of the fuselage to which the pivoting wings are attached. In fatigue tests in 1968, cracks appeared in the wing box at less than one-half of the design life of the aircraft.[69] Subsequent modification and test efforts were thwarted by two additional failures in fatigue tests. In response to these failures, a special committee of outside experts and contractor engineers (called the Advisory Committee on D6AC Steel) was assembled to analyze the problem and to propose solutions. The deliberations of the Committee led to "great advances in the state of the art on fatigue," and to the design of a new wing box with clearly

---

[69] "Fatigue" is a deterioration of metal caused by the repetitive application of stress. The problem was manifested on the F-111 wing box (during tests) by the appearance of hairline cracks. See *TFX Hearings—Second Series*, Part 1, pp. 169–171, 233–236, Part 2, pp. 259–264, 288–293, and Part 3, p. 658.

sufficient fatigue life.[70] This box was installed in all new F-111s as they came down the production line. For those F-111s already produced, a test, modification, and retrofit program costing nearly 100 million dollars was initiated to bring the old wing boxes up to full fatigue life.[71]

It had always been recognized that a variable-sweep wing would have unique fatigue characteristics. With a fixed wing, structural loads are borne by multiple attaching points and by the aircraft's skin. But with a variable-sweep wing, all loads for each wing are concentrated in a single wing pivot. In a marginal adjustment of standard practice similar to that observed on the engine-inlet compatibility problems, fatigue requirements were tightened for the design of the F-111.[72] Instead of the usual design practice, which was to design to a static strength specification with the expectation of acceptable fatigue life as a by-product, the F-111 was to be designed specifically with fatigue considerations in mind.[73]

This approach defined acceptable fatigue life throughout the design and early production efforts. A new measure of acceptable fatigue life would emerge only with the advent of fatigue tests on an actual F-111 specimen. Yet these tests, which mainly required placing a heavily instrumented F-111 in a fatigue test facility, were not scheduled to occur until late in the program, after volume deliveries of the aircraft were already being made to operational commands. The tests were scheduled for that date *simply because they*

[70] U.S. Senate, Committee on Armed Services, *Fiscal Year 1972 Authorization For Military Procurement*, 92d Cong., 1st Sess. (1971), p. 3925; and Interview 16.

[71] *TFX Hearings—Second Series*, Part 2, pp. 262, 289–290, and Part 3, p. 658; and U.S. Senate, Committee on Armed Services, *Fiscal Year 1972 Authorization for Military Procurement*, p. 3925. Later, an unrelated static strength problem appeared, the result of a manufacturing defect. It cost approximately 35 million dollars to correct.

[72] Recall that, while its basic suitability was unexamined, the F-111 distortion index was more demanding than that employed in prior programs.

[73] Interview 16.

always had been.[74] Consequently, a refined measure of acceptability *could not* emerge until late 1968. For all the acknowledged difficulty of the fatigue problem for variable-sweep wings, no one had paid attention to the timing of fatigue tests. Disconfirmation of the initial wing box design thus would not occur until late 1968, when full production of the aircraft was under way. The result of this disconfirmation was an intense technical search process and an advance in the state of the art on fatigue—but also a grounding of all operational F-111s and a costly test, modification, and retrofit program.

We can see this pattern again in the treatment of the drag problems on the F-111. In the first year of the development, wind tunnel tests revealed unexpectedly high drag levels on the aircraft. A number of committees (most prominently, the Aerodynamics Study Group) were formed over the next few years in an attempt to find means to reduce the drag levels.[75] But these attempts were successful in achieving only a marginal reduction in drag.

The F-111 requirements placed great importance on the minimization of aerodynamic drag. The incorporation of afterburning turbo-fan engines in the aircraft complicated the achievement of minimum drag levels, since the extra air from the fan (the air which by-passed the core engine) would create unique aft-end flow characteristics and engine nozzle requirements on the plane. To understand these effects, new techniques were required for testing aircraft and nozzle designs, and new parameters were needed for applying test data.[76] Such tools were developed, but only in response to the aft-end drag problems of the F-111. These tools were not available for the early years of the F-111/TF-30 development, when the configurations of the engine and aircraft were being established and refined. Indeed, during that period, NASA's aerodynamic research efforts

[74] *TFX Hearings—Second Series*, Part 2, p. 263; and Interview 12.
[75] *TFX Hearings—Second Series*, Part 2, pp. 339–365.
[76] Greathouse, "Blending Propulsion With Airframe," p. 68.

were curtailed. "As a result, the TF-30's nozzle suffers a performance loss and the aircraft a backend drag increase that was not accounted for in original estimates."[77] (Aftend drag on the F-111 accounts for between 30 and 40 percent of the plane's total drag, while later research has apparently established less than 5 percent as an ideal.)[78] In consequence, the plane suffered serious degradation in its sea-level, supersonic dash range, as well as in its ferry range.[79] As we saw earlier (Chapter III), when Dr. Flax confronted indications of the drag increase in 1964, he knew that new aerodynamic principles would be required to achieve desired drag levels. Such principles would become available, but only in response to the problems he was confronting—too late for incorporation in the F-111.

There was, of course, one area of technical uncertainty in the F-111 program where few problems were experienced —the variable sweep wings, which were the primary technical advance in the airframe design. As noted in the overview in Chapter II, NASA had done intensive wind tunnel studies of variable-sweep configurations prior to proposing this option to TAC. "By early 1959 there was conclusive evidence that the major obstacles to the successful employment of variable sweep either had been overcome or were clearly vulnerable."[80] It was at that point that NASA began actively seeking an application, just as TAC was formulating its requirements for a successor to the F-105.[81] The Air Force technical people were highly skeptical at first. Their skepticism induced NASA to perform additional tests on specific aircraft configurations. These later tests resolved the Air Force's skepticism and led to acceptance of the

---

[77] Ibid.   [78] Levin, "F-15," p. 42.

[79] *TFX Hearings—Second Series*, Part 1, p. 59; "U.S. Air Force Selected Acquisition Report on the F-111A/D/E/F," dated December 31, 1969, p. 2; and Interview 12.

[80] Robert L. Perry, *Innovation and Military Requirements: A Comparative Study*, Rand Memorandum No. RM-5182-PR (August 1967), p. 67.

[81] Ibid., p. 68.

variable-sweep concept in the new operational requirement.[82]

Though more extensive comparison would be required to make the case conclusive, we may surmise that the variable-sweep technology was successfully adapted because the extensive testing performed by NASA served to reduce the uncertainty of incorporating it. Indeed, this search process was required before the Air Force would accept a configuration of such relative novelty.[83] It was the kind of intensive search effort notably absent in the other problems we have examined. We can speculate that such additional research will be undertaken only when a pre-existing satisfactory approach to the problem does not exist. Though they were to prove inappropriate, previously satisfactory design approaches did exist for integrating the propulsion system, accommodating the fatigue loads, and minimizing the drag on a supersonic aircraft. Consequently, additional research was not necessary to define acceptable approaches for these design problems. However, earlier attempts to establish satisfactory variable-sweep wing configurations—attempts that included two flying research vehicles—were widely held to have been unsatisfactory.[84] There had never been an operational aircraft with such wings. The NASA tests in 1959 served to provide the appropriate, acceptable structure.

The development process, then, was generally averse to long-range anticipation of technical problems. Instead of resolving acknowledged areas of uncertainty, it proceeded routinely with the concepts and tools in hand and responded only to unequivocal information of a technical deficiency. Only for design problems lacking an acknowledged structure did research efforts precede the problems and actually reduce the uncertainty. As Allison suggests in his formula-

[82] Ibid., pp. 69–70.
[83] Ibid., pp. 67–70. This uncertainty reduction was also required to overcome the Air Force's negative reaction to earlier research prototypes that had used a different method of sweeping the wings (see Chapter I).
[84] Ibid., pp. 44–57, 69–70.

tion of Model II, organizations engage in search only where situations cannot be construed as standard—that is, where the problem decomposition is not a matter of accepted organization routine.[85] When design problems can be construed as standard, research effort will be allocated to their resolution only in response to unequivocal information on unfavorable performance. (Unfortunately, that information on unfavorable performance will itself often be "timed" or scheduled in the development process according to pre-existing routines, not according to analytic recognition of areas of uncertainty—witness the fatigue tests.) When design problems cannot be construed as standard, research effort will be allocated to their resolution in anticipation of unfavorable performance.[86]

The new concepts and research methods produced in response to problems become a part of the tools in hand as the next development approaches. They constitute an important source of technical learning in the development process. In addition to the technical advances and reallocations of research resources they induce, the perceived prob-

---

[85] Allison, *Essence of Decision*, p. 84.

[86] One dimension of the problem that we will not pursue in detail here is the fact that non-DOD organizations (particularly NASA) are responsible for the performance of much of the research. NASA serves an advisory role in aircraft developments and, by contract, performs much of the aerodynamic testing that these developments require. NASA's scientific concerns can conflict with the immediate needs of specific weapon developments, and occasionally the efforts of NASA and DOD will be insufficiently integrated for a program. An example of this problem is the sharp curtailment of NASA's aerodynamic efforts that occurred with the rise of NASA's ballistic-missile and space efforts in the late 1950s. The problem is further reflected in an observation made in a Rand study of the F-104 development of the early 1950s. The F-104 development involved a number of theoretical concerns of particular concern to (what was then) NACA. In consequence, "By comparison [to other fighter developments], the F-104 . . . was able to command an unusual amount of wind tunnel time for proving its aerodynamics." NASA's *own* interests can thus influence the amount of testing a weapons program receives. See Thomas Marschak, "The Role of Project Histories in the Study of R&D," in Marschak, Glennan, and Summers, *Strategy for R&D*, p. 113.

lems of prior developments induce alterations in subsequent procurement practices. Thus, in response to the severity and the dynamic nature of the F-111's engine-inlet compatibility problems, the Air Force moved in the F-15 program (and the Navy moved in the F-14 program) to map the entire engine-inlet interface before the first flight of the aircraft.[87] (On its part, General Dynamics, in one of its first design proposals after the F-111 development—a design proposal for the B-1 strategic bomber—placed the engines and inlets as far as possible from the "armpit" location of the F-111's engines and inlets: in pods hung under the *moveable* part of the B-1's swing wings.)[88] Similarly, in response to the wing box fatigue problems of the F-111, major structural testing of the F-15 was also moved to a period before the first flight of the aircraft. The NASA effort on fighter-type research has continued since it was reactivated in the mid-1960s. The tools NASA developed for studying back-end drag and nozzle performance have been applied early to the subsequent developments.[89] All of these changes are surely adaptive responses to the problems of the F-111 development. However, as we shall see later in this chapter (when we examine the role of intense schedule pressure in complicating the solution of engine-inlet compatibility problems), these responses are highly selective. They leave nearly all development organizations and sequences untouched. By the logic of our argument, they serve mainly to alter the timing of new measures of acceptability for design efforts in the structural and engine-inlet areas. They build into future programs the possibility for a technical search *in these particular problem areas* to be triggered earlier in the development, when it can have

[87] "F-15 Engine-Inlet Simulator Installed at AEDC," pp. 44–45; and U.S. Senate, Committee on Armed Services, *Fiscal Year 1972 Authorization for Military Procurement*, p. 4016.

[88] Michael P. London, "B-1: The Last Bomber?" *Space/Aeronautics*, Vol. 53 (April 1970), pp. 31–32.

[89] Greathouse, "Blending Propulsion With Airframe," pp. 59–60, 63–68; and U.S. Senate, Committee on Armed Services, *Fiscal Year 1973 Authorization for Military Procurement*, p. 3593.

more impact. They are the "new routines" for test scheduling. However, future developments are likely to have problems in different areas. The complexity and uncertainty of fighter developments are such that sources of technical problems are likely to be highly variable from generation to generation. (For example, the propulsion problems of the F-15 development were not integration problems but durability problems.)[90] If the development process is modified only to anticipate the problems of the previous generation of aircraft, it will doubtless miss the problems of the new generation of aircraft, except to react to them late in development and to be modified for yet a third generation of aircraft.

We now have a partial explanation of the engine-inlet compatibility problems on the F-111. These difficulties resulted from the application of old design approaches to new design problems. The development process tended to avoid acknowledging technical uncertainties by stereotyping them—that is, by construing them as extensions of the familiar, in spite of the grounds that existed for examining the problems in greater depth. Only the emergence of the severe stalls in flight tests induced the research efforts necessary to understand the peculiarities of the new technology engines.

Clearly, if the development process is not forward looking, then the structure of development and production schedules assumes greater significance. Hypothetically, the short-range focus of the development process would be of lesser consequence if schedules allowed sufficient time and flexibility for program management to provide a full re-

[90] See "Air Force Review Group Probes F100 Engine; Findings Imminent," *Aviation Week and Space Technology*, Vol. 102 (May 12, 1975), p. 18; Cecil Brownlow, "New Engine Standards Raise F-15 Costs," *Aviation Week and Space Technology*, Vol. 98 (May 21, 1973), pp. 18–19; "F-15 Durability Problems," *Aviation Week and Space Technology*, Vol. 98 (April 30, 1973), p. 93; and U.S. Senate, Committee on Appropriations, *Department of Defense Appropriations: Fiscal Year 1974*, Hearings, 93d Cong., 1st Sess. (1973), pp. 402–407.

sponse to emergent problems. But as we will see, the development and production schedules in the F-111 development were highly compressed and yet, at the same time, gave rise to a particularly inflexible form of development organization that would impede the formulation of technical remedies.

The Role of Intense Schedule Pressure

An important part of any aircraft development is its tentative scheduling of development and production milestones. Contractors are usually instructed to provide this scheduling information as a part of their design proposals. In the case of the TFX, these milestones were programmed to obtain a high degree of "concurrency"—that is, overlap between the testing of R&D prototypes and the commencement of series production of the aircraft. The concept is generally attributed to the "Cook-Craigie" plan of the early 1950s.[91] Its central purpose is to reduce the lead time between the initiation of a program for a weapon system and the attainment of an operational capability of that system. This reduction in lead time is to be accomplished by: (1) increasing the number of R&D prototypes of the weapon; (2) producing the R&D prototypes on "hard" production tooling (versus having them hand-built on "soft" tooling, which delays the availability of the production tooling); (3) accelerating the testing phase of the development, by using the increased number of R&D prototypes; and (4) commencing production of the weapon system during the testing phase, to avoid delays in securing long lead-time production items. Implicitly, concurrency assumes that flaws in a weapon system discovered during the testing of it will be minor in nature. Because of the inherent compression of development time, concurrency also implies the elaboration of highly detailed development plans early in

[91] Thomas K. Glennan, "Issues in the Choice of Development Policies," in Marschak, Glennan, and Summers, *Strategy for R&D*, p. 47; and Marschak, "The Role of Project Histories," pp. 102–103.

203

the development, plans which allow the rapid integration of complex development tasks for early production.[92] (An example of these plans is the extensive specification detail covering the F-111 development, observed in Chapter III.)

Concurrency was planned for the TFX at the outset. The first flight of the aircraft was to take place in December 1964, and orders for inventory production were to be placed in 1965. First production units were to be delivered in 1967. TAC had insisted throughout the design competition that development schedules were to be maintained.[93]

This application of concurrent schedules magnified the technical risks of the program. It imposed a severe time pressure on all development efforts. Design choices had to be made early, without extensive verification, because it was necessary to firm design details to meet schedule dates.[94] (For example, General Dynamics froze its inlet design in the fall of 1963, as scheduled; but this design freeze clearly occurred before the resolution of technical uncertainties on engine-inlet compatibility.)[95] The R&D proto-

[92] Glennan, "Issues in the Choice of Development Policies," p. 47.

[93] Richard Austin Smith, "The $7 Billion Contract That Changed the Rules," *Fortune*, Vol. 67, Part I (March 1963), pp. 99, 188, and Part II (April 1963), p. 191; *TFX Hearings—First Series*, Part 2, p. 478, Part 6, p. 1606, and Part 9, pp. 2292–2298; U.S. Senate, Committee on Armed Services, *Military Procurement Authorizations: Fiscal Year 1966*, p. 950; and U.S. Senate, Committee on Armed Services, *Military Procurement Authorizations for Fiscal Year 1968*, 90th Cong., 1st Sess. (1967), p. 113. These schedules represented a two-year delay in the original TFX program as approved by the Air Force in 1960.

[94] Glennan, "Issues in the Choice of Development Policies," pp. 46–47; and Marschak, "The Role of Project Histories," pp. 102, 104, 107.

[95] Interview 16. Of course, the Air Force, Pratt & Whitney, and General Dynamics did not know that substantial uncertainties remained unresolved. In fact, apart from the data on which standard practice focused their attention, they lacked hard evidence to confirm or to challenge the engine and inlet designs available at this time. The point here is that under normal development practices, this lack of information was common. Concurrency assumed that all important development problems could be anticipated by careful development planning. However, if development plans failed to anticipate certain

types had to be built on hard production tooling, which made subsequent changes in the aircraft's configuration especially time consuming and costly.[96] Given the early commitment to production, if defects were not discovered and resolved early in the testing of the aircraft, production aircraft would be built in ever-increasing numbers, incorporating the defects.

But concurrency did more than simply reduce the time available for the development process to resolve technical problems. It also reduced the flexibility of the development process itself. By directly coupling development efforts to a complex production process, it forced these efforts to proceed within the elaborate administrative framework required for production planning. Development had to be planned and sequenced in detail so as smoothly to mesh

---

critical problems, the development process would proceed in relative ignorance of them. At least until flight tests imposed new measures of acceptability on design efforts, the process would proceed according to plans, *as if* the resolution of uncertainties marked out by the plans were the same as the resolution of uncertainties in the actual design problems. In many cases (cases where plans accurately forecast problem areas), the two sets of uncertainties—the anticipated and the real—would be the same. But as a succession of unfortunate concurrent developments has demonstrated, the two sets are frequently not the same; and, by the time flight tests or other tests reveal this difference, concurrent systems will be well on their way into volume production. Thus, conformity to schedules early in development efforts does not necessarily signify that there was a reasonable analytic expectation that uncertainties had been resolved. Conformity to schedules may most of all signify conformity, in the sense described by our cybernetic assumptions.

[96] Hard tooling was necessary for two reasons: (1) given the time pressure on the program, there was insufficient time for two tooling cycles (i.e., soft tooling for the R&D prototypes, then hard tooling for the production aircraft); and (2) the 23 R&D prototypes required for the program was too large a number to be produced on soft tooling. Recent advances in tooling technologies, such as numerical control, have made it easier to modify initial tooling designs and thus have reduced the time pressure somewhat on design changes which require tooling changes. See Glennan, "Issues in the Choice of Development Policies," p. 47; and Marschak, "The Role of Project Histories," p. 102.

with the rapid production buildup. The development organization had to be large and "bureaucratic" to manage this process.[97] As drawings were released for the fabrication of production tooling, for the placement of orders at foundries and forges, and for the performance of the thousands of other tasks which fed into the production of the plane, design changes became increasingly disruptive and difficult to make. To be sure, the production of any complex system *ultimately* requires that design flexibility be surrendered, to allow acquisition of items with long lead-times and to permit replication of the design in volume. However, because it schedules production so early, concurrency extensively intertwines production and development and forces these rigidities back into development efforts, even though development efforts still face substantial technical uncertainties that require resolution.[98]

[97] The F-111 design organization ranged in size from 4,000 to 6,000 people, and the Air Force supervisory office exceeded 200 people. Personnel levels in other concurrent programs, like the F-15 and the B-1, are of a similar order of magnitude. By contrast, design groups and supervisory offices for non-concurrent projects, projects uncoupled from production processes, have generally contained 75 to 90 percent *fewer* people. Levels of documentation, reporting requirements, and other indicators of the administrative burden in the non-concurrent projects reflect a similarly drastic reduction, versus concurrent projects. Because of these reductions, the design process in non-concurrent projects is typically more informal and flexible than in concurrent projects. This informality and flexibility are great assets in resolving large technical uncertainties, as they permit more rapid adjustment of design approaches in response to technical information as development proceeds. Obviously, this flexibility is acquired at the price of postponing the production buildup of the system. However, as noted momentarily in the text, this production delay does not directly translate into a delay in the operational availability of the system. See "Lightweight Fighter Gets New Impetus," *Aviation Week and Space Technology*, Vol. 101 (July 15, 1974), p. 127; and, especially, Robert L. Perry et al., *System Acquisition Strategies*, Rand Memorandum No. R-733-PR/ARPA (June 1971), pp. 23–38.

[98] In Chapter III, we discussed at length the narrow vision of "design problems" that existed within the development process. (See p. 119.) That discussion emphasized how the development process exhibited little tendency to update performance choices on the basis of development results. Instead, the development process was ob-

The decision to employ concurrency thus introduced important time pressures and rigidities into the F-111 program, thereby notably complicating the resolution of such technical problems as those with engine-inlet compatibility. In light of these disadvantages, why was concurrency employed? The common reason given for adopting concurrency is that it would save time and money.[99] The operational command was obviously anxious to have the aircraft as soon as possible, and concurrent schedules were thought to insure early availability and, through a more abbreviated contractor support period, lower program costs. This justification, hardly unique to the F-111 program, is logically plausible. *On paper*, compressed schedules self-evidently promise earlier availability and a shorter period of contractor support than is the case with more relaxed schedules. However, promised availability is not the same thing as actual availability. In fact, a Rand study of fighter developments of the 1950s concluded that the lead-time advantages attributed to concurrency were not borne out by development experience—the lengthy retrofit programs, tooling changes, and design modifications characteristic of concurrent programs tended to consume the time advantages concurrent schedules had promised.[100] Moreover, much as described above, concurrency's emphasis on exten-

---

served to have focused on dimensions of performance emphasized in the formal requirements. The discussion above in the text (and that to follow in this chapter) extends the argument presented in Chapter III. It suggests important additional sources of the pressures to avoid acknowledging trade-offs within the development process.

[99] See, for example, Memorandum for the Secretary of the Air Force, from Air Force Chief of Staff Curtis LeMay, dated August 14, 1963, re Prototype competition for F-111 program, printed in *TFX Hearings—First Series*, Part 9, p. 2296.

[100] Burton H. Klein, T. K. Glennan, Jr., and G. H. Schubert, *The Role of Prototypes in Development*, Rand Memorandum No. RM-3467-PR (1963). Note that the structural problems of the F-111 caused it to be repeatedly grounded from 1968 through mid-1972, and the Mark II avionics problems delayed operational availability of the F-111Ds by at least two years.

sive development planning and on early commitments to production tended to suppress technical uncertainties and to reduce the flexibility of the design process, with notable effects on the cost and quality of operational systems.[101] It is fair to say that the empirical case for concurrency as an efficient means of hastening aircraft development was ambiguous at best in the late 1950s and early 1960s, when the F-111 development was planned.

The common reason given for F-111 concurrency is thus difficult to accept at face value. Other influences were at work, and they seem to conform to our cybernetic assumptions. Meehan and Millett have noted that management arrangements in weapon system developments do not characteristically derive from rational "efficiency" criteria, but derive instead from the procuring agency's having "traditionally used" a given management arrangement.[102] In other words, the basic structure of a development is characteristically a routine extension of past practice. Hence, we might profitably consider the scheduling arrangements that the Air Force has traditionally used.

After concurrency was established in development doctrine in the early 1950s, it almost was universally applied in subsequent programs. Both of the Century series tactical fighter-bombers preceeding the F-111—the F-100 and the

---

[101] On this issue, see Ibid.; Glennan, "Issues in the Choice of Development Policies," pp. 46–47; Burton H. Klein, "A Radical Proposal for R&D," *Fortune*, Vol. 57 (May 1958), pp. 112–113, 218–226; Marschak, "The Role of Project Histories," pp. 105–107; and Robert L. Perry, *System Development Strategies*, Rand Memorandum No. RM-4853-PR (August 1966), pp. 101–138. A later study suggested that, for airborne weapon systems of the 1950s and 1960s, a strong negative correlation existed between the degree of schedule concurrency and the ultimate quality of system performance. See Richard A. Stubbing, "Improving the Acquisition Process for High-Risk Electronics Systems," *Congressional Record—Senate*, Vol. 115, 91st Cong., 1st Sess. (February 7, 1969), pp. 3171–3176.

[102] John D. Meehan and Thomas O. Millett, "Major Weapon System Acquisition: An Analysis of DOD Management Arrangements" (unpublished M.Sc. thesis, Air University, Wright-Patterson Air Force Base, Ohio, 1968), pp. 20–22.

F-105, the latter of which the F-111 was intended to replace—were produced under the concurrency concept. The F-105 in fact has been described as "one extreme" of development-production concurrency. The three major General Dynamics developments preceding the F-111—the F-102, the F-106, and B-58—were all produced under the concurrency concept. Indeed, of all the Century series fighters, interceptors, and fighter-bombers—the F-100, F-101, F-102, F-104, F-105, F-106 and F-107—only the F-104 could be said to have been developed under a prototyping (or separated-development-and-production) arrangement. Notably, the F-104 was also the only one of the Century series aircraft to have few design details specified at the outset.[103]

If aircraft developments of the 1950s had made concurrency merely routine, the ballistic missile developments in the latter part of the decade sanctified the approach. These developments—the Atlas, Thor, Titan, and Minuteman—were conducted under unique institutional arrangements, arrangements reflecting the national urgency of the programs and the widespread consensus that normal Air Force development organizations were ill-equipped to manage the programs. In effect, the regular Air Force development establishment was by-passed for these programs, with management control vested in an elite group of scientists and a small group of high-ranking Air Force officers. Schedules for these programs were indeed compressed. However, actual development efforts were not characterized by the elaborate development planning and early production commitments (before extensive tests) typical of the concurrent aircraft developments. Instead, the missile developments were characterized by multiple prototype approaches

[103] Klein, Glennan, and Schubert, *The Role of Prototypes*, pp. 11–29; and Marschak, "The Role of Project Histories," pp. 92–110, 117. The F-106 actually grew out of the F-102 development. The F-104 was a product of Lockheed's unique "skunkworks," a design bureau also responsible for the U-2 design of the 1950s and the YF-12/SR-71 design of the 1960s.

to major development tasks and early testing of hardware prototypes before production commitments were made. The unique environment and institutional arrangements for the missile programs made this opportunistic strategy possible. The flexible management that resulted made the programs a technical success. Unfortunately, when the perceived lessons of the ballistic missile experience were translated into organizational ritual in 1959, the scheduling aspects of the missile programs, their nominal concurrency, received great attention, while the institutional preconditions for that scheduling were ignored. The larger lesson of these programs, if acknowledged, would have implied major disruption of established development organizations.[104]

In the wake of the extremely challenging development of the first-generation ballistic missiles, aircraft seemed relatively easy design problems, within an easily extended state of the art.[105] Given the widespread misconception that concurrency had been responsible for success in the exotic missile developments, and given the routine application of the concept to fighter developments of the 1950s, concurrent schedules were applied rather naturally to the aircraft development that followed: the TFX.[106] After all, if aircraft were "relatively easy" design problems, why not save money and time and insure development success by concurrent development? That this inference might not be

[104] Perry, *System Development Strategies*, chaps. 3–5.

[105] Interviews 11 and 12. Moreover, DDR&E, McNamara's primary advisor on the early TFX decisions and later OSD's overseer for actual development efforts, was formed in 1958 primarily in response to the urgency and technical demands of the ballistic missile programs. DDR&E's formative experiences were in the missile programs, and the deputy directors of the organization had backgrounds in missile technologies (that is, in missile and related electronics technologies). The Director of DDR&E was a physicist. See U.S. House of Representatives, Committee on Government Operations, *Eleventh Report: Organization and Management of the Missile Programs*, Report, 86th Cong. 1st Sess. (1959), pp. 18–19.

[106] This view was articulated in Interviews 5, 9, 10, 11, and 12; cf. Adam Yarmolinsky, *The Military Establishment: Its Impacts on American Society* (New York: Harper and Row, 1971), p. 268

relevant to an advanced aircraft like the TFX—particularly in light of the stringent, bi-service requirements it had to meet—seems not to have entered the calculation. Concurrency simply was planned from the outset.

Hence, the Air Force's tradition of concurrent developments serves to explain why the development and production schedules of the TFX were so compressed. By the time of the TFX program, concurrent schedules had become the norm in fighter developments and had been notably sanctified by selective interpretations of the high-visibility missile programs. Concurrency was not a written rule for weapon developments, and its benefits in terms of development time were actually debatable. Nevertheless, it was simply the way the Air Force did business at the time of the F-111 program.[107]

To see the way in which concurrency constrained the time available for problem resolution, it is useful to examine the implications of schedule dates in the context of the development. Following the contract award, the contractor took his broad initial design and began to elaborate it into ever greater detail. The timing of this intensive design effort was determined by the scheduled date for the first flight of the aircraft, December 1964. If the plane were to fly then, it would have to roll off the production line for ground testing in October 1964. If the plane were to roll out in October 1964, then major assembly had to begin in June 1964. If major assembly were to begin in June 1964, then the first aircraft parts had to be fabricated in Decem-

---

[107] While there are exceptions, concurrency remains the norm on major programs, in spite of the outcry against concurrency in the late 1960s, and in spite of the "fly before you buy" policy of the early 1970s. The F-111 actually "flew" before it was "bought" (it was first flown four months before the initial production commitment). The F-15, showcase of the procurement reforms of the early 1970s, was scheduled for initial production commitment four months after its first flight, the same lapse as on the F-111. More will be said on this issue in Chapter VI. See U.S. Senate, Committee on Armed Services, *Fiscal Year 1973 Authorization for Military Procurement*, pp. 3598–3599.

ber 1963, only one year after the awarding of the development contract. If parts were to be fabricated then, drawings of these initial parts had to be released—that is, the design efforts on these parts had to be substantially completed—by October 1963, ten months after the contract award; and so forth.

In turn, the first flight date of the aircraft was derived from the scheduled operational dates of the F-111A and F-111B.[108] Yet these operational dates were dates for which there was "no rational requirement" other than that they were established before the contract competition and were only slightly adjusted thereafter.[109] Without anyone's having paid much attention to the consequences for resolving technical problems, these operational dates "worked back" to structure the time allocations for the entire development process.[110] Even though the operational dates were later

[108] Interview 16.

[109] The schedules were adjusted by six months during the source selection competition, to account for the unexpected delays in choosing the prime contractor for the program in 1962. Memorandum for the Director of Defense Research and Engineering, from Leonard Sullivan, Jr., dated October 1, 1964, re Report of PHOENIX/F-111B ad hoc group, printed in *TFX Hearings—Second Series*, Part 3, p. 481; *TFX Hearings—First Series*, Part 9, p. 1931; and Interview 11.

[110] This phenomenon is not rare: prominent schedule dates often take on a "life of their own," independent of any rationale behind their original establishment and in spite of their implications for the sequencing of technical efforts. A low-level example in the F-111 program is the scheduling of the second and third R&D prototypes of the F-111B: the first flight dates (and hence the timing of the design effort) on these planes was geared " 'to meet the PHOENIX development schedule,' " even as, simultaneously, the PHOENIX development schedule was geared to " 'having something available to put in [F-111B] aircraft #2 and #3 since they will be available.' " The tautology was lost on development organizations, although both the aircraft and the avionics design groups preferred more time. See Memorandum for the Director of Defense Research and Engineering, from Leonard Sullivan, Jr., dated October 1, 1964, re Report of PHOENIX/F-111B ad hoc group, printed in *TFX Hearings—Second Series*, Part 3, p. 481. Another striking example of this general phenomenon can be found in the Navy's DD-963 (DX) destroyer program. See J. W. Devanney III, "The DX Competition," *U.S. Naval Institute: Proceedings*, Vol. 101 (August 1975), p. 21.

modified, all development efforts had presumed the earlier operational dates and were, accordingly, sequenced by them.

Hence, the F-111 development was structured in its time dimension by the inflexible operational dates that concurrency assumed. The intense schedule pressure that resulted made it more difficult to integrate the new technology engines. Fixed design choices had to be made early: witness the selection of inlet designs in late 1963, only a year after the contract award. By the time engine-inlet problems were fully apparent and by the time the development process responded, the production of the aircraft was building up according to previously formulated schedules that in no way anticipated the inlet problems. As the efforts to resolve the stall problem proceeded, the production build-up continued unabated.[111] The incorporation of remedies became increasingly costly.

The fact that the schedules were maintained is, of course, a key to these problems, and in the F-111 program, schedule adherence is often attributed to the program's controversial nature.[112] Congress, it is said, would have looked upon any delay in the F-111 program as a manifestation of failure. Because of this latent political problem, it is argued, schedules had to be maintained. However, by looking at other, less controversial programs than the F-111, we can see the pattern of the F-111 development to be symptomatic of the rule, not an exception to it.

For example, the F-3H-1, an all-weather Navy fighter developed in the early 1950s, went through approximately five modifications in its engines in the course of its development. In June 1954, the Navy finally acknowledged that an entirely different engine was required. But by that time, 60 planes had already been produced, 38 of which had no engine at all, and only 30 of which could be retrofitted with

---

[111] *TFX Hearings—Second Series*, Part 3, p. 636.
[112] For example, Interview 15.

the suitable engine.[113] Another example is the F-100, an Air Force development, also of the early 1950s. The program was heavily concurrent. When signs of development problems appeared, suggestions were made for a relaxation of the schedules. No relaxations occurred, and a costly retrofit program was later required to cure a severe stability problem.[114] More recently, the Navy F-14 was to have had a significantly more powerful engine for all but the first three lots of its production. But when the more powerful engine lagged in development, the Navy maintained its schedules and ". . . rushed into buying the inferior engine."[115] Finally, when the F-15's engine failed an important qualifying test, all of the contractual innovations of the early 1970s did not alter the predictable result: schedules were maintained.[116]

This list could be extended indefinitely. The point is that schedules for development and early production are not characteristically revised. They tend to be maintained, and hence the fact that they are established a certain way is itself important.

[113] U.S. Senate, Committee on Armed Services, Preparedness Investigating Subcommittee, *Eighth Report, Navy Aircraft Procurement Program: Final Report on F-3H Development and Producement*, Report, 84th Cong., 2d Sess. (1956), pp. 3–7.

[114] Marschak, "The Role of Project Histories," pp. 92–96.

[115] Interview 11. See Michael Getler, "Navy Drops Hotter Model of the F-14," *Washington Post* (July 28, 1971), p. A1; U.S. Senate, Committee on Armed Services, *Fiscal Year 1973 Authorization for Military Procurement*, pp. 4019–4061; and U.S. Senate, Committee on Armed Services, *Fiscal Year 1975 Authorization for Military Procurement*, Hearings, 93d Cong., 2d Sess. (1974), pp. 5119–5122.

[116] "Air Force Probes F100 Engine," p. 18; Brownlow, "New Engine Standards," pp. 18–19; and U.S. Senate, Committee on Armed Services, *Fiscal Year 1975 Authorization for Military Procurement*, p. 2852. Note the contrast to one example of a non-concurrent development, the F-104. The F-104 was the only non-concurrent development among the Century Series fighters. The flexibility of the F-104's schedules allowed a complete change of engines after the first test flight and before production commenced—the only such change among the Century Series fighter developments. Ultimately, 2500 F-104s were produced, 2200 of them for American allies. See Marschak, "The Role of Project Histories," pp. 90–117, especially p. 115.

In the F-111 program, then, the highly compressed schedules were not likely to change much to accommodate the additional engine and inlet development time that was needed. As a result, delays in the formulation of inlet and engine remedies would translate into cost penalties—modifications would be increasingly expensive to perform as the production buildup continued—and performance penalties —anything other than minor "fixes" would be prohibitively expensive to incorporate in units whose assembly was nearly complete. There in fact were many delays in formulating compatibility remedies, delays occasioned by the suppression of the compatibility problems until the flight tests, the lull in wind-tunnel testing in 1965 when most participants avoided acknowledging the seriousness of the problems, the time-consuming frictions between General Dynamics and Pratt & Whitney, and the contractual ambiguities that left it to the government itself to develop a complete solution. Some of these delays, especially the inter-contractor frictions and the contractual ambiguities, could have been reduced by more aggressive initiatives from Defense Department civilians. However, like the lower-levels of the development process, high-level officials were insensitive to the costs of delay, even as they sanctioned adherence to established program schedules. The next section will describe their actions and their evolving perceptions in detail.

The View from the Pentagon

As regards the Air Force version of the F-111, there was very little Secretarial involvement in the development process prior to the first flight of the aircraft.[117] Following the contract award in 1962, but before the first flight in 1964, McNamara reportedly did not attend any meetings dealing

---

[117] However, numerous meetings were held in 1964 to address the problem of weight growth in the Navy version. These will be discussed in Chapter v.

215

specifically with the F-111A development. Instead, his involvement was confined to a routine monitoring of the program. He kept informed of certain aspects of the program through memoranda from his service Secretaries.[118] For example, in early 1964 McNamara requested that a report on the program's status be submitted to him. This report was to detail ". . . original versus the currently estimated force requirements, development costs and production costs."[119] It was, in addition, to provide the then-current performance estimates for the aircraft.

After the first flight of the aircraft, however, McNamara and his Secretarial colleagues became more extensively involved. Their greater involvement was first occasioned by the scheduled requirement to establish contractual commitments for production, shortly after the first flight. Later, of course, the persistence of major technical problems intensified their involvement.

The first flight of the aircraft took place, on schedule, in December 1964. To high-level defense officials, this timely first flight was an event of considerable significance. As Harold Brown, the Director of Defense Research and Engineering (and soon to become Secretary of the Air Force), said in subsequent testimony, "There is no question that the Air Force version is going to be extremely successful. The first flight occurred only two years after the award of the contract, which is a remarkable achievement."[120] Eugene Zuckert, then Secretary of the Air Force, recalled the first flight achievement in the following terms, shortly after he left office in 1965: "The first flight of the TFX (now the F-

[118] Interview 13. The bulk of the memoranda that the Secretary is known to have seen dealt with the Navy version. See, for example, *TFX Hearings—Second Series*, Part 2, pp. 401–410.

[119] Memorandum for the Director of Defense Research and Engineering, the Secretary of the Navy, and the Secretary of the Air Force, from Robert S. McNamara, dated January 18, 1964, re TFX program status, printed in *TFX Hearings—Second Series*, Part 2, p. 400.

[120] U.S. Senate, Committee on Armed Services, *Military Procurement Authorizations: Fiscal Year 1966*, p. 489.

111 and FB-111) in December, 1964, just two years after the contract was signed, may well prove to have been the most effective documentation of the McNamara technique of 'project definition.' "[121] The meeting of contractual schedules was being viewed as testimony to self-evident development success. This impression of success is important in light of two facts. First, it was belied by the existence of the severe compressor-stall problem. The people in the Pentagon were not aware of the severity of the problem until July 1965, even though the F-111A had stalled on the ground on its first flight and had, by the end of June, accumulated 105 hours of test time and experienced repeated stalls in flight.[122] Second, in April 1965, before the awareness of the stall problem, and before the government had any flight test data of its own, the commitment to production of the aircraft was made on schedule.[123] The commitment to production was in part rationalized on the basis of established schedules' having been met by the contractor.[124]

The justification for the commitment to production, however, went beyond the simple recognition of schedule adherence by the contractor. In April 1965, Secretary Zuckert wrote a long memorandum to McNamara, detailing the current status of the program and the pros and cons of entering production.[125] The memorandum begins by noting various performance deficiencies in the F-111A: combat ceiling, ferry range, and sea-level, supersonic dash range. But the memorandum fails to mention the stall problem.

[121] Eugene M. Zuckert, "The Service Secretary: Has He a Useful Role?" *Foreign Affairs*, Vol. 44 (April 1966), p. 474.

[122] General Dynamics, "GD F-111 Category I Flight Test Progress Report," dated 30 June 1965, p. 14; and Interview 14.

[123] *TFX Hearings—First Series*, Part 2, p. 478; and *TFX Hearings—Second Series*, Part 3, pp. 498, 633.

[124] Memorandum for the Secretary of Defense, from Secretary of the Air Force Eugene Zuckert, dated April 13, 1965, re F-111 Program (from the files of the Permanent Subcommittee on Investigations, Committee on Government Operations, U.S. Senate, Exhibit 26W-51 of *TFX Hearings—Second Series*).

[125] Ibid.

Indeed, the thrust of the memorandum is optimistic, as is Zuckert's summary appraisal that the Air Force is satisfied that the F-111A will "meet the requirements of the tactical air mission in the future." In support of this appraisal, Zuckert goes on to assert: "The Air Force believes that the improvement normal in any aircraft will take place here. To the extent that the Research and Development program does not produce an aircraft according to specifications in the contract, the Air Force intends to employ the strict *remedy of deficiencies clause.*"[126] This rationalization was to be repeated subsequently in other memoranda by other Pentagon officials commenting on the desirability of continuing production. The "improvement normal in any aircraft"[127] would likely relieve any deficiencies that devel-

[126] Ibid. Emphasis added.

[127] This is a common assumption in weapons acquisition programs. When development problems appear, it will quickly be assumed that adequate technical improvements and performance remedies will ultimately be forthcoming, either in time to be phased into the production process or, at least, in time to be retrofitted in systems already produced. The assumption is a convenient one, as it sanctions acquiescence in an on-going development and production process in spite of any revealed development problems. While often realistic, it can in other instances be a self-deceiving and very costly assumption for defense officials to make. The important points on this issue, as on many others in this study, are: (1) whether or not the weight of objective evidence realistically indicates that problems are sufficiently tractable to admit to timely, cost-effective solutions; and (2) whether decision makers seem actually to respond to this evidence as it develops over time, or whether, by contrast, they seem to be locked into self-deceiving myths of future improvement and to resist indications that the improvements will not be forthcoming (the latter being an interesting phenomenon in cybernetic terms). In the discussion of engine-inlet and other problems that immediately follows in the text, we will encounter examples of self-deceptive expectations of timely product improvements. For examples of how costly these expectations may prove to be, see discussions of the Mark II avionics program, the F-111 wing box modifications, and the C-5A wing fatigue/retrofit problems in John W. Finney, "C-5A Jet Repairs to Cost 1.5 Billion," *New York Times* (December 15, 1975), pp. 1, 21; Robert R. Ropelewski, "C-5A Category 2 Test Finish Near," *Aviation Week and Space Technology*, Vol. 94 (May 3, 1971), pp. 36–44; *TFX Hearings —Second Series*, Part 2, pp. 262, 289–290; U.S. Congress, Joint Economic Committee, Subcommittee on Economy in Government, *Mili-*

oped. If this failed, the "remedy of deficiencies" clause in the contract[128] would provide the leverage necessary to secure adequate performance.

By the logic of the cybernetic paradigm, contracts are uncertainty-absorbing devices, which impose highly structured plans on an uncertain environment, *plans which are followed as if they foreordained an optimal course of events.*[129] While there may be substantial evidence available to challenge the wisdom of the plans contained in the contract, ultimate program outcomes remain a matter of great uncertainty. This uncertainty provides decision makers with wide interpretive latitude for unconsciously conceptualizing problems in such a way that trade-offs among important program attributes seem to disappear. In spite of unfavorable information on the progress of the program, decision makers still will tend to reconcile them-

---

tary Budget and National Economic Priorities, pp. 799–835; and U.S. Senate, Committee on Armed Services, *Fiscal Year 1973 Authorization for Military Procurement,* p. 1190.

[128] The F-111 production contract contained a so-called "correction of deficiencies" (COD) clause, which placed a financial onus on the contractor for any performance shortfalls versus specifications. The contract was a fixed-price contract; however, if the contracted price (the "target price") was exceeded in the efforts to meet existing specifications, the government and the contractor would share the additional expense, in proportions of 85 percent and 15 percent respectively. They would do so up to 120 percent of the target price (i.e., up to the "ceiling price"), at which point the contractor would assume the complete additional financial burden for meeting specifications. On government-directed changes in specifications, the government would assume the full burden for the negotiated target cost of the change, but the COD clause would be effective on increments over that cost (*TFX Hearings—Second Series,* Part 2, pp. 269–272; and Interview 16). By contrast, on a so-called cost-plus-fixed-fee contract, the government covers the full expense for (and hence assumes the risk of) obtaining performance and design goals that it has established.

[129] See Richard M. Cyert and James G. March, *A Behavioral Theory of the Firm* (Englewood Cliffs: Prentice-Hall, 1963), pp. 105–106; and John D. Steinbruner, *The Cybernetic Theory of Decision: New Dimensions of Political Analysis* (Princeton: Princeton University Press, 1974), chaps. 3 and 4.

selves to the programmed course of events. Characteristically, they will infer favorable outcomes for programmed alternatives and will impute unwarranted certainty to these inferences. They will selectively process information in order to confirm the inferences and to resist the threatening implications of unfavorable data.[130]

These theoretical propositions accord reasonably well with Secretarial decisions on maintaining schedules. The deficiencies clause in the F-111 contract established a legalistic attribution of risk to the contractor, which, in the minds of the Secretaries, shifted to the contractor the full responsibility and the financial burden for meeting specifications. Whatever the test reports on performance or the disagreements between General Dynamics and Pratt & Whitney, production could continue, since the Secretaries presumed that, in the end, the prime contractor would be contractually required to achieve specified performance—and with little financial risk to the government, since development efforts were governed by a fixed-price contract.

Clearly, this was a consummate avoidance of uncertainty, particularly when associated with the expectation of "improvements normal in any aircraft." In the first place, it ignored the actual legal prospects for the enforcement of the deficiencies clause. Defense officials now uncritically assumed that the clause would be effective; yet no one, including these officials, had really paid much attention (or would pay much attention) to the provisions of the contractual interface documents, documents which defined the mutual obligations among the prime contractor, the engine contractor, and the government.[131] Legal responsibility for

---

[130] Steinbruner, *Cybernetic Theory*, chap. 4.

[131] As the Air Force F-111 System Program Director (SPD) surmised in 1969: "Well, we feel that [the fault] is about a halfway split down the middle between the engine manufacturer and the airframe manufacturer" (U.S. House of Representatives, Committee on Armed Services, *Hearings on Military Posture* [1969], p. 3212). We noted earlier in the text that General Dynamics' inlet met the distortion index criterion defined in the interface documents of the

the engine-inlet problems proved impossible to assign. On these problems, as on others, the deficiencies clause was unenforceable.[132] At the same time, apart from the legal specifics of the situation, the Secretaries' expectation of future improvements ignored the realistic technical prospects for resolving the stall problems and achieving specified performance. Later events would confirm that most of the expectations of "normal improvements" were exaggerated.[133] Nevertheless, the uncritical inferences of contractor responsibility and inevitable improvements served, in the Secretaries' minds, to make the trade-off between continuing production and achieving specified performance seem to disappear. By conceptualizing the program in this way,

---

contract. We should add here that Pratt & Whitney's engines met that company's performance obligations to the government. According to Air Force Secretary Harold Brown, "The engine contractor contracted on the basis of engine performance demonstrated on the ground. The airframe contractor contracted for inflight performance on the basis that the Government would provide an engine with a certain performance." In the end, the stall responsibility was the government's, as the Pratt & Whitney engines in effect did not allow the government to meet its contractual obligations to General Dynamics. See London, "VFX—The Navy's Choice," pp. 55–56; and Memorandum for the Record, by John F. Dealy, Office of the General Counsel, Air Force, dated May 1, 1967, re contractual requirements for production of F-111 engines, excerpted in TFX Hearings—Second Series, Part 3, p. 636. See also p. 623 of these hearings.

The deficiencies clause also proved difficult to enforce on other major development problems. This was in part a result of government oversights in writing the contracts (oversights similar to those that occurred in specifying engine and inlet requirements). It was also a result of the large volume of contract changes enacted to accommodate specification changes and other exigencies. These changes proved difficult to trace. Finally, it was the result of ultimate government acceptance of the production aircraft. Once the government accepted production aircraft, as predictably it would when the aircraft became available, there was some question as to whether this acceptance implied that the contractor had discharged its responsibility. London, "VFX—The Navy's Choice," pp. 55–56; and TFX Hearings—Second Series, Part 3, pp. 561, 631–637.

[132] Interviews 12 and 16.

[133] These performance deficiencies were described in detail in Chapter II.

221

the Secretaries avoided difficult choices in the months and years ahead when the performance estimates of the aircraft gradually declined, while production continued relatively unabated.[134]

In 1965, for example, estimates indicated that high drag levels on the F-111A would decrease the aircraft's ferry range and its sea-level, supersonic dash range. Optimistic performance projections were made at the time, based upon assumptions that General Dynamics would reduce the drag to acceptable levels. But as a former Air Force R&D official observed, "This [the drag problem] is the classic 'correction of deficiencies' problem. We thought General Dynamics would clean it up."[135] For the drag problem—as for most performance deficiencies at this stage of the program—the contractor's onerous legal responsibility for attaining specified performance was seen as inducing intensive efforts that would, in the future, resolve the problems. After all, the contractor was *required* to achieve specified performance. But General Dynamics could not clean up the drag, and F-111A performance never achieved the

---

[134] Note here and in the discussion that follows in the text how aptly Steinbruner's notion of "inferences of transformation" or "wishful thinking" describes the Secretarial behavior we observe. Steinbruner argues that decision makers frequently engage in long-range projections and take these projections seriously for decision purposes: "Many of these projections, of course, follow normal logic and are established on the basis of available evidence and deductive inference. However, there is a class whose strength derives not from objective evidence, but from the role they play in managing complex belief structures. When a set of beliefs is under pressure from inconsistent information being processed in a short time frame, it is possible to maintain consistency without changing the beliefs by casting them in a long-range time frame and adopting the inference of transformation; namely, that the immediate situation will succumb to a favorable trend over time. . . . The strength of transformation beliefs in terms of cognitive theory derives from the fact that they protect the established belief structure from negative evidence and from the necessity which would otherwise arise of undergoing massive restructuring." See Steinbruner, *Cybernetic Theory*, pp. 116–117.

[135] Interview 12.

levels projected in the optimistic estimates.[136] After a prolonged period of being "ratcheted down," bit by bit, to the performance levels ultimately attained, the government accepted the planes anyway.[137]

There are other cases in which we can see a similar imputation of favorable future performance, drawn from the deficiencies clause. In May 1965, one month after the production letter contract was signed, the Air Force General Counsel's office acknowledged that the government could not reject any of the planned 23 R&D prototype aircraft for failure to meet specifications; however, the General Counsel's office went on to argue that: "This is an immaterial omission in a development program of this type. The important thing is the Government's right to specific performance established in the Correction of Deficiencies clause."[138] A year later, after Air Force and Navy flight tests had begun to reveal performance deficiencies in the F-111, Air Force Secretary Brown wrote a memorandum to McNamara recommending a definitive production contract (that is, final approval of detailed terms for the contract).

[136] *TFX Hearings—Second Series*, Part 3, p. 514; "U.S. Air Force Selected Acquisition Report on the F-111A/D/E/F," dated December 31, 1969, pp. 2–6; and Interview 12. In his memorandum recommending the authorization of production in 1965, Zuckert noted that the projected shortfall in sea-level, supersonic dash was "particularly troublesome." The contract specification was 210 miles, the General Dynamics estimate was 176 miles, and the Air Force estimate was 106 miles. Yet, in the end, the actual dash was only 30 miles. Memorandum for the Secretary of Defense, from Secretary of the Air Force Eugene Zuckert, dated April 13, 1965, re F-111 program (from the files of the Permanent Subcommittee on Investigations, Committee on Government Operations, U.S. Senate, Exhibit 26W-51 of the *TFX Hearings—Second Series*).

[137] The careful reader will have noted that the argument being presented in this section offers an important supplement to Chapter III's discussion of nuclear-mission issues. The concluding section of the present chapter will make the connections explicit.

[138] Memorandum for the Record, from Edmund J. Kelly, Office of Air Force General Counsel, dated May 14, 1965, excerpted in *TFX Hearings—Second Series*, Part 3, p. 635.

After recognizing certain performance deficiencies, Dr. Brown concluded that the correction of deficiencies clause "preserves the Government's position to obtain acceptable aircraft performance."[139]

Yet the flight-test evidence was revealing that anticipated improvements, such as the reduction in drag, were not forthcoming. Consequently, the Air Force assembled a review group to evaluate the performance status of the F-111s. In establishing the review group, the Air Force requested that General Dynamics and Pratt & Whitney each present "their company's plan for achieving contract required performance of the F-111A and F-111B. . . ."[140] The companies were still expected to solve the problems and achieve contract-specified performance—in spite of the fact that performance was seriously deficient versus specifications, that the basic F-111 configuration was firm, and that aircraft were coming down the assembly line. As Dr. John Foster (who had earlier replaced Harold Brown as Director of Defense Research and Engineering) wrote in July 1966, the philosophy of the F-111 contract negotiations ". . . assumes that an 'acceptable' aircraft will be achieved. . . ."[141]

The Air Force review concluded that the General Dynamics drag estimates were optimistic. However, the report went on to say that a significant part of the problem was "the lack of progress on the part of the airframe and engine contractors in obtaining credible data from which to reliably determine the extent to which the deficiencies in

[139] Memorandum for the Secretary of Defense, from Secretary of the Air Force Dr. Harold Brown, dated July 2, 1966, re definitive contract for F-111 production, excerpted in *TFX Hearings—Second Series*, Part 3, p. 635.

[140] Telegram from Aeronautical System Division, USAF, to General Dynamics and Pratt & Whitney, dated July 21, 1966, re executive management review on performance of F-111A and F-111B, excerpted in *TFX Hearings—Second Series*, Part 3, p. 510.

[141] Memorandum to the Deputy Secretary of Defense, from Director of Defense Research and Engineering Dr. John S. Foster, dated July 6, 1966, re definitization of F-111 production contract, excerpted in *TFX Hearings—Second Series*, Part 3, p. 636.

cruise performance can be corrected."[142] More generally, there was at this time (mid-1966) an emerging awareness among high-level officials that General Dynamics and Pratt & Whitney were not fully cooperating with each other. Each contractor was seen as blaming the other for propulsion-related deficiencies, particularly the stall problem.[143]

Hence, there was now evidence not only that the plane would have performance deficiencies (there had been estimates of this all along) but also evidence that the contractors, the parties that the Secretaries expected to resolve the problems, were not themselves working together to accomplish this resolution. Each was blaming the other for performance deficiencies. Since the engines and airframe operate in complicated interdependence, it would be difficult under the circumstances to allocate responsibility for these deficiencies between the two contractors.

Needless to say, this inability to assign legal responsibility severely threatened Secretarial mechanisms for suppressing uncertainty and avoiding hard choices in the program. In particular, it threatened the means by which the contract allowed them to conceptualize the program so that the trade-off between continuing aircraft production and achieving specified performance disappeared. If the prime contractor no longer bore full responsibility for meeting performance, he could no longer be expected to engage in the intense problem-solving effort necessary to secure specified performance in the future. Indeed, the evidence indicated that the ambiguity of legal responsibility had actually impeded these problem-solving efforts, as relations between General Dynamics and Pratt & Whitney had deteriorated.

To compound these problems, Senator McClellan's Permanent Subcommittee on Investigations at this time (Au-

[142] Aeronautical Systems Division, USAF, "F-111 Independent Review Group and Supporting Tabs: 1–3 August, 1966," pp. 9 and 10 (from the files of the Permanent Subcommittee on Investigations, Committee on Government Operations, U.S. Senate, Exhibit 23 of *TFX Hearings—Second Series*).

[143] Interview 12.

gust 1966) resumed its investigation of the F-111 program.[144] (The investigation had been suspended in December 1963, following President Kennedy's assassination.) The renewed interest of this powerful skeptic was a further threat to the Secretaries. The promise of favorable *future* performance now might not be enough. A perceived foe of the program now would be fully aware of the severity of present problems.

In response to these threats, the Secretaries did not question the basic premise that allowed them to avoid acknowledging the seriousness of program problems—that is, they did not question that the contractors would or could satisfactorily meet performance specifications in the future. Instead, in the face of the threatening information, they in effect restored the premise itself by instituting the "Icarus" meetings in August 1966.

As one participant in the meetings suggested to the author, "The Icarus meetings were a way of getting General Dynamics and Pratt & Whitney to cooperate with each other, by forcing them to sit down together."[145] The weekly Icarus meetings between the Secretary of Defense and the Chairmen of the Board and Presidents of General Dynamics and Pratt & Whitney (plus their staffs) brought the highest possible level of pressure to bear on the contractors. With the contractors working together again, the attribution of responsibility would again seem feasible to the Secretaries. The achievement of specified performance again could be required, and the inherent contradiction between continuing production and meeting specified performance would be dissolved for the Secretaries.[146] Moreover, as

---

[144] *TFX Report*, p. 2.   [145] Interview 12.

[146] This interpretation explains why Grumman officials, as well as Air Force and Navy program officials, were not invited to these meetings at the outset. The efforts of all of these officials would clearly be required for any rescuing of the *program*. The focus of the Icarus meetings on General Dynamics and Pratt & Whitney followed naturally from the key inferences that had, in the minds of the Secretaries, reconciled the continued production bulid-up with the growing evidence of development problems.

specified performance was achieved, the political problem of the McClellan investigation would diminish.

Thus, the common interpretation of the Icarus meetings—that McNamara assumed personal management of the program to rescue it and to salvage his reputation—is only part of the story.[147] The interpretation offered here suggests that what McNamara really was rescuing was a key premise for maintaining cognitive consistency, a premise that had served to resolve the inconsistency presented by the continuation of production in the face of pessimistic flight reports and ever-decreasing performance projections. As Steinbruner has postulated, such threats to consistency will be resolved by the simplest inference necessary to restore consistency and to maintain belief structures.[148] In the F-111 program, the simplest inference to restore consistency was the one drawn from the deficiencies clause, which had been at the center of the Secretaries' earlier maintenance of program schedules and performance expectations.[149]

The Icarus meetings appropriately began with a list of sixteen "problems": that is, sixteen performance specifications and the current estimates of performance against these specifications.[150] It seemed that one could talk of meeting

[147] See, for example, *TFX Report*, p. 69.

[148] Steinbruner, *Cybernetic Theory*, pp. 101–102, 114–121.

[149] As noted earlier in the text, many people contend that the schedules of the F-111 program were maintained because schedule delays were politically infeasible. The argument above suggests that such political considerations might actually have provided an additional simple inference to restore consistency when schedules were maintained. In confronting reports of deficient performance, McNamara might well have said that schedules could not be altered because "McClellan would kill the program if we delayed it." An inference of this type would be fully consistent with the assumptions of the cybernetic paradigm. The simple imputation of a potential political problem would not itself imply an analytic understanding of the problem, any more than the imputation of a "deficiencies-clause" solution indicated a deep analytic understanding of the efficacy of that clause.

[150] See "Original F-111 Problem List," a list of problems with which the Icarus meetings began, in *TFX Hearings—Second Series*, Part 3, p. 543.

specifications again. According to one observer, there was a "binary atmosphere" in these meetings. Where a performance deficiency existed, something was "wrong" that had to be "fixed."[151]

The engine-inlet compatibility problems were a recurrent theme of the meetings, as a cycle of attempted stall improvements and resulting performance measurements was pursued. In the course of these efforts, McNamara was concerned that engine and inlet specifications be firmly established, in order to clarify stall responsibility:

> "Continuing the discussion, Mr. McNamara asked where responsibility for the engine stall problem might lie: with the airframe contractors? With engine contractor, or we just don't know? Dr. Brown said we don't know. . . . [A DOD engineer] said that no engineer knows enough about the stall mechanism to write specifications. The Secretary replied that there should be no production contract until specifications can be written. . . ."[152]

Of course, there already was a production contract, but for McNamara to recognize its full implications for the correction of performance problems would be for him once again to threaten the premises that had sustained his adherence

[151] Interview 9. One possible contributing factor to the Secretaries' underestimation of the complexity of the problems they confronted was the lack of aeronautical engineering expertise in DDR&E. The DDR&E was dominated by experts from strategic missile technologies throughout this period and tended to underestimate the difficulty of aeronautical engineering problems (Interviews 10 and 11). To strengthen DDR&E's expertise in this area, McNamara and Foster brought William R. Laidlaw to the Pentagon in November 1966, to be Foster's special assistant on F-111 issues. Laidlaw, a Vice President of Research and Engineering for North American Aviation, had a doctorate in aeronautical engineering from Massachusetts Institute of Technology and was hired to keep McNamara and Foster "better informed on the technical problems of the F-111." See the interview with Dr. Laidlaw in "William R. Laidlaw: Defense's F-111 Expert," *Armed Force Management*, Vol. 13 (December 1966), p. 29.

[152] Notes of the preliminary Icarus meeting, March 30, 1967, quoted in *TFX Hearings—Second Series*, Part 3, p. 558.

to development and production schedules. Indeed, it would threaten the *raison d'être* of the Icarus meetings themselves. In addition to the stall problem, the Icarus meetings focused on the need to meet a broad range of performance specifications and the impossibility of allowing production unless specifications were met. As McNamara indicated in the first Icarus meeting, "1963 specifications must be met and . . . lesser performance would not do."[153] But by this time, the basic configuration of the aircraft was already beyond the stage of substantial design improvement. Since early 1965, the design efforts could at best only be problem- and refinement-oriented.[154] Moreover, the production cycle had commenced sixteen months earlier, in April 1965. Whatever the decisions McNamara made on production schedules, he would be dealing with a full-scale production line.[155] The expectations of future achievement of specified performance (the premise drawn from the deficiencies clause) were again being threatened, since the "future" was now beign foreclosed by the production build-up.

McNamara and his associates resisted the full meaning of this build-up, however. A sampling of comments made in the course of the Icarus meetings graphically demonstrates their resistance:

[153] Notes of the Icarus meeting, August 25, 1966, quoted in *TFX Hearings—Second Series*, Part 3, p. 544. In spite of McNamara's enhanced awareness of conventional-mission problems by this time, his focus in these meetings was on established specifications within the existing design, which emphasized performance criteria for the nuclear mission. In the previous chapter we noted that the specifications which structure the design effort also structure the definition of performance problems. Where conventional mission problems would be reported in qualitative terms (e.g., "underpowered," "lack of maneuverability," etc.) or relatively unrecognized quantitative terms, the nuclear-mission deficiencies would be reported in specific, widely recognized, contract-relevant, quantitative terms. See notes of the Icarus meetings, excerpted in *TFX Hearings—Second Series*, Part 3, pp. 542–568.

[154] Interview 16. For one indication of the degree of improvement possible at this point, see *TFX Hearings—Second Series*, Part 3, pp. 500–501.

[155] *TFX Hearings—Second Series*, Part 3, p. 633; and Interview 16.

"Mr. McNamara repeated that he could not allow production until he was sure of aircraft performance. . . . With the F-111A, the problem essentially was when to go into production."—*September 10, 1966*

"Mr. McNamara cautioned that no contract could be signed until he was assured of resolution on a number of the outstanding problems. Dr. Foster pointed out that production was already taking place."—*November 4, 1966*

Mr. Vance: "We do not want to go into production until we have satisfactorily completed R&D." . . . Dr. Flax observed that we are already proceeding with production, to which Mr. Davis [President of General Dynamics] added that General Dynamics had been committed to production since April 1965.—*January 14, 1967*

Dr. Foster said that proceeding now ran counter to the "philosophy of not accepting aircraft or allowing production, until satisfactory performance were demonstrated. Dr. Foster suggested that the program was in need of [a] 6-month, or longer, slippage to accommodate performance proof. . . ." Mr. Widmer [a General Dynamics engineer] replied that the airplanes were 90 percent built already.—*April 29, 1967*[156]

The Secretaries were not aware of the extent or the complexity of the production process that they had authorized back in April 1965. As an Icarus participant indicated to the author, "High DOD officials had the image that they had authorized only a few, long lead-time forgings. They

[156] Notes of the Icarus meetings (for dates indicated in the text), quoted in *TFX Hearings—Second Series*, Part 3, pp. 548, 552, 555–556, 560. In the quotations above, those portions offset by quotation marks are taken directly from the notes of an Air Force officer in attendance at the meetings. Those portions not in quotation marks represent paraphrasings of the officer's notes by McClellan Committee staff members. The general veracity of this material was confirmed by a confidential interview with an Icarus participant.

sustained the illusion that they could still choose."[157] By sustaining this illusion, the Secretaries avoided recognizing the costs of delays in developing inlet remedies. The Triple Plow I remedies could be incorporated in those planes already well along in production, but by that time these modifications were expensive and could not remove certain enduring performance penalties.

The F-111 production contract is again important for understanding Secretarial perceptions, in this case the Secretarial illusions on production. The Secretaries confused the evolution of the production *contract* (from letter contract to definitive contract), with the evolution of production *itself* (from "a few, long lead-time forgings" to full-scale manufacture).[158] Because of their confusion and because they believed that "the contractor was going to fix any problems under the deficiencies clause," they allowed the production line to gather momentum as the deficiencies persisted.[159]

When the production contract was actually definitized in May 1967, the Triple Plow I modifications had just been approved for production.[160] Later in 1967, the Triple Plow II inlet was flight tested and shown to be a complete solution to the stall problem, one that would allow the retrofitting of larger engines. However, by that time the inexorable prior movement of planes down the production line had made a larger inlet for these planes out of the question.[161]

[157] Interview 12.

[158] See, for example, notes of the preliminary Icarus meeting of November 4, 1966, quoted in *TFX Hearings—Second Series*, Part 3, p. 552.

[159] Interview 12.

[160] Notes of the Icarus meeting, April 27, 1967, quoted in *TFX Hearings—Second Series*, Part 3, p. 559–560.

[161] Summary report to Tristan J. Keating, Chief, Systems Engineering Division, Aeronautical Systems Division, Air Force Systems Command, from F. T. Rall, Chief, Aeromechanics Division, F-111 System Program Office, dated May 11, 1967, re F-111 Inlet Status, printed in *TFX Hearings–Second Series*, Part 3, p. 519; and Interview 16.

ACCOMMODATING THE PROGRAMMED
COURSE OF EVENTS

The engine-inlet compatibility problems are more or less typical of the difficulties that are encountered in major weapons programs. The compatibility problems were substantially "solved" in the end, but not without large, unanticipated expenditures—approximately 100 million dollars —and certain enduring performance penalties. Together, the engine-inlet and nuclear-mission problems offer a useful perspective on the frequently troublesome responses of the development process to normal development difficulties.

The compatibility problems resulted from a pattern of applying old design approaches for propulsion integration to a new design problem. Because this new design problem was construed as a standard one, development efforts concentrated on satisfying traditional measures of engine-inlet compatibility. Yet these measures camouflaged important technical uncertainties. Only the persistently negative information produced by actual flight tests forced the development process to reconceive the integration problem and to modify initial design approaches.

This delayed appreciation of the integration problem would not have been so serious if development and production schedules, as well as the whole intricate maze of program plans, had provided greater leeway for problem-solving efforts. However, in a carryover of standard development practices of the 1950s, the concurrency concept was routinely applied to the program, imparting important rigidities to development organizations even as it imposed potentially intense schedule pressures on all problem-solving efforts. This potential for pressure was in fact realized, as the schedules were substantially maintained through the initial years of production of the plane. The costs of altering the schedules were an important analytic reason for maintaining them. But given this schedule adherence, remedies were destined to be expensive, especially if they were delayed. Unfortunately, some serious delays did occur. The

Secretaries appear to have been insensitive to the costs that resulted. Indeed, they appear to have avoided acknowledging the costs inherent in *any* decision on the compatibility problems. They assumed that favorable performance could be contractually required of the contractors and would (through "normal improvements") be achieved in the future. Later, they resisted acknowledging the full scope of the production effort. These Secretarial inferences made the costs of adhering to established schedules seem to disappear. The prime contracts were a strikingly fertile source for these unrealistic inferences. The compatibility solutions were expensive and incomplete as a result.

This explanation supplements the previous chapter's argument that the development process acted slowly and with few dramatic initiatives to resolve the multi-purpose deficiencies stemming from the F-111's nuclear-mission emphasis. If, as the Secretaries presumed, favorable performance could be required of the contractor and would be achieved in the future, the need for aggressive initiatives would disappear—performance deficiencies would be remedied in the natural course of events. *The same pressure that was expected to induce the contractor to develop compatibility improvements would induce the contractor to develop performance improvements.* Recall, for example, Secretary Zuckert's memorandum urging a commitment to production in 1965. After noting numerous deficiencies in the F-111's performance, Secretary Zuckert nonetheless recommended an early production commitment, since "the improvement normal in any aircraft will take place here" and, to the extent specified performance is not achieved, the Air Force "intends to employ the strict remedy of deficiencies clause."[162] At least through 1967, the Secretaries' conceptualization of the program helped them to avoid con-

[162] Memorandum for the Secretary of Defense, from Secretary of the Air Force Eugene Zuckert, dated April 13, 1965, re F-111 Program (from the files of the Permanent Subcommittee on Investigations, Committee on Government Operations, U.S. Senate, Exhibit 26W-51 of the *TFX Hearings—Second Series*).

fronting not only compatibility problems but also performance problems.

This experience emphasizes the tendency of the development process to avoid acknowledging major uncertainties
and to adhere instead to previously established methods
and sequences. Along with the discussion of design decomposition in Chapter III, it underscores the importance of the
basic structures and plans imposed at the outset of a development. Since the uncertainties in major weapon programs are too great for all significant development problems to be anticipated,[163] these plans and structures almost
inevitably will fail to accommodate critical dimensions of
the development task. Nonetheless, the development process will proceed as if all uncertainties had been anticipated.
By the time unforeseen development problems are revealed,
substantial commitments already will have been made to a
specific design. At that point, the revision of technical approaches and program plans will be costly and disruptive.
Program officials will face powerful pressures to reconcile
the unanticipated problems to the established program
schedules. These officials will avoid acknowledging the hard
choices with which they are presented. They will, irrepressibly it seems, see the problems in ways that make the hard
choices disappear. The inevitable uncertainty surrounding
such problems will provide wide interpretive latitude for
officials to make these selective, frequently self-deceiving
interpretations. Defense officials, then, are unlikely to institute aggressive actions to resolve emergent development
problems. Characteristically they will make conservative
choices that accommodate the programmed course of
events, even as the development process over which they

[163] Even on relatively low-risk developments, developments which
seem to require no major advances in the existing state of the art,
design goals are frequently unattainable and important uncertainties are not wholly anticipated in initial development plans. For a
graphic illustration of this point, see Robert L. Perry, A Prototype
Strategy for Development, Rand Memorandum No. RM-5597-1-PR
(July 1972), pp. 16–26.

preside will act slowly to revise established technical approaches. This behavior necessarily makes "normal" problems costly, in terms of the performance and lead time as well as the expense of major weapon systems. Moreover, it identifies the critical limits to Secretarial initiative and perception once a major weapons program has begun. These limits constituted an important part of McNamara's dilemma on the mission and inlet problems. As we will observe in the next chapter, they constituted an equally important part of his dilemma on Navy development problems.

The F-111B: The Navy Version of the F-111 (Courtesy of the General Dynamics Corporation).

CHAPTER V

"Born in Sin": The Development and Cancellation of the F-111B

The inlet and mission problems addressed thus far in this study are fairly typical of the ones encountered in major weapon system developments. However, the central issues of the development of the Navy version—the weight growth, the redesign decisions, and the program's cancellation—go to the heart of the unique, bi-service character of the F-111 program. An examination of these latter issues will reveal how the basic organizational innovation of the F-111 program—commonality in the development and procurement of a major weapon system—was thwarted.

The chapter begins by presenting the Navy's own analytic explanation for the main anomalies of the F-111B development. A critical review of the Navy's position will suggest a different explanation, one emphasizing how the Navy's subordinate role influenced Navy behavior in the program. The third section of the chapter will examine how McNamara and his colleagues responded to this Navy behavior. Drawing upon the results of the F-111B development and of the other recent bi-service acquisition programs, the final section hints at certain guidelines for achieving success in bi-service ventures.

THE APPROPRIATE CANCELLATION: THE NAVY'S POSITION ON THE F-111B DEVELOPMENT

The key question was whether Navy requirements were to be taken seriously; if they were, the F-111B was an inadequate airplane.
                                        —Navy Program Official[1]

[1] Interview 9.

The Navy's position on the F-111B is a key to understanding what went wrong in the plane's development. Although subordinate in the management of the program, the Navy was the service that would be using the F-111B. For the F-111B to be deployed, the Navy would ultimately have to be satisfied with its capabilities (or, at least, to acquiesce in its deficiencies). In the end, however, the Navy was neither satisfied nor acquiescent. In late 1967, after a long string of attempts by General Dynamics to improve the F-111B's performance, high-level Navy officials began their successful effort to cancel the F-111B.

The present section will briefly examine the Navy's position on the F-111B throughout the program and will explore the assumptions behind the Navy's argument in 1968 that the F-111B should be cancelled. It will thus attempt to clarify the debate on whether the F-111B's cancellation was indeed appropriate, as the Navy contended.

The F-111 program began in 1962 on a basis that the Navy had opposed throughout earlier debates. Against its will, the Navy was placed in a distinctly subordinate position in the management structure for the program. McNamara had stipulated a structure wherein Navy officials would be merely appended to the regular Air Force System Program Office (SPO) for the F-111 program. The Air Force was, in effect, the executive service for obtaining Navy requirements. The Navy was on record in opposition to this program structure, having argued that the distinctiveness of the carrier environment demanded Navy management of the program. Moreover, the Navy had argued that the basic Air Force requirements were ill-suited to the limited-war environment and would impose severe penalties on carrier compatibility. The Navy lost on both counts, however; in the face of McNamara's determination to secure a joint program, the Navy was ultimately forced to participate in an Air Force-managed development of a fighter based on an Air Force requirement.

This acquiescence by the Navy continued through the first year of development (1963). However, in December 1963, General Dynamics reported a substantial increase in weight on the F-111B, an increase from the specified *weight empty* of 38,804 pounds to a projected weight empty of 45,259 pounds. The Navy viewed the weight growth as a confirmation of its original skepticism, particularly since the projection of 45,259 pounds assumed 3,226 pounds of weight savings that the government had not, at that time, formally approved.[2] Later in the development, the higher drag and

---

[2] *TFX Hearings—Second Series*, Part 2, pp. 367–369; and Interview 16. While this weight growth was substantial in any case, it was measured against a specified weight empty (38,804 pounds) that had not been adjusted since the fourth-round evaluations of the source selection competition, in September and October of 1962. This failure to adjust the proposal weight of General Dynamics' design represented a departure from the normal practice. Development programs usually include a negotiation to adjust the proposal weight of a contractor's design, based on the more detailed definition of configuration and requirements obtained during the first year of development. (The adjusted figure is then incorporated in the definitized RDT&E contract.) The following table suggests the normal magnitude of these adjustments:

Aircraft	Time in Months from Proposal to the Establishment of Weight Guarantee	Percent Increase in Guarantee vs. Proposal
F-111B	3	0
A-3A	4	2.0
A-4A	4	Negligible
A-5A	7	1.2
A-6A	6	8.2
F-4B	8	4.8
F-8A	3	7.5

SOURCE: Interview 16. Obviously, this failure to adjust the F-111B's weight guarantee made the weight growth of the F-111B appear relatively larger than it otherwise might have appeared. But in the environment of controversy surrounding the program during the 1963 McClellan Hearings, "adjustments" in the proposal weight would have been construed as "concessions" to an inferior design. Moreover, the Navy would have resisted any attempt to relax the weight

weight of the airframe, plus a five per cent deficiency in the fuel economy of the TF-30 engines, created limitations on the F-111B's ability to "loiter" on station in its fleet air defense role. Additional fuel was thus required, increasing the *take-off weight* of the aircraft by as much as 6,800 pounds.[3] Weight saving programs were ultimately able to save a net amount of 2,373 pounds, but the expected take-off weight of the plane remained approximately 16,000 pounds heavier than the contract specification of 62,788 pounds.[4]

Surprisingly, the sources of this substantial weight growth are difficult to specify. No single part of the airframe was responsible for the airframe weight growth. Instead, it resulted from rather diffuse weight increases throughout the aircraft's structure, deriving from a variety of causes.[5] The fuel-economy deficiency of the TF-30 engine

---

specification, since that service felt that the joint requirement already specified a higher weight empty than was desirable.

[3] Memorandum to the Chief of Naval Operations, from the Chief of the Bureau of Naval Weapons, dated February 5, 1964, re F-111B status, printed in *TFX Hearings—Second Series*, Part 2, pp. 402–404.

[4] This weight figure applies to F-111B R&D prototype number eight, which was to have been the first prototype representative of a production F-111B, as it incorporated the SWIP modifications, the P-12 engine (an engine of improved thrust), and the N-1 modifications (a package of modifications to enhance the F-111B's carrier suitability). The Naval Air Systems Command estimated the take-off weight of F-111B number eight to be 79,212 pounds. This figure can be compared to the contract specification of 62,788 pounds and the Bureau of Naval Weapons' official weight estimate during the fourth round of the source selection (October 15, 1962) of 63,500 pounds. F-111B number eight was never delivered to the Navy, as the program was canceled before General Dynamics completed work on it. This information from Interview 13; and from "F-111B Estimated Performance Chart, July 1967," a document supplied by the Navy to the McClellan Committee in 1970 (from the files of the Permanent Subcommittee on Investigations, Committee on Government Operations, U.S. Senate, Exhibit 7 of the *TFX Hearings—Second Series*).

[5] The original 9,681-pound increase in weight empty (that is, the increase before any weight reductions: 45,259 pounds, plus the assumed savings of 3,226 pounds, minus the specified weight empty of

—which, together with drag increases and weight growth on the airframe, led to the need for additional fuel—was apparently the result of Pratt & Whitney's inability to achieve specified performance.[6]

Consequently, the basic cause of the weight growth was that the achievement of the F-111A/B engineering and performance requirements within the specified weight constraint was technically impossible—that is, it was beyond the technical state of the art of the 1960s. Though most program participants recognized this, they disagreed on its implications for the program.[7] In the 1964 reviews of the program, the Navy contended that the weight growth was proof of a fundamental lack of compatibility between the Air Force and Navy performance needs. As a result of the

---

38,804 pounds) was broken down by the contractor in the following way:

	Increase in Pounds
Omissions from Estimates in 1962 Proposal	1,019
Specification Review (i.e., tighter specifications)	684
Various Minor Configuration Alterations	1,862
Load and Stiffness Changes	772
Government-Furnished Equipment (primarily engines and avionics)	351
Other Government Requirements Changes	385
Miscellaneous	4,608
Total Projected Weight Increase, 12/17/63	9,681

No single, identifiable component was responsible for the large, "Miscellaneous" weight growth. The Miscellaneous growth was instead a composite of many small weight increases.

[6] *TFX Hearings—Second Series*, Part 1, p. 81, and Part 2, p. 323; and Interview 16.

[7] Compare, for example, Memorandum to the Chief of Naval Operations, from the Chief of the Bureau of Naval Weapons, dated February 5, 1964, re F-111B status; and Memorandum for the Secretary of Defense, from Secretary of the Air Force Eugene Zuckert, Secretary of the Navy Paul Nitze, and Director of Defense Research and Engineering Harold Brown, dated February 15, 1964, re F-111B Weight Review; both memoranda printed in *TFX Hearings—Second Series*, Part 2, pp. 401–404, 435–438. Similar contrasts in opinion were obtained from Interviews 6, 9, 11, 12, 13, 14, 16, 17, 19, 20, and 26.

weight growth, the Navy argued, the F-111B would be marginally compatible with the demands of carrier operation and would be unacceptably deficient in various characteristics of performance.[8] The Navy argued for a redesign of the F-111B, a course tantamount to the establishment of a separate Navy program. The Navy was thus reiterating the position advanced during the initial debates on the joint program. In 1961 the Navy had argued that its needs could not be met in a bi-service program based on Air Force requirements. The weight growth was now viewed by the Navy as confirmation of that position.

However, the weight growth was viewed differently by high-level DOD officials—McNamara, Navy Secretary Nitze, Air Force Secretary Zuckert, and Director of Defense Research and Engineering Brown—who recognized the seriousness of the weight growth, but maintained that an "acceptable" aircraft could still be provided by the joint program.[9] They differed from the Navy on one central issue: the interpretation of requirements. The Navy contended that its requirements represented critical capabilities for performing the fleet defense mission, while the high-level officials considered them to be only approximate indicators of necessary performance. High-level civilian officials were willing to accept less-than-specified performance, as long as the F-111B still offered a "missile platform" capability more cost-effective than any alternative aircraft.[10]

[8] Memorandum to the Chief of Naval Operations, from the Chief of the Bureau of Naval Weapons, dated February 5, 1964, re F-111B status, printed in *TFX Hearings–Second Series*, Part 2, pp. 401–404.

[9] Memorandum for the Secretary of Defense, from Secretary of the Air Force Eugene Zuckert, Secretary of the Navy Paul Nitze, and Director of Defense Research and Engineering Harold Brown, dated February 15, 1964, re F-111B Weight Review, printed in *TFX Hearings—Second Series*, Part 2, pp. 435–438.

[10] *TFX Hearings—Second Series*, Part 2, pp. 446–463. Some actual cost-effectiveness studies performed by the Navy supported the Secretaries' conclusion. For example, a study done by the Office of Naval Operations, comparing the F-111B to the A-6A (configured with Phoenix missiles) and the F-4, found the F-111B preferable in terms of cost, performance, and deck space when considered against "the

As a result, these officials refused the Navy request for redesign. At the same time, they approved a program for intensive weight reduction efforts by the contractor: the Super Weight Improvement Program, or SWIP. The SWIP program would ameliorate the problems of the weight growth, and the marginal deficiencies versus specifications that remained were an acceptable trade-off to obtain a bi-service aircraft.

The Navy was not convinced that the SWIP program really could reduce the F-111B's weight to acceptable levels. Over the next three years, as flight tests got under way and as other performance remedies were attempted, the Navy remained skeptical of the F-111B's suitability for carrier operations and of its capabilities for the fleet air defense mission. Indeed, to the Navy, results of the flight tests and performance remedies served only to confirm again that the Air Force and Navy needs were not compatible. Qualitative judgments by Navy test pilots were uniformly negative.[11] Quantitative measurements of the plane's performance continued to report deficiencies versus the original requirements, as Table II reflects:[12]

---

high-level threat of the type to be seen in the seventies." See U.S. Senate, Committee on Armed Services, *Military Procurement Authorizations for Fiscal Year 1968*, Hearings, 90th Cong., 1st Sess. (1967), p. 728.

[11] See *TFX Hearings—Second Series*, Part 1, pp. 103–104, and Part 3, pp. 498–513.

[12] Ibid., Part 1, p. 59. These figures apply to F-111B number eight, which, as noted in footnote 4, would have been the first production-representative F-111B. Note that this prototype incorporated approximately 4,500 pounds of Navy-directed changes (the N-1 modifications) of the structure and fuel weight of the basic SWIP aircraft. These changes will be discussed in detail later in the chapter. For some perspective on the F-111B's take-off weight, note its comparison to operational Navy aircraft: the F-4J has a take-off weight between 47,000 and 56,000 pounds, the A-3B has a take-off weight between 70,000 and 73,000 pounds, the RA-5 has a take-off weight over 76,500 pounds, and the A-7E has a take-off weight between 30,500 and 42,500 pounds. The F-14A has a take-off weight between 58,180 pounds in its air superiority configuration and 72,566 pounds with maximum bomb and missile loads. The significance of the wind-

Table II. F-111B: Specified Performance
Versus Actual Capability

Category	Specified Performance	Actual Performance	Deficiency
Weight Empty	38,804 lbs.	46,112 lbs.	20 percent
Take-off Weight	62,788 lbs.	79,000 lbs.	26 percent
Loiter Altitude	35,000 ft.	30,000 ft.	12 percent
Loiter Time at 150 Mi. from Carrier	3.5 hrs.	3.0 hrs.	14 percent
Launch Wind-Over-Deck	−8 knots	+19 knots	+27 knots
Landing Wind-Over-Deck	+5 knots	+12 knots	+7 knots

In November 1967, with a formal commitment to F-111B production imminent, Navy admirals moved to have the F-111B canceled. By that time, some high-level officials agreed with the Navy that the F-111B's problems were more basic than any fixes could remedy. As a high-level Navy official later commented, "It had become clear that, even if you could lick each individual problem, the complete aircraft would still be a 'dog.' "[13] Moreover, by the beginning of 1968, McNamara's resignation as Defense Secretary had been announced, and his departure from the Pentagon was only a few weeks away.[14] McNamara was the single DOD official with the greatest personal stake in the success of the

over-deck terms in the chart will be discussed below (footnote 21). For weight data, see *Jane's All the World's Aircraft, 1961–1962* (New York: McGraw-Hill, 1961), p. 245; U.S. Senate, Committee on Appropriations, *Lightweight Fighter Aircraft Program,* Hearings, 94th Cong., 1st Sess. (1975), p. 64; U.S. Senate, Committee on Armed Services, *Military Procurement Authorizations: Fiscal Year 1966,* Hearings, 89th Cong., 1st Sess. (1965), p. 97; and "What's Ahead," *Aerospace Daily* (February 14, 1972), p. 249.

[13] Interview 17.

[14] McNamara's departure was announced November 27, 1968. He left the Department of Defense on February 29, 1968.

bi-service program. The officials who remained after he left were not so closely identified with the program. Some of these officials had begun to consider the Navy's negative opinion of the aircraft "precisely correct."[15] Cancellation of the F-111B was then the logical course. The Navy soon succeeded in its move to cancel the F-111B and embarked on a program to develop its own air superiority fighter—the F-14 (called the VFX at that time).

To the Navy, then, the cancellation of the F-111B was a sound decision. In the Navy's professional military judgment, the specifications established for the F-111B in 1961 represented a minimum acceptable capability for performing the fleet air defense mission. After extended efforts to improve the F-111B's performance, the plane was clearly deficient versus these requirements and judged unsuitable for operational use. By this logic, the primary lesson of the F-111B development was that the Navy and Air Force performance needs could not be met in a single aircraft, a lesson that the Navy felt was a vindication of its original predictions in 1961.[16] McNamara had simply asked for more performance than could be provided by this basic aircraft. Hence, to the Navy, the great error of the F-111B development was McNamara's failure to heed the advice of military professionals and technical experts at the outset of the program.[17]

Implicit in the Navy's position are two key propositions:

[15] Interviews 17 and 18.

[16] *TFX Hearings—Second Series*, Part 2, pp. 408–410, 462; *TFX Report*, pp. 90, 92; U.S. House of Representatives, Committee on Armed Services, *Hearings on Military Posture*, 90th Cong., 2nd Sess. (1968), pp. 9363–9364; Naval Air Systems Command study made available to the author; and Interviews, 9, 17, and 19.

[17] This Navy appraisal of the F-111B program corresponds to a common criticism of McNamara's administration of the Defense Department: he failed to take seriously the judgment of military professionals. See, for example, Colonel Robert N. Ginsburgh, USAF, "The Challenge to Military Professionalism," *Foreign Affairs*, Vol. 42 (January 1964), pp. 254–256; and John C. Ries, *The Management of Defense: Organization and Control of the U.S. Armed Services* (Baltimore: Johns Hopkins University Press, 1964), chaps. 3 and 12.

(1) a normative proposition that judgments derived from specialized, professional knowledge of warfare—judgments expressed in formal weapon requirements and in service interpretations of these requirements—should be the primary definition of what constitutes an acceptable weapon system; and (2) an empirical proposition that the judgments made by Navy professionals on the F-111B were in fact based on this specialized knowledge and not on more parochial considerations.

Both propositions are necessary to the Navy's position. If one accepts both propositions, then one can reasonably conclude that the F-111B was an inadequate airplane and rightly was canceled.

Although the first proposition does not admit to empirical verification, the second proposition does, and the Navy position on it is vulnerable. There is considerable evidence to indicate that Navy judgments were animated by antipathy to the bi-service program. This conclusion emerges from a comparison of the Navy's behavior on the F-111B program to its behavior on the F-14 program (the latter being the Navy-managed program that followed the F-111B's cancellation). In this comparison, one observes a more lenient Navy attitude toward requirements and deficiencies in the F-14 program, a difference in attitude that seems best explained by the Navy's basic antipathy toward the bi-service F-111 program.

A first point of comparison between the two planes is their cost. At the time of cancellation, the F-111B was estimated to cost over eight million dollars per plane. This high cost (five million dollars per plane over original estimates) was an additional reason that the Navy urged cancellation of the F-111B. In 1968 testimony before the House Armed Services Committee, Rear Admiral Thomas F. Connolly (Deputy Chief of Navy Operations for Air, the head of naval aviation) criticized the cost of the F-111B and urged adoption of the VFX (F-14) to replace the F-111B. He indicated in his testimony that the same critical standards would be applied to VFX cost increases as had been applied to F-111B increases: "If these people come in with soaring prices . . . I personally am going to go back and look at the F-4 and see what we can do with that. There are some things that can be done with that F-4. I would just as quickly go to my CNO [Chief of Naval Operations] and Secretary of the Navy and say, 'Sir, I do not recommend that we proceed with VFX-1. It is not satisfactory. It is going to be too expensive, and we're not going to get the people's money for it.' But I don't expect that is going to happen."[18]

It did happen, however. The F-14 will cost between 18 and 21 million dollars per plane, making the F-14 the most expensive fighter plane available in the western world.[19] The Navy, however, has gone ahead and produced the F-14 in volume. A second point of comparison between the two planes is their "loiter" time on station for the fleet air defense mission. The F-14 is 20 percent deficient against a *lower* loiter requirement than that against which the F-111B was measured. The F-111B was only 14 percent deficient against its higher requirement.[20] A third point of comparison for the

[18] U.S. House of Representatives, Committee on Armed Services, *Hearings on Military Posture* (1968), pp. 9363–9364.

[19] The figure of 18 million dollars represents F-14 production costs per unit as of late-1975 and includes the costs of an initial provision of spare engines and other parts. The figure of 21 million dollars represents program acquisition costs per unit (for the approved 390-plane program) and includes a per unit allocation of research and development expenditures. Because of the high cost of the F-14, the Navy has been forced to consider cheaper alternatives for follow-on procurement. See "Procurement Costs Continue Upward Spiral," *Aviation Week and Space Technology*, Vol. 103 (September 22, 1975), p. 15; and U.S. House of Representatives, Committee on Appropriations, *Department of Defense Appropriations for 1974*, Hearings, 93d Cong., 1st Sess. (1973), Part 6, p. 558; and U.S. Senate, Committee on Appropriations, *Lightweight Fighter Aircraft Program*, pp. 35–66, 104.

[20] David A. Brown, "Accelerated Testing Set for F-14A," *Aviation Week and Space Technology*, Vol. 95 (December 20, 1971), p. 53; Members of Congress for Peace Through Law, Committee on Military Spending, "Report on Military Spending," in U.S. Senate, Committee

two planes is on two approximate measures of carrier compatibility—launch wind-over-deck and landing wind-over-deck. The F-14's performance on launch and landing wind-over-deck is slightly improved over that of the F-111B, but is measured with a missile load that is 4,200 pounds lighter than was on the F-111B for the measurement of this characteristic.[21] (The F-111B's wind-over-deck was, in any case, approximately 11 knots lower than that of the F-4 Phantom.[22]) The latter two points of comparison reflect essential measures of capability for the fleet air defense mission: ease of launch, time on station, ease of recovery. The F-111B fares well in the comparison, with superior performance in the time-on-station category.

---

on Armed Services, *Authorization for Military Procurement, Research and Development, Fiscal Year 1970, and Reserve Strength*, Hearings, 91st Cong., 1st Sess. (1969), p. 4284; *TFX Hearings—Second Series*, Part 1, p. 59; U.S. Senate, Committee on Armed Services, *Fiscal Year 1973 Authorization for Military Procurement*, Hearings, 93d Cong., 1st Sess. (1973), p. 3872; and Interview 20.

21 Brown, "Accelerated Testing Set for F-14A," p. 53; and *TFX Hearings—Second Series*, Part 1, p. 59. Landing wind-over-deck is a term relating the weight, strength, and minimum landing velocity of an aircraft to the momentum-absorbing capabilities of the arresting equipment on an aircraft carrier. A landing wind-over-deck of 20 knots, for example, means that on a calm day the carrier must travel at 20 knots through the water (creating a "wind" over its deck of 20 knots) to land the given aircraft. The aircraft then can approach the carrier at a safe velocity relative to the air and land at a safe velocity relative to the carrier (that is, at a velocity that falls within the momentum-absorbing limits of the carrier arresting gear and the structural strength limits of the aircraft itself). The launch wind-over-deck relates the power of the carrier catapults to the weight, structural strength, and launch velocity of an aircraft. To be launched from a carrier, an aircraft requires a certain minimum velocity relative to the air. The portion of this velocity that a given catapult can impart is limited by an aircraft's weight and strength: the heavier or weaker the aircraft, the less the velocity the given catapult can impart. The remaining velocity necessary for launch is provided by the wind-over-deck of the carrier. The measure of this wind-imparted, relative velocity is the launch wind-over-deck.

22 *TFX Hearings—Second Series*, Part 1, p. 59; and Memorandum for the Director of Defense Research and Engineering, from Leonard Sullivan, Jr., dated October 1, 1964, re Report of Phoenix/F-111B ad hoc group, printed in *TFX Hearings—Second Series*, Part 3, p. 480. The F-4 datum reflects Phantom performance as of late 1964.

It can be argued that the Navy compromised on the F-14's loiter time in order to obtain a better all-around fighter —that is, one capable of close-range aerial combat ("dog-fights").[23] However, this aspect of the F-14's performance illustrates vividly how much less seriously a service treats requirements when that service is committed to a program. Originally, the Navy intended to build an interim version of the F-14 (the F-14A), using the basic TF-30 engine from the F-111B. Only 67 out of the planned total of 463 F-14s were to be F-14As. The remaining units were to be F-14Bs and F-14Cs, equipped with the Advanced Technology Engine (ATE), which has a thrust-to-weight ratio 51 percent greater than that of the TF-30 engine—the largest improvement in thrust-to-weight ratio between engine generations that Pratt & Whitney has ever accomplished.[24] Development problems on the ATE led the Navy to cancel the F-14B/C program, while maintaining R&D on the engine. All F-14s will now be delivered as F-14As with the basically unimproved TF-30 engine. Yet the difference in performance between the F-14A and F-14B is dramatic, and the Navy never formally considered dropping the F-14A to get the F-14B.[25] *Implicitly, the Navy is not taking its own requirements seriously.* Interestingly, Navy pilots have reported the F-14A to be underpowered in Military Power (that is, when the afterburner is not being used). Navy admirals are now quick to explain how these complaints are a prod-

[23] However, this was a new requirement for the Navy's fleet air defense aircraft. The Navy's Missileer, whose mission the F-111B assumed once the bi-service program was established, was to have been deployed along with a tactical fighter (initially the F-4) to do the dogfighting.

[24] Cecil Brownlow, "Navy Plans Procurement of 463 VFXs," *Aviation Week and Space Technology*, Vol. 89 (December 23, 1968), pp. 18–19; and U.S. Senate, Committee on Armed Services, *Fiscal Year 1973 Authorization for Military Procurement*, pp. 3753–3755, 4019–4027, 4046–4047.

[25] That is, Pratt & Whitney never received a request from the Navy for cost estimates on dropping the TF-30-P-412 engine to get the ATE (the F-401-PW-400). See U.S. Senate, Committee on Armed Services, *Fiscal Year 1973 Authorization for Military Procurement*, p. 4041. Note that only in 1975, after the final buys had been approved, did

uct of the unique characteristics of the turbo-fan engines used in the F-14A. The admirals missed this subtlety on the F-111B when it was labeled "underpowered."[26]

The point of this contrast is simple: if the Navy had been genuinely committed to the F-111B—as it would have been to a normal Navy program—it would have procured the plane. But the Navy was not thus committed to the F-111B. It felt that it had been " 'ratcheted down' in its requirements and could not give more."[27] Unlike the Navy-developed F-14, the F-111B had to demonstrate its basic suitability; this suitability was not assumed in advance.

Yet the requirements being sought in the bi-service F-111 program were beyond the state of the art. Deficiencies vis-à-vis these requirements were assured, and the Navy would take these relative deficiencies as evidence of the F-111B's unacceptability. Versus other aircraft, and certainly for its fleet defense mission, the F-111B provided substantial increases in Navy capabilities. For example, the F-111B had a greatly increased loiter capability and a lower landing wind-over-deck than the Navy's F-4 Phantom. But versus its own contract specifications, the F-111B was deficient in both categories, and these deficiencies served to confirm the Navy's basic doubts about the plane.

---

the Navy begin to consider proposals to replace the F-14's original engine with a more powerful engine. See "F-14 Engine," *Aviation Week and Space Technology*, Vol. 103 (July 14, 1975), p. 16. For an indication of the F-14B's performance, see Speedletter to the Commander of the Naval Air Test Center, from the Commander of the Naval Air Systems Command, dated 3 April 1974, re F-14B Navy Flight Evaluation, printed in U.S. Senate, Committee on Armed Services, *Fiscal Year 1975 Authorization for Military Procurement*, Hearings, 93d Cong., 2d Sess. (1974), pp. 5119–5121.

[26] U.S. Senate, Committee on Armed Services, *Fiscal Year 1973 Authorization for Military Procurement*, p. 3873. Afterburning, turbo-fan engines have a different power curve than afterburning, turbo-jet engines have. Specifically, for a given maximum thrust, the Military Power thrust is lower in a turbo-fan than in a turbo-jet (or, put differently, for a given maximum thrust in Military Power, the after-burner augmentation of a turbo-fan engine is greater). More will be said on this subject later in the chapter.

[27] Interview 9.

Thus, the situation was set up for Navy rejection of the F-111B. The important point here is the existence of a burden of proof on the F-111B. Since the F-111 program was managed by the Air Force, the Navy took the view that the plane's acceptability was to be proved. But on the later F-14 program, there was no similar burden of proof. The F-14 program was managed by the Navy. Deficiencies that had been unacceptable on the F-111B in such areas as cost and loiter time suddenly became acceptable, indeed became the object of strenuous Navy defenses. *In other words, there is a powerful organizational difference between an option whose acceptability is taken for granted—because it originated with the organization—and an option whose acceptability is doubted—because it originated with a competing organization.* For an option whose acceptability is taken for granted, deficiencies represent problems only at the margin of a fundamentally acceptable capability. But for an option whose acceptability is doubted, deficiencies represent confirmation that the option itself is fundamentally unsuitable.

One searches in vain for a case to corroborate the Navy's position: a truly major, service-initiated program that the service itself moved to cancel in the face of performance deficiencies. Indeed, unless Pentagon civilians force an end to service-initiated programs, the services typically support them, whatever their deficiencies—witness the C-5A, the Cheyenne helicopter, the DD-963 destroyers, the MBT-70 (Main Battle Tank), the B-70, and the Skybolt missile, not to mention the Air Force versions of the F-111.[28] A service rarely acts to terminate its *own* failures on major programs.

[28] J. W. Devanney III, "The DX Competition" *U. S. Naval Institute: Proceedings*, Vol. 101 (August 1975), p. 21; Alain C. Enthoven and K. Wayne Smith, *How Much Is Enough? Shaping the Defense Program, 1961–1969* (New York: Harper and Row, 1971), pp. 243–262; U.S. House of Representatives, Committee on Armed Services, *Review of Army Tank Program*, Hearings, 91st Cong., 1st Sess. (1969); U.S. Congress, Joint Economic Committee, *Economics of Military Procurement*, Hearings, 90th Cong., 2d Sess. (1968); U.S. Senate, Committee on Armed Services, *Fiscal Year 1972 Authorization for Military Procurement*; Hearings 92d Cong., 1st Sess. (1971), pp.

Moreover, the services resist bi-service development, or bi-service use, of virtually *any* weapon system. After the Army's MBT-70 tank development was terminated, the Army refused to consider buying Germany's "Leopard" tank.[29] When the Air Force's Aerospace Defense Command (ADC) performed a study that concluded that the Navy's F-14 would be better for the bomber-intercept mission than the Air Force's F-15, the Air Force Chief of Staff insisted that the "F-14 be eliminated from ADC planning and threat project scenarios."[30] When the Congress directed that the Army and the Navy develop only one heavy-lift helicopter, to be used in common, the services defiantly continued their separate programs.[31] When the Air Force and the Navy each moved to put a gun in its respective version of the A-7 attack aircraft, each refused to use the other's gun. (The same was true on engine improvements sought in the A-7, with the Navy wanting an improved Pratt & Whitney engine instead of the already-developed Air Force Allison engine.) Indeed, the Air Force version of the A-7, procured after the basic A-7 (that is, the Navy version) was already undergoing flight tests, ended up having only 30 to 40 percent commonality with the Navy version. The two planes differed in such large items as engines and basic avionics, as well as in details (wiring, cockpit instruments, oxygen systems, wheels, tires, brakes, and starters). The cost savings inherent in having two services use the same aircraft were substantially reduced.[32] More recently, Air Force and Navy

---

3005–3007; and U.S. Senate, Committee on Armed Services, *Fiscal Year 1973 Authorization for Military Procurement*, pp. 3623–3685.

[29] U.S. Senate, Committee on Armed Services, *Fiscal Year 1973 Authorization for Military Procurement*, p. 3629.

[30] Cecil Brownlow, "U.S. To Modernize Air Defense," *Aviation Week and Space Technology*, Vol. 97 (November 27, 1972), p. 12. The ADC is the Air Force command charged with defending the U.S. from attacking enemy bombers.

[31] John W. Finney, "Pentagon Scored on Copter Costs," *New York Times*, May 22, 1972, p. 7.

[32] "Aerospace in Perspective: Tactical Warfare," *Space/Aeronautics*, Vol. 51 (January 1969), p. 97; and Richard G. Head, "Decision-Making on the A-7 Attack Aircraft Program" (unpublished Ph.D.

positions in the A-7 program were reversed: the Navy was directed to evaluate the Air Force's two Lightweight Fighter prototypes (the YF-16 and YF-17), to choose one for procurement as a Navy Air Combat Fighter. OSD attempted to commit the Navy to the Air Force selection, the YF-16. Congressional appropriations language *required* a common choice. The Navy resisted, however. It chose the YF-17 and specified a series of design changes which would cost over one billion dollars to develop and test—virtually the cost of starting from scratch. Like Air Force behavior in the A-7 program, these Navy actions reduced the savings anticipated from Navy procurement of a flight-tested Air Force prototype.[33]

This list could be extended, but we need not belabor the point. On items major and minor, the services resist common development or use. They struggle to maintain their independence in establishing requirements and in developing weapon systems. They see the weapons of a competing service to be critically different from their own and to be

---

dissertation, Syracuse University, 1970), pp. 351–356, 369, 393–397, 498–522. The A-7 was a subsonic Navy attack aircraft, intended for close air support and battlefield interdiction. In 1965, the Air Force was forced into this development by strong OSD pressures and by competition for the close-support mission from the Army's Cheyenne helicopter. Predictably, when the Cheyenne was canceled—thereby reducing the Army threat to an Air Force mission—the Air Force moved to cancel the A-7 program. It very nearly succeeded in doing so, but the cencellation ultimately proved too expensive.

[33] U.S. Senate, Committee on Appropriations, *Lightweight Fighter Aircraft Program*, pp. 1–66. Note that engineers at the Naval Air Systems Command (NASC, formerly part of the Bureau of Naval Weapons) performed the analyses that underlay the design changes the Navy proposed. Since the YF-16 and YF-17 were Air Force planes, these Navy engineers had not had their normal hand in designing and evaluating the planes through a Navy development. Asking these engineers to evaluate the planes after the Air Force had already developed them was thus certain to lead to extensive suggestions for revisions. Civil servants working for the services exert a powerful influence on all weapon developments. As we shall see in our analysis of the F-111B program, any program which excludes or downgrades the participation of these civil servants assumes some very important risks.

insufficiently sensitive to the particular operational contingencies they face. We plausibly can deduce, then, that the basic problem for the Navy in the F-111B program was that, unlike the F-14, the F-111B was not a Navy plane. We are not necessarily suggesting that, in terms of some particular conception of desirable force capabilities, the Navy "should" have procured the F-111B. *Arguably*, the F-111B should not have been procured and was rightly canceled. But this contention is only arguable, not self-evident or certain. The case against the F-111B was ambiguous. In a service-initiated program, such ambiguity normally works to sustain the service's support in spite of deficiencies, as it allows the service to perceive in the conflicting evidence sufficient reasons to maintain the program. However, in the F-111B program, this ambiguity worked to precisely the opposite effect. A skeptical Navy could see in the program's mixed results a confirmation of its genuine doubts about the plane.

In other words, the objective case against the F-111B does not provide a sufficient explanation for the plane's cancellation. In addition to the objective case, we must examine how the Air Force origins and management of the program gave the F-111B's deficiencies a unique meaning to the Navy and led logically to program cancellation. The next section will perform that task.

NAVY SKEPTICISM AND THE DEMISE OF THE F-IIIB

Young man, you'll never see this airplane fly off the deck of an aircraft carrier.
>   —Navy Admiral, speaking to an
>   Air Force officer, 1963.[34]

---

[34] "New Plane Seen More Costly, Little Better Than F-111," *Congressional Quarterly Weekly Report*, Vol. xxvi (May 3, 1968), p. 1008.

From the outset of the F-111 program, the Navy was skeptical about the F-111B's suitability for the carrier air environment and its capabilities for the fleet air defense mission. This section will examine the sources of Navy antipathy to the F-111 program and demonstrate how this hostility burdened development efforts. Furthermore, it will consider how the Navy's opposition to the program created a political problem for the plane with Congress, a problem that proved to be decisive with the efforts at cancellation of Senator McClellan and high-level Navy officers. This discussion will demonstrate the widespread and rather subtle effects of Navy antipathy to the program. It will show how McNamara's attempt to alter a central organizational prerogative of the services—their autonomous specification and development of weapon systems—was fatally vulnerable to the Navy's necessary control of critical development decisions.

The Threat of Commonality

Robert McNamara's early years as Secretary of Defense were particularly innovative ones in the massive Pentagon bureaucracy. In James Schlesinger's words, a "very stale mill pond" was stirred by the activism and initiative of McNamara and his colleagues.[35] The services, of course, were unsettled by the increasing centralization of power in OSD, and the Navy felt this disruption as severely as any of them. Many moves by McNamara in his early years upset important Navy interests: his questioning the value of nuclear propulsion in ships, his emphasis on airborne cargo and troop transport at the expense of ocean transport, and his expansion of the U.S. Strike Command (an interservice operational command which, if expanded, would use more Navy ships and would thus reduce the Navy's control of its

---

[35] James R. Schlesinger, "Organizational Structures and Planning," in Roland McKean (ed.), *Issues in Defense Economics* (New York: National Bureau of Economic Research, 1967), p. 214.

own ships).[36] More generally, McNamara's much-publicized implementation of program budgeting in the Department of Defense portended (although it never achieved) a shift in the nexus of service rivalry from budget "ceilings" to mission capabilities. Since the Air Force was made executive agent for obtaining Navy mission capabilities in the F-111 program—the only major aircraft development anticipated for the 1960s—the Navy perceived the program as an important political setback under the new Pentagon regime.[37]

Consequently, the F-111 program and the Navy's behavior in it cannot be considered in isolation from the larger changes wrought in the McNamara years. To the Navy, the F-111 program was, of necessity, one contest in a larger bargaining game, as it (along with the other services and DOD agencies) resisted McNamara's encroachment on its professional prerogatives. The specific influence of this larger threat on Navy behavior in the F-111 program is difficult to document. But the Navy was particularly sensitive to the trend toward centralization, since it had always feared control by civilian officials who lacked a proper appreciation of sea power.[38] Certainly, this sensitivity created a generalized resistance that might have focused on the F-111 program, one of McNamara's more inflammatory early actions.

[36] Hanson W. Baldwin, "The Navy at Ebb Tide," *The Reporter*, Vol. 30 (January 30, 1964), pp. 35–38; and James M. Roherty, *Decisions of Robert S. McNamara* (Coral Gables: University of Miami Press, 1970), chap. 4.

[37] Robert J. Art, *The TFX Decision: McNamara and the Military* (Boston: Little, Brown, 1968), p. 2; and Richard Austin Smith, "The $7 Billion Contract that Changed the Rules," Part I *Fortune*, Vol. 67 (March 1963), p. 99. An early observation on the weapon system rivalry implicit in program budgeting is Katherine Johnsen, "New Budgeting Plan Shifts Rivalry from Services to Weapon Systems," *Aviation Week and Space Technology*, Vol. 75 (July 31, 1961), p. 24. A good study on how and why the effects of this change proved to be less than anticipated is John P. Crecine and Gregory Fischer, *On Resource Allocation Processes in the U.S. Department of Defense*, Institute of Public Policy Studies, University of Michigan, Discussion Paper No. 31 (1971).

[38] Ries, *The Management of Defense*, pp. 210–211.

But even apart from the larger bargaining game, commonality itself was a sufficient threat to arouse Navy antipathy. We noted in the previous section that, on major and minor weapons, the services resist common development or use. In part, this resistance derives from the importance of weapon system developments to the mission capabilities and operational roles of the services. The autonomous definition and development of weapon systems is an important source of power to them.[39] Moreover, it is a significant component of their professional doctrine, which portrays military (and particularly combat) experience as the most important background for making choices on weapon system characteristics.[40] On relatively minor hardware items (such as the A-7's gun, mentioned earlier), operational roles and professional status are hardly at stake. But these items nonetheless will reflect certain service idiosyncrasies as, for example, in certain minor operational features they incorporate. An attempt to merge the development or procurement of these minor items will generate controversy. In such a controversy, the services generally will be able to make an argument for their own weapon—or against that of another service—since there is enough complexity in weapon capabilities (absolute and relative, quantitative and qualitative) for a service to observe evidence that supports its interests. In these situations, the easier course always will be for the services to go their separate ways.

But in the F-111 program, the Navy failed in its attempt to go a separate way and was forced to join in what had been an Air Force program. In the process, the distinctiveness of the aircraft carrier environment, an important proposition of Navy doctrine, virtually had been ignored by the new civilian regime in the Pentagon. However, the F-111 program did more than strike at the heart of the professional

[39] Paul Y. Hammond, *Organizing for Defense* (Princeton: Princeton University Press, 1961), pp. 58–59.
[40] Head, "Decision-Making on the A-7 Attack Aircraft Program," pp. 66–68.

257

military prerogatives of the Navy. In the particular form proposed—commonality in development and production—the program also was a threat to the Navy's civilian technical staff at the Bureau of Naval Weapons (BuWeps, now a part of the Naval Air Systems Command). This staff normally held major responsibilities for the oversight and technical direction of Navy aircraft programs. However, in the F-111 program, Navy program officials, civilian and military, were merely to be appended to the regular Air Force development organizations. While Navy officials would look to the Bureau for special evaluations throughout the program,[41] the Bureau's engineers would remain in a subordinate, advisory role in the day-to-day management of the program. The prospect of this subordination triggered an enduring negative reaction from the Bureau immediately after McNamara proposed the joint program in 1961. Of all the many opponents to a bi-service program, the Bureau was widely recognized to be the most persistent—to the point that, throughout the program, its analyses and advice were discounted by non-Navy audiences.[42]

Both civilian and military officials thus resented their subordinate position in this program to obtain a plane largely tailored to Air Force requirements. They felt, with some justification, that they had been required to make all the basic compromises necessary to obtain a joint program. They remained skeptical that this Air Force plane could become an appropriate weapon system for the carrier environment.

Though the Navy's antipathy to the F-111B was widespread, Navy program officials were, by all accounts, totally dedicated to securing a plane that the Navy community would accept.[43] But the Navy community would not accept

[41] Given the Bureau's unyielding opposition to the bi-service program, Navy officials were certain to get highly critical evaluations of F-111B development progress and problems. Evidence of this criticism will be noted throughout this chapter.

[42] Interviews 6, 9, 11, and 12.

[43] Interviews 6, 9, and 16.

just any plane that the program produced. Program officials were placed in a uniquely difficult position. Since high-level officers felt that Navy desires had been compromised to a minimum acceptable level[44]—a feeling that would be perceived, if not shared, by subalterns—these subordinate officers could not easily compromise on technical issues. No Navy program official could become too eager an advocate of the program, too willing a compromiser on issues of technical specification and performance, too enthusiastic an exponent of making the program work at further expense to the Navy. Any program official's advocacy of concession would be greeted by the broad Navy skepticism at every level. For a program official to maintain his credibility in the Navy, he would have to demonstrate his serious intent to secure Navy needs that had been reduced to their "minimum" in the establishment of the joint requirement.

In the context of the development process, this meant inflexibility. The joint requirement established in 1961 had burdened the proposed aircraft with the additional weight that would be generated by each service's unique demands. As we shall see, Navy inflexibility further burdened the development. The specifications for a weapons development are extensive and often mutually contradictory. Since they confront a physical reality that imposes tight constraints, they cannot be applied inflexibly if major program goals are to be met. Consequently, a successful development is contingent upon their being intelligently modified as a matter of course. The character of Navy behavior was explicitly at odds with this imperative for program success. (Congressional opposition to the program, dating from the contract

[44] Vice Admiral Robert Pirie, Deputy Chief of Naval Operations for Air (the head of naval aviation), went into "early retirement" because of the stridency with which he asserted this position. A number of other Navy admirals were "reassigned" for the same reason. See Richard Austin Smith, "The $7 Billion Contract That Changed the Rules," Part II, *Fortune*, Vol. 67 (April 1963), p. 191. Due to Civil Service regulations, opponents of the bi-service program in BuWeps could not be similarly punished.

award, deepened the Navy's resistance, for McClellan's "dare-it-to-work" attitudes mirrored the Navy's own.)[45] In addition, these specifications framed the issues that became the key arguments for program cancellation, when Navy officials moved to terminate the program in 1967. While cost problems and performance deficiencies on the F-14 would be portrayed as being offset by the increased capability that the plane provided, the F-111B would simply be judged deficient.[46]

The essential impact of commonality—particularly in the form McNamara imposed, which visibly subordinated the Navy—was thus to create in the Navy a low tolerance to deficiencies against its own requirements. While (relative to their respective requirements) the Air Force F-111s were arguably more deficient than the Navy F-111Bs, the Air Force procured its versions in volume.[47] The Air Force, however, operated on an assumption of the F-111's basic suitability that the Navy could not share.

[45] See Thomas Alexander, "McNamara's Expensive Economy Plane," *Fortune*, Vol. 75 (April 1967), p. 91. The timing of this Congressional opposition was important, coming as it did in the first year of the development. As soon as the McClellan hearings ended, the substantial F-111B weight growth was revealed, thus commencing a "cycle of problems" on the F-111B. These will be discussed in detail in the text.

[46] See statement and testimony of Admiral Elmo R. Zumwalt, Chief of Naval Operations, and testimony of Rear Admiral Thomas R. McClellan, Commander, Naval Air Systems Command, in U.S. Senate, Committee on Armed Services, *Fiscal Year 1973 Authorization for Military Procurement*, pp. 3743–3751, and 3837–3877. This statement and testimony provide a representative Navy discussion of how the F-14's capabilities outweigh its deficiencies.

[47] *TFX Hearings—Second Series*, Part 2, p. 59; and U.S. Senate, Committee on Appropriations, *Department of Defense Appropriations for Fiscal Year 1973*, Hearings, 92d Cong., 2d Sess. (1972), p. 781. By suggesting that the F-111A is "arguably more deficient" than the F-111B, we are not suggesting that the F-111A is less capable for its nuclear interdiction mission than the F-111B would have been for its fleet defense mission. Unless done with considerable sophistication, such a comparison would be virtually meaningless. We are simply suggesting that, as compared to contract specifications, the F-111A *could* be considered more deficient than the F-111B.

We will move now to examine Navy behavior in the program in detail, beginning with the early years of the program.

Establishing Requirements and Commencing Development

According to a high-ranking Navy officer close to the TFX deliberations in 1961, the Navy "knew its needs would not be met in a joint program" at a very early stage of the program: in September 1961, when McNamara's memorandum establishing the joint requirement specified a take-off weight of 55,000 pounds for the Navy version, a 5,000-pound increase over the maximum take-off weight the Navy had said it could accept.[48] With the Navy thus convinced that its broad needs were neglected, the service resisted concessions on many detailed specifications for the proposed aircraft.[49] First, at Navy insistence, a self-contained pilot escape capsule was incorporated as a design requirement. This feature added approximately 400 to 500 pounds to the airframe. The F-14, indeed all other American fighter planes, have ejector seats. Second, the Navy required that the plane be able to carry two Phoenix missiles internally, in addition to the four external missiles. This demand enlarged the bomb bay and added further weight. No other Navy tactical fighter—the F-14 included—carries or is planned to carry missiles or bombs internally. Third, the Navy insisted that

[48] Interview 26. Note that the Missileer was expected to weigh 52,000 pounds. Larry Booda, "New Delay Raises Doubts on TFX Future," *Aviation Week and Space Technology*, Vol. 77 (July 9, 1962), p. 26.

[49] The information that follows in the text is drawn from Michael P. London, "VFX—The Navy's Choice," *Space Aeronautics*, Vol. 50 (November 1968), p. 52; Staff Report, "TFX: Mission and Design," *Space/Aeronautics*, Vol. 47 (June 1963), p. 74; *TFX Report*, p. 8; and Interview 16. One qualification should be added to the information that follows in the text: the Navy does have one attack aircraft, the A-5, which possesses limited provisions for carrying internal ordnance. No Navy fighter aircraft has such provisions, however.

an extraordinarily large volume of the aircraft be set aside for Phoenix avionics (the so-called AWG-9 system), a volume three times that projected at the time by Hughes (the Phoenix contractor). These avionics, to be supplied separately by the Navy to General Dynamics, ultimately grew to fill the large space. In the F-14 program, where internal aircraft space was a more pressing problem to the Navy (the F-14 was shorter and narrower than the F-111B), the AWG-9 system was reduced from the 1,900 pounds it weighed for the F-111B to a weight of 1,300 pounds for the F-14, even as additional firing capabilities were added to it.[50] Finally, the Navy required 3.5 hours loiter at 150 miles from the carrier and 1.0 hours loiter at 750 miles from the carrier. Both of these F-111B specifications exceeded the earlier specifications for the F-6 Missileer, as well as the later specifications for the F-14 (although, we note again, the F-14's mission is broader than was the F-111B's or the Missileer's).[51]

To be sure, a supporting case could be made for each of these Navy demands. The demands were not necessarily

[50] U.S. Senate, Committee on Armed Services, *Fiscal Year 1973 Authorization for Military Procurement*, p. 4064. Hughes and the Navy describe the size reduction as being the result of state-of-the-art advances, which, in part, it was. But the important point here is the difference in Navy concern for limiting the size of the avionics. For the F-111B program, the avionics, like the engines, were Government Furnished Aeronautical Equipment (GFAE). Hughes was the prime contractor to the Navy for the Phoenix avionics and missile and an associate contractor to General Dynamics. The provision of the larger space for the avionics in the F-111B, in effect, would have given Hughes a contract performance advantage, as the stringency of design trade-offs would be eased substantially. Needless to say, it would also ease the weight standard for Hughes. The Phoenix missile itself may have increased considerably in weight, though Hughes disputes this. See Paul Alelyunas, "Air-to-Air Missiles," *Space/Aeronautics*, Vol. 44 (November 1965), p. 75; and "Perspective: Navy Says It Wants the F-111B, Heavy or Not," *Space/Aeronautics*, Vol. 46, (November 1966), p. 34.

[51] Brown, "Accelerated Testing Set for F-14A," p. 53; Members of Congress for Peace Through Law, "Report on Military Spending," p. 4284; *TFX Hearings—First Series*, Part 6, pp. 1391–1393; *TFX Hearings—Second Series*, Part 1, p. 59; and Interview 20.

ill-conceived. Moreover, the Navy's persistence on these issues of detail was matched by the Air Force's own resistance to conceding any of its requirements. For example, in 1961, when the joint program was established, the Air Force informally agreed with the Navy to accept whatever sea-level dash capability was provided by the winning contractor's design proposal. General Dynamics' winning proposal was evaluated to achieve 135 nautical miles of supersonic dash. However, General Dynamics advocated certain design changes to the Air Force that held out the possibility of achieving over 200 miles of dash capability. In spite of the implications of these changes for Navy-mission performance, and in spite of its informal agreement to accept the dash capability of the winning proposal, the Air Force approved the proposed changes and moved early in the development to achieve the higher capability.[52] This angered the Navy, of course, and hardly encouraged that service toward compromise.

It is obvious that, in a bi-service development, conflicts of this sort were almost inevitable. The adversary relationship of the two services insured that each would resist concessions to the other. Thus, while the Navy did make a number of unique demands early in the program, demands that belied the service's stated weight consciousness and imposed certain penalties on the Air Force, these demands were matched by the Air Force's own demands and were a predictable outgrowth of the Navy's position in the program.[53] They were typical of the problems that McNamara

[52] Government Report II.

[53] Note an additional example of the Navy's unwillingness to concede on marginal requirements. After the Work Statement and RFP's had been sent out to the aerospace industry in October 1961, the Navy apparently "moved heaven and earth in vainly trying to insert a requirement that its version be able to do 0.6 Mach at 35,000-foot altitudes, a speed that would virtually have put the plane in a stall." Clearly, the Navy was pressing further to burden an already difficult list of requirements. See Smith, "The $7 Billion Contract," Part I, p. 184.

and his associates failed to foresee in forcing the Navy into a joint program.

Once the development began, the Navy's commitment to the program was expressed in a subtle way: it sent a minimal number of Navy personnel to participate in the direct government management of the program at the Air Force's F-111 System Program Office (SPO).[54] At the outset of the development, the Navy delegation at the SPO comprised less than 10 percent of the SPO's total personnel, "when [the Navy] could have insisted on 50 percent."[55] Moreover, the Navy delegation was originally headed by a "relatively low-ranking officer," a captain.[56] The small size and relatively low rank (and hence minimal independent authority) of this Navy contingent to the Air Force SPO apparently resulted from the Bureau of Naval Weapons' (BuWeps') desire to maintain close control of its technical staff associated with the SPO. Navy personnel in the SPO would, over time, naturally acquire a sense of being part of a new "team"—an F-111 team, an Air Force-dominated team, and certainly a less Navy-controlled team. But through mid-1965, when the Navy's SPO contingent was increased at Secretary Nitze's behest, the contingent remained small, and BuWeps maintained control of it.[57]

[54] Interviews 5, 6, and 11. The ground rules of the development provided only that the SPO would include "appropriate" naval personnel. There was no specific direction on the size of the Navy's SPO contingent, and there is no evidence of the Air Force's having limited Navy participation in the SPO. See Memorandum for the Secretary of the Navy, from the Chief of the Bureau of Naval Weapons, dated March 20, 1963, re Navy participation in the management of the F-111 (TFX) program, printed in TFX Hearings—First Series, Part 7, pp. 1817–1822.

[55] Interview 5.

[56] Memorandum for the Secretary of the Navy, from the Chief of the Bureau of Naval Weapons, dated March 20, 1963, re Navy participation in the management of the F-111 (TFX) program, printed in TFX Hearings—First Series, Part 7, p. 1818; and Interview 5.

[57] Government Report II; and Interview 19. An effective geographic separation of technical staffs resulted from this control, as the Navy's technical staff was headquartered just outside Washington, while the Air Force's staff was at Wright-Patterson Air Force Base

The Navy's commitment to the program during these early years was also reflected in Navy actions on a related program. Recall that the Navy requirement for a close-support aircraft (the so-called VAX requirement, or attack aircraft, experimental) was separated from the TFX negotiations in May 1961. Historically, Navy attack planes had been specialized, subsonic aircraft. The Navy felt that subsonic planes were best suited to the demands of battlefield interdiction and of close support for ground troops.[58] In-

in Ohio, where the SPO was located. Reportedly, during the F-111 development, whenever a problem arose that would require changing design specifications, the Air Force people would write the Navy people, the Navy people would write the Air Force people, back and forth, until it was too late to make the change being considered. Face-to-face contact, it was alleged, could have resolved many of these issues in a matter of hours or days. (This information is from a DDR&E official close to the program.) Hence, the geographic separation of the technical staffs reinforced the inflexibility of the Navy on development issues.

[58] This Navy doctrine is an excellent example of the propositions in Chapter III on the evolution of requirements. The Navy specializes its pilots into two groups: supersonic fighter pilots and subsonic attack pilots. Each group represents a separate line of training and promotion. Moreover, there is little cross-training or lateral movement between the two groups. As a result, there is a firm organizational base within the Navy for pilots who fly subsonic aircraft and who subscribe to doctrine placing positive value on subsonic speed for the attack mission. Their requirements for new aircraft reflect this tradition: from the A-1 of the 1940s to the A-7 of the mid-1960s, only the A-5 (ultimately used for reconnaissance, not attack, missions) possessed a supersonic capability, and did so at the behest of OSD, not the Navy. While the advance of technology has made the achievement of supersonic speed a routine design goal, the Navy attack pilots have never seen fit to press their speed capabilities into the supersonic regime, save for the uniquely biased requirement to be described in the text. Since subsonic planes are generally less costly and complex than supersonic planes, Navy attack aircraft tend to be cheaper and simpler than Air Force and Navy fighter aircraft (although the attack aircraft at times have very costly avionics).

The Air Force, by contrast, does not separate its pilots into specialized subgroups with distinctive doctrine and equipment. As a major article of doctrine in the past, TAC pilots and aircraft were assumed to be capable of performing the full scope of tactical aircraft missions. Accordingly, the Air Force had no organizational base or tradition on the virtue of subsonic speed, and its aircraft were opti-

265

deed, the vehemence of the Navy argument on this point, as well as the plausibility of the argument itself, were the main reasons that the VAX requirement had been separated from the TFX negotiations. However, by mid-1962—the middle stages of the TFX source selection competition—the Navy had formulated its new VAX requirement, and the requirement was completely at odds with prior Navy doctrine for attack aircraft: "The proposed attack aircraft . . . was planned by the Navy around the concept of a swing-wing supersonic aircraft about one-half the size, weight, and cost of the TFX. . . . As the concept was defined by the Navy in 1961–1962, the VAX proposal envisioned an aircraft capable of Mach 2 supersonic flight at high altitude, but only high subsonic (Mach .9) speed at sea level. . . . The VAX had many features similar to those of the TFX/F-111; in fact, the Boeing VAX design proposal looked so much like the losing Boeing F-111 design, Pentagon staffers immediately named it the F-55.5."[59]

Systems analysts and DDR&E officials objected to the VAX requirement formulated by the Navy, since the Navy was proposing a supersonic aircraft to perform a mission (i.e., ground attack) for which supersonic flight had never been a Navy requirement. On the advice of his systems analysts, Secretary McNamara postponed the VAX program late in 1962, pending the Navy's re-evaluation of its requirement.[60] The VAX requirement the Navy had for-

---

mized to the most demanding of the tactical missions, the supersonic missions. See W. T. Gunston, *Bombers of the West* (New York: Charles Scribner's Sons, 1973), p. 228; and Head, "Decision-Making on the A-7 Attack Aircraft Program," pp. 125–134, 190. More recently, Air Force and Navy doctrine on these issues appeared to be somewhat in flux, following the disruptive influences of recent combat experience (both in Vietnam and the Middle East) and of procurement dollar shortages.

[59] Ibid., pp. 180–181. Apart from what it implies about the Navy's commitment to the F-111 program, this Navy design proposal is interesting for its suggestion of the kind of plane that would have been possible had the F-111 not been designed around a *supersonic* sea-level dash.

[60] Ibid., pp. 181–182.

mulated—the same in its essentials as the "alternate TFX" that the Navy had proposed, unsuccessfully, during the joint TFX negotiations of 1961—was clearly a calculated attempt to use the VAX program as a foot-in-the-door for later TFX cancellation. We need not doubt that, when built, the VAX would have been preferred to the F-111B. The complexity of weapon capabilities will nearly always allow a preferred alternative to be favorably compared to unwanted substitutes, especially substitutes from another service. However, with McNamara's disapproval of VAX, this option was closed off to the Navy. (The Navy's reevaluation of the VAX program later led to the development of the A-7, a plane perfectly in keeping with prior Navy doctrine on attack aircraft.) Shortly thereafter, in March 1963—and perhaps as a consequence of the Navy's realization that the F-111B was its only present program for obtaining a fleet air defense capability—the Navy increased its planned purchase of the aircraft from the 235 units projected in October 1961 to 359 units.[61]

If increases in planned procurement of the aircraft are an indication, then the Navy at this point finally had resigned itself to the bi-service program. However, development effort was proceeding apace at this time, and Navy antipathy was manifested in subtler ways than overt resistance to the program. Following the contract award, General Dynamics began to translate its contract proposal into a more detailed design. An important constraint for the contractor in performing such design work is the so-called Mil-Specs, or Standard Military Specifications. Incorporated in (literally) a five-foot shelf of documents, Mil-Specs codify the requirements to be met by the myriad of detailed parts that go into an aircraft—bolts, brackets, wires, complete subsystems, wings, fuselage, and the total aircraft itself. They automatically apply to all weapon-system developments.[62]

[61] U.S. House, Committee on Armed Services, *Hearings on Military Posture*, 91st Cong., 1st Sess. (1969), p. 3202.
[62] Interviews 5, 9, and 11.

Characteristically, the Mil-Specs are applied somewhat flexibly, as indeed they must be, since: (1) in so complex and tightly interdependent a mechanism as a modern jet aircraft, many of these detailed specifications inevitably come into conflict with each other; and (2) these specifications are not systematically updated—they have simply "accumulated over the past fifty years without any systematic review to see how cost-effective they are."[63] When Mil-Specs lead to conflicts in design specifications, they are compromised in order to achieve a reasonable design. Generally, the working-level engineers apply the Mil-Specs, but the executive-level people decide on the trade-offs.[64]

But in the case of the TFX development, by virtually all accounts, the Navy applied these specifications inflexibly, thus contributing to the weight growth of the aircraft.[65] As a former Navy program official commented, "Mil-Specs were overly used by the Navy technical people to argue against the plane. The Navy did take advantage of the fact that they had these unbending requirements and could make a rational case for them."[66] Or, as a DDR&E official described it, "Well, the Navy sure followed the book."[67] Even though Navy procurement people were dedicated to the program, it was the executive-level people who would decide the trade-offs, and they were not so dedicated to the program. A knowledgeable supporter of the Navy's position on the program estimated that the Navy's Mil-Spec inflexibility generated 1,000 pounds of additional weight for the F-111B.[68]

[63] Interview 9.   [64] Interview 9.
[65] Interviews 1, 6, 9, 10, 11, and 12.
[66] Interview 9.   [67] Interview 11.
[68] Interview 10. This Navy behavior is not unique. Since, in formal terms, Mil-Specs are universal requirements, their application, even their unwise application, always possesses an immanent, authoritative rationale. Thus, if a service wants to erode the performance of a proposed system in order to avoid having to procure it, Mil-Specs provide a ready means of doing so. Reportedly, in 1972, one of the services (not the Navy) was "Mil-Speccing to death" a foreign-made missile it did not want to be forced to procure, in spite of the foreign missile's alleged superiority over its American counterpart (Interview 9).

But the greatest source of additional weight for the aircraft was simply the extreme performance and structural demands placed upon the aircraft.[69] This growth became fully apparent in December 1963, when General Dynamics reported a 5,000-pound increase in projected F-111B empty weight, to 45,259 pounds (versus the 38,804 pounds specified in the contract). The projected weight increase was actually 3,000 pounds greater than this, but General Dynamics was assuming the acceptance of proposals to reduce the weight by 3,000 pounds.

Secretary McNamara was apparently apprised of this growth, since he called for a complete review of the F-111 development in January 1964.[70] The Bureau of Naval Weapons immediately began to review the project, and ultimately concluded: "The fact that the F-111B has the highest weight empty of any design yet started by the Navy, coupled with the fact that the growth is the greatest, both in absolute and percentage terms, at this stage of design is a matter of grave concern. . . . The overall level of performance at the current weight is unacceptable. . . ."[71]

---

[69] Commonality further exacerbated these demands in an intriguing way. In aircraft design, there is a static strength specification called the "g" requirement. Essentially, the g requirement is a stipulation of how many times the force of gravity the structure of the plane must be capable of withstanding, under certain static test conditions. For example, a 3-g requirement on a 10,000-pound airplane means a static strength requirement of 30,000 pounds. The Navy g requirement for tactical aircraft was 6.5 g's; the TAC requirement was 7.33 g's. Commonality brought the Navy up to the higher common denominator. By way of comparison, the Navy's subsonic Missileer (which, as we noted earlier, was the Navy's predecessor to the TFX) was not classified as a fighter aircraft, so it had only a 4-g requirement. This information from *TFX Hearings—First Series*, Part 3, p. 646; and Interview 11.

[70] Memorandum for the Director of Defense Research and Engineering, the Secretary of the Navy, and the Secretary of the Air Force, from Robert S. McNamara, dated January 18, 1964, re TFX program review, printed in *TFX Hearings—Second Series*, Part 2, p. 400.

[71] Letter to the Chief of Naval Operations, from the Chief of the Bureau of Naval Weapons, dated February 5, 1964, re F-111B status, printed in *TFX Hearings—Second Series*, Part 2, p. 401–404.

Thus, according to the report, there was a need for "major redesign." In subsequent meetings the Deputy Director of Defense Research and Engineering for Tactical Air and the Assistant Secretary of the Navy for Research and Development agreed to halt the development of the F-111B pending its redesign. Since the development of the F-111A would continue, this meant an end to commonality. George Spangenberg, a distinguished Navy engineer and the author of the BuWeps study, later admitted that, "The ploy that we were using of saying stop and redesign the Navy airplane would have, in effect, made two different airplanes, one for the Navy and one for the Air Force."[72]

However, by orders given at the Secretarial level—Zuckert of the Air Force, Nitze of the Navy, or Brown of DDR&E (its director)—this agreement was recast to recommend instead a series of options whose primary effect would be to continue the joint development of the F-111A and F-111B and to focus contractor efforts and management attention on weight improvement (the Super Weight Improvement Program, or SWIP). In addition, fall-back redesigns of the F-111B were to be prepared, in the event that the weight control programs failed.[73]

The contractor and the services thus began the SWIP program, the process of taking weight out of the existing structure. This was a painstaking effort, involving the removal even of ounces of metal from some parts. During this difficult weight improvement program, the Navy refused a number of specification compromises that would have removed large amounts of weight: (1) the replacement of the unique, 400- to 500-pound escape capsule by conventional ejection seats; (2) a reduction in the required loiter time, which would permit less fuel and structural weight in the aircraft; (3) a reduction (from the specified number of six) in the number of 1,000-pound Phoenix mis-

[72] *TFX Hearings—Second Series*, Part 2, p. 408.
[73] Ibid., pp. 428–438.

siles to be carried on the aircraft; and (4) a relaxation of the static strength or "g" requirement of the airplane.[74]

The Navy's inflexibility on F-111B specifications contrasts sharply with the subsequent F-14 experience. We have already noted how the F-111B's capsule and loiter requirements exceeded those of the F-14. The analogies for the Phoenix missile are similarly instructive. On the F-14, the Phoenix missile load was placed in an "overload" condition. This meant, first, that the F-14's basic load was not six, 1,000-pound Phoenix missiles; instead, it was six, 300-pound Sparrow missiles, a 4,200-pound saving. All formal F-14 performance measurements, from carrier landing to gross weight, would be made with the lighter Sparrow load. One source calculated that if the Navy had given up four Phoenix missiles (or if the Navy and the Air Force had given up the bomb bay), the basic loiter and carrier compatibility goals could have been met on the F-111B.[75] The Navy could not realistically have given up four of the missiles; however, the Navy was unwilling to concede any of them. The second implication of placing the Phoenix in overload condition on the F-14 was that the F-14's structure would not have to meet the specified static strength (or "g") requirement when it carried the Phoenix missile. The F-14's specified static strength is 6.5 g's with an 1,800-pound missile load.[76] In other words, when the F-14 carries Phoenix missiles, the g requirement is relaxed—precisely the relaxation in requirements that the Navy refused on the F-111B, with a resultant weight penalty.[77]

[74] Interview 16. The escape capsule is unique to the F-111 among tactical fighters. However, the F-111 shares this feature with the B-1 strategic bomber, a plane in development at this writing.

[75] Interviews 6 and 11. For a good description of the implications of the overload condition, see "Tactical Warfare," *Space/Aeronautics*, Vol. 53 (January 1970), p. 74.

[76] Brown, "Accelerated Testing Set for F-14A," p. 53; and Interview 11.

[77] To be sure, the Air Force was also resistant to changing its g requirement, as it considered the weight problem to be less severe than did the Navy. If commonality were enforced, this Air Force

The Navy's argument in remaining inflexible on the F-111B specifications was that Air Force needs were dictating the aircraft the Navy would get. In particular, the Navy pointed to the Air Force's supersonic sea-level dash mission, which had dictated the configuration and much of the detailed design of the aircraft.[78]

Given the Navy inflexibility on specifications, weight reductions could only be achieved through the SWIP effort. The SWIP changes were formally approved in July 1964 and ultimately reduced F-111B empty weight to 43,162 pounds.[79] At that time, the Navy estimate of F-111B weight

---

resistance would prevent any compromise of the g requirement. The point here is that the Navy itself opposed any relaxation. The problem never reached the stage where commonality with the Air Force impeded compromise on this specification.

[78] Interview 16. See also Larry Booda, "Rift May Affect TFX Role, Configuration," *Aviation Week and Space Technology*, Vol. 79 (September 9, 1963), p. 26.

[79] The SWIP program saved 4,060 pounds, an earlier weight improvement program (WIP, initiated by the contractor prior to the December 1963 presentation) saved 595 pounds, and other weight reduction efforts saved 668 pounds, for a total decrease of 5,323 pounds. This decrease, subtracted from the 48,485-pound projected F-111B weight of December 1963 (the weight before proposed reductions), gives the final SWIP prototype weight of 43,162 pounds (Interview 16). This figure is only 164 pounds greater than General Dynamics estimated in high-level reviews of July 1964. Compared to the proposal weight of 38,804 pounds, this represented an 11.3 percent weight growth. (See footnote 2 of this chapter for an explanation of the significance of the proposal weight, as opposed to the contract-specified weight.) To place this weight growth in context, we can compare it to the growth for other Navy fighters:

Aircraft	Percent Increase in Actual Weight vs. Proposal Weight
F-111B (Initial SWIP aircraft)	11
A-3A	7
A-4A	−3
A-5A	20
A-6A	13
F-4B	8
F-14A	8

SOURCE: Interview 16

Obviously, the F-111B fares reasonably well in this comparison

was 3,000 pounds greater than that of the contractor, because the Navy estimate allowed for "normal growth" of the aircraft as it approached fleet introduction.[80] Later, as a result of *Navy-directed* changes to improve carrier compatibility, the plane grew to within 150 pounds of the Navy estimate.[81]

In spite of the differing estimates of weight-empty between the contractor and the Navy, the Navy did agree that all feasible airframe weight reductions had been accomplished by the contractor in the SWIP effort.[82] Of the 43,000 to 46,000 pounds that the SWIP aircraft would weigh, once built, only 25,000 pounds would be in the airframe, down from roughly 30,000 pounds before SWIP. The other 20,000 pounds were composed of the engines, avionics, and other equipment over which the contractor had no control—these items were government-supplied and were provided largely under the aegis of the Navy.[83]

---

with operational Navy aircraft (though we should add that, by comparison with most of these aircraft, the F-111B was heavier in *absolute* terms, also an important issue). Later changes in the SWIP aircraft (to accommodate added fuel and other modifications) increased the SWIP weight to 43,592 pounds, a 12.3 percent increase over the proposal weight. The Navy-directed N-1 package of fixes brought the weight of the aircraft up to 46,121 pounds, an 18.9 percent increase over the proposal weight (and a mere 0.4 percent less than the Navy's estimate of July 1964). See Erwin J. Bulban, "General Dynamics Defends F-111 Program," *Aviation Week and Space Technology*, Vol. 87 (November 13, 1967), p. 34; and Memorandum for the Deputy Secretary of Defense, from Paul H. Nitze, dated July 29, 1964, re F-111, printed in *TFX Hearings—Second Series*, Part 2, p. 461.

[80] Memorandum to Adm. Emerson Fawkes, from George Spangenberg, Bureau of Naval Weapons, dated August 14, 1964, re F-111B design review, printed in *TFX Hearings—Second Series*, Part 2, pp. 452–455.

[81] *TFX Hearings—Second Series*, Part 2, p. 456; and Interview 16. These Navy-directed changes will be discussed in detail later in the text.

[82] Interview 16.

[83] Interview 16. The development of the Phoenix missiles and avionics was funded and controlled by the Navy. The development of the Pratt & Whitney engines was funded by the Air Force, but was supervised by the Navy.

The contractor made suggestions later in 1964 for improvements to reduce the weight and volume of the missile and fire-control systems (the latter system, it will be recalled, taking up a great deal of volume in the aircraft). But the Navy "wouldn't hear of it."[84] Such frictions are common in associate contractor relationships. When the prime contractor has a weight-growth problem but is required to integrate a subsystem whose weight he must take as given, the potential for friction is clear. But the Navy's unwillingness to modify these subsystems to reduce their weight effectively closed off any further weight reductions beyond those obtained through SWIP.

The SWIP program stabilized the weight of the planned R&D prototypes of the F-111B at approximately 43,000 pounds, where it would remain until 1966. Further weight reductions would require substantial configuration changes, which were unacceptable to McNamara, and/or Mil-Spec relaxations—such as the static strength requirements for the aircraft structure—which were variously unacceptable to the Navy and the Air Force.[85] The Navy's technical staff at the Bureau of Naval Weapons felt at this point (late 1964) that more refined evaluation of the aircraft would have to await flight tests, which were to follow in a few months.[86] At this same time, however, the Navy's planned procurement of the F-111B, which had been increased to 705 units the prior March, was decreased to 335 units. This procurement level was slightly under the planned F-111B procurement of mid-1963 (that is, under the 359 F-111Bs planned after the original, "TFX-like" VAX requirement had been disapproved by OSD) and commenced a progression of cuts in firm production plans down to 50 units in 1966.[87]

[84] Interview 16.
[85] Interview 16; and TFX Hearings—Second Series, Part 3, p. 462.
[86] Interview 19.
[87] U.S. House of Representatives, Committee on Armed Services, Hearings on Military Posture (1969), p. 3202. The rising cost of the F-111B was also a factor in this volume reduction. As Richard

Since all participants agreed that the maximum weight reductions had been achieved for the existing F-111B design and specifications, those weight problems that remained would become performance problems—after all, weight *per se* was a problem mainly in terms of its impact on aircraft performance. Although the first of the SWIP F-111Bs (R&D prototype number four of the F-111B) would not be delivered until September 1966, a relatively firm baseline (between 43,000 and 46,000 pounds empty) now existed for making performance projections. On this basis, a carrier landing problem was anticipated for the new aircraft. The Navy said in late 1964 that it wanted a reduction in the 130-knot landing-approach speed of the aircraft. This problem was recognized by the contractor as well as the Navy. Carrier-arresting gear must absorb the momentum of a landing aircraft. This momentum is, in turn, a function of the aircraft's weight or mass times its landing velocity (Newton's familiar mv). At its given weight and approach speed, the F-111B neared the momentum-absorbing limits of Navy arresting gear. Since the weight of the aircraft was not considered susceptible to further reduction, the 130-knot approach velocity had to be reduced.[88]

To do this would require increasing the "lift" of the

Lorette has demonstrated, unit cost increases in weapon systems are commonly offset by reductions in the number of units to be procured, a step which reduces the growth in total program cost. See Richard J. Lorette, "The Relationship Between Pressures on the System Program Director and the Growth of Weapon System Cost Estimates" (unpublished D.B.A. dissertation, Harvard Business School, 1967), chap. 10.

[88] Memorandum for the Director of Defense Research and Engineering, from Leonard Sullivan, Jr., dated October 1, 1964, re Report of the PHOENIX/F-111B ad hoc group, printed in *TFX Hearings—Second Series*, Part 1, p. 68; "Washington Roundup: F-111B Weight Loss," *Aviation Week and Space Technology*, Vol. 85 (July 25, 1966), p. 25; George C. Wilson, "Variable-Geometry F-4 Proposed to Navy," *Aviation Week and Space Technology*, Vol. 85 (July 11, 1966), p. 30; and Interview 16.

wings. But the F-111B already had highly efficient wings in this aerodynamic sense. Achievement of the 15-knot reduction that the Navy required was considered beyond the state of the art.[89] General Dynamics began, however, to design modifications to the wings that would increase their lift without increasing aircraft drag (the plane did, of course, have higher-than-expected drag levels, which General Dynamics did not want to exacerbate). In April 1965, in his letter to McNamara advising a commitment to production, Air Force Secretary Zuckert was confident that the F-111B weight increase would, "[to] a considerable extent . . . [be] offset by the addition of high-lift flap devices improving landing and take-off capabilities."[90]

In this memorandum, Zuckert went on to describe two other changes in the F-111B program in 1965, changes that were considered necessary to reduce the risk of an unsatisfactory aircraft emerging in the years ahead. First, there were changes in the Navy contingent at the Air Force F-111 program office (SPO) at Wright-Patterson. Rear Admiral, W. E. Sweeney, was assigned to the SPO as Deputy Director for the F-111B/Phoenix program, and the size of the Navy contingent in the SPO was increased.[91] The original Navy contingent to the SPO had been small and was headed by a lower-ranking officer (a captain). The problems with the F-111B's weight, plus the difficulties being experienced in the integration of the Phoenix avionics (the AWG-9 system) with the airframe, suggested the need for a more in-

[89] Interview 16. One can infer this from the remarks of a chief Navy aeronautical engineer (also a critic of the program), who admitted that General Dynamics' solution to the problem "was really an advance in the state of the art." See *TFX Hearings—Second Series*, Part 2, p. 456.

[90] Memorandum for the Secretary of Defense, from Secretary of the Air Force Eugene Zuckert, dated April 13, 1965, re F-111 Program (from the files of the Permanent Subcommittee on Investigations, Committee on Government Operations, U.S. Senate, Exhibit 26W-51 of the *TFX Hearings—Second Series*).

[91] Ibid., p. 7.

tegrated management team to supervise the development.[92] The possibility of establishing a separate prime contractor-customer relationship between Grumman and the Navy (in effect, establishing a separate Navy program office and contractor) was also explored at this time. However, the plan was rejected due to strong opposition by high-level officials in the Air Force and General Dynamics.[93] The remedy of expanding and upgrading the Navy contingent was selected instead. The Bureau of Naval Weapons disliked this choice, since it created the expanded SPO contingent that the Bureau had successfully prevented in the first three years of the program.

The second change in the program that took place in 1965 was the initiation of work to increase the thrust of the F-111B's engine. While program officials anticipated that the General Dynamics work on higher-lift wings would alleviate the weight-induced carrier landing problem, a higher-thrust engine would be required to offset the weight growth in other performance areas (e.g., acceleration and rate-of-climb). Engine improvements were discussed throughout the early months of 1965. Actual specification and development of the improved engine (the so-called P-12 version of the TF-30 engine) began late in 1965, after

[92] Ibid. Recall that the Phoenix system was developed under Navy supervision outside the F-111 SPO. By these changes in 1965, procedures were established to coordinate the efforts of the Navy and the SPO for the Phoenix development; and contractual obligations were established between General Dynamics and Hughes (the Phoenix/AWG-9 contractor). Formalized obligations of this sort frequently fail to anticipate critical integration difficulties. In the Navy's A-7 program, for example, the development of an advanced avionics system (Integrated Light Attack Avionics System, or ILAAS) was placed under a separate project manager from the airframe development, and insurmountable integration difficulties resulted. See Head, "Decision-Making on the A-7 Attack Aircraft Program," p. 321.

[93] This conclusion is the author's surmise, based on testimony of Dr. Thomas Cheatham, in 1965 the Deputy Director of Defense Research and Engineering for Tactical Warfare, in *TFX Hearings—Second Series*, Part 3, pp. 521–540; and on Interviews 10, 11, 14, and 16.

flight tests commenced.[94] (The engine itself would not be available for three years).

With these technical and management changes in effect or under way, initial flight testing of the aircraft began. Before considering the nature of these flight tests and the later efforts devoted to resolving F-111B problems, we should summarize our discussion of the F-111B's development through 1965. The main cause of the F-111B's weight growth was the demanding joint requirement established in 1961. However, early in the program, the Navy sought and received certain performance and configuration guarantees that placed further weight burdens on the plane's design. As development efforts proceeded, the Navy sustained a broad range of specifications in the face of weight data that urged specification relaxation. The weight growth set in motion efforts to reduce the weight and approach speed of the aircraft, as well as to increase the thrust of the F-111B's engines; however, the weight and thrust improvements, at least, would not be available for a few years. Finally, as suggested by numerous examples throughout our discussion, the Navy's relatively inflexible position on

[94] Following its delivery that month, the first F-111B flew in May 1965. In August 1965, detailed design studies for the improved Navy engine began. Flight tests continued throughout this period and culminated in a formal Navy Preliminary Evaluation (NPE) in October 1965. The early report on the NPE was issued on November 3, 1965. On November 22, 1965, in a meeting attended by Deputy Secretary Vance, Navy Secretary Nitze, Air Force Secretary Brown, Director of Defense Research and Engineering Foster, and Deputy Assistant Secretary (Systems Analysis) Murray, McNamara gave a formal go-ahead on the new engine development. *TFX Hearings—Second Series*, Part 1, p. 105, and Part 3, pp. 498–500; Memorandum for the Record, by H. B. Robertson, Jr., Special Counsel to the Secretary of the Navy, dated November 22, 1965, re F-111B Program Meeting, printed in *TFX Hearings—Second Series*, Part 3, pp. 500–501; and Memorandum for the Secretary of Defense, from Eugene Zuckert, dated April 13, 1965, re F-111 Program (from the files of the Permanent Subcommittee on Investigations, Committee on Government Operations, U.S. Senate, Exhibit 26W-51 of the *TFX Hearings—Second Series*).

F-111B problems represented a decided contrast to the service's later, more lenient attitude toward F-14 problems. With this background, we will move first to consider the nature of the flight tests that the Navy conducted, tests important for the information they generated and the biases they embodied. We will then be prepared to observe the later technical efforts devoted to improving the F-111B, which ultimately failed to prevent the plane's cancellation.

Controlling "Hard" Data: The Navy Flight Tests

The beginning of flight tests marked a change in the basis of development decisions. Where "projections" and "estimates" were at issue in earlier decisions, actual flight test data would now be available. Since these tests were Navy controlled, the Navy would have an important, virtually autonomous ability to define the problems. Although the data would be drawn from flying aircraft, much of it would be qualitative. A Brookings Institution study notes: "The military services have what amounts to a conflict-of-interest problem. They identify military requirements, specify the system needed to fulfill them, and then serve as judge and jury over each weapon project."[95] There were important problems in the F-111B development. But the decisive voice in defining these problems would now be that of the Navy, a service skeptical of the F-111B's suitability.

Three characteristics of the tests enhanced the likelihood that the Navy would find severe faults with the F-111B. First, the F-111B's mission placed it at a disadvantage in the testing process, particularly with respect to the pilots who would fly the tests. The F-111B was not a "dogfighting" aircraft; in effect, its missiles and sophisticated avionics were to do the dogfighting. This was essentially the Missil-

[95] Charles Schultze, Edward R. Fried, Alice M. Rivlin, and Nancy H. Teeters, *Setting National Priorities: The 1973 Budget* (Washington: The Brookings Institution, 1972), p. 156.

eer's mission, which the F-111B had inherited. Since the time of the Navy debates on the Missileer back in the late 1950's, Navy pilots had remained skeptical of the concept of relying upon missile rather than aircraft performance for intercepting enemy aircraft.[96] The shift to the F-111B from the Missileer in 1961 had sustained this "missile-performance" concept for the fleet defense mission; yet without overt notice, it changed the type of pilot who would test and operate the Navy's fleet defense aircraft. The light, subsonic Missileer was to have been flown by Navy attack pilots, the subgroup of Navy pilots who fly the Navy's universally subsonic attack aircraft; however, the heavier, supersonic F-111B would be flown by Navy fighter pilots, the subgroup of Navy pilots who fly the Navy's universally supersonic tactical fighter aircraft.[97] Understandably, these latter pilots were the Navy group most opposed to the concept of placing a premium on missile rather than aircraft performance—whether that concept was embodied in a Navy-managed Missileer or an Air Force-managed F-111B. Consequently, the test pilots for the F-111 would have a doctrinal prejudice against the F-111B, beyond their sharing the wider Navy prejudice against this Air Force program. Moreover, in performing the tests, these pilots would use the more agile, lighter-weight F-4 Phantom as the bench mark of performance for the F-111B.[98] Though ade-

[96] Brownlow, "Navy Stresses Simplicity, Reliability," p. 79; and testimony of the Secretary of the Navy, Fred Korth, in *TFX Hearings—First Series*, Part 6, p. 1476.

[97] *TFX Hearings—Second Series*, Part 3, p. 483. As noted in footnote 58 of this chapter, the Navy's (supersonic) fighter pilots and (subsonic) attack pilots are virtually distinct suborganizations of the Navy. Each group has its own unique forms of training, equipment, and doctrine. Moreover, lateral mobility between the two groups is minimal. See Head, "Decision Making on the A-7 Attack Aircraft Program," pp. 124–134.

[98] Memorandum for the Director of Defense Research and Engineering, from Leonard Sullivan, Jr., dated October 1, 1964, re Report of PHOENIX/F-111B ad hoc group, printed in *TFX Hearings—Second Series*, Part 3, pp. 479–482.

quate power *was* a real problem in the program, the F-111B, burdened with 8,000 pounds of Phoenix missiles and avionics, inevitably would seem underpowered compared to the F-4, which had been designed for air-to-air combat and which had a mission configuration consisting of lighter weight missiles than the Phoenix.[99] As a DDR&E official foresaw in 1964, ". . . there is a very real and practical problem of 'pilot acceptance' of lower performance than the F-4. . . . The magnitude of this hurdle cannot be overemphasized; if the pilots don't like it, it will never reach the fleet."[100] But this lower performance was virtually assured, simply by the size and low relative power—that is, in effect, by the mission—of the F-111B.

The second point to be made about these tests is the way in which they discounted what was in fact a state-of-the-art advance, the afterburning, turbo-fan engine. The power curve of a turbo-fan engine is different from that of a turbo-jet engine. For a given maximum engine thrust, the military power of the turbo-fan engine (that is, the full thrust of the engine without its afterburner in operation) is generally less than that of a turbo-jet engine. However, the afterburner's augmentation of engine thrust is greater for the turbo-fan engine.[101] Many military flight tests are required to be performed in military power. These tests at military power,

[99] *TFX Hearings—Second Series*, Part 1, p. 71.

[100] Memorandum for the Director of Defense Research and Engineering, from Leonard Sullivan, Jr., dated October 1, 1964, re Report of PHOENIX/F-111B ad hoc group, printed in *TFX Hearings—Second Series*, Part 3, p. 480.

[101] Leon H. Dulberger, "Advanced Fighter-Attack Aircraft," *Space/Aeronautics*, Vol. 45 (April 1966), p. 87; Captain John Francis, Jr., USAF, "F-111: A Pilot's View," *Air Force Magazine*, Vol. 54 (April 1971), p. 36; Michael P. London, "Tactical Air Superiority," *Space/Aeronautics*, Vol. 49 (March 1968), p. 208; *TFX Hearings—Second Series*, Part 1, pp. 206–208; and Interviews 11 and 12. For the TF-30 engine, the thrust augmentation provided by the afterburner is approximately 80 percent. For a normal turbo-jet engine, the thrust augmentation is approximately 50 percent, though there are, of course, wide variations from engine to engine.

simply by the nature of the engine's power curve, would show the plane in a less favorable light.[102] The pilots flying the tests would be accustomed to the higher military-power performance of turbo-jet aircraft, such as the F-4. It is hardly surprising that these Navy test pilots returned reports emphasizing that the plane had "limited performance in military power" and that the "MIL Thrust [military power] performance of the vehicle is totally unsatisfactory from mission accomplishment and safety of flight aspects."[103] In the F-111B development, these evaluations were taken at face value; however, in the F-14 development, when pilots also complained of a lack of thrust in military power, high-level Navy officers were quick to recognize the subtleties of the turbo-fan's power curve. For example, Admiral Thomas McClellan, Commander of the Naval Air Systems Command, argued in Senate testimony that "the intermediate thrust [which was claimed to be deficient] is what was known in the past as military power. The [F-14A's] engine is meeting the specs and the power is there. What you have here is a fan engine which has different characteristics than a turbo-jet that the average pilot is used to flying. So there is some difference of opinion as to whether [the F-14A] lacks thrust."[104] Fine points of meaning such as this were

---

[102] Memorandum to the Chief of Naval Operations, from the Chief of the Bureau of Naval Weapons, dated February 5, 1964, re F-111B status, printed in *TFX Hearings—Second Series*, Part 2, pp. 401–404. These tests also showed the Air Force plane in a less favorable light. See, for example, *TFX Hearings—Second Series*, Part 3, p. 514.

[103] Navy speed-letter report for the Chief of the Bureau of Naval Weapons, dated November 3, 1965, re Phase I Navy Preliminary Evaluation of the Model F-111B Airplane: First Interim Report, p. 3; and Abstract and Performance Summary from the Navy Preliminary Evaluation of the F-111B Final Report, dated January 7, 1966, p. 54 (both test reports are from the files of the Permanent Subcommittee on Investigations, Committee on Government Operations, U.S. Senate, Exhibits 19 and 20A of the *TFX Hearings—Second Series*).

[104] U.S. Senate, Committee on Armed Services, *Fiscal Year 1973 Authorization for Military Procurement*, p. 3873. The Navy had a particular incentive to argue that the F-14A possessed sufficient

lost in the controversy of the F-111B development, which meant that the "overweight" F-111B would simply be judged "underpowered." Moreover, it meant that the F-111B would be harshly judged on a standard carrier compatibility test—the single-engine, rate-of-climb test, which is made to show whether a plane that is landing can take off again from a carrier, in military power, with only one engine in operation, after "missing" its landing. The Navy told the Secretaries, for example, that a "wave-off" (a landing that, at the last moment, could not be completed) could mean an ordered ejection from the aircraft. It is hardly surprising that McNamara responded by saying, " 'That kind of aircraft could not be accepted.' "[105]

The third point to be made about these tests is the apparent attitude of the pilots conducting them. As one DDR&E official commented in 1966, the "Navy test pilot . . . had a single-minded approach—did the plane meet the specifications?"[106] A brief survey of other flight test reports corroborated this observation. For example, in a May 1966 flight test report on the high-lift devices General Dynamics had developed, the Navy test pilot first noted the serious need for greater directional stability; he then went on to cite the source of the instability: "[Various] means of

---

power: it had cancelled the F-14 B/C program, which was to have equipped all but the first 67 units of the F-14 with a more powerful engine.

[105] Notes of the Icarus meeting, September 17, 1966, quoted in *TFX Hearings—Second Series*, Part 3, p. 549. The single-engine, rate-of-climb test simulates a missed landing when one engine and both afterburners are out of commission, such as might occur after combat.

[106] Notes of the Icarus meeting, October 1, 1966, summarized in *TFX Hearings—Second Series*, Part 3, p. 550. We should emphasize that Navy test pilots are widely recognized for the rigor of their evaluations. The problem with the "specification orientation" of their F-111B evaluations was simply that their professional rigor could not be separated from the wider Navy skepticism. Indeed, "professional rigor" would be a natural medium for the expression of Navy bias.

artificial stability compensation have been used to circumvent basic airplane design requirements for stability in the high-lift configuration. . . . The improved high-lift characteristics failed to offset the weight growth of the F-111B airplane to permit compliance with performance guarantees . . . carrier operations specification requirements . . . and fleet operational needs."[107] We should note that Air Force pilots also criticized the directional instabilities of the plane.[108] The point here, however, is that Navy tests were far the more specification-oriented, conceding little to the plane whenever specifications were not being met, even as the Navy remained inflexible on compromising any specifications. "Basic airplane design requirements" had been

[107] Abstract from the Navy Evaluation of the Production F-111B High-Lift Devices, Final Report, dated November 23, 1966 (from the files of the Permanent Subcommittee on Investigations, Committee on Government Operations, U.S. Senate, Exhibit 22B of the *TFX Hearings—Second Series*).

[108] Abstract from the report entitled, "Preliminary Air Force Evaluation of the Low-Speed Handling Qualities of the F-111," dated February 1970 (from the files of the Permanent Subcommittee on Investigations, Committee on Government Operations, U.S. Senate, Exhibit 22A of *TFX Hearings—Second Series*). By contrast to the requirements orientation of the Navy test reports, this Air Force test report notes that, with the stability augmentation system turned on, "the aircraft was easy to land in smooth air . . . even at an aft center of gravity," but with parts of the system inoperative, control became more difficult—for example, angle of attack control was "very difficult" under these circumstances. The Air Force report is, then, a fairly balanced appraisal, citing weaknesses as well as strengths in the various performance remedies being attempted. Nowhere in the Air Force report is the stability augmentation system described in such terms as a "means of artificial stability compensation" to circumvent "basic design requirements."

It may appear that the distinction between Air Force and Navy test reports is being exaggerated. We would argue, however, that the differing evaluations of the Air Force and Navy test reports are a concise reflection of the thesis of this chapter. They indicate that, for the Air Force, which took the acceptability of the F-111 for granted, deficiencies represented problems only at the margin of a fundamentally acceptable capability; while for the Navy, which doubted the acceptability of the F-111B, deficiencies were a confirmation that the plane's "basic requirements" were unsuitable.

284

circumvented—there is perhaps no simpler expression of the Navy's skepticism of the F-111B's basic suitability. Moreover, these tests and other performance estimates would be strictly interpreted by the Navy. For example, the landing wind-over-deck of the F-111B would be cited as deficient, which it was (by seven knots) compared to the contract specifications. However, it was only deficient by one knot versus the Navy's original requirements of 1961, and it was superior to that of the F-4 Phantom by approximately eleven knots.[109] To be sure, one or two qualitative measurements cannot fully describe a plane's "carrier compatibility." They can only suggest what the compatibility might be. Hence, the F-111B's superiority to the F-4 on landing wind-over-deck is only a clue to, and not conclusive proof of, the F-111B's actual compatibility. But the very complexity and uncertainty of the compatibility issue (in common with most performance issues) allowed organizations possessing inevitably conflicting evidence on F-111B compatibility to observe a confirmation of their working assumptions on the program. The Navy, which doubted the F-111B's basic suitability, which maintained a single-minded attention to specifications because it believed it had been "'ratcheted down' in its requirements and could not give more,"[110] observed quantitative performance deficiencies

[109] Memorandum for the Director of Defense Research and Engineering, from Leonard Sullivan, Jr., dated October 1, 1964, re Report of PHOENIX/F-111B ad hoc group, printed in *TFX Hearings—Second Series*, Part 3, p. 480; and *TFX Hearings—First Series*, Part 6, p. 1414. The specification incorporated in the contract was the evaluated wind-over-deck for the 1962 General Dynamics design proposal, rather than that of the Navy's original requirement. Moreover, sometime after the contract award in 1962, but before July 1964, the Navy changed the way it measured wind-over-deck, from a so-called standard day measurement to a "hot day" measurement. This increased the *measured* wind-over-deck by about 3 to 4 knots in tests, though the *specified* wind-over-deck would remain unchanged. Hence, the apparent performance discrepancy on this characteristic was artificially inflated. See Memorandum for the Deputy Secretary of Defense, from Paul Nitze, dated July 29, 1964, re F-111, reprinted in *TFX Hearings—Second Series*, Part 2, p. 461.
[110] Interview 9.

relative to the contract as conclusive evidence of the F-111B's incompatibility with the carrier environment. The contractors' test pilots, whose bias was naturally different from the Navy's, judged that the F-111B would easily land on a carrier.[111]

A negative bias thus inhered in the flight tests, because of a skeptical Navy's control of the tests, because of the type of pilots who would be flying the tests, and because of a systematic technical feature of the tests. Deficiencies serve to confirm an organization's doubts about options whose acceptability is not assumed in advance. Clearly, the bias of the Navy-controlled flight tests would generate extensive documentation of such deficiencies on the F-111B. The tests did reveal legitimate and important problems, but given the uncertainty surrounding key notions of operational suitability—like "carrier compatibility"—it would be inordinately difficult for high-level officials to separate what was true from what was biased. Moreover, since high-level officials could not readily have manipulated test procedures to eliminate bias, these officials had to take the pilot complaints seriously, even if the complaints were distorted.[112] Flight tests represent the most authoritative evaluation of a weapon system, and Congress would not likely approve an aircraft that the Navy pilots, fairly or not, had rated unacceptable.

[111] Interview 16. The pilots who made this judgement were from Hughes (the Phoenix contractor) as well as General Dynamics.

[112] As we shall see later in this discussion, these officials consciously preferred to allow the testing process to proceed uninhibited. This is understandable, given the obvious service resentment that would follow any meddling with their testing prerogatives, as well as the obvious and compelling they're-the-ones-who-have-to-use-it-so-they-should-be-the-ones-to-test-it arguments that would be leveled against any Secretarial intrusion in this area. The F-111 program had enough political problems as it was, without adding this one. The point, however, is not that the Secretaries necessarily could have overcome the bias of the tests; it is rather that this bias was virtually inevitable in a common development. Consequently, the bias of the tests is yet another area where the Navy would have critical control in the implementation of McNamara's decision to establish a bi-service development.

The technical efforts devoted to the F-111B between 1965 and 1967 were primarily responses to the evolving understanding of F-111B capabilities demonstrated in the flight tests. These technical efforts took the form of a sequential pursuit of development problems, where the solution of one problem only created yet another problem. The next section will examine these efforts—the final attempts to secure an acceptable airplane before the Navy moved to cancel it.

The Cycle of Problems: 1965–1967

The flight tests were a continuing process during this period. Generally, they returned pessimistic information about the aircraft's power and performance (in addition, of course, to evidence about the engine-stall problem). In October 1965, the first formal government flight test of the F-111 was conducted by Navy pilots on a pre-SWIP F-111B —"The Navy wanted to evaluate the plane as quickly as possible."[113] In a move "without precedent," the Navy publicly released portions of the test reports on this pre-SWIP F-111B (the SWIP F-111B would not be available until September 1966). Naturally, since it was the first government test, and since a pre-SWIP aircraft was being tested, a large number of faults were cited (some, of course, major in scope) giving a particularly unfavorable impression of the aircraft.[114]

[113] Interview 12. This first test was a so-called Navy Preliminary Evaluation (NPE). For a general description of NPEs, see J. J. Hernandez, "Steps in Preliminary Evaluations," *Naval Aviation News* (November 1966), p. 37. For a description of the F-111B's first NPE, see *TFX Hearings—Second Series*, Part 3, pp. 498–499, 510. The pre-SWIP F-111B (that is, the F-111B without the SWIP weight reductions) had a weight empty approximately 3,000 pounds greater than that of the SWIP F-111B. The first three F-111B prototypes were pre-SWIP aircraft.

[114] Erwin J. Bulban, "General Dynamics Defends F-111 Program," p. 34; "Washington Roundup: F-111B Weight Loss," p. 25; and Wilson, "Variable-Geometry F-4 Proposed to Navy," p. 30. Though an unfavorable impression of the plane was created by release of the report, some idea of the actual status of the F-111B can be gained by

Technical efforts were devoted to resolving the problems anticipated earlier and those now being revealed in the flight tests. By 1966, General Dynamics' efforts to reduce the F-111B's landing speed bore fruit. General Dynamics resolved this problem by adding a unique second slat to the leading edge of the F-111B's wing, and by increasing the area and deflection angle of its wing flaps.[115] A 20 percent improvement in the wing's maximum coefficient of lift was achieved, as was the desired 15-knot reduction in landing approach speed—down to 115 knots with six Phoenix

comparing its first flight tests to those of other Navy aircraft. (This first Navy flight test is called a Phase I [airworthiness] Navy Preliminary Evaluation.) Taking the Phase I NPEs for the Navy's F-14 and (lower technical risk) A-7 gives the following comparison:

	Number of Specific Deficiencies		
	F-111B	F-14	A-7
Major Deficiencies (i.e., "Safety of Flight" or "Mandatory" corrections)	29	43	18
Minor Deficiencies (i.e., "Desirable for Correction")	112	75	Not Known

These numbers are not directly comparable. However, they do make the point that all planes have numerous deficiencies in the first stage of testing and that a mere citation of limitations does not convey much meaning about the capability of the aircraft. The results must be handled carefully—something the Navy did not do in its public release of the findings of the F-111B tests. See "F-14 Deficiencies," *Aviation Week and Space Technology*, Vol. 97 (July 24, 1972), p. 18; *TFX Hearings—Second Series*, Part 3, p. 498; and U.S. Senate, Committee on Armed Services, *Fiscal Year 1973 Authorization for Military Procurement*, p. 3762.

[115] Interview 16. These changes in moveable surfaces of the wing resolved the landing-speed problem without adversely affecting the performance of the plane in normal flight operations. With the new flaps and slats retracted, the wing's cross-section was no different than it had been before the changes were made. However, with its flaps and slats deployed, the new wing could assume a greater curvature— and hence provide more lift—than the original wing. This greater lift allowed the plane to approach the carrier safely at a lower landing speed.

missiles on the aircraft.[116] Some stability problems remained, but the essential reduction in approach speed had been obtained.

The Navy had not anticipated that this reduction in landing speed would be successful, as a state-of-the-art advance was required to achieve it. But once the reduction in landing speed was obtained, a new problem appeared: the reduction in landing speed meant reduced aerodynamic force on the control surfaces of the aircraft, since the aircraft moved more slowly through the air when landing.[117]

The Navy then complained of directional change and control sluggishness. The low drag of the F-111B relative to other aircraft, coupled with the plane's low approach speed, meant that the engines would have to run very near idle in landings, where the engines had a very slow response. En-

[116] By comparison, the Navy's A-6 attack aircraft has an approach speed of 126 knots, its A-7 has an approach speed of approximately 130 knots, and its F-8 air superiority fighter has an approach speed of between 130 and 140 knots. The Navy's F-14 has a specified approach speed of 123 knots, with a significantly lighter missile load. One report indicates that the F-14's actual approach speed is 117 knots. These are not all-other-things-equal comparisons; among other differences, these planes are all lighter than the F-111B. However, there is a high correlation between safety and landing speed. Stuart Levin notes: "Even on land, with a nice fixed airstrip, the accident frequency increases with the 2-2½ power of landing speed. Navy [sic] has found it worse on carriers, increasing with roughly the cube of speed." See Brown, "Accelerated Testing Set for the F-14A," p. 53; Stuart M. Levin, "Why the Swing-Wing?" *Space/Aeronautics*, Vol. 50 (November 1968), p. 73; Brooke Nihart, "Navy's F-14," *Armed Forces Journal*, Vol. 109 (December 1971), p. 41; *TFX Hearings—First Series*, Part 6, pp. 1542–1545; *TFX Hearings—Second Series*, Part 1, p. 135; and U.S. Senate, Committee on Appropriations, *Lightweight Fighter Aircraft Program*, p. 58. Information on the technical performance of the wing modifications is from Abstract from the Navy Evaluation of the Production F-111B High-Lift Devices, Final Report, dated November 23, 1966; and Abstract from the report entitled "Preliminary Air Force Evaluation of the Handling Qualities of the F-111, May, 1966," dated February, 1970 (both abstracts from the files of the Permanent Subcommittee on Investigations, Committee on Government Operations, U.S. Senate, Exhibits 22A and 22B of the *TFX Hearings—Second Series*).

[117] Interview 16.

gine thrust could not be used easily for correctional maneuvers. Allegedly, if the aircraft did not come into its final approach properly oriented, the pilot was required to go from minimum to maximum throttle settings, back and forth, to achieve the proper orientation. In these circumstances, there was risk of the airplane's "running away" from the pilot.[118]

General Dynamics argued that Pratt & Whitney should be required to increase engine responsiveness in the lower performance ranges. There had been a number of problems with the engine fuel controls (indeed, these controls were one source of the stall problem).[119] The engines, however, were Government Furnished Aeronautical Equipment, the development of which was being supervised by the Navy. General Dynamics tried to get binding contractual responsibilities from Pratt & Whitney, but both Pratt & Whitney and the Navy refused, the former saying that it was "selling engines to the Navy, not General Dynamics."[120] The Navy argued that General Dynamics should put greater drag on the aircraft—the Navy had never liked the extremely "clean" configuration that the Air Force mission had dictated for the plane. With higher airframe drag during landings, the Navy argued, the engines could be run at higher throttle settings (where they had more rapid response) without increasing the plane's existing landing speed. General Dynamics proved mathematically that the Navy's de-

---

[118] Interview 9. For more information on this problem, see "Aerospace in Perspective: Tactical Warfare," *Space/Aeronautics*, Vol. 49 (January 1968), p. 116; London, "VFX—The Navy's Choice," p. 55; and Donald C. Winston, "Navy Studies F-111B Offensive Missions," *Aviation Week and Space Technology*, Vol. 87 (October 23, 1967), p. 29.

[119] Interviews 13 and 16; and General Dynamics, "GD F-111 Category I Flight Test Progress Report," dated June 30, 1965, p. 12a (from the files of the Permanent Subcommittee on Investigations, Committee on Government Operations, U.S. Senate, Exhibit 18F of the *TFX Hearings—Second Series*).

[120] Interview 16.

mand for additional drag would require enlarging the wing "spoilers" to the size of barn doors![121] Nonetheless, General Dynamics increased the spoiler area as much as was practicable. Pratt & Whitney attempted to improve engine response but did so without performance obligations to General Dynamics. With the advent of these Navy-only changes to the airplane and the anticipation of further changes, the Navy began for the first time to fund development efforts peculiar to the F-111B aircraft on July 1, 1966.[122]

As these remedies were being pursued in the latter part of 1966, General Dynamics sat down with Navy people to ask them what, finally, the Navy needed to make the F-111B an acceptable aircraft. The Navy agreed to specify its needs and soon detailed the desired changes. The Navy contended that the weight increase in the F-111B (even as reduced by the SWIP effort) had forced the aircraft into a higher angle of attack—a higher "nose up" attitude—in landings. The Navy argued that the resulting decrease in over-the-nose visibility required modification.[123] There was initially some controversy over the need for additional visibility, for General Dynamics test pilots considered the visibility of-

[121] Interview 16. Spoilers are flat, moveable plates that conform to the upper surface of a wing. They can be angled sharply upward from the wing to disturb the smooth flow of air over the wing. When this is done, the spoilers increase the drag and reduce the lift of a wing. In the usage proposed by the Navy, the spoilers would in effect have been acting as drag brakes.

[122] *TFX Hearings—Second Series*, Part 3, p. 653; U.S. Senate, Committee on Armed Services, *Authorization for Military Procurement, Research and Development, Fiscal Year 1969, and Reserve Strength*, Hearings, 90th Cong., 2d Sess. (1968), p. 953; and Interview 16.

[123] "Aerospace in Perspective: Tactical Warfare" (January 1968), p. 116; notes of the Icarus meeting, March 11, 1967, quoted in *TFX Hearings—Second Series*, Part 3, p. 557; U.S. Senate, Committee on Armed Services, *Authorization for Military Procurement, Research and Development, Fiscal Year 1969, and Reserve Strength*, p. 953; Winston, "Navy Studies F-111B Offensive Missions," p. 29; and Interview 16.

fered by the F-111B in landings to be sufficient.[124] Flight tests (including cockpit movies) through December 1966 were intended to resolve this controversy, as well as to provide a basis for determining any other needed changes. After these tests, all parties accepted the need—at least for purposes of securing Navy acquiescence—to incorporate a package of modifications called the "N-1 package of fixes."[125]

The N-1 modifications included visibility improvements (raised pilots' seats, a sharper windshield angle, and a higher wing-flap deflection angle) and balance improvements (a two-foot extension of the nose, an eight-inch rearward shift of the landing gear, and a forward redistribution of the moveable avionics). These improvements were to be phased into the production of F-111B prototypes along with the improved (10 percent more powerful) version of the TF-30 engine (the P-12). Initially, the improvements were expected to be available in late 1967 with the delivery of F-111B prototype number six.[126]

In all, these improvements added approximately 2,500 pounds to the empty weight of the aircraft. It was these Navy-directed N-1 changes that brought the F-111B's weight-empty within 0.4 percent of the earlier-noted Bu-

[124] Notes of the Icarus meeting, October 1, 1966, quoted in *TFX Hearings—Second Series*, Part 3, p. 550.

[125] Ibid; and Memorandum for the Deputy Secretary of Defense, from Secretary of the Air Force Harold Brown, dated May 2, 1966, re F-111 flight test review (from the files of the Permanent Subcommittee on Investigations, Committee on Government Operations, U.S. Senate, Exhibit 26W-33 of the *TFX Hearings—Second Series*). The Brown memorandum of May 1966 states that F-111B performance will be evaluated in flight tests by December 1966, and that changes required to achieve acceptable performance will be incorporated in the Navy's number one production aircraft. In other words, in mid-1966, Brown and his superiors were anticipating the "final" set of Navy changes required to make the F-111B an "acceptable" aircraft.

[126] *TFX Hearings—Second Series*, Part 1, pp. 109–110; U.S. Senate, Committee on Armed Services, *Military Procurement Authorizations for Fiscal Year 1968*, p. 784; and U.S. Senate, Committee on Armed Services, *Authorization for Military Procurement, Research and Development, Fiscal Year 1969, and Reserve Strength*, p. 953.

reau of Naval Weapons weight estimate of 1964. Moreover, they increased the aircraft's fuel capacity by 2,000 pounds, thereby increasing the take-off gross weight by this additional amount.[127] The additional fuel would aid in the achievement of the specified loiter time. But it would also degrade measures of carrier compatibility and cause an additional weight increase in a plane whose central political problem lay in its overweight condition and in the compatibility difficulties thought to result. As an aerospace journal noted in late 1966, "the F-111B has run into an overweight problem and it is on this point that [Senator] McClellan has refocused his investigative fire."[128] Finally, the N-1 changes, particularly the windshield angle change, would increase the aerodynamic drag of the plane, thereby tending to decrease the F-111B's loiter range.[129] In 1967, *Armed Forces Management*, a publication with close relations to the services, alluded to the negative impact of the N-1 changes: "What [the N-1 changes] may do to the aerodynamic performance of the aircraft is not being discussed, even on a non-attributable basis, by Navy and Industry engineers."[130] In spite of all these disadvantages, the N-1 changes had one central advantage in the eyes of the contractor and of high-level defense officials: these changes represented what the Navy acknowledged, in writing, was finally necessary to make the F-111B an "acceptable" aircraft.[131]

The flight tests of those F-111B's already delivered con-

[127] "Aerospace in Perspective: Tactical Warfare" (January 1968), p. 116; "F-111B Estimated Performance Chart, July 1967," a document supplied by the Navy to the McClellan Committee in 1970 (from the files of the Permanent Subcommittee on Investigations, Committee on Government Operations, U.S. Senate, Exhibit 7 of the *TFX Hearings—Second Series*); *TFX Hearings—Second Series*, Part 2, pp. 455–456; and Interview 16.

[128] "Perspective: Navy Says it Wants the F-111B, Heavy or Not," p. 29.

[129] Interview 22.

[130] "An AFM Essay: The F-111B—White Hope or White Elephant?" *Armed Forces Management*, Vol. 13 (July 1967), pp. 28–29.

[131] Notes of the Icarus meeting, March 11, 1967, quoted in *TFX Hearings—Second Series*, Part 3, p. 557.

tinued throughout this period. The first SWIP F-111B (F-111B prototype number four) was delivered in the fall of 1966 and was used in late 1966 and early 1967 to perform preliminary "check-out" tests on the SWIP modifications. The second SWIP F-111B (the fifth F-111B prototype) was delivered in early 1967. It was used in March and April for the initial stages of the first formal Navy evaluation of the SWIP aircraft.[132] The conclusions of the Navy test were negative:

> The F-111B remains unfit for service use as previously reported [in the October 1965 preliminary evaluation] and was found to be incapable of carrier-based operations. . . . The large disparity between observed performance and the specification performance requirements of the airplane is a cause for concern. . . . The climb performance in Military [non-afterburner] thrust remains poor, with little improvement over that previously reported and compares unfavorably with other Navy airplanes. . . . Acceleration in Combat [full afterburner] thrust . . . was found to be unacceptable. . . . The performance of the propulsion system of the airplane continues to not only be unacceptable in a service airplane but imposes distinct safety hazards [this relates to the stall problem and the lack of engine responsiveness]. . . .[133]

To make matters worse, these tests had to be cut short after the tragic crash of the other SWIP F-111B in April. The completed formal evaluation would be delayed by eight months—until February 1968—as only one SWIP aircraft would now be available to perform both the basic tests and the formal evaluation.[134]

---

[132] *TFX Hearings—Second Series*, Part 1, p. 68, and Part 3, p. 512.

[133] Abstract from the Phase IB Navy Preliminary Evaluation of the SWIP F-111B, Final Report, dated June 1, 1967, printed in *TFX Hearings—Second Series*, Part 3, pp. 512–513.

[134] *TFX Hearings—Second Series*, Part 1, p. 68.

This unexpected delay was a serious blow to the program, as it slowed the program's general progress and delayed carrier suitability trials of the aircraft. Successful carrier landings of the aircraft, after all, would be the most convincing demonstration of the plane's carrier suitability. But early trials could not be held. All that existed in terms of a formal evaluation was the Navy's harshly critical one quoted above, which revealed legitimate problems but also reflected the biases of the testing process discussed earlier. Increased engine thrust perhaps could alleviate some of the difficulties. However, the more powerful, Navy-developed P-12 engine was itself delayed. The first P-12 engines were to be incorporated in the sixth F-111B prototype, which was, in turn, due to be delivered in the fall of 1967. The engine delays now necessitated postponement of delivery of this aircraft until the spring of 1968.[135]

The negative test reports, the delay in further tests, and the delayed engine availability all exacerbated a central problem of the program—the political problem. In 1966, Senator McClellan had led a successful move to block funds for long lead-time production items on the F-111B.[136] In

[135] U.S. Senate, Committee on Armed Services, *Military Procurement Authorizations for Fiscal Year 1968*, p. 784; and U.S. Senate Committee on Armed Services, *Authorization for Military Procurement, Research and Development, Fiscal Year 1969, and Reserve Strength*, p. 953. The sixth F-111B prototype also was to incorporate the nose extension and high-lift modifications of the N-1 package of fixes, but not the windshield, landing gear, and seat modifications.

[136] U.S. Senate, Committee on Armed Services, *Military Procurement Authorizations for Fiscal Year 1968*, pp. 699–700, and George C. Wilson, "McClellan to Resume F-111 Investigation," *Aviation Week and Space Technology*, Vol. 85 (August 22, 1966), p. 17. In blocking F-111B production, Senator McClellan wanted to prevent the Defense Department from tying the Navy into the program by committing it to production—or, as one former Navy official described it, McClellan wanted to prevent the Department from "getting the Navy half-pregnant so that it would compromise" (Interview 9). For an indication of the degree to which the Air Force, by contrast, was anxious to have binding commitments made to its part of the program, see U.S. Senate, Committee on Armed Services, *Authorization for Military Procurement, Research and Development, Fiscal Year 1969, and Reserve Strength*, p. 394.

the wake of the new difficulties with the program in 1967, he successfully blocked production funding once again. Senator McClellan actually wanted to have the program terminated at this point. However, he did not have the votes, primarily because many Congressmen feared that canceling the F-111B would leave the Navy without a fleet air defense capability.[137] (McDonnell had earlier proposed a variable-sweep version of its F-4 Phantom as a substitute for the F-111B, but this alternative lacked a Phoenix capability.)[138]

In short, what McClellan and the Navy lacked in 1967 was an alternative aircraft to fulfill the Phoenix, fleet-air-defense mission. With such an alternative in hand, Congressional termination of the program would become politically feasible.

The alternative was not long in coming.

Forward to Cancellation: 1967–1968

In our examination of the program through mid-1967, we have observed the F-111B going through a cycle of problems, as the contractor and defense officials sought to secure a satisfactory airplane. The initial weight growth led to high-lift remedies and the development of a higher-thrust engine, then to enlarged spoilers and improved engine controls, and finally to the N-1 package of fixes. The solution to each problem only led to yet another problem. This pattern of problem-solving conforms to the short-range, reactive pattern of technical effort observed earlier for the F-111A's performance and compatibility problems (see Chapters III and IV). It is important here because political moves in Congress could foreclose the effort. While high-level defense officials presumed an acceptable aircraft could be achieved, the Navy, hostile to the program, would seek

---

[137] London, "VFX—The Navy's Choice," p. 57; and Interview 10.
[138] *TFX Hearings–Second Series*, Part 1, p. 91; and Wilson, "Variable-Geometry F-4 Proposed to Navy," p. 30–31.

cancellation. The technical remedies pursued through mid-1967 would prove to be insufficient and overdue in the face of the increasing Navy desire for program cancellation.

The chain of cancellation events commenced in July 1967, even as the Congress was about to delete funds for long lead-time, production items for the F-111B. In July the Soviet Union held its first major air show in six years. The six advanced fighters that the Soviets displayed at the show "touched off new Navy fears that Soviet aerospace technology was making greater strides than that of the United States."[139] As Admiral E. R. Zumwalt, Jr., Chief of Naval Operations, later observed: "[At] the Domodedovo air show, the Soviets [unveiled] six new fighter prototypes that possessed predicted aerodynamic and weapons performances which would surpass those of the F-4. Facing military obsolescence in its fighter aircraft, and with the unsatisfactory F-111B program failing to provide an acceptable alternative, the Navy set about to produce an advanced fighter able to cope with the entire air threat spectrum foreseen through the mid-1980's."[140] The Navy fears expressed at the time were an atypical reaction to the air show. For example, *Aviation Week* editorialized: "The Soviets appear to have exhausted their creative design capability in the current generation of aerospace technology and are leaning more heavily than at any time since the end of World War 2 on foreign concepts. . . . [One] of the lessons of Domodedovo may be that the Soviets are having difficulty in keeping up with the accelerated pace of western technology."[141] Another trade journal reported: "Although the Moscow Air Show last month was the most important dis-

[139] "Navy Facing Dilemma Over Decision on Fighter Plane," *Congressional Quarterly Weekly Report*, Vol. xxvi (February 16, 1968), p. 286. See also Robert Hotz, "Echoes from Domodedovo," *Aviation Week and Space Technology*, Vol. 87 (July 17, 1967), p. 21.

[140] U.S. Senate, Committee on Armed Services, *Fiscal Year 1973 Authorization for Military Procurement*, pp. 3744–3745.

[141] Hotz, "Echoes from Domodedovo," p. 21. See also Robert D. Archer, "The Soviet Fighters," *Space/Aeronautics*, Vol. 50 (July 1968), pp. 64–72.

play of new Soviet aircraft in years, Pentagon experts tended to downgrade the importance of the planes exhibited. In fact, the Soviet display, they felt, was of more psychological and propaganda importance than of technical significance. Considering the very poor performance of Russian equipment [in the Six Day War in the Middle East], the Soviets had to do something to recoup some of their lost prestige."[142]

In spite of this general downgrading of the air show, the fears of the Navy were taken seriously at the time. There was "some feeling" among high-level Navy civilians that the "F-111B solution"—that is, a pure philosophy of extended-range intercept, with little close-range "dogfighting" capability—was perhaps the wrong solution to fleet defense in light of the new Soviet fighters.[143] Moreover, as noted earlier, there had always been considerable ambivalence within the Navy (particularly among Navy fighter pilots) about this solution to the fleet defense problem. Events of the mid-1960s—notably the Vietnam air war—heightened the Navy's (and the Air Force's) awareness of the need for aerial combat capability in tactical fighters.[144] The Soviet air show only increased this sensitivity; and it was, of course, in the Navy's interest to act upon it, since the F-111B lacked close-range capabilities.

Consequently, the Navy commissioned Grumman, a long-time builder of Navy aircraft and a major subcontractor on the F-111 program, to evaluate the F-111B's capabilities relative to the "heightened" Soviet threat. Grumman submitted its study in October. The study concluded that the F-111B would not meet the Navy's needs for an air superiority fighter capable of successfully mixing in dogfights with Soviet fighters. However, Grumman did more than study

[142] "Pentagon Unimpressed by New Soviet Fighters," *Armed Forces Management*, Vol. 13 (August 1967), p. 13.
[143] Interview 18.
[144] Levin, "Why the Swing-Wing?" p. 71; London, "Tactical Air Superiority," pp. 62–63; and London, "VFX—the Navy's Choice," p. 51.

the F-111B. It submitted an "unsolicited proposal" for the plane's redesign.[145] The Grumman proposal incorporated the F-111B's Phoenix missile system and its P-12 engines in a smaller and lighter airframe of swing-wing design. Shortly thereafter, three other companies having long and close relationships with the Navy—Ling-Temco-Vought, McDonnell-Douglas, and North American Rockwell—also submitted proposals. At approximately this time, the Navy told General Dynamics that it "didn't really want the F-111B"— this in spite of its earlier agreement in writing that the N-1 changes would make the F-111B an acceptable aircraft.[146]

The Grumman submission represented a critical defection from the program, since, along with the other contractors' proposals that followed, it provided the kind of discrete alternative to the F-111B that had been lacking in the 1967 Congressional hearings. It occurred in the midst of General Dynamics' efforts to develop a final set of major changes for the F-111B on which the Navy had agreed. And it was hardly an "unsolicited" set of proposals. As a former Navy program official commented, "No one does something for nothing."[147] This was not the first time that Grumman had broken ranks with General Dynamics. Back in 1964, Grum-

[145] "Navy Evaluates F-111B Substitutes," *Aviation Week and Space Technology*, Vol. 88 (January 29, 1968), p. 22; "Navy Facing Dilemma Over Decision on Fighter Plane," p. 286; and U.S. Senate, Committee on Appropriations, *Department of Defense Appropriations for Fiscal Year 1969*, Hearings, 90th Cong., 2d Sess. (1968), pp. 1058–1059. For a different interpretation of these proposals—an interpretation which links the proposals to the OSD-approved redesign studies of 1964–1965—see letter to the Editor of the *Washington Post*, from George A. Spangenberg, Director of the Evaluation Division of the Naval Air Systems Command, dated May 2, 1972, printed in "The F-14 Deal: An Inside Story," *Armed Forces Journal*, Vol. 109 (June 1972), p. 10.

[146] Interview 16. For a discussion of the alternatives being proposed, see "Case Studies in Military-Industrial Pressures," *Congressional Quarterly Weekly Report*, Vol. xxvi (May 24, 1968), p. 1165; "Navy Evaluates F-111B Substitutes," p. 22; and "Navy Facing Dilemma Over Decision on Fighter Plane," p. 286.

[147] Interview 9.

man had exerted a great deal of effort in developing F-111B redesign proposals following the initial weight growth.[148] At that time, Grumman concluded that the achievement of Navy mission requirements was contingent on a significant departure from commonality.[149] Grumman's new, 1967 proposal was essentially a reiteration of this earlier position. Grumman was widely suspected to have been less than fully committed to the F-111 program.[150] In any event, because of the promise of the "unsolicited" design proposals, the Chief of Naval Operations initiated a fighter study to evaluate the F-111B against possible alternative aircraft.[151]

This study would serve to sharpen and refine the alternatives to the F-111B.[152] Even as the F-111B improvements and flight tests were being further delayed, attractive alternatives, free of the troubled past of the bi-service F-111B, were emerging. Clearly, the Navy was being given greater latitude than it had known previously in the F-111 program.[153]

This sudden latitude was a result of high-level personnel

---

[148] *TFX Hearings—Second Series*, Part 2, pp. 446–451. These so-called CWIP (Colossal Weight Improvement Program) studies created some animosity between General Dynamics and Grumman (Interviews 9 and 16).

[149] *TFX Hearings—Second Series*, Part 2, pp. 448–450.

[150] "Aerospace in Perspective: Tactical Warfare," *Space/Aeronautics*, Vol. 51 (January 1969), p. 100; and Interviews 14 and 16.

[151] U.S. Senate, Committee on Appropriations, *Department of Defense Appropriations for Fiscal Year 1969*, p. 1059.

[152] Ibid., pp. 1058–1059. According to public reports at the time, the study concluded that it was too soon to make a decision between the F-111B and the proposed alternatives. However, as will be discussed in the text, Navy officials privately moved for cancellation at approximately this time.

[153] Compare this new Navy latitude to earlier restrictions placed on efforts to improve the F-111B. As late as September 1966, Secretary McNamara and Air Force Secretary Brown admonished the Icarus participants to avoid proposals for F-111B improvements that reduced commonality. Now, in late 1967, the Navy was allowed to define alternatives that were more than departures from commonality —they were completely new airframes. Notes of the Icarus meeting, September 10, 1966, excerpted in *TFX Hearings—Second Series*, Part 3, p. 549.

changes within the Defense Department. In June 1967, Paul Nitze, Secretary of the Navy, was named to replace Cyrus Vance as Deputy Secretary of Defense.[154] In effect, this was an appointment to become executive manager of the Pentagon, for McNamara was preoccupied with Vietnam-related business.[155] Nitze had earlier felt that the Navy's antipathy to the program was a product of bureaucratic parochialism; but by the time he left the Navy Department, Nitze thought that the Navy's negative opinion might be accurate.[156] Moreover, Paul Ignatius, appointed as Nitze's successor in August 1967, held some reservations about the program when he assumed office.[157] (Note that the Navy commissioned the Grumman study in July, during the transition period from Nitze to Ignatius.) Ignatius was convinced that the F-111B had real technical problems—this had been a long program and there was still no production aircraft—but he also recognized that the Navy had an "emotional problem" with the plane.[158]

The Gruman proposal, as well as the Navy fighter study, followed these personnel re-alignments. In combination with McNamara's relative distraction, these shifts in key personnel gave the Navy greater latitude for maneuvering. When the proposals of Grumman and the other contractors were received, Ignatius reportedly felt that these proposals would provide useful back-up designs in the event that the F-111B's problems proved insurmountable.[159]

In November 1967 the move for outright cancellation crystallized. The budget for Fiscal Year 1969, then in the final stages of preparation, required a major budgetary commitment by the Navy to the F-111B program: a total of 585 million dollars, including 389 million dollars for

---

[154] *New York Times* (June 16, 1967), p. 42.

[155] Interview 9.

[156] Interviews 9 and 17.

[157] Interviews 9 and 18. The initially appointed successor to Nitze, John McNaughton, died in a tragic plane crash in July, before being sworn into office. Ignatius was sworn into office September 1, 1967.

[158] Interview 18.   [159] Interviews 9 and 18.

the procurement of 30 production aircraft.[160] The Navy had always considered the F-111B program a significant opportunity cost. Now the Navy viewed the program as a major budgetary threat as well, one which would draw funds away from more favored Navy programs.[161]

Moreover, on a related matter, a joint Air Force-Navy planning effort for a follow-on to the F-4 Phantom had reached the stage of commitment to advanced development for the engines—and the Air Force had been named the executive service.[162] Since the planning effort had been established as a joint effort in order to explore possible development of a common aircraft, the Navy was in a critical position. It faced the distinct prospect of yet another common development. The missions being proposed for the

[160] See U.S. Senate, Committee on Appropriations, *Department of Defense Appropriations for Fiscal Year 1969*, pp. 1398–1399.

[161] Interviews 9, 22, and 26.

[162] Dulberger, "Advanced Fighter-Attack Aircraft," p. 93; Dulberger, "Advanced Interceptor Aircraft," *Space/Aeronautics*, Vol. 46 (November 1966), p. 61; U.S. House of Representatives, Committee on Armed Services, *Hearings on Military Posture* (1968), pp. 9546–9547; and U.S. Senate, Committee on Armed Services, *Military Procurement Authorizations for Fiscal Year 1967*, Hearings, 89th Cong., 2d Sess. (1966), p. 452.

The Air Force called its follow-on the FX (fighter-experimental), while the Navy called its version the VFAX (fighter-attack aircraft, experimental). The Air Force emphasis throughout the planning stages was on air superiority with a secondary emphasis on interdiction capability. The Navy VFAX plans of 1966–1967 reversed these priorities, stressing air-to-ground bombing capability with a secondary air-superiority capability. The events of the second half of 1967, which portended an end to the F-111B program and the institution of a substitute Navy program, led the Navy to shift its VFAX emphasis back to air superiority. While this then made Air Force and Navy mission priorities the same, the Navy could at that point expect to avoid a joint program, for reasons to be discussed shortly. Note that, as early as 1966, the aerospace industry considered VFAX the likely answer to the Navy's problems with the F-111B. See "Aerospace in Perspective: Tactical Warfare" (January 1968), p. 112; Dulberger, "Advanced Fighter-Attack Aircraft," p. 82; London, "Tactical Air Superiority," pp. 70–71; and U.S. Senate, Committee on Armed Services, Preparedness Investigating Subcommittee, *U.S. Tactical Air Power Program*, Hearings, 90th Cong., 2d Sess. (1968), pp. 113–121.

new fighter by both of the services were substantially similar (certainly more similar than the F-111A and F-111B missions). As an aerospace trade publication speculated, "The big question now is whether VFAX will be merged with the FX, for the similarities are striking and DOD inclinations toward commonality have been previously established."[163] However, if the Navy could tie the 8,000 pound Phoenix system (missiles and avionics) into its plans for the new fighter, the Air Force and Navy missions—and designs—would diverge. Consequently, the Navy needed to justify a Phoenix capability for the VFAX. To do this, in turn, the Navy needed to eliminate all alternatives to the VFAX for carrying the Phoenix system—that is, the Navy needed to eliminate the F-111B.

Accordingly, in early November, top Navy admirals, including the Chief of Naval Operations, began to push specifically for F-111B cancellation.[164] Later that month, McNamara was appointed to the presidency of the International Bank for Reconstruction and Development, though he would not be leaving until late February. With the prospective departure of McNamara, many saw F-111B cancellation as a matter of time.[165] On its part, the Navy had already begun to conserve resources on the program.[166]

It is hardly surprising, then, that Navy carrier trials of the F-111B were delayed without explanation until April, when the Senate Armed Services Committee already would have completed its authorization hearings.[167] In Icarus meetings in 1967, these carrier trials had been seen as "'a *sine qua non* prior to the next Congressional hearings.'"[168] This

[163] "Aerospace in Perspective: Tactical Warfare" (January 1968), p. 112.

[164] *New York Times* (November 4, 1967), p. 1.

[165] "Navy Evaluates F-111B Substitutes," p. 23; and Interview 6.

[166] Interview 9.

[167] U.S. Senate, Committee on Armed Services, *Authorization for Military Procurement, Research and Development, Fiscal Year 1969 and Reserve Strength*, p. 205.

[168] Notes of the Icarus meeting, September 21, 1963, quoted in *TFX Hearings—Second Series*, Part 3, p. 563.

judgment accurately reflected the importance of the trials, for in 1967, when the Senate Appropriations Committee blocked long lead-time production funding, the Committee specified that series production of the F-111B should not start until after carrier suitability tests by the Navy and a review of the program at that time by Congress.[169] But the trials were delayed. Navy Secretary Ignatius felt that the working-level test officials (pilots, technicians, and others) should be left alone in their performance of the carrier suitability tests—that is, left free from high-level civilian and Navy meddling, so that they could perform the tests in a safe and professional manner. This freedom meant that there would be no tests in time for the hearings.[170]

As the budget hearings approached, it was clear that the F-111B authorization would face a Congressional struggle. Congress was as resistant as the Navy to the major production commitment contemplated that year.[171] McNamara made the initial presentation to the committee. However, McNamara stepped down on February 29, 1968, to be formally replaced by Clark Clifford on March 1.[172] By that time, the Navy had completed its fighter study (the one begun in late 1967 after the Domodedovo air show and the

[169] Katherine Johnsen, "Senate Unit Slashes F-111B Funds," *Aviation Week and Space Technology*, Vol. 87 (August 14, 1967), p. 26.

[170] Interview 18. For an example of service behavior when the opposite incentive is unambiguously present—that is, when the service has a clear interest in hastening the test process to confirm a production commitment—note that the Navy discovered a method in 1971 to speed F-14A testing by eighteen months. This acceleration of F-14A tests occurred as the F-14A was moving into production and followed a year of particularly intense Congressional criticism of the program. See Brown, "Accelerated Testing Set for F-14A," pp. 49–53.

[171] Donald C. Winston, "$350 Million F-111B Request Facing Congressional Struggle," *Aviation Week and Space Technology*, Vol. 88 (February 5, 1968), p. 22.

[172] *New York Times*, February 22, 1968, p. 39; and *New York Times*, March 2, 1968, p. 3.

submission of design studies by Grumman and others). The Navy study recommended, and OSD agreed, that the Fiscal Year 1969 procurement authorization should be reduced from 30 units to 8 units, with money added to the request to allow initial definition of the VFX design. A decision would be made in Fiscal Year 1969 as to which was the better aircraft for the fleet defense mission.[173] According to *Congressional Quarterly*, the agreement included an additional provision not publicly revealed—the F-111B was to be cancelled quietly after the elections in November.[174]

Defense officials approached the Senate Armed Services Committee with the proposed revision in funding and the proposed post-election cancellation on March 27, 1968. To the Committee, which had hesitated to cancel the F-111B for fear of delaying deployment of a "vitally needed" Phoenix capability, the proposed deal was a clear signal that delay could be afforded. Since, in addition, the Navy admirals made clear their desire for outright cancellation,[175] the Committee voted on March 28 to terminate the F-111B

[173] U.S. Senate, Committee on Appropriations, *Department of Defense Appropriations for Fiscal Year 1969*, pp. 1396–1397. Before he left the Pentagon, McNamara was apprised of the revised approach that the Navy Department had formulated (Interview 18). The VFX that was to be defined grew out of the earlier VFAX (see footnote 162 of this chapter). When the Navy was given greater latitude to study alternatives in the fall of 1967—that is, when the likelihood of F-111B cancellation increased—the Navy shifted the operational emphasis of its planned fighter from attack-air superiority to air superiority-attack. With this reversal of priorities, the "A" was dropped from the VFAX acronym.

[174] "New Plane Seen More Costly, Little Better Than F-111," pp. 1008–1009.

[175] See U.S. Senate, Committee on Armed Services, *Authorization for Military Procurement, Research and Development, Fiscal Year 1969, and Reserve Strength*, pp. 1125–1140. See also the later House testimony of Vice Admiral Thomas F. Connolly, Deputy Chief of Naval Operations for Air, for similar expressions of the Navy preference for outright cancellation; in U.S. House of Representatives, Committee on Armed Services, *Hearings on Military Posture* (1968), pp. 9360, 9363–9364, 9387.

program. In its place, they substituted additional funds for the VFX (which was to become the F-14). Funds for the Phoenix missile system were maintained.[176]

Subsequent testimony by defense officials before other committees of Congress—the House and Senate Appropriations Committees and the House Armed Services Committee—was "only a formality."[177] The Navy carrier trials that were to have taken place in April were rescheduled again until June because of "small difficulties with the aircraft and bad weather."[178] No doubt. By this later time, it would be too late for the tests to make any difference. Time had run out on the F-111B. The program was terminated on July 10, 1968.[179]

In summary, cancellation of the F-111B derived from a confluence of Secretarial-level personnel changes, Congressional moves to forestall F-111B production, and a final Navy drive to have the program cancelled. To the new Secretarial personnel, F-111B cancellation was a more plausible course than it had been for McNamara, since they did not share McNamara's unusually close identification with the

[176] U.S. Senate, Committee on Armed Services, *Authorizing Appropriations for Military Procurement, Research and Development, Fiscal Year 1969, and Reserve Strength*, Report No. 1087, 90th Cong., 2d Sess. (April 10, 1968), pp. 2–3.

[177] "New Plane Seen More Costly, Little Better Than F-111," p. 1009.

[178] U.S. House of Representatives, Committee on Armed Services, *Hearings on Military Posture* (1968), p. 8727.

[179] *TFX Report*, p. 74. At the insistence of Navy Secretary Ignatius, the Navy later performed the carrier trial—in virtual secrecy and after the formal cancellation of the F-111B. According to the contractor, the carrier trial was a clear success, proof of the F-111B's excellent potential for carrier operations (Interview 16). A former Navy officer disputed this appraisal, alleging that the competence of the Navy test pilot was responsible for the successful carrier takeoffs and landings that occurred during the trial (Interview 26). These opinions are difficult to evaluate, since the public record provides no reliable information on the conduct or results of the trial itself. However, the evident contrast between the opinions suggests that, even down to this last, ironically quiet event in the controversial F-111B program, the different participants in the program saw what they expected to see as they evaluated ambiguous test results.

program. To the Congress, F-111B cancellation was feasible for the first time in 1968, since a delay in Phoenix deployment could be afforded, *by the Secretaries' own admission*, and alternatives to the F-111B were now available for development.[180] To the Navy, F-111B cancellation was imperative since a production commitment was imminent, and a bi-service development for the next generation of fighter aircraft was possible. The Navy had failed to kill the program subtly, through its repeated attempts in previous years to institute major redesigns of the plane. A more overt political move was necessary in 1968. Since McNamara was gone and Congress was on its side, the Navy could make that move in 1968 without losing face—and without admirals' losing their jobs.

With the commencement of the VFX (F-14) program, the Navy had at last achieved a return to normalcy in weapons procurement. As with the F-111B, the F-14 would be plagued by serious problems. But where the F-111B was "born in sin,"[181] the F-14 was the Navy's own. Whatever its problems, the F-14 would be supported by the Navy. An order more fundamental than any specifications had been restored.

The Demise of the F-111B: Unanswered Questions

The unique significance of the F-111 program resides in the history of the ill-fated F-111B. That history has now been examined in considerable detail, and it will be useful here to bring the explanation into focus.

The F-111B program began on a basis that the Navy had consistently opposed. Air Force dominance of program management aroused the hostility of Navy development organizations. At the same time, the size and weight specified for the F-111B marked the plane as an Air Force design and

180 Interview 10.
181 This phrase was coined by a staff member of Senator McClellan's Permanent Subcommittee on Investigations.

undermined the Navy's doctrinal preconceptions on the size appropriate for carrier operations and fighter-mission performance. These preconceptions were later challenged to the limit, when development efforts revealed a substantial weight increase on the F-111B. The weight increased primarily because the specifications governing the program were beyond the state-of-the-art of the 1960s. Specified performance levels could not be achieved within the Navy's weight constraint. The supersonic dash requirement of the Air Force was the key cause—yet another reason that the basic Air Force mission should have been compromised. From the beginning to the end of the development, the Navy exacerbated the problem, however, through its inflexibility on specification and configuration requirements. Inevitably, the weight problem translated into performance deficiencies—both quantitative deficiencies, as defined against contractual specifications, and qualitative deficiencies, as defined by Navy pilots in Navy-controlled tests. The revelation of these deficiencies led to a cycle of development problems, which delayed the completion of the development program and sorely tried the patience of Congress. But the deficiencies endured and confirmed to the Navy that the F-111B was fundamentally unsuitable. Moreover, the Phoenix mission concept behind the F-111B, a source of controversy in the Navy since Missileer days, was itself the subject of an important challenge. As the air war in Vietnam intensified, the Navy perceived the need for a plane of greater aerial combat capability than the F-111B. To the argument that the F-111B failed to meet its requirements was added the argument that the requirements themselves defined the wrong type of aircraft, an aircraft too limited in its specified role to be useful on a carrier.[182] Since the

[182] These arguments against the F-111B did not urge abandonment of the Phoenix capability. The Soviet Union had continued to deploy air-to-sea missiles on its aircraft, and the Phoenix was thought to be the only weapon capable of countering this threat to Navy ships. However, it was argued that the Phoenix capability ought to be augmented by a "dogfight" capability. The F-111B could not, of

Navy did not want the plane, and since alternatives to the F-111B had become available, the Congress, with virtual support from the Defense Department, moved forcefully in 1968 to end the long and painful program.

Throughout this chapter's discussion of the F-111B program, we have kept the analytic and cybernetic paradigms more or less in the background, concentrating instead on the complicated substantive narrative. This method allowed a more coherent presentation of the narrative, but it perhaps obscured the role of the paradigms in developing the explanations we have offered. Here, very briefly, we should reflect on the role of the paradigms in our explanations.

The cybernetic paradigm emphasizes a central phenomenon of the F-111 development, a phenomenon which was introduced early in this chapter: namely, that when an organization has severe doubts about an option, "deficiencies" will serve to confirm to the organization that the option is *fundamentally* unsound. There will be a low tolerance to any shortfalls from promised results. Thus, after being forced to accept a large plane of "Air Force design" and to concede on major specifications, the Navy would not naturally accommodate itself to the deficiencies that appeared. (By contrast, the Air Force and McNamara readily accommodated themselves to "deficiencies," as they proceeded on the different assumption that the F-111 was a basically suitable aircraft.) In the popular metaphor, a glass of water acceptably full to the Air Force seemed dangerously empty to the Navy. This difference in frame of reference powerfully influenced the Navy's perception of the evolving results of the program. From this difference, Navy behavior in the program followed: that service's resistance to the weight growth, its inflexibility on specifications, and its sustained dissatisfaction with the succession of technical

course, provide this combined capability. "Navy Evaluates F-111B Substitutes," p. 22; U.S. Senate, Committee on Armed Services, *Fiscal Year 1973 Authorization for Military Procurement*, pp. 3744–3745; and Interview 18.

remedies. Of particular importance in the cybernetic explanation are two basic features of the program: (1) the optimism of the joint requirement, which sanctioned a large plane with performance goals beyond the attainable state of the art; and (2) the character of the testing process, in terms of the biases of the tests and the kind of pilots who flew the tests. Given these two features of the program, the Navy was sure to receive quantitative and qualitative confirmation of the "basic deficiencies" of the F-111B. This confirmation insured that the Navy would consider the F-111B, as developed, a fundamentally unsuitable aircraft.

The analytic paradigm, on the other hand, emphasizes the more consciously calculating, self-interested behavior of the Navy. It focuses more on the "parochial" bases of Navy resistance, particularly the loss of position and power implied by that service's subordinate position in this major program. Evidence of such behavior can be found throughout the program: recall how the Navy attempted to avoid the program at the outset, then tried to use the VAX requirement in 1962 as a means to the TFX it really wanted, then sought major redesigns of the plane in 1964, and, all else having failed, made a clearly calculated move to cancel the plane in late 1967, as a binding production commitment approached. The underlying theme of this interpretation is that the Navy never really made a genuine commitment to the F-111B.

We need not doubt that the Navy's commitment was uneasy at best, especially at the beginning and end of the program, when the Navy's stakes were clearest and the Navy's calculating behavior most pronounced. But we ought not to slip into a simplistic "Navy sabotage" argument to explain the F-111B's demise. Many people in the Navy (for example, Navy program officials) worked very hard to develop an F-111B suitable for Navy use. Yet these people were honestly dissatisfied with the program's results at each stage. In spite of their best efforts, they could not see the F-111B as an adequate airplane, even though they arguably would not have been so dissatisfied with analogous results from a Navy-initiated program. To describe the resistance of these people as being simply calculated, self-serving oposition is to miss much of the style and flavor of Navy opposition. It is, we would argue, to miss a major part of the difficulty of accommodating the Navy to this "Air Force program."

Both analytic and cybernetic assumptions are thus useful to our explanation of Navy behavior in the program. The analytic explanation emphasizes the service's calculus of relative position and advantage. It is the explanation most plausible and natural to our political analysis, as it details the "not invented here" reaction that we reasonably expect when, as in the F-111B program, a powerful bureaucracy has suffered a major loss of traditional prerogative and has been forced to accept as its own an option developed by a separate, competing organization. But the cybernetic explanation offers an important supplementary perspective: it emphasizes the role played by a deep-rooted structure of simplified doctrinal beliefs in the Navy (beliefs analogous to the Air Force doctrines described in Chapter III). These Navy beliefs articulated the size, weight, and margin for performance growth and modification appropriate to the main components of the naval fighter forces. They provided the points of reference from which the evolving results of the F-111B program would be judged by the Navy. Because the original F-111B requirement strained those beliefs, and because the development effort could not meet the relaxed standards embodied in the requirement, the F-111B results were sure to be judged negative. By contrast, say, to the Air Force's acquisition of the Navy's F-4, the Navy could not be reconciled to the Air Force's F-111.[183] It could not, in the course of the program, be "brought around" to accept

[183] Unlike the Navy's bitter experience with the F-111B, the Air Force's acquisition of the F-4 was highly successful and proceeded without any major problems. More will be said on the contrast between the F-111B and F-4 programs in the final section of this chapter.

the F-111B. In other words, the cybernetic explanation focuses upon the conflict or dissonance between the Navy's doctrinal preconceptions and the evolving program results. It emphasizes how the Navy was forced to "ratchet down" in the course of the program. As we will argue later in this chapter, bi-service developments can succeed if (among other things, to be sure) they minimize this dissonance. Cybernetic assumptions serve to draw the attention of the political analyst to this key feature of any bi-service effort.

With these understandings of Navy behavior in the F-111B development, we have but half of the story of the F-111B's demise. The other half, only partially discussed thus far in our study, is how McNamara and his colleagues responded to the Navy's behavior. Of central importance is the question of why redesigns of the F-111B were never undertaken, since observed deficiencies in the existing F-111B design were sure to sustain Navy resistance to the plane and to provide powerful Navy arguments for cancellation. Our discussion of Navy behavior assumed, in passing, that redesigns were not undertaken as a consequence of McNamara's own inflexibility. He was too committed to the program to allow the reduction of commonality that such redesigns would have entailed. He must have considered the Navy to be "crying wolf" in its redesign requests. But if McNamara were thus aware of Navy inflexibility on its redesign requests, why did he acquiesce in Navy tactics on the other issues? Allowing the Navy (as well as the Air Force) to sustain certain of its specifications, to pursue an open cycle of technical problems, and to delay carrier trials was self-defeating, since it also delayed F-111B fleet introduction and provided time for Congressional opposition to mount.

It can reasonably be argued that this acquiescence was necessary. Secretarial intervention to alter Navy behavior would have imposed substantial costs. For example, OSD-altered flight tests would have been viewed with a skeptical eye by the Congress. Moreover, such meddling by OSD cer-

tainly would have eliminated any vestiges of support for
the program in the Navy. (Obviously, any attempt to speed
up the tests would have led to a complaint by the Navy—
conceivably true, but in any event difficult to refute—that
it could not endanger the lives of its test pilots.) As a result, the Secretaries had to accept most of the inevitable
decentralization of the actual development effort that would
implement their early decisions, even though this decentralization placed certain key decisions and processes under
the control of the Navy.

But if the Secretaries were really aware of this decentralization, they would not have embarked on a bi-service development in the first place, or they at least would have
examined more critically the basic development plans, particularly the performance specifications and program
schedules. If our examination of the inlet problems is any
guide, the Secretaries probably did not have a full awareness of the impact of Navy behavior. On the inlet problems,
the Secretaries were not really aware that a mile-long production line was in full-scale operation in 1967. Though
the Secretaries certainly knew, all too well, that the Navy
had an "emotional problem" with the F-111B, it is not apparent that they had a broad understanding of the impact
of Navy behavior. An important indication of their lack of
understanding is provided by an analogy that they felt confirmed the soundness of the bi-service concept: the Air
Force's successful acquisition of the Navy-developed F-4.
This analogy was inaccurate in at least one critical respect.
The F-4 had already been developed and thoroughly tested
when the Air Force acquired it. There was little uncertainty
regarding the plane's performance capability, and hence
little possibility for deficiencies to appear that would in-
flame Air Force doubts about this Navy plane. Nonetheless,
at the outset of the program, the Secretaries viewed the bi-
service *procurement* of the F-4 as support for the bi-service
development of the F-111. In spite of the continual Navy
resistance to the program, in spite of the technical and ad-

ministrative uncertainty attending the bi-service development of a complex weapon system, and in spite of the political problem for the program portended by Senator McClellan's criticisms in 1963, Secretary McNamara anticipated that the Navy would ultimately be as happy with the F-111B as the Air Force was with the F-4. Indeed, McNamara apparently expected that the F-111 would be *more* suitable for bi-service use than the F-4, since the F-111 was being designed from the start as a bi-service aircraft. This was, to say the least, an extreme misconception of the hazards of a bi-service development.[184]

He and his colleagues allowed the development effort to proceed in a pattern that is by now familiar in our study of the F-111 program: the emergence of a problem, such as the weight-growth, would trigger a proposed solution, such as the SWIP program, while the pace of development was maintained. Generally, the result of this behavior was late SWIP aircraft, late P-12 engines, late N-1 changes, and a severe political problem. Recall that the Secretaries were

[184] Interview 24; and Smith, "The $7 Billion Contract," Part II, p. 111. A suggestion of this belief can be found in *TFX Hearings— First Series*, Part 2, p. 429. The Smith article notes, from its author's 1963 interview with McNamara, that McNamara thought that if commonality worked on the F-4, a plane already developed, it should "certainly work for the TFX, which was being specially designed to suit the Navy and the Air Force." This assumption not only ignored the difficulties of getting two services to work together in a single development program. It also ignored the peculiar difficulties of adapting an "Air Force plane"—conceived originally for operations from land—to operate from the far less permissive environment of an aircraft carrier. The alleged problems of securing "carrier compatibility" from Air Force designs were highlighted by the Navy throughout the F-111B program. They provided the basis for powerful Navy arguments against the F-111B, as they rested on the intuitively compelling image of the hazards of landing on a small, undulating carrier deck, as opposed to a large, fixed airfield. The F-4 example was not particularly relevant as an answer to these arguments, since the second service to buy the F-4 was the Air Force, the service that faced the more permissive operating environment. Indeed, the Navy would argue that bi-service acquisition could *only* work from the Navy to the Air Force, and not in the other direction, because of the less stringent operating environment the Air Force confronted.

apprised of a potentially serious weight problem in late 1962, before the development even began.[185] Yet concentrated weight-reduction efforts did not commence until the actual report—as opposed to the prediction—of substantial weight growth. Prior to that time, development proceeded routinely. Recall further that the P-12 engine improvements were not initiated until twelve months after the *minimum* weight of the F-111B was known and eighteen months after the first reports of major weight growth.[186]

In important ways, the process appears once again to have been focused on short-range information cycles, to have been adverse to speculation, and to have proceeded routinely until problems were *faits accomplis*. The cybernetic paradigm makes this general pattern of behavior understandable. In the next section of this chapter, cybernetic assumptions will be used to observe more closely the behavior of the Secretaries during the F-111B development. This analysis will complement our discussion of Navy inflexibility. It will reveal how the Secretaries were in a weak position to neutralize the effects of the Navy's behavior.

THE COMPLEMENT TO NAVY INFLEXIBILITY: CYBERNETIC BEHAVIOR ON F-IIIB TECHNICAL PROBLEMS

In our discussion of the engine-inlet compatibility problems in Chapter IV, we observed that development routines "timed" the awareness of propulsion integration difficulties. Development schedules were established with reference to prior development experience and planned F-111 operational dates with no effective anticipation of integration difficulties. As a result, the severe stall problem was not re-

---

[185] Interview 1.

[186] The minimum weight of the F-111B was ascertainable in July 1964, when the SWIP reductions were approved. Specification and development of the P-12 engine did not begin until August 1965. *TFX Hearings—Second Series*, Part 1, p. 105; and Interview 16.

vealed until flight tests began, a mere four months before the production commitment. Since the schedules were maintained while the problems resisted resolution, the remedial efforts were costly and only partially successful.

A similar pattern is apparent on the technical problems of the F-111B. The contractor's weight reporting system determined when the weight growth would be revealed. Once it was revealed, the configuration was maintained, as the larger development effort continued. Weight reduction and compensation efforts were initiated in sequence. This process was open-ended until Congressional impatience foreclosed all of the problem-solving efforts.

The Timing of "Awareness": General Dynamics' Weight Reporting System

Prior to the contract award in 1962, McNamara was apprised of a potentially serious weight problem in the F-111B. There were, however, no special measures taken to monitor or to control the weight of the F-111B. The development process proceeded routinely until December 1963, when the substantial weight-growth was reported as a fact. At that time, the normal operation of the contractor's weight reporting system produced a new weight estimate that confirmed the 1962 prediction.[187]

General Dynamics' weight reporting system was based upon the weight projections made in the final round of the source selection competition. In that competition, the most important weight estimate was the so-called "statistical base" calculation. To prepare this figure, the contractor performed mathematical stress analyses of various structural sections of the aircraft. These analyses gave the necessary information on which to base decisions about the metallurgical composition of the plane, the thicknesses of parts, and so on. Though individual parts were not yet designed, ap-

---

[187] The information in this section on the contractor's weight reporting system is drawn from Interview 16.

proximate dimensions of structural sections could be estimated and factored with thickness and materials information to determine approximate structural weights by section. These weights, plus the anticipated weight of non-structural items (such as the plane's radar, engines, and canopy) were added together to determine an estimated weight for the proposed design.

After the contract award, as designs were detailed, weight was monitored as a variance against the statistical base estimate. The resulting total weight estimate could only be as accurate as the statistical base, since, for reporting purposes, that base represented all of the weight of a section except the unanticipated increment.[188]

Variance estimates were the essential weight monitoring tool through November 1963. To that time, the total weight growth was 825 pounds.[189] However, after the earlier mock-up inspection of August 1963, the foundation for a new, more accurate weight estimate (called a "grass roots" estimate) was prepared. With the completion of the mock-up inspection, design detail down to the individual part level had commenced. Accompanying this effort was the development of a highly detailed weight estimate to replace the original, statistical base estimate.

Variance estimates were reported through November 1963, and received the routine concurrence of all concerned, including the Navy. The new grass roots estimate was reported in December 1963, and we know the bad news that it conveyed—an 8,000-pound weight increase over the prior estimate.[190] It is impossible to determine when this addi-

[188] Clearly, the accuracy of increment estimates was also important to the accuracy of the total weight estimate. There was, however, a substantial difference in the variance of potential errors, as between the statistical base and the increment.

[189] TFX Hearings—Second Series, Part 2, p. 369.

[190] That is, an 8,000-pound increase over the November 21, 1963 (variance-estimated) report, the increase before weight savings. It was inferred in the 1970 McClellan hearings that General Dynamics purposely concealed the weight growth until after the first series of Congressional hearings ended in November 1963. A Navy weight

tional weight actually was designed into the aircraft. No doubt, the accretion was gradual and occurred more or less evenly over the prior months.[191] The important point here is that, because of the way the weight was reported, the Secretaries would not have an accurate weight estimate until one year after development commenced. For this program, weight control was vital, since weight had been a major point of contention in early program debates. Yet by the time of the more accurate estimate, drawings were already being released for the fabrication of parts, and only six months remained before the first F-111B prototype entered major assembly.[192] It was only in response to this report of weight growth that remedial efforts were launched, efforts that the warnings and anticipation of the weight problems had failed to trigger.

The Decisions on Redesign: 1964

As detailed earlier in this chapter, General Dynamics' report of substantial weight growth led to a request by McNamara for a complete review of the TFX program. The Bureau of Naval Weapons initiated its own review and concluded in February 1964 that a halt in the development of the F-111B was needed to provide the opportunity to redesign the aircraft. With the 1963 McClellan hearings still a fresh memory, the Bureau recommended an end to com-

---

engineer admitted in testimony, however, that General Dynamics might not have been aware of the weight growth, "perhaps because of the manner in which they maintained the weight data." Inasmuch as the hearings ended when President Kennedy was assassinated—an event General Dynamics could not predict—and inasmuch as no direct evidence of concealment was ever revealed, the timing of the reported increase was probably keyed to the weight reporting system, as surmised in the text. Nonetheless, it is still true that the timing of the report was advantageous from a political, if not a technical, standpoint. See discussion in *TFX Hearings—Second Series*, Part 2, pp. 368–370, 373, 419.

191 *TFX Hearings—Second Series*, Part 2, p. 372; and Interview 16.
192 Interview 16.

mon development.[193] This proposal received the concurrence of others, including the Assistant Secretary of the Navy for Research and Development, Dr. James Wakelin, and the staff of Defense Research and Engineering. However, by orders given at the Secretarial level—either Zuckert of Air Force, Nitze of Navy, or Brown of Defense Research and Engineering—this agreement was recast to recommend instead: (1) the continuation of the program on its previously established schedules; (2) the continuation of special efforts to reduce the weight of the aircraft (that is, continuation of what was later called the SWIP program); and (3) the institution of immediate design studies of the F-111B to provide fall-back options to be instituted later, if warranted.[194]

In essence, there was to be no change in the F-111B program, save for the initiation of the fall-back design studies. Though this decision had little practical impact (beyond what it did *not* provide for—a redesign of the aircraft), the way in which it was justified is of particular interest.

The decision was explained in a joint memorandum from Brown, Nitze, and Zuckert to Secretary McNamara.[195] The memorandum itself described the primary problems created by the weight growth, the nature of disagreements between the Navy and Air Force on F-111B performance, and the need to wait three to four months for more "hard data" to establish more accurate performance estimates. The memorandum is thus fairly straightforward. There is an attachment to the memorandum, however, that provides a revealing glimpse of the way in which the Secretaries weighed

---

[193] Ford Dixon, "McNamara, General Dynamics, and the F-111: A Business and Political History" (unpublished Ph.D. dissertation, Texas Christian University, 1972), pp. 132–134.

[194] Memorandum to the Secretary of Defense, from Director of Defense Research and Engineering Harold Brown, Air Force Secretary Eugene Zuckert, and Navy Secretary Paul Nitze, dated February 15, 1964, re F-111 Weight Review, printed in *TFX Hearings—Second Series*, Part 2, pp. 435–438.

[195] Ibid.

alternatives to their specifically recommended course of action.

Four alternatives are listed in the attachment, with "pros" and "cons" noted for each one. The alternatives themselves range from the one actually chosen (a continuation of the program as originally planned) to the one the BuWeps review had urged (a complete halt in the F-111B development, pending the redesign of the aircraft). It will be instructive to quote in full the arguments for which the net advantages were presumably the greatest—namely, the recommended choice:

ALTERNATIVE COURSES OF ACTION CONSIDERED

1. Continue with [the] present program. Maintain in force the extraordinary weight reduction efforts. Back up this approach with prepared alternative design options for the F-111B to be instituted if warranted.

Pros:

a) Retains contractual commitments without reopening [sic] to increased costs.

b) Maintains schedules.

c) Keeps the pressure on to reduce weight but retains commonality and specification performance.

d) Provides the opportunity to measure actuals achieved in weight and performance as the design and test progress.

e) Time is available in the F-111B schedule between the first five R&D aircraft and subsequent deliveries to incorporate changes.

f) Even if heavy, in terms of tactical mission standards, the R&D aircraft would be of great benefit for test purposes and for Phoenix weapons system integration and development.

Cons:

a) Based on present Navy predictions of performance and expected growth this course leads to a Navy airplane with little or no margin for future growth. If Navy predictions come true, the resultant airplane would not meet all of the Navy's stated requirements.

b) Probably forecloses [the] possibility of extensive fixes through redesign except at still larger cost.[196]

Though this argument is in the paradigm form of an analytic choice, its content reveals something else again. All of the listed advantages for this alternative refer to what might be called *administrative values*. "Contractual commitments" and "schedules" will be maintained. Performance and weight "actuals"—the main issues of this February program review—might not improve, but whatever they are, they will be "measured." Even if the design is heavy, it will be useful for "test" and "integration" purposes. In keeping with this scheme, all of the listed disadvantages relate to projected aircraft performance: the margin for growth and for the achievement of requirements will be reduced, and the possibility of extensive fixes will be foreclosed. The value integration in this decision is more apparent than real. Until a more immediate reality presented itself—that is, until more hard data were available—the trade-off between performance and administrative values would be dissolved.

There is a parallel between this redesign decision on Navy weight and the redesign decision made shortly thereafter in March 1964 by Dr. Flax (Assistant Secretary of the Air Force for Research and Development) when the F-111 drag increases were revealed. As discussed in earlier chapters, Dr. Flax was presented in March with NASA recommendations for redesign because of the alarming drag increases. Dr. Flax decided to sustain the existing program on its original schedules, but he also gave the "insurgent" group that argued for redesign (NASA) a postponed opportunity to vindicate its position (through accelerated wind tunnel

[196] Ibid., p. 437. For the other three alternatives listed in the memorandum, the "pros" become progressively more performance-oriented—even as the alternatives themselves become more radical in their implications for the previously planned program.

testing and the provision of a more sophisticated test model). In the February redesign decision, the program had also been continued, with the insurgent group (the Navy) given a postponed opportunity to vindicate its position (through a hypothetical redesign—that is, through design studies of the aircraft). In both cases, goals were sequentially addressed with the "need for hard data" providing the mechanism for this value separation. A confrontation with the information that would force recognition of the trade-off was postponed.

The F-111B program continued with only Grumman putting any effort into the redesign studies. Upon the completion of these efforts at a regular executive management review in July attended by high-level military officials, the Secretaries of the Air Force and Navy, and, for part of the meeting, by contractor representatives, the various redesign versions were compared to the various existing F-111B design estimates. The most important data presented are shown in Table III.[197] The Navy, Air Force, and contractor still could not agree on the likely maximum weight of the

Table III. F-111B: July 1964 Design Review Presentation.

| Estimated by: | 1963 Original Presentation | July 1964 Projections | | | Grumman Redesign |
	Navy	Navy	Air Force	Gen. Dyn.	Navy
Weight Empty (pounds)	39,500	46,284	43,994	42,099	42,360
Take-off Weight (pounds)	70,000	77,692	74,501	72,630	72,280
Loiter Time at 150 Miles From Carrier (hours)	5.0	4.0	4.2	4.4	4.5

[197] Memorandum for the Deputy Secretary of Defense, from Navy Secretary Paul H. Nitze, dated July 29, 1964, re F-111, printed in *TFX Hearings—Second Series*, Part 2, p. 461. See also p. 436 of the hearings. The *minimum* weight was known, as the SWIP changes were approved at the meeting. The main point of contention was the degree to which the F-111B would grow in weight as fleet introduction approached.

existing F-111B, in spite of the Secretaries' anticipation in February that they would have "much better information" in about four months. Note that the General Dynamics estimate of the empty weight of the existing F-111B was actually *less* than the Navy estimate of the Grumman redesign, and that the Air Force estimate is substantially closer to that of the contractor than to that of the Navy.[198] The situation had not improved appreciably since February, when Air Force and Navy estimates (the only estimates involved at that time) also differed considerably.

The Secretaries' decision in July did not significantly differ from their decision in February. The Grumman redesign was not approved. Instead, the Secretaries chose to continue development of the F-111B (SWIP version), but to have the Navy and Air Force get together "to develop a mutually acceptable common basis for calculation and presentation of weight and performance data."[199] Whatever the performance results might be, the *estimation* of per-

[198] This "structure of optimism" was a recurrent phenomenon in the F-111B development. On virtually all performance estimates, General Dynamics, followed closely by the Air Force, was the most optimistic, while the Navy was usually very pessimistic. For other F-111 examples, see *TFX Hearings—Second Series*, Part 2, pp. 349–350, 436 and Part 3, pp. 501, 543, 548. For an example in a program of the 1950s (the F-102 interceptor program) see Thomas Marschak, "The Role of Project Histories in the Study of R&D," in Thomas Marschak, Thomas K. Glennan, Jr., and Robert Summers, *Strategy for R&D: Studies in the Microeconomics of Development* (New York: Springer-Verlag, 1967), p. 106. For an example in a program of the 1970s (the Navy Air Combat Fighter), see U.S. Senate, Committee on Appropriations, *Lightweight Fighter Aircraft Program*, pp. 76–79.

[199] Memorandum for the Secretary of the Air Force, from Navy Secretary Paul H. Nitze, dated July 31, 1964, re F-111B program, printed in *TFX Hearings—Second Series*, Part 2, pp. 462–463. The delivery schedule for later R&D prototypes of the F-111B (numbers two through five) was slipped approximately 7 months to allow the incorporation of weight improvement changes. However, the overall F-111 program was not slowed nor was the fleet introduction date (1968) of the F-111B. Later decisions were to change both of these dates, when the Navy-controlled Phoenix development lagged. The production line at General Dynamics was relatively unaffected in any event, as that line performed final assembly only for the Air Force F-111s, while the Navy F-111Bs were assembled at Grumman. See *TFX Hearings—Second Series*, Part 2, p. 427, and Part 3, pp. 482–494.

formance would at least be made on a "common basis." (In fact, until much later in the program, the estimates of the Air Force, the contractor, and the Navy continued to differ.)[200] Once again, the development momentum of the existing F-111B configuration was sustained, as the ambiguity of weight and performance data allowed the Secretaries to avoid acknowledging an explicit trade-off between the routine continuation of development and the achievement of Navy performance specifications. The SWIP program reinforced this Secretarial predisposition, for it promised weight improvements (the key to ameliorating the Navy problems) without substantial revision of schedules or costs.[201]

As noted earlier, the SWIP program imposed strict weight-monitoring procedures on the design process and directed design efforts toward the removal of all unnecessary structural weight from the aircraft. This weight reduction mainly involved the removal of weight from existing designs rather than the redesign of whole parts and subsystems.[202] The SWIP effort thus accords well with our

[200] See, for example, TFX Hearings—Second Series, Part 3, pp. 501, 548.

[201] This program was expensive—it cost approximately 50 million dollars, of which the government paid 85 percent, the contractor 15 percent. Substantial redesign, however, would have cost approximately 480 million dollars and would have involved major disruptions of the program. See Memorandum to Admiral Fawkes, from BuWeps engineer George Spangenberg, dated August 14, 1964, re F-111B Design Review, printed in TFX Hearings—Second Series, Part 2, pp. 452–455.

[202] Interview 16. The SWIP program removed 5,000 pounds of weight from a 30,000-pound airframe. In the opinion of most observers, further weight reductions were inadvisable. Hence, we can conclude that as much as 16 percent of the weight in the original design (the design preceding the weight improvement programs) was physically "unnecessary." Readers familiar with the literature on organizations will note that this reduction suggests the magnitude of organizational slack in the design process, in terms of the design latitude (a "resource") provided engineers during the formulation of the original design. The SWIP reductions are analogous to the experience of a corporation which, under the pressure of falling profits, suddenly "finds" ways to cut costs substantially. Richard M.

earlier depiction of design evolution as a progressive decomposition of the proposed configuration with fairly stable parameters established around each successive level of design detail. Few of the parameters were altered in the course of the SWIP effort. The SWIP effort was, in effect, an accelerated repetition of the initial design effort, but with an exclusive focus on weight reduction.

By the end of 1964, redesign of the F-111B had been foreclosed. Since the SWIP program took weight-reduction efforts as far as they could be taken within the existing F-111B configuration, all subsequent attempts to resolve F-111B problems would have to take the weight as given. The F-111B's weight was still a focal point for emotional opposition to the plane. But for program engineers, the irreducible weight was now a problem to be addressed in terms of its specific effects on performance.

Led Down a Path, Problem by Problem

The redesign decisions in 1964 reflected the same pattern of Secretarial response to development problems that we have observed in prior chapters. To the reports of F-111B weight growth, the Secretaries responded by approving an essentially conservative weight-reduction program that maintained the pace of development efforts. Thereafter, as flight tests began, the Navy would be in a stronger position to define what the F-111B's problems were. The Navy's doubts about the basic suitability of the F-111B would then translate into a cycle of problems, wherein the solution of one problem only created another. Since the Secretaries acted on the assumption that an "acceptable" aircraft would be developed that would satisfy the Navy, they followed the Navy through this cycle, problem by problem, without a

Cyert and James G. March, *A Behavioral Theory of the Firm* (Englewood Cliffs: Prentice-Hall, 1963), pp. 36–38. Cf. footnote 140, Chapter III, supra.

decisive comprehension of the larger pattern to which the effort conformed.

In late 1964, after the extent of actual SWIP weight reductions proved less than anticipated, the Secretaries were forced to confront the inevitable landing-momentum problem that resulted.[203] It was thought in early 1965 that, "[to] a considerable extent, the weight increase would be offset by the addition of the high-lift flap devices."[204] One performance impact of the now irreducible weight increase was to be offset by another remedy, the high-lift flap devices. A second impact of the weight increase was on the adequacy of the engine's power. "Based on the flight performance of [the] first R&D aircraft, development of an engine with increased thrust (TF-30-P-12) was authorized."[205] The flight-test reports of a lack of power spurred approval of the development of an advanced engine, although the F-111B's overweight condition had been known for 18 months and the maximum feasible reductions in weight had been known for over a year. Finally, when all of these changes led to Navy allegations of pilot visibility problems in tests conducted through late 1966, the N-1 package of "carrier suitability" improvements was inaugurated, which added over 2,500 pounds of additional weight to the aircraft.[206]

[203] *TFX Hearings—Second Series*, Part 2, p. 333.

[204] Memorandum for the Secretary of Defense, from Air Force Secretary Eugene Zuckert, dated April 13, 1965, re F-111 Program (from the files of the Permanent Subcommittee on Investigations, Committee on Government Operations, U.S. Senate, Exhibit 26W-51 of the *TFX Hearings—Second Series*). See also the testimony of Paul Nitze, Secretary of the Navy, in U.S. Senate, Committee on Armed Services, *Military Procurement Authorizations: Fiscal Year 1966*, p. 777.

[205] Statement of Robert A. Frosch, Assistant Secretary of the Navy for Research and Development, in U.S. Senate, Committee on Armed Services, *Military Procurement Authorizations for Fiscal Year 1968*, p. 784. See also the detailed chronology presented in footnote 94.

[206] Notes of the Icarus meeting, for September 10, 1966; October 1, 1966; October 22, 1966; January 12, 1967; and March 11, 1967, all quoted in *TFX Hearings—Second Series*, Part 3, pp. 549–551, 555, 557. Also, Interview 16.

The Secretaries' expectations for the N-1 package were as optimistic as their earlier expectations for the high-lift devices. They believed that these final improvements would make the F-111B acceptable to the Navy:

"By way of review, Mr. McNamara said he wanted to cover the following three points:
1. Has the Navy accepted the carrier suitability package?
2. Is the statement in writing as to what the Navy requires to make the F-111B an acceptable aircraft?
3. Is there a good possibility of having the specifications met?"
Mr. Nitze replied affirmatively to all three questions.

". . . If anything productive has come out of these meetings, [McNamara] felt, it has been this evolution of a satisfactory aircraft for the Navy."[207]

However, shortly thereafter, the initial stages of the first Navy evaluation of a SWIP aircraft were performed, and the Navy concluded that the SWIP F-111B was "unsuitable for service use."[208] (The formal evaluation itself was not completed, as the other SWIP test plane crashed in April, thereby delaying further tests by eight months.)

The pessimistic results of this evaluation of the SWIP aircraft were at odds with the expectations invested in the SWIP program. Indeed, the results of this Navy test read like the results of the first evaluation of the pre-SWIP F-111B in October 1965.[209] To make matters worse, there were now to be further delays. Although an F-111B with the ten-percent-more-powerful P-12 engine was due to be delivered a year later, this F-111B would also have 2,500 pounds (or six percent) more structural weight than the SWIP F-111B, as it would also incorporate the N-1

[207] Notes of the Icarus meeting, March 11, 1967, quoted in *TFX Hearings—Second Series*, Part 3, p. 557.
[208] *TFX Hearings—Second Series*, Part 1, p. 103, and Part 3, p. 512.
[209] *TFX Hearings—Second Series*, Part 3, p. 498.

changes. The SWIP/N-1 aircraft would thus have a net power improvement of relatively marginal significance over the SWIP-only aircraft. If the SWIP F-111B was *fundamentally* unsuitable, the SWIP/N-1 F-111B was not likely to be suitable either. In consequence, the whole cycle of improvements—the SWIP program, the high-lift devices, the P-12 engine, the N-1 changes—was called into serious question. Steinbruner notes: "When a set of beliefs is under pressure from inconsistent information being processed in a short time frame, it is possible to maintain consistency without changing the beliefs by casting them in a long-range time frame and adopting the inference of transformation; namely, that the immediate situation will succumb to a favorable trend over time."[210] After many months of technical effort, the "favorable trend" had decisively failed to materialize.

It is hardly surprising, then, that Paul Nitze had some doubts about the plane when he left his post as Secretary of the Navy in mid-1967. His reservations were but a small reflection of the skepticism felt in the Congress (and particularly in the Senate Armed Services and Appropriations Committees) about the plane.[211] Congress began to see the F-111B development as a program of endless difficulties and recurrent delays, where promised solutions were never final, where there was always a new problem and a new remedy that in the end never worked out. To the Secretaries, operating from within the process, each complication seemed to

---

[210] John D. Steinbruner, *The Cybernetic Theory of Decision: New Dimensions of Political Analysis* (Princeton: Princeton University Press, 1974), p. 117.

[211] See, for example, Johnsen, "Senate Unit Slashes F-111B Funds," p. 26; "Navy Evaluates F-111B Substitutes," pp. 22–23; and Winston, "$350 Million F-111B Request Facing Congressional Struggle," p. 23. The definitive expression of Congressional impatience is, of course, the 1968 authorization report of the Senate Armed Services Committee, the report that initiated the process of program cancellation in Congress. See U.S. Senate, Committee on Armed Services, *Authorizing Appropriations for Military Procurement, Research and Development, Fiscal Year 1969, and Reserve Strength*, pp. 2–3.

have a solution. To the Congress, observing the process from a distance, the problems increasingly seemed to reflect the F-111B's basic unsuitability. The Secretaries seemed to be chasing an endless cycle of problems. The negative SWIP test report and the subsequent flight-test delays only confirmed Congress' observation.

Until McNamara's departure, he and the other Secretaries continued publicly to defend the program. But even as their defense continued, they were setting in motion, unwittingly at first, the alternatives that were ultimately to seal the F-111B's fate.

In the end, the observed Secretarial behavior proved unsuited to the exigencies of a bi-service development. The inevitable control of critical development decisions and processes by a skeptical Navy served to create an overwhelmingly negative image of the aircraft and to set in motion a chain of problems for development efforts to address. This pattern demanded aggressive compensatory initiatives from the Secretaries, such as earlier engine-thrust improvements. In the actual context of the program—where busy decision makers confronted problems shrouded in uncertainty, presented to them by subordinate organizations —these aggressive initiatives might not have been possible. Moreover, whatever the political and organizational necessities, these initiatives might not have been practical in technical or engineering terms, until the program was further advanced. But to acknowledge these obstacles to more aggressive action is only to emphasize the problematic course on which the Secretaries embarked in the F-111 program. While they understood and successfully blocked early Navy moves to end common development, they clearly underestimated other, more subtle implementation difficulties of such a program. Their characteristic responses to development problems were reactive and short range. They were also inadequate to the success of the program. Indeed, their major *initiative* in the course of the program was their decision in 1965 to upgrade and to augment the Navy's representation at the Air Force program office—a move deriving primarily from the recommendations of a high-level DDR&E official who was relatively new to the Pentagon when he made the recommendations.[212]

But more generally, the development process proceeded routinely, much as it did on the engine-inlet compatibility problems. In a sequence rendered understandable by the cybernetic paradigm, the Secretaries were led down a path, problem by problem, not realizing until the end that it led logically to program cancellation. If their similar behavior on the inlet and mission problems led them to approve aircraft with important deficiencies, it worked on the Navy version to subvert the distinctive characteristic of the F-111 program. As the admiral had predicted back in 1963, the Secretaries were never to see this bi-service aircraft "fly off the deck of an aircraft carrier."

GUIDELINES FOR SUCCESS IN BI-SERVICE PROGRAMS

This unfortunate experience in bi-service development provides a basis for an interesting set of comparisons among various forms of bi-service acquisition. Two other major, bi-service acquisitions were attempted in the 1960's; the F-4 and the A-7. Both were more successful than the F-111 development (at least, if procurement in volume can be taken

---

[212] The newly appointed official was Leonard Sullivan, Jr., who came to the Defense Department in July 1964 from Grumman. At that time, he assumed the office of Deputy Assistant Director for Combat Systems in DDR&E. In the fall of 1964, he chaired an ad hoc study group on the Phoenix/F-111B. The conclusions of the study group, written up by Sullivan, led to the expansion and upgrading of the Navy contingent at the SPO. See Memorandum for the Director of Defense Research and Engineering, from Leonard Sullivan, Jr., dated October 1, 1964, re Report of PHOENIX/F-111B ad hoc group, printed in *TFX Hearings—Second Series*, Part 3, pp. 479–482. See also Sullivan's 1970 testimony in the same volume of hearings, pp. 465–479, 482–494.

as an indicator of success). There were differences in the degree of "commonality" in the two programs, however, and the differences are instructive.

The F-4 acquisition by the Air Force was the first bi-service acquisition of the McNamara era. With substantial assistance from systems analysts in OSD in 1961, McNamara was able to induce the Air Force to terminate its F-105 acquisition in favor of the F-4. At the time, the Navy already was deploying the F-4. The plane's performance characteristics and costs were well known and relatively firm. It was the equal of the F-105 in most respects, but possessed superior acceleration and speed, and what OSD considered superior capability for conventional operations. Air Force pilots liked the speed characteristics of the F-4, but Air Staff people preferred the F-105's optimization for the delivery of tactical nuclear weapons.[213]

The F-4 fit well the conception of fighter aircraft held by the Air Force, save for its de-emphasis of the delivery of tactical nuclear weapons. It was thus ideally suited, from McNamara's point of view, for bringing about a greater emphasis on conventional capabilities. Because the high-performance F-4 fit the Air Force's doctrinal image of a fighter aircraft, only minor changes in the Navy version were made prior to Air Force acquisition of the plane. Because the F-4 represented an implicit de-emphasis of nuclear weapons, however, the initial Air Force procurement of the F-4 was relatively small and slow. But because the F-4's performance appealed to pilots who had flown the F-105, the Air Force was ultimately very pleased with the aircraft and procured it in great quantity.[214]

By contrast, the Air Force procurement of the A-7 was

[213] Unless otherwise indicated, the information that follows in the text is drawn from Head, "Decision-Making on the A-7 Attack Aircraft Program," passim.

[214] Ibid., pp. 156–170, 215–216; and Jacob A. Stockfisch, *Swords into Ploughshares: Managing the American Defense Establishment* (New York: Mason & Lipscomb, 1973), p. 145.

very difficult and less successful. Since World War II, the Air Force had not developed a single aircraft optimized for the close support mission. TAC had long held that the close support mission could be performed well by its expensive, supersonic fighter planes. Indeed, since the F-100 had broken the sound barrier for operational aircraft, TAC had not even developed a subsonic fighter plane. All of the TAC doctrine on aircraft survivability and weapons delivery emphasized the need for the highest attainable performance in its aircraft.[215]

Systems analysts in OSD felt different and challenged the TAC contention that the close support mission could be adequately performed with supersonic aircraft. Through a series of deliberations between 1963 and 1965, they ultimately coerced TAC into accepting the Navy's subsonic A-7 to improve Air Force capabilities for performing the close support mission.[216]

The A-7 had commenced initial flight tests by that time. Its performance characteristics and costs could be predicted with some confidence. However, it distinctly differed from TAC's conception of what a fighter plane ought to be. In TAC's terms, the A-7 was too slow and lacked a sufficient avionics capability. Before procuring the A-7 in quantity, the Air Force made major changes in it. It developed a more powerful engine to substitute for the Navy-developed engine. It also developed an expensive, highly sophisticated avionics system to replace the more austere avionics in the Navy version. It added a whole variety of subsystems of Air Force design—wiring, cockpit instruments, oxygen systems, wheels, tires, brakes, and starters—to replace Navy-developed versions. While the Air Force made only five changes in the Navy F-4 prior to procuring that plane, it

[215] Head, "Decision-Making on the A-7 Attack Aircraft Program," pp. 104–121, 155–158, 248–255.

[216] An important pressure on the Air Force during these deliberations was the implicit threat of an Army takeover of the close support mission, a threat given credibility when the Army initiated its Cheyenne helicopter development in 1964. See Ibid., p. 250.

made between 19 and 42 changes in the A-7.[217] In 1969, when the Cheyenne helicopter was cancelled and the Army threat to TAC control of the close support mission was reduced, the Air Force reduced its planned purchase of the A-7D from four wings to three. By the early 1970s, new A-7Ds were routed to Air National Guard units.[218]

In the A-7 acquisition, the Air Force was in a position similar to that of the Navy in the F-111B program. It was forced to buy an aircraft that it considered fundamentally unsuitable for its particular operations. However, the position of the Air Force differed from that of the Navy in one obvious respect: the A-7 was a flying hardware article at the time the Air Force was forced to agree to procure it. The A-7 did not, as did the F-111, exist only on paper. Hence, the Air Force could not avoid procuring it by using performance deficiencies to suggest the plane's unsuitability. Instead, the Air Force did the next best thing: it made the A-7 over into an Air Force plane, in ways corresponding to its doctrinal preconceptions on survivability. Later, it used the rise in cost that resulted to argue for a reduced procurement of the plane. The A-7D does share a common shell with the original Navy A-7. However, beneath that shell lies a proliferation of Air Force subsystems (some of

---

[217] The exact number of changes counted for the A-7 depends on what one defines as a change (a smaller number of changes will be counted if many minor changes are grouped together to constitute a single "change"). However, under any plausible counting rules, the number of A-7 changes far exceeded the F-4 changes. The F-4 changes were minimal: larger wheels, belled-out wheel wells, reconfigured rear cockpit (so the plane could be flown from the rear), new inertial navigation system, and Air Force life-support systems.

[218] Head, "Decision-Making on the A-7 Attack Aircraft Program," pp. 490–522; and U.S. Senate, Committee on Armed Services, *Fiscal Year 1973 Authorization for Military Procurement*, pp. 3512–3514, 3520. The cancellation of the Cheyenne also produced an unsuccessful Air Force attempt to cancel the A-7D entirely. If the cancellation could have been achieved inexpensively, the attempt might have succeeded. But it could not (too many A-7Ds had already been procured or authorized), so the Air Force instead reduced its planned procurement.

which, like the Allison engine, the Navy itself later procured, under pressure from OSD). The expense of developing these unique Air Force subsystems reduced the savings to be had from an Air Force procurement of an already-developed Navy aircraft.[219]

The F-111, F-4, and A-7 examples suggest some of the limits of bi-service programs for reducing acquisition costs. For reasons discussed throughout this chapter, bi-service programs will always be resisted by the second service in the program. But the hazard presented by this resistance—its potential for undermining the benefits of bi-service acquisition—seems most importantly the product of two variable factors: (1) how uncertain the attributes of the weapon are, at the time the second service is added; and (2) how closely the weapon fits the second service's doctrine, its preconceived image of what that type of weapon ought to be. For a given service and weapon type, if uncertainty is low (e.g., after testing and production are well under way) and the doctrinal conflict is small, the probabilities of success in bi-service acquisition are high.[220] If uncertainty is low but the doctrinal conflict is large, the probabilities of success are mixed. The low uncertainty portends ultimate acquisition in some volume, but the large doctrinal conflict augurs costly service modifications. If both the uncertainty and the doctrinal conflict are large, the probabilities of success are low. Finally, if the uncertainty is high but the doctrinal conflict is small, the probabilities of suc-

[219] In fact, the cost more than doubled, versus original estimates. See U.S. Comptroller General, *Report to the Congress: Acquisition of Major Weapon Systems* (Washington: U.S. Government Printing Office, 1971), pp. 31–32.

[220] Relatively, if not absolutely. The "obvious" reasons that the services "always" resist bi-service acquisition will have different implications for different services and weapon types. If the weapon is central to a service's dominant mission, this resistance will be intense. For more peripheral missions, the resistance might be less intense. Hence, the propositions in the text assume these variables (and others we can imagine) to be constant or given, with only uncertainty and doctrine allowed hypothetically to vary.

cess are difficult to predict. High uncertainty alone may be sufficient to allow full expression of the second service's resistance. Yet if that service is left with no alternative to the bi-service program, it might well acquiesce in procuring it.[221]

Note that, when the second service is the Navy, the minimal doctrinal conflict is unavoidably large for tactical aircraft. Navy doctrine emphasizes the peculiarities of the operational environment aboard aircraft carriers and the subtle problems of adapting aircraft to that environment. The Navy's unique experience and expertise in performing, and in developing the aircraft which perform, carrier landings make the determination of "carrier compatibility" a virtual Navy monopoly. The aircraft of other services will normally fail to incorporate the features necessary for carrier landings (such as, strengthened tail structures and arresting hooks), and the other services will be unable to argue *from experience* on what is required to make a plane "carrier compatible." As a result, any attempt to impose another service's aircraft on the Navy is likely to lead to major modification efforts that are difficult to limit or prevent. Even when the other service's aircraft is fully tested and seems to fit Navy mission doctrines, the Navy possesses a powerful doctrinal argument for making changes in it. This Navy leverage is unique—certainly, the Air Force can make no comparably exclusive claims to tactical expertise—

[221] These guidelines serve to extend the logic of our earlier discussion of the importance of "hard options" for increasing OSD's leverage over the requirements process. (See footnote 146 of Chapter III.) We should emphasize here that these guidelines do not ignore the calculated, "not invented here" reaction of the services against any attempts to force them to procure another service's weapon. The guidelines are based on the proposition that doctrinal differences play a central part in any "not invented here" reaction, as doctrine establishes the major points of reference from which the distinctive features of another service's weapon will be evaluated. By this logic, the resistance of a service can be overcome more easily—a service can be "brought around" more readily to accept a second service's weapon—when the doctrinal conflict is small.

and it gives the Navy an effective path of resistance to *any* OSD attempt to impose another service's aircraft. Carrier-compatibility arguments helped to kill the F-111B, a plane designed from the start to incorporate compatibility features. More recently, such arguments allowed the Navy to escape from procurement of a flight-tested, doctrinally harmonious Air Force fighter plane, the Air Combat Fighter (F-16), even after Congress had expressly prohibited the Navy from considering any alternatives to the F-16.[222]

Our discussion of guidelines to successful bi-service programs surely abstracts the problem to an unacceptable degree, particularly since the data base is too small to permit confident generalization. However, the implied lesson is clear and plausible. The second service in any bi-service program will doubt the suitability of an option formulated by a competing organization. At the same time, the second service will control important parts of the process of adapting that option to its use. For a bi-service program to succeed in the existing political and institutional environment, the organizational foundations for the doubts must be minimized (by avoiding sharp conflicts with central tenets of service doctrine, an especially difficult task in the Navy's case) and the latitude for second-service control must be kept small (by avoiding options with uncertain configurations, costs, and performance). Otherwise, problems of implementation are likely to prove insurmountable, even to a strong-willed Defense Secretary seeking to "revolutionize" the management of defense affairs.

[222] For a good overview on this case, see U.S. Senate, Committee on Appropriations, *Lightweight Fighter Aircraft Program*, pp. 1–66. In these hearings (p. 47), Vice Admiral W. D. Houser, Deputy Chief of Naval Operations for Air Warfare, compares the F-16 to the plane that the Navy preferred and selected, the F-18: "Of course, the big difference is that the [F-16] won't land on a carrier, so that characteristic makes it unsuitable. Several versions of the F-16 were looked at for Navy use powered by different engines and for one reason or another they were not suitable; therefore the F-18 was selected."

CHAPTER VI

The F-111 and the Prospects for Acquisition Reform

The F-111 program began in 1962 as the symbol of a new order in the Department of Defense. It ended ten years later as a measure of the failures of that order. In the intervening period, much had gone wrong, technically and politically. In all of these unfortunate problems, the underlying influence of cognitive simplifications and organization routines was decisive. While McNamara and his associates seemed to have "won" on a few early program decisions, they were insensitive to the inevitable complexities of a biservice program and were in no position to control the vast apparatus that implemented their will. The story of the F-III is an important story of cybernetic processes overwhelming the program of a determined set of leaders, owing as much to the evident cybernetic behavior of the leaders themselves as to the "perversities" of development processes. It is a story that epitomizes Allison's dictum that government leaders can substantially disturb, but not substantially control, the behavior of large organizations.[1]

This was first evident in the design emphasis of the F-111. For McNamara to achieve his doctrinal goals, it was imperative that the Air Force requirements be related coherently to the shift in capabilities he sought. At the same time, for him to get the Navy to accept this "Air Force plane" for deployment, it was imperative that the Navy's goals be attainable in technical terms. The joint requirement ultimately established met neither criterion. The Air Force's supersonic dash mission was a routine extension of that service's dominant mission of nuclear inter-

---

[1] Graham T. Allison, *Essence of Decision: Explaining the Cuban Missile Crisis* (Boston: Little, Brown, 1971), p. 67.

diction at low altitudes. Supersonic speed did not promise major survivability benefits on the low-altitude dash, and the capability conflicted with the doctrinal goals explicitly articulated by the new administration. Nonetheless, conceiving the program in the same simplified terms as did the advisory organizations on which he relied, McNamara established the Air Force requirement as the basis for a joint program. Because that requirement dominated the F-111's design and structured the efforts of development organizations, broader considerations of performance for Air Force missions were neglected. When the costs of the dash mission became apparent, it was too late.[2] A nuclear bomber had been developed for limited-war missions, and an important burden had been added to the achievement of Navy goals— a technical burden that translated into a political obstacle to the program's larger goal of bi-service use of a common aircraft.

The Navy, of course, exacerbated these burdens and remained skeptical of the F-111B's appropriateness for Navy needs. While the Navy would hold a lenient attitude toward its own F-14, it was intolerant of deficiencies in the F-111B. Problem followed problem, until the Navy and the Congress acted with passive DOD support to terminate the program.

Finally, a major difficulty in the integration of propulsion and airframe served to increase program costs, to complicate development and test efforts, and to handicap a large portion of the Air Force F-111s that ultimately were built. The integration of turbo-fan engines had been construed as an extension of the familiar, turbo-jet integration problem. By the time the difficulties emerged, major improvements would be costly and difficult. The highly compressed schedules, for which no "rational requirement" existed, provided insufficient leeway for full resolution of the problem. Yet the schedules were maintained, with the result that major improvements could not be incorporated in the first 141 F-111s that had been produced.

[2] Notes of the Icarus meeting, September 10, 1966, quoted in *TFX Hearings—Second Series*, Part 3, p. 548.

McNamara and his associates were not in a good position to deal with these problems. They could not plausibly have ferreted out detailed information on performance problems, when the process itself did not acknowledge them. Officials could not easily manipulate the processes of development, such as the flight tests, through which the Navy antipathy was expressed. And they could not easily redirect the technical efforts for integrating the propulsion and airframe, particularly when integration responsibilities, necessarily delegated to two separate organizations (General Dynamics and Pratt & Whitney), were so narrowly defined in the relevant contracts. In important respects, then, development processes were too decentralized and fragmented, and development problems were too uncertain, for McNamara and his associates to take decisive action. Instead, they repeatedly acted on the basis of simplified images of emergent problems—images conforming to pre-existing requirements and schedules—and avoided the implications of information threatening to these images. Initial development plans decisively structured the development efforts that followed.

Within that structure, development processes proceeded routinely. Predictions of development problems, such as the early anticipation of weight and compatibility difficulties, went unrecognized. Only the actual emergence of problems, as revealed by such sub-routines of the development as the weight reporting system, fatigue tests, and flight tests, directed technical attention toward them. But even then, the basic structure of the development remained intact. Decisions were made that essentially reconciled the emergent difficulties to the foreordained course of events. Remedial efforts were instituted, while development or production proceeded apace. No one undertook the aggressive initiatives necessary to the program's success.

While it was critical to the implementation failures of the F-111 program, this pattern of behavior is not really surprising. Organizations inevitably factor activities into manageable pieces. Once the organization is set in motion on a given activity, it is difficult to modify, or *even to know to modify*, important elements of the process. To say that the success of the F-111 program required fine-tuning of this process is to say that the program had a high probability of unsatisfactory results from the beginning.

It was thus insufficient for McNamara to calculate shrewdly in getting the services together for a bi-service development. What was required, in addition, was a thorough consideration of the structure of development that was being established—most importantly, a consideration of the flexibility of development organizations, the leeway for problem resolution in development schedules, and the nature of the services' performance requirements. It was in the beginning that McNamara and his associates could perhaps have avoided irreversible choices, choices with unfortunate consequences for their doctrinal goals and their bi-service aspirations. Once the development was under way, the possibilities for modifying the program became increasingly limited and illusory.

This analysis of the F-111 development suggests key characteristics of the conduct of American acquisition programs. The next section of this chapter will provide a brief summary of these characteristics. The final sections of this chapter will attempt to demonstrate their generality, to explore their relationship to our paradigms of decision, and to suggest their implications for improving the conduct of major acquisition programs in this country.

CHARACTERISTICS OF THE DEVELOPMENT PROCESS

Weapons development is a problem in the management of uncertainty: a learning process.[3] It is a process suffused with "surprises" that cannot be foreseen at the outset of

[3] This characterization of the development process of course is not original. It is implicit in most of the microeconomic studies of the subject and is explicitly discussed, for example, in Burton H. Klein, "The Decision-Making Problem in Development," in Richard Nel-

development efforts.[4] A key to successful development is thus the ability of development organizations to respond to these surprises—the sensitivity of development organizations to new information, their ability to formulate new technical approaches according to this information, and their ability to integrate the new technical approaches into an existing design. For optimal development outcomes, design organizations must clearly be flexible, highly adaptive organizations. To the degree these organizations are inflexible, they will be unable to accommodate any but the smallest surprises. Yet rigidity is a primary feature of the acquisition process we have observed in the F-111 program.

This inflexibility is first apparent in the typical origin of American acquisition programs: a service-unilateral requirements process. Service requirements are formulated by user commands. These commands develop routine conceptions of their roles and missions, conceptions which find elaborate foundation in the doctrine, training,[5] hardware, and in-

---

son (ed.), *The Rate and Direction of Inventive Activity: Economic and Social Factors* (Princeton: Princeton University, 1962), pp. 477–508.

[4] See A. W. Marshall and W. H. Meckling, "Predictability of Costs, Time and Success of Development," in Nelson (ed.), *Rate and Direction*, chap. 5; Merton J. Peck and Frederick M. Scherer, *The Weapons Acquisition Process: An Economic Analysis* (Boston: Harvard Business School, 1962), chaps. 2 and 17; and Robert L. Perry et al., *System Acquisition Experience*, Rand Memorandum No. RM-6072-PR (November 1969), passim. These studies demonstrate the extraordinary uncertainty of development outcomes throughout the 1950s and 1960s. For example, costs characteristically increased 100 to 200 percent over predictions for programs in this period. The level of technical advance sought in a program was typically high, and cost overruns were most importantly a function of this level of advance.

[5] Note, for example, the Air Force assumption that high top speed insured adequate air superiority capability, an assumption that routinely extended the *subsonic* lessons of World War II and the Korean War into the *supersonic* requirements for new fighters in the 1950s and 1960s (see discussion in Chapter II, p. 88n). Given the lack of combat experience at supersonic speeds, the only test the high-top-speed assumption confronted was that presented by training and maneuvers. Yet this training and maneuver experience was largely enacted by similar planes—that is, by planes embodying the high-

341

formal expectations of the organization. These conceptions represent highly selective (and, at times, objectively arbitrary) simplifications of the combat environment. Since future combat contingencies and the desirable weapons for them are a matter of great uncertainty and are necessarily conjectural, these simplifications will face few unambiguous

---

top-speed assumption. The faults of the assumption were accordingly camouflaged.

The advent of the Vietnam air war, however, pitted these planes against highly maneuverable Soviet MIG-21s and revealed the weaknesses of the high-top-speed assumption (as well as the weaknesses of American armament and tactics for air-to-air combat). To explore the implications of this revelation, the Air Force and Navy in 1967 instituted training activities that pitted dissimilar aircraft aganst each other for the first time. These activities revealed the critical importance of transonic maneuverability, as opposed to high top speed, for aerial combat. They helped to break fighter-tactic evaluations out of standard conceptions of formation and maneuver. The subsequent Navy and Air Force requirements for new tactical fighters (the F-14 and F-15, respectively) emphasized maneuverability in lieu of highest top speed. The pressure of unfavorable combat experience once again proved to be a key impetus for doctrinal innovation and refinement. As Steinbruner has noted, the objectively biased and simplified cognitive structure imposed on a problem tends to endure in an uncertain environment, since an uncertain environment mutes any challenge to the simplification and provides no unambiguous criteria for rejecting or modifying it. Change is to be expected only when uncertainty is low and an awareness of the full complexity of the problem (the "reality principle") is imposed on the organization—as in a crisis caused by unfavorable combat experience. See Captain Donald C. Carson, USAF, "Dissimilar Aerial Combat Tactics—New Techniques in Battle Training," Air Force Magazine, Vol. 56 (March 1973), pp. 57–61; Michael Getler, "The MIG and the Phantom," Space/Aeronautics, Vol. 51 (May 1969), p. 83; Richard G. Head, "Decision-Making on the A-7 Attack Aircraft Program" (unpublished doctoral dissertation, Syracuse University, 1970), p. 262; Michael P. London, "Tactical Air Superiority," Space/Aeronautics, Vol. 49 (March 1968), p. 63; John D. Steinbruner, The Cybernetic Theory of Decision: New Dimensions of Political Analysis (Princeton: Princeton University Press, 1974), chap. 4; Edgar Ulsamer, "TAC's Focus Is On Lean and Lethal," Air Force Magazine, Vol. 58 (March 1975), pp. 29–30; U.S. Senate, Committee on Armed Services, Fiscal Year 1974 Authorization for Military Procurement, Hearings, 93rd Cong., 1st Sess. (1973), pp. 4390–4408; and U.S. Senate, Committee on Armed Services, Fiscal Year 1975 Authorization for Military Procurement, Hearings, 93rd Cong., 2nd Sess. (1974), pp. 4143–4162.

or clear-cut disproofs. They may initially be adaptive responses to new information (such as, responses to combat experience). However, over time they may be carried to extremes and into inappropriate regimes. New requirements will embody these conceptions, often in spite of important changes in the tactical environment or in national defense goals.

The new requirement characteristically will specify a "total weapon system"—that is, a weapon whose major subsystems have yet to be developed. As a result, the requirement will envision an acquisition program requiring the simultaneous development and integration of most or all major system components.[6]

Only a single program proposal will be presented by a user command for the approval of service headquarters. (Multiple options would reveal user command uncertainty, an ostensible lack of firm deduction from the strategic or tactical threat, and would provide an opening for others, ultimately including DOD civilians, to exercise choice.) The process of securing headquarter's approval is an advocacy process, wherein the user command is under pressures to "sell" its new program. Technical agencies such as NASA frequently are excluded from this process, even though it is a time when the inducements to aggrandize performance goals are substantial. (Recall the increase to supersonic speed on the F-111's sea-level dash that occurred when TAC secured approval of its proposed TFX.) By the time technical agencies re-enter this process, a formalized consensus has been established within the service on the new requirement. Technical warnings at this point will count for little, as the user command will now have an approved program in hand and will have made major commitments to it. The major goal now will be to begin the actual development program.

Technical agencies (and, later in the process, contractor

[6] As opposed to the development, say, of a new airframe to use engines and avionics that have already been developed and tested.

343

engineers) will be pressured to generate means to attain the new requirement. Any problems that the efforts of these agencies reveal will be filtered out before reaching the service-secretary or OSD level. In any event, the extensive low level consultations between the user command and the technical agencies may act to co-opt the latter. (In public testimony, NASA never revealed either TAC's increase in dash speed or the agency's criticisms of it. Furthermore, there is no evidence that NASA ever apprised OSD of the problem.)[7]

Hence, the service organization is relatively insensitive to technical warnings and fairly rigidly committed to a single option at a very early stage of the program. As this option receives the approval of successively higher levels of the service department and OSD, it gains an increasingly broad consensus that becomes increasingly difficult to arrest. A TAC requirement becomes an approved Air Force requirement, then in turn becomes an approved Air Force Department program and a Defense Department program. For Air Force secretaries, OSD officials, or Congressmen, it is strikingly difficult to modify this single option. The powerful consensus behind the option provides elaborate sources of persuasion. Because the ultimate capabilities the program will provide remain uncertain at this point, and because the capabilities that actually would be useful are a matter of inevitable conjecture, it will be difficult to prove analytically the weaknesses of the proposed program. Arguments *always* will be available to support the proposed program, and information served up by the service will

---

[7] Throughout the public record on the program, it is suggested or assumed that the dash requirement was Mach 1.2 from the beginning —and *with NASA's technical blessing*. This assumption has implied to most observers that, were it not for McNamara's imposition of Navy requirements, the original Air Force requirements could have been achieved and that, as a result, performance deficiencies on the F-111 were caused by the burden of Navy requirements. Inferentially, McNamara's bi-service goal, not Air Force neglect of technical warnings, was responsible for F-111 deficiencies—clearly, a convenient impression from the Air Force's point of view.

make the proposed program appear suitable and feasible.[8] While OSD possesses its own sources of analysis and information—mainly, DDR&E and Systems Analysis (the latter now called Program Analysis and Evaluation)—these suborganizations must rely substantially on information provided by the services. Their interests often will be at odds with those of the Defense Secretary, and, in any event, they have little in the way of standing or independent position to formulate discrete options.[9] They certainly can modify service proposals, but only through a protracted, intensely political process that cannot be a normal way of doing business in OSD, at least as the requirements process now is structured. Consequently, OSD can in general approve or deny only a single option, suffused with uncertainty at what is still a very early stage of the program—that is, before any hardware testing reveals what the critical trade-off relationships actually are and even before contractor design proposals suggest what these trade-off relationships might be. (Recently, a few austere prototype programs have provided higher quality information on performance trade-offs and costs before the designs were coupled to normal development and production processes. However, the value of the prototypes for reducing uncertainties may have been undermined by the services' practice of specifying major performance changes—which introduce new uncertainties—when the prototypes enter advanced development and production.)

Once its option receives approval, the sponsoring service

[8] A former assistant secretary for one of the services *never* received a service requirement that was not portrayed as being within the state of the art. Interview 4.

[9] The limits of OSD initiative became more pronounced following the change of administrations in 1969. In a "treaty" with the Joint Chiefs of Staff, the incoming Defense Secretary, Melvin Laird, agreed to change Systems Analysis' role to one of "evaluation and review," thereby reducing Systems Analysis' prerogative to initiate independent proposals. See Benjamin Schemmer, "*How Much is Enough?* Tells a Lot . . . But not Enough," *Armed Forces Journal*, Vol. 108 (February 1, 1971), p. 37.

sends out requests for proposals to the aerospace industry and begins a source selection competition. The contractor proposals that follow are often a product of an exhaustive search among technical alternatives to meet the service goals. However, since the service prescribes performance (and many technical features) in great detail, the contractor is constrained from making the most cost-effective trade-offs among service-desired attributes. Hence, while OSD and the services make commitments to a single option before design proposals—and relevant trade-offs—can be known more clearly, the contractor is constrained from making those trade-offs in formulating a design proposal.

Once a single design proposal is accepted, on the basis of service evaluations, broad design flexibility is quickly lost, *even though uncertainties have not been reduced commensurately.* The approved proposal by this time has been handed over to the service development organization and must adapt to whatever structures prevail there. Connections are made to the incredible complex of reporting and communication links, and development is conducted according to pre-existing rules without regard to the eccentricities and uncertainties of the specific program.[10] The contractor's development organization and the service's program office are massive and thoroughly bureaucratized. (For example, they are nine or ten times as large as their French counterparts designing roughly equivalent hardware articles under a more austere and flexible mode of development organization.)[11]

[10] This discussion follows Robert L. Perry, *System Development Strategies: A Comparative Study of Doctrine, Technology, and Organization in the USAF Ballistic and Cruise Missile Programs, 1950–1960,* Rand Memorandum No. RM-4853-PR (August 1966), p. 128. See also J. Ronald Fox, *Arming America: How the U.S. Buys Its Weapons* (Boston: Harvard Business School, 1974), passim; Robert Perry, *A Prototype Strategy for Aircraft Development,* Rand Memorandum No. RM-5597-1-PR (July 1972), pp. 21–26; and U.S. Senate, Committee on Armed Services, *Weapon Systems Acquisition Process,* Hearings, 92nd Cong., 2nd Sess. (1972), pp. 1–43.

[11] See development personnel totals for the French Mirage IV and the F-111A, in Robert L. Perry et al., *System Acquisition Strategies,*

The winning proposal is decomposed and detailed through this highly structured process. The proposal sets the basic physical shape of the ultimate design and, through a process of progressive disaggregation, the shape of component subsystems as well. Since the design proposal was itself constrained by and keyed to the extensive service requirements and specifications, this process of decomposition extends the emphases of the requirement throughout the design. Levels of acceptability on the decomposed pieces of the design will be determined by an elaborate unfolding of initial specifications. Extensive reporting and monitoring procedures reinforce attention to these criteria. The result is a narrow vision of what constitutes a "design problem" within program organizations.

This process is poorly suited to make continuing trade-offs among conflicting system attributes as development proceeds. Dimensions of performance inadequately captured in the elaborate specification detail will not be integrated into design efforts. Interdependencies at the margin among specified (and unspecified) attributes will be neglected. Consequently, while performance on dominant performance attributes may itself ultimately be deficient, design efforts structured to obtain the dominant performance attributes will tend to ignore and often to subsume other capabilities.[12] As the OSD approvals and contractor proposals neglect high-order trade-offs among program attributes, so, too, do the design efforts. Moreover, the services often will have set performance requirements beyond the state of the art, on the assumption that by "holding the engineers' feet to the fire" they will induce maximum technical advance and performance; yet these extreme perform-

---

Rand Memorandum No. R-733-PR/ARPA (June 1971), pp. 28–29. See also U.S. Senate, Committee on Armed Services, *Weapon Systems Acquisition Process* (1972), pp. 1–43.

[12] Recall that the dominant design imperative of the F-111 was the demanding nuclear mission. Performance on that mission was ultimately quite deficient; yet design efforts structured to attain it had subsumed broader aircraft capabilities.

347

ance demands actually may work to preclude attaining the maximum performance, even per unit, as the pursuit of these demands through an inflexible development process can prevent optimizing trade-offs among *desired* performance attributes.[13]

This process concentrates on fulfilling preplanned commitments. The sequence of development operations is determined by the routine carryover of sequences and practices from prior programs (perhaps selectively updated according to particularly prominent schedule difficulties of the previous development).[14] These sequences presume, above all, that the resolution of development uncertainties is assured by the elaborate planning that is routinely imposed on the program. Little time is provided to accommodate the unanticipated. Rarely do the particular problems posed by a given program determine the character of its development sequences. Yet development efforts will conform to these sequences with the result that appropriate feedback on the technical uncertainties of a specific program is only fortuitously available at the time of firm design commitments.

Design efforts thus will proceed routinely, operating with reference to elaborate specifications and measures of ac-

[13] Demanding performance goals are often defended as being a choice by the services to opt for high quality per unit, rather than for higher numbers of cheaper, less exotic units. Given the inflexibility of American development organizations, we would argue, the services are not getting the highest quality per unit for the resources they expend. Inflexible development organization translates the "quality per unit" design philosophy of the services into an inefficient solution in terms of the services' *own* objectives. Recall in this context the Mark II avionics and the sea-level, supersonic dash of the F-111, discussed in Chapter III. For a provocative discussion of this issue, see Jack N. Merritt and Pierre M. Sprey, "Negative Marginal Returns in Weapons Acquisition," in Richard G. Head and Ervin J. Rokke (eds.), *American Defense Policy, Vol. III* (Baltimore: Johns Hopkins University Press, 1973), pp. 486–495.

[14] Note again the selective changes in test schedules enacted for the F-15 program, discussed on p. 201. See also Erwin J. Bulban, "F-111 Lessons Applied to Other Projects," *Aviation Week and Space Technology,* Vol. 96 (June 26, 1972), pp. 123–125.

ceptability (such as the F-111's distortion index), as if the satisfaction of these measures were equivalent to the resolution of actual technical uncertainties in the design problems. The onset of certain key tests, especially flight tests, will impose a new awareness of technical difficulties on the design process, as these tests provide definitive new measures of acceptability for design efforts. Problem-solving efforts will proceed incrementally in a cycle of design modifications and reports on resultant performance effects. However, early in these efforts, as scheduled, a production build-up will begin. This build-up will be integrated loosely with the extended problem-solving efforts, often in spite of the integration efforts of high-level officials. Perhaps the most notable decision of high-level officials during this period will be to reduce planned production volumes to hold down program costs in the face of rising unit procurement costs.

The operational hardware that results from this process will have performance characteristics that are a by-product of problem-solving efforts, triggered by routinely scheduled tests, and a foreordained production velocity for the early production years at best marginally modified in light of development results. Where the performance of the weapon is particularly unsatisfactory, retrofit and modification programs may be initiated for those units already produced. More generally, however, the user service and the Defense Department will have been "ratcheted down" to acceptance of the de facto result.

In light of the above characterization, is it any wonder that weapons developments seem to have a "life of their own"? Is it surprising that technical problems, however severe, seem always insufficient to re-orient a program or to induce fresh approaches? By this point in our analysis, it should not be surprising. Yet it may properly be argued that our analysis has covered only one program in detail. While frequent reference has been made to other programs, this reference has not been systematic. To provide a better idea of the generality of the F-111 experience, the next

349

section will place the F-111 development in historical context, by surveying the major Air Force acquisition programs of the postwar era. It will describe some notable, yet short-lived, exceptions to our characterization of the development process. In its discussion of these exceptional cases, and particularly in its examination of why the exceptions were established and why they were so short-lived, it will reaffirm the general propositions derived from our analysis of the F-111 development.

ACQUISITION STRATEGIES OF THE POSTWAR ERA

The postwar years brought a shift in Air Force acquisition strategy and organization. Weapons became more complicated—they became integrated "systems"—and the fairly austere practices that had characterized development during World War II were replaced by less flexible, more highly structured processes. Exceptions to this trend toward inflexibility existed throughout the period. But these exceptions barely could be sustained for the duration of a single major program, much less for successive generations of programs. Even the most exceptional programs of the period—the first-generation ballistic-missile developments—ultimately succumbed to the pressures of routine practices that had become the norm in service development organizations.

In the 1940s, the standard development strategy was different from that we have observed in the F-111 program. During that period, prototyping was the normal strategy for system acquisition.[15] In the Air Force, an engineering

[15] The information following in the text is drawn from Arthur Alexander, *Weapons Acquisition in the Soviet Union, the United States, and France*, Rand Memorandum No. P-4989 (March 1973), pp. 14–19; Clarence J. Danhof, *Government Contracting and Technological Change* (Washington: Brookings Institution, 1968), chap. 3; Perry, *System Development Strategies*, pp. 13–21; Perry, "The Atlas, Thor, Minuteman, and Titan," in Eugene Emme (ed.), *The*

project office in the Air Materiel Command (AMC) would supervise subsystem development through a hardware testing period at which time control passed to a production engineering project office of the command. Subsystem development was the responsibility of the project offices, with integration of subsystems for production the task of the manufacturer.[16] There was little government intervention in the details of contractor design efforts—the average size of an Air Force project office overseeing an aircraft or missile development was only ten people (roughly one-twentieth the size of the Air Force's F-111 project office).[17] Since subsystems were not elaborately interdependent and were not preprogrammmed for a specific weapon and delivery schedule, specifications were few and design configurations could change fairly rapidly. (Note, for example, that in the 1944 to 1950 period the basic design of the B-47 medium-range bomber changed three times before the ultimate swept-wing configuration was established, and that the basic design and performance goals of the B-52 long-range strategic bomber

---

History of Rocket Technology (Detroit: Wayne State University Press, 1964), chap. 7; and W. D. Putnam, *The Evolution of Air Force System Acquisition Management*, Rand Memorandum No. R-868-PR (August 1972).

[16] Wartime development of the B-29 bomber was an exception. A single project office managed development and production, as the B-29 was considered too complex to be managed within the standard framework. Later, when B-47 production was accelerated tenfold during the Korean War (1951), joint project offices were formed that were physically co-located in order to smooth the transition from engineering to procurement. Joint project offices became standard practice by 1953, even as the research and development project offices were split off from AMC into a separate Air Research and Development Command (ARDC, designed to give greater status to research and development efforts, outside a command [AMC] that had long been production-oriented). In 1961, AMC and ARDC were recombined into the Air Force Systems Command, as the separate-command organization had made the transition from development to procurement quite difficult. Also, ballistic-missile programs of the late 1950s had demonstrated the desirability, it was thought, of more centralized control. See Putnam, *Evolution*.

[17] Perry, *System Development Strategies*, pp. 17–18.

changed at least seven times before a firm requirement and configuration was approved.)[18]

By the early 1950s, however, this flexible process was transformed under increasing Air Force adherence to the "weapon system concept." Weapons were becoming increasingly complex, and their subsystem components were becoming increasingly interdependent. Post-war design studies of potential missile systems, as well as the experience of developing the first jet aircraft, indicated that the traditional practice of designing components to be fitted into an aircraft or missile as necessary should be replaced by a policy of specifying the total system and designing components to perform within it. The Air Force concluded that "the complete weapon system—the aircraft or guided missile, its components, supporting equipments, and USAF preparation for its implementation as a weapon—should be planned, scheduled, and controlled, from design through test, as an operating entity."[19] Underlying this concept was the notion that the extent and duration of uncertainty were predictable. Because the system was to be elaborately pre-programmed, its operational use had to be specified clearly at the outset: development should not begin until a program proposal had defined "the operational need for a weapons system to be used under specific warfare conditions in stated time periods" and until military requirements statements had defined "the exact technical capability of individual weapons required to meet these operational needs. . . ."[20] Finally, in

[18] Thomas Marschak, "The Role of Project Histories in the Study of R&D," in Thomas Marschak, Thomas K. Glennan, Jr., and Robert Summers, Strategy for R&D: Studies in the Microeconomics of Development (New York: Springer-Verlag, 1967), pp. 118–129.

[19] Letter from Major General D. L. Putt, Vice Commander of ARDC, to Commanding General, Wright Air Development Center, dated 8 December 1952, re General Policy Guidance on Use of Single Prime Contractor for Development of a Complete Weapon System, quoted in Putnam, Evolution, p. 6.

[20] Study by Colonel B. A. Schriever, for Air Staff, dated April 1951, re Combat Ready Aircraft, quoted in Perry, System Development Strategies, p. 20. See also Perry, "The Atlas, Thor, Minuteman, and Titan," p. 148n.

an effort to reduce lead times by minimizing delays in the transition from development to procurement, it was contemplated that a production commitment would be made well in advance of the completion of subsystem development—a logical policy, given the underlying assumption that uncertainties could be accommodated by adequate planning.[21]

These policy changes were the roots of the development strategy that was later applied to the F-111 program: firm military requirements were to precede the development, elaborate plans were to be established to allow the simultaneous development and integration of complex subsystems, and an early commitment to production was to be enacted to allow the early operational availability of the system. Nearly all major aircraft programs of the 1950s reflected the policy shift. The relatively austere prototype development of the F-100 was accelerated dramatically into concurrency; although the F-100A was a low-risk development, concurrency had results for the program that we now consider to be synonymous with the concurrency concept itself: costly modification and retrofit programs.[22] With some variation, all other major aircraft programs of the period— the F-101, F-102, F-105, F-106, F-107, B-58, and B-70— incorporated the weapon system-concurrency concept, with familiar results.[23] Indeed, of all major aircraft developments

[21] Marschak, "The Role of Project Histories," pp. 102–103; Perry, *System Development Strategies*, pp. 20–21; and Perry, "The Atlas, Thor, Minuteman, and Titan," p. 148.

[22] B. H. Klein, T. K. Glennan, Jr., and G. H. Shubert, *The Role of Prototypes in Development*, Rand Memorandum No. RM-3467-PR (1963); and Marschak, "The Role of Project Histories," pp. 90–98.

[23] Klein, Glennan, and Shubert, *The Role of Prototypes*, pp. 1–29; Marschak, "The Role of Project Histories," pp. 98–110; and U.S. Senate, Committee on Armed Services, *The B-58 Program* and *The B-70*, Committee prints, 86th Cong., 2nd Sess. (1960). For example, the F-100 required a retrofit program to cure a troubling stability problem; and the F-102 (the first system fully to embody the weapon system concept) required extensive modification and retrofit programs, cost twice as much as original plans, and suffered performance deficiencies and many delays in operational introduction.

of the 1950s, only the F-104 deviated from the weapon system-concurrency norm. This deviation was for fairly idiosyncratic reasons, and the system was never a major procurement program for the Air Force.[24]

Hence, in the 1950s, Air Force development strategy assumed the major characteristics we have ascribed to it. The only important exceptions to this rule were the strategic missile developments, which represented a new class of weapons for the Air Force. In the 1950s, the Air Force developed two different species of strategic missiles: (1) cruise missiles, which resembled "pilotless aircraft"; and (2) rocket-powered ballistic missiles. Cruise missiles conformed to the norm for development programs of the 1950s, while ballistic missiles were exceptions. The differences between the two sets of programs are instructive and warrant brief discussion.

Cruise missiles presented technical problems of equal difficulty to those presented by ballistic missiles.[25] However, because of the visual and operational analogy of cruise missiles to long-range bomber aircraft, it was thought that these missiles could be inexpensively developed by the mere diversion of aircraft technology: "The conception of cruise missiles as a routine evolutionary extension of the long range bomber was imperfectly supported by experience with

[24] Marschak, "The Role of Project Histories," pp. 110–117. Lockheed had lost an earlier Air Force source selection competition (for the F-102 interceptor program) and needed a new aircraft program to stay in the fighter business. At the same time, there was some sentiment in the Air Force among fighter pilots in favor of a lightweight fighter, devoid of the "luxury items" many ex-Korea pilots considered useless. Hence, Lockheed proposed a cheap, austere prototype program for a lightweight fighter. The program perhaps allowed the Air Force to support a contractor and mollify an Air Force subgroup (the pilots wanting a "hot rod" fighter) without great resource commitments. However, the air superiority F-104 was at odds with the increasing interdiction emphasis of the Air Force in the 1950s and was never procured in volume in this country (though 2,200 units were procured by foreign countries). For a discussion of the considerations behind the F-104 program, see Joseph Goodyear, "The Lightweight Fighter," *Ordnance*, Vol. 39 (November-December 1954), pp. 388–392.

[25] Perry, *System Development Strategies*, p. 119.

[earlier missiles] such as Regulus and Matador, and the relative technical simplicity of the earliest cruise missiles was not properly appreciated. Yet the basic premise survived, largely unquestioned."[26]

Accordingly, the Air Force cruise missile programs of the 1950s, Snark and Navaho, were formulated under the weapon-system concept and were routinely handled by the regular Air Force development organization. The extreme technical uncertainty of these projects defied the elaborate pre-planning, however.[27] As Perry notes in his penetrating study of Air Force missile developments,

> The Navaho program reflected a development philosophy that did not acknowledge the possibility of failure in a comprehensive planned system program. It began in the expectation that several ambitious requirements for technological excellence would be satisfied quickly and at a reasonable cost. . . . In neither [the] Snark nor Navaho development were there serious efforts to provide alternative subsystems or applications. . . . In the case of Snark there were some important substitutions and additions, but they almost invariably came *after the original item had been carried through to the point of flight test.* They were, at best, patchwork repairs to a system troubled by basic defects. Yet in the context of the establishment and doctrines that characterized [Air Force program organization] during the late 1950s, there was essentially no alternative to the sort of last-minute desperation measures that marked the close of both [the] Snark and Navaho development. Provisions for another course had not been made—*indeed could not be made without overturning the [Air Force development] institution.*[28]

[26] Ibid., p. 55.

[27] A 1971 Rand study judged that the Navaho system was the most formidable technical challenge of *all* Air Force developments of the 1950s, including the first-generation ballistic-missile developments. See Perry et al., *System Acquisition Strategies*, p. 13.

[28] Perry, *System Development Strategies*, pp. 50–51. Emphasis added.

Allowing for the greater uncertainty of the cruise-missile programs, this characterization corresponds closely to our description of the F-111 development process. In the end, development organization and strategy for the cruise-missile programs proved unsuitable for meeting the extreme technical challenge the programs presented—a challenge that had been muted by the cruise missiles' analogy to long-range bomber aircraft. The Navaho was cancelled in 1957, and the Snark, widely regarded as a failure, was deployed in a single token squadron in 1961.[29]

While cruise missiles were considered an extension of bomber aircraft technology and operations, rocket-powered ballistic missiles were considered to be without analogy in Air Force operational or development experience. There was no operational user command in existence that had deployed ballistic missiles, established doctrine on their characteristics and use, or formulated a requirement for their development. Air Force acquisition organizations had never supervised a major ballistic-missile program. The technical problems of such developments were considered to be surmountable only in the distant future. Ballistic missiles thus were considered a major change, so highly uncertain that the Air Force made no specific plans to develop them immediately after the war, opting instead for the seemingly evolutionary cruise-missile approach. A low-level research effort on ballistic-missile technology was maintained, to keep abreast of technical possibilities.[30]

By 1954, however, the picture had substantially changed. In that year, the prestigious Strategic Missiles Evaluation Committee (headed by John Von Neumann) reaffirmed the opinion of a number of scientific groups at the time that an effective intercontinental missile could be developed by 1960, *if* exceptional management techniques were applied. Multiple projects were to be instituted in parallel to insure the success of technical efforts. The technical direction of the program was to be vested in an unusually well-qualified

[29] Ibid., pp. 39, 47. [30] Ibid., pp. 54–57.

group of scientists and engineers, headed by a high-ranking Air Force officer. Following the Von Neumann Committee's recommendations, the Air Force established a special field office with complete control over the program and placed the program on highest priority status. Within weeks, the Air Force Scientific Advisory Committee (an Air Force advisory board composed of civilian scientists and engineers) reviewed the development plans and concluded that no single prime contractor could manage the ICBM program adequately and that neither the civil service nor the military could attract the required engineering talent to provide technical control. It was agreed that the newly created private firm of Ramo-Wooldridge, an elite group of engineers, should be made responsible for systems engineering and technical direction under contract to the program office. This arrangement effectively by-passed the existing project offices and technical support groups in the regular Air Force development organization. Communications between the ballistic-missile program office and Ramo-Wooldridge were unimpeded by organizational formalities, as they sat side by side in daily contact. Through these arrangements, the Air Force acquired two valued abilities: (1) direct control over the actions of the technical program managers without having to invest in ritual correspondence; and (2) rapid and continuous cognizance of the details of program activity which was dependent neither on periodic reporting nor inexpert observation. By 1955, when it became clear that this efficiently concentrated program authority required companion financial authority to expedite decisions, procedures were enacted that gave the program office a unique, single point of review in the entire Air Force for funding authority.[31]

While the missiles developed through the late 1950s—the Atlas, Thor, Minuteman, and Titan—were "complete sys-

[31] Until that time, the ICBM programs required the normal financial approvals of the regular chain of command in the Air Materiel Command. See Ibid., p. 65; and Alexander, *Weapons Acquisition*, pp. 15–16.

tems," the development strategy and organization established to oversee these developments provided unique flexibility to cope with the uncertainties of the programs. In part because there were not many pre-existing design or test routines in place for these new weapons, organization and strategy had been tailored to the development task (in "non-exempt" programs, the reverse was true). The ballistic-missile programs emphasized early testing and such conservative techniques as sequential planning and the simultaneous exploration of several alternatives ("parallelism").[32] There was an explicit awareness of and provision for the possibility that some particular component might not be available when required. Advance planning was constantly invalidated by changing technology and test experience. Contrasting the ballistic- and cruise-missile programs, Perry notes:

> In the ballistic missile programs, technical decisions were made in the light of program experience; they were inherently sequential. That decisions could actually be made along the way, that the course of the program could be changed to accommodate technical reality, was largely because real alternatives existed. These had not occurred by nature; they had in every case been deliberately created, preserved, and enriched, although the [normal Air Force development] doctrine of the time virtually forbade such actions. Because the program was structured so as to encourage a ready interchange of information and a considerable flexibility of outlook, there was no great difficulty about taking advantage of alternatives and options. The illusion of a rigidly programmed development [an illusion held by the general Air Force community and the

[32] Indeed, Perry et al., characterize the ballistic-missile development effort as "the most comprehensive application of deliberate system parallelism in the post-war period . . . ," and, except for the Manhattan Project of World War II, the most thorough exploitation of parallelism *ever* attempted. Perry et al., *System Acquisition Strategies*, p. 114.

public] was in part the product of the rapidity of decision-making and its general effectiveness.

[By contrast, in] the cruise missile programs, decisions were nominally sequential, but, because of the absence of feasible alternatives, it was virtually impossible to change the course of the program once it was underway. When technology proved stubborn the developers had no choice but to try to bend it to their will; it would not readily bend, causing many of the difficulties the cruise missiles encountered during development.[33]

In sum, because the ballistic missiles were construed as different, and because of high-level intervention to lift their development out of standard organizations, the ballistic-missile programs provided the flexible, program-oriented strategy and organization necessary to reconcile the high uncertainty of the projects to the demands of a total system development. This flexibility "ignored the dicta of the 'weapon system concept' so recently enunciated and so diligently honored elsewhere," and, in practicing extensive prototyping, violated the doctrine of overlapped development and procurement—concurrency—that was observed by the rest of the research and development establishment.[34] But by tailoring development strategy to development tasks, the program succeeded.

Unfortunately, by the late 1950s, the regular Air Force organization reasserted its influence. The ballistic-missile procedures had been under attack from their inception, as they so obviously cut into the functional authority of existing organizations. In effect, both of the major acquisition command headquarters (Air Materiel Command and Air Research and Development Command) and Air Staff were by-passed in the ballistic-missile review channels. As the missiles moved into production, Air Materiel Command

---

[33] Perry, *System Development Strategies*, p. 137. See also pp. 82–85, 89–101.

[34] Ibid., p. 116.

began performing financial reviews through more routine channels. These channels provided an avenue of penetration for normal organizations into the "exempt" ballistic-missile programs.[35] Accordingly, program management grew more rigid, project offices enlarged (even though the major development tasks were complete), and the exceptional ballistic-missile management became increasingly similar to the norm for the 1950s.[36]

Notably, a similar pattern of exception evolving into rule occurred in the Navy's development of the Polaris missile system and its follows-ons.[37] For both the Air Force and Navy, then, ballistic missiles initially were construed as exceptional, received unusual management arrangements, but then faded back into established channels in the end. Following the development of these first generation missiles, ICBMs were no longer "different"—development and operational experience with missiles had been acquired, user commands had been established, and doctrine had been formulated. Succeeding generations of missile programs were organizationally routine and were required to adapt to the inflexibilities of existing acquisition organizations for their development and procurement.[38]

In 1959 the perceived pattern of success in the ballistic-missile organizations was "translated into organizational ritual and imposed on the balance of the research and devel-

[35] The Air Materiel Command was the Air Force command which supervised procurement. Its organization for the ballistic-missile programs was less substantially modified than was the ARDC program organization. See Ibid., pp. 68–72, 131; and Putnam, *Evolution*, pp. 9, 21.

[36] Perry, *System Development Strategies*, pp. 76–77, 104–105, 131.

[37] Harvey M. Sapolsky, *The Polaris System Development: Bureaucratic and Programmatic Success in Government* (Cambridge: Harvard University Press, 1972), chaps. 1, 7, and 8.

[38] Ibid.; A. Ernest Fitzgerald, *The High Priests of Waste* (New York: W. W. Norton, 1972), pp. 110–123; Perry, *System Development Strategies*, pp. 116–117, 129–132; and U.S. House of Representatives, Committee on Armed Services, *Hearings on Military Posture*, 91st Cong., 1st Sess. (1969), pp. 2399, 3266–3269.

opment command."[39] In this transfer (which was discussed in Chapter IV), the scheduling aspects of the ballistic-missile programs—their nominal concurrency[40]—received great attention, while the organizational preconditions for this scheduling did not. In particular, the importance of the accumulated rights and priorities of the ballistic-missile program were neglected. This neglect was understandable, for the organizations translating the ballistic-missile experience into new development practice were precisely the organizations that had been circumvented by the special rights and procedures of the ballistic-missile programs. Given the increasing "weapon system" emphasis of the early 1950s, the detailed planning and concurrent schedules of the ballistic-missile programs fit the routines of these organizations. The flexibility of the ballistic-missile programs did not fit these routines at all and promised severe institutional disruption. Ultimately, the only visible change enacted as a result of the acquisition experience of the late 1950s was a recombination of the development and procurement functions into a single Air Force command, the Air Force Systems Command (established in March 1961).

Hence, by the time Robert McNamara assumed office in 1961, a decade of interpreted acquisition experience had firmly established the major features of structure and organization that were observed in the analysis of the F-111 program. The basic assumption underlying this interpreted experience was that technical uncertainties could be predicted and managed according to plan. McNamara was hardly one to do battle against that assumption. He was the consummate rationalist, the ultimate advocate of the

[39] Perry, *System Development Strategies,* pp. 116–117, 129–132. See also Putnam, *Evolution,* pp. 9–20.

[40] Recall that ICBM schedules were highly compressed, but that subsystems were prototyped, multiple options were developed in parallel, and hardware was extensively tested before firm commitments were made. The Air Force adopted the scheduling sequences of the programs, but not their parallel development and extensive testing features.

power of analytic reason to anticipate and to accommodate all relevant contingencies. Nowhere in his record does one find real appreciation of uncertainties, of the need to promote flexibility in the face of highly uncertain organizational tasks. "Parallel developments" were "needless duplication" to him and to many of his associates. Development could be planned exactly, even to the point of fixing the price of development *and production* at the outset of a program.[41] Hardware needs could similarly be predetermined by sufficient analytical attention before a program began.[42] In all, McNamara was not one to question the very characteristics of organization that ultimately would overwhelm his goals in the F-111 program. He not only would accept the rigidities of acquisition organization established in the 1950s, he would reinforce them.[43]

The F-111 program thus was handled by the normal Air Force development organization, modified mainly by the attachment of Navy program officials to the regular program office. The F-111 would be a typical development, in its essentials handled routinely by a rigid development organization.

PARADIGMS OF DECISION AND THE PROGRAM IMPLEMENTATION PROBLEM

The processes responsible for the unfortunate results of the F-111 program were thus common to most Air Force system developments of the post-war era. McNamara failed to un-

[41] See John Mecklin, "The C-5: The Ordeal of the Plane Makers," Part II, *Fortune*, Vol. 72 (December 1965), pp. 158–159, 280–284, 288–292; and Harold Meyers, "For Lockheed, Everything's Coming Up Unk-Unks," *Fortune*, Vol. 80 (August 1, 1969), pp. 81, 131–134.
[42] Robert J. Art, *The TFX Decision: McNamara and the Military* (Boston: Little, Brown, 1968), pp. 89–99; Alain C. Enthoven and K. Wayne Smith, *How Much is Enough? Shaping the Defense Program, 1961–1969* (New York: Harper and Row, 1971), pp. 31–72; and William H. Kaufmann, *The McNamara Strategy* (New York: Harper and Row, 1964), pp. 194, 199.
[43] Changes in acquisition practice since McNamara's tenure will be discussed in the final section of this chapter.

derstand and to anticipate their influence both in the establishment of the bi-service program and in the conduct of actual development efforts. Instead, he seemed to think that the far-flung bureaucratic network that would implement his decisions would respond to his will and determination. Failing to recognize the problems of implementation, he failed to foresee how the diverse operations of this network could overwhelm the bi-service program he had established.

A phenomenon more general than the F-111 program or the weapons acquisition process is evident here: many scholars have argued that decision processes regularly neglect the importance of long-range implementation problems.[44] The press of immediate events on very busy decision makers, plus the tendency for options to be conceptualized in terms of traditional analytic dimensions of cost and benefit, work to minimize the recognition of implementation difficulties in the decision process. At the same time, it is readily apparent, the resolution of these difficulties can constitute the better part of success in organizational activity.

The analysis of the F-111 program confirms that a powerful body of theory is presently available for conceptualizing the implementation problem and, more generally, for understanding the behavior of large public organizations. The primary theoretical reference in this study has been Steinbruner's formulation of the cybernetic paradigm, which owes a major acknowledged debt to the prior work of Allison and to the impressive founding efforts of Simon and others at the Carnegie School. At the collective level of decision making, the cybernetic paradigm emphasizes the conglomerate, semi-feudal character of organizational activity. It draws attention to the factoring of problems to organizational subunits, to the goals and standard operating procedures ("sops") of these subunits, to their regularities

---

[44] See, for example, Allison, *Essence of Decision*, chaps. 4, 6, and 7; and Steinbruner, *Cybernetic Theory*, Part 2. For a different treatment of this general issue, see Jeffrey L. Pressman and Aaron Wildavsky, *Implementation: How Great Expectations in Washington Are Dashed in Oakland* (Berkeley: University of California Press, 1973).

of behavior, and to their search patterns when problems are perceived. It suggests the constraints of agenda and information faced by higher-level decision makers nominally presiding over these subunits.[45] Overall, at the collective level of decision making, the cybernetic paradigm focuses on persistent patterns of behavior at the subunit level, such as the TAC emphasis on nuclear weapons, and suggests the difficulties higher-level officials confront in attempting to redirect that behavior. With these propositions in mind, an analyst examining McNamara's proposal for a bi-service TFX program could hardly have missed a key feature of the proposal: the Navy, inevitably, would have a virtual monopoly on F-111B flight tests and hence an extraordinary power to define what constituted a "problem" in the later stages of development. Such an analyst would also have noted the limited capacity in OSD for countering this Navy control.

These characteristics of collective decision making described by the cybernetic paradigm represent the paradigm's direct incorporation of earlier theoretical work, most prominently Cyert and March's behavioral theory of the firm (and Allison's derivative Model II).[46] However, Steinbruner's formulation deepens our understanding of these characteristics of organization behavior by rooting them in a conception of the *individual* decision maker drawn from experimentally verified principles of cognitive psychology and information theory. His formulation describes the individual behavior that lies behind the aggregate, subunit behavior described in the earlier theories. In so doing, Steinbruner provides a more complete behavioral view of the decision process. More than that, however, he places this observation in the mainstream of a relatively new, but well-developed, body of knowledge having a core logic different from standard rational assumptions. He provides persuasive

[45] Allison, *Essence of Decision*, chap 3.
[46] Ibid.; and Richard M. Cyert and James G. March, *A Behavioral Theory of the Firm* (Englewood Cliffs: Prentice-Hall, 1963), chaps. 1–6.

evidence that this formulation represents a coherent understanding of decision processes, a "paradigm," distinct from the logic of rational choice (that is, from the intellectual tradition embodied in the analytic paradigm). The paradigm thus makes a serious claim to structure the understanding of decision processes, and describes behavior that is presumed to be neither aberrant nor unintelligent, but eminently human and consistent with what is known about the cognitive operations of the mind under uncertainty.[47]

In terms of its practical value to the analyst or scholar, Steinbruner's formulation provides a clear alternative framework for understanding ubiquitous features of behavior in large organizations: the tendency of decision makers to believe in extraordinary problem simplifications, to conceptualize problems so that conflicting objectives "actually" seem consonant, to impute unwarranted certainty to the future benefits (and impossibility to the future costs) of chosen actions, and to sustain this behavior in the face of accumulating evidence urging change. This framework is particularly useful for understanding individual behavior in organizations, behavior which theories of aggregated, subunit behavior (like Model II) do not by themselves readily capture. This is an important benefit, since much "organization" behavior must be interpreted by the scholar or analyst using the documentation of individuals: memoranda, testimony, and so on. More generally, the paradigm alerts the analyst to a central phenomenon: decision makers, even when very experienced in their business, will tend to develop stable simplifications over time which render the decision process insensitive to important segments of complex problems.[48] The paradigm provides a rich set of clues on the mechanisms by which individuals will sustain these simplifications in spite of contradictory information. (Recall the Secretaries' "correction of deficiencies" assumptions and their confusion of the evolution of program contracts with

---

[47] Steinbruner, *Cybernetic Theory*, pp. 103–108.
[48] See Steinbruner, *Cybernetic Theory*, p. 340, for a fuller discussion of the implications of this point.

the evolution of actual production, as they addressed the engine-inlet compatibility problems.) While these assumptions may seem bizarre to the outside observer, they are perfectly logical to the cybernetic analyst. For example, a cybernetic analyst examining the F-111 program might note that program schedules would provide little time or flexibility for resolving problems that development efforts revealed. The paradigm would alert the analyst to look further, to probe for unrealistic assumptions being made about how development efforts were expected to resolve any problems in spite of the compressed schedules. The analyst would not have to look very far: defense officials had great faith at the outset of the program in the efficacy of contract devices to secure positive results without any underlying organizational change. To the cybernetic analyst, this presumption of *de jure* contractor responsibility would be a warning signal, especially in light of the procurement experience of the 1950s.[49]

To be sure, explanations drawn from the analytic paradigm could be used to explain significant features of this behavior—the cybernetic paradigm holds no exclusive claim to understanding in this area. However, the cybernetic paradigm significantly broadens our understanding, as it powerfully evokes the rigidities, the narrow vision, the objectively strange assumptions that, even casual observation informs us, suffuse much of the activity of large organizations. It may be true that the logic of the analytic paradigm could be strained to explain the cybernetic behavior observed in the F-111 program. But why should one endeavor to explain all varieties of government behavior in terms of analytic logic, when much of that behavior can be readily understood in terms of a rigorous alternative logic? The logic by which the analyst structures and interprets inevi-

---

[49] Another excellent example is McNamara's belief, at the outset of the program, that the F-111B would be more suitable for bi-service use than the F-4, since the F-111B was being designed from the start for bi-service use. This belief ignored the obvious potential for difficulties in a bi-service development. However, it was ideally suited to sanction the course upon which McNamara had embarked.

tably fragmentary evidence will critically influence the understandings he reaches. By applying the cybernetic paradigm as a competing framework of analysis, the analyst at least will be constrained from too easily bending the evidence to the demands of established analytic assumptions.[50]

An additional payoff to the separate application of the cybernetic paradigm is suggested by an intriguing result of the present study: those aspects of the decision process to which McNamara and his associates—supreme rationalists all—were insufficiently sensitive were precisely the ones evoked by the cybernetic paradigm. Of course, this result does not imply that, had these individuals only been sensitized to the assumptions of the cybernetic paradigm, the F-111 program necessarily would have had different results. It does, however, suggest that an appropriate sensitivity would have led them to act with greater caution. Had their conception of the defense management problem recognized the significance of implementation difficulties, it is likely that they would not have been so confident in imposing an undeveloped aircraft on two resisting services through so inflexible a development organization.

REFORMING THE ACQUISITION PROCESS: THE POLICY IMPLEMENTATION PROBLEM

The most frustrating thing is that we know how we ought to manage—you, me, all of us—and we refuse to change based on what we know.

> —Deputy Defense Secretary David Packard,
> addressing the Armed Forces Management
> Association, 1970[51]

---

[50] See Steinbruner, *Cybernetic Theory*, pp. 328–329, for an extended discussion of this issue.

[51] See the text of Packard's speech before the Dinner of the Armed Forces Management Association, Los Angeles, California, August 20, 1970, reprinted in U.S. House of Representatives, Committee on

With a greater sensitivity to program implementation difficulties, McNamara and his associates might have avoided choices harmful to their goals. However, to accomplish anything more affirmative, to achieve positive results in terms of their goals, more than a concern for program implementation problems was required. Existing acquisition practices—the organization and procedures of the process that would develop *any* likely weapon system they approved—sharply reduced their ability to take affirmative action. It limited the amount and certainty of the information they received; it structured the timing of all important program commitments they would have to make; it restricted the agenda of options they faced; and it determined the degree of control they would have over actual development efforts.

For surmounting these organizational constraints, reform of the acquisition process was required. Having neglected program implementation difficulties, McNamara and his associates did not perceive or confront this larger problem of acquisition policy.[52] But if they had confronted it, they would have faced a set of particularly difficult problems that have neutralized most attempts to reform acquisition policies. Past attempts at reform have employed some of the brightest and most experienced analysts of defense affairs in the country. Yet these efforts generally have met with little success. Our analysis offers clues on why reform has been so difficult, and it indicates possible future directions

---

Government Operations, *Policy Changes in Weapon System Procurement*, Hearings, 91st Cong., 2nd Sess. (1970), p. 323. The argument to be presented in this section of the text draws upon the author's submissions to the Commission on the Organization of Government for the Conduct of Foreign Affairs (the so-called Murphy Commission).

[52] As discussed in the text, McNamara believed that appropriate analysis and contract incentives would insure desirable development outcomes. This conception of the acquisition problem ignored the need for general reform in the acquisition process as much as it ignored the potential for difficulty in the TFX program he instituted. This subject will receive more attention momentarily.

for acquisition reforms. The present section will explore these clues and reforms. The fundamental problem, this discussion will suggest, is the difficulty of implementing the major reforms that we can conceive.

Outside the services and the contractors, there is a surprising contemporary consensus on the appropriate future basis for acquisition programs. Rand studies since 1958, the 1969 report of the Defense Blue Ribbon Panel, the 1971 report of the Comptroller General on the acquisition of major weapon systems, the policy pronouncments of a recent Deputy Defense Secretary, David Packard, and the studies of most independent scholars have reached essentially the same conclusions. With varying emphases, each of these sources has urged a reduced reliance on detailed performance requirements, a greater separation of development and procurement to allow extensive testing before production commitments, a reduced emphasis on exotic subsystems, and an increase in the autonomy and flexibility of program management.[53] This contemporary consensus ex-

[53] For Packard's testimony, see U.S. House of Representatives, Committee on Government Operations, *Policy Changes in Weapon System Procurement*, pp. 1–42, 313–339. For a sampling of the Rand studies, see Alexander, *Weapons Acquisition*; Alvin J. Harman, *Analysis of Aircraft Development*, Rand Memorandum No. P-4976 (March 1973); Burton H. Klein, W. H. Meckling, and E. G. Mesthene, *Military Research and Development Policies*, Rand Memorandum No. R-333-PR (December 1958); and Perry, *A Prototype Strategy*. For the Blue Ribbon Panel's conclusions, see U.S. Defense Blue Ribbon Panel, *Report to the President and the Secretary of Defense on the Department of Defense* (Washington: U.S. Government Printing Office, 1970), chap. 2. For the Comptroller General's conclusions, see U.S. Comptroller General, *Report to the Congress: Acquisition of Major Weapon Systems* (Washington: U.S. Government Printing Office, 1971), pp. 1–3, 41, 51–56. Finally, for examples of recent scholarly efforts, see Graham T. Allison and Frederic A. Morris, "Armaments and Arms Control: Exploring the Determinants of Military Weapons," *Daedalus*, Vol. 104 (Summer 1975), pp. 99–130; Robert J. Art, "Restructuring the Military-Industrial Complex: Arms Control in Institutional Perspective," *Public Policy*, Vol. 22 (Fall 1974), pp. 423–459; and John D. Steinbruner and Barry Carter, "Organizational and Political Dimensions of the Strategic Posture: The Problems of Reform," *Daedalus*, Vol. 104 (Summer 1975), pp. 131–154.

tends an already long line of past recommendations for acquisition reform. Surveying twenty years of attempted reforms, Arthur Alexander notes:

> In the last two decades alone, over 20 high-level studies have been conducted on the problem of Air Force and Defense Department R&D, and most of these studies have identified the same symptoms—diffused authority, increased detailed directions [sic], overconstrained regulation at the working level. Organizational boundaries have shifted frequently and new sets of regulations have attempted to cut through the morass of existing rules, but the problems remain.[54]

Given this extended continuity in diagnoses of the problem and the contemporary consensus on the appropriate directions for change, why has so little change actually occurred? Why is it that, in Packard's words, "we refuse to change based on what we know?"

The lack of change is not a result of the objective necessity of present acquisition practices—that is, it is not a result of the inherent qualities of technology or the peculiar character of the enemy threat repeatedly forcing this country back to its dominant acquisition practices. The United States is the only country in the world that regularly employs this elaborately structured, heavily bureaucratized strategy; yet foreign weapons are not to be feared less because of it.[55] The problem of integrating complex subsystems into a complete system should not be underestimated; yet this country is not the only country integrating all-weather avionics, accurate navigation systems, and refined fire control systems into its aircraft.[56] Moreover, for

---

[54] Arthur Alexander, *Design to Price from the Perspective of the United States, France, and the Soviet Union*, Rand Memorandum No. P-4967 (February 1973), p. 7.

[55] Ibid., passim; and Alexander, *Weapons Acquisition*.

[56] Foreign weapons rely on complex avionics and other advanced subsystems to a lesser degree than do American weapons. However, when foreign countries do adopt advanced subsystems, they do not

its own weapon systems, in between major programs, the United States has secured substantial capability improvements by incorporating new (at times radically new) subsystems in an existing airframe. (Recall, for example, the major thrust improvements obtained for the F-111Fs, and the more sophisticated avionics installed in the F-111Ds and F-111Fs.)[57] If this integration can be accomplished for new versions of a given system, why must all subsystems be elaborately pre-programmed for an entirely new system? Certainly not because the inherent qualities of technology dictate it.

The normal reason given for this concurrent pre-programming of new subsystems is a time-and-performance argument: if the United States developed prototypes using off-the-shelf subsystems (the "incremental approach"), its weapons would not incorporate the maximum performance, performance available from *new* subsystems, for meeting the enemy threat; alternatively, if this country were to prototype the basic system (airframe, engines, and basic support subsystems, for example) prior to integrating new subsystems, development would require an inordinately long time before the weapon were operationally available. While this argument is intuitively plausible, there is little empirical data to support it. On the issue of timing, there is no hard

simultaneously emulate American acquisition practices, suggesting that the adoption of complex subsystems does not require the adoption of practices common in American acquisition programs.

[57] Other examples include the substantial capability improvements achieved through successive versions of the F-4 Phantom, the A-4 Skyhawk, and other fighter and attack aircraft. Note also the major thrust increase formerly planned for the B version of the F-14: the difference in power between the F-14A and F-14B would have represented the largest generation-to-generation increase in engine thrust relative to engine weight *ever achieved* by Pratt & Whitney, a strong suggestion of the magnitude of improvement that may be possible through subsystem improvements on a fully developed airframe. See U.S. Senate, Committee on Armed Services, *Fiscal Year 1973 Authorization for Military Procurement*, Hearings, 92nd Cong., 2nd Sess. (1972), p. 4026.

evidence available to prove that concurrent pre-programming is as a rule a quicker way to develop and deploy a wholly new system. *Planned* schedules may indicate a more rapid deployment; but the delays caused by retrofit, modification, and other corrective efforts typical of concurrent pre-programmed developments tend to eliminate the planned schedule advantage.[58] In this context, recall the extended delays in F-111 operational capability occasioned by the fatigue and avionics problems. The Air Force necessarily accepted these delays, yet would not have agreed to more relaxed development schedules in the first instance.[59]

On the issue of attaining maximum performance across successive generations of developments, the evidence is not

[58] At the same time, as we have observed throughout this study, these compressed schedules have a notably unfortunate impact on design flexibility and, through the resulting suppression of important trade-offs, on system cost. For a discussion of these problems, see Klein, Glennan, and Shubert, *The Role of Prototypes*, pp. 1–29; Marschak, "The Role of Project Histories," pp. 90–126; and Perry et al., *System Acquisition Strategies*, pp. 31–45.

[59] The pattern of later accepting, time after time, what we earlier refuse to acknowledge and recognize in our plans is an interesting phenomenon in the terms of the cybernetic paradigm. Acquisition officials at nearly every level repeatedly are able to deceive themselves as to the fitness of standard acquisition practices. Programs are initiated with confidence that all uncertainties have been anticipated; development efforts are keyed to early plans and proceed as if all uncertainties in fact have been anticipated; unexpected problems are revealed after large commitments have already been made; and expensive retrofit and modification programs then ensue. Participants in this process generally fail to read the larger lessons of the experience. In subsequent developments, they will change certain matters of detail associated with conspicuous problems of the prior development (e.g., if drag problems plagued the prior effort, they will increase the wind tunnel time and drag monitoring efforts in the subsequent effort). But basic organization and policies will remain unchanged. A new program thus tends to "solve" the specific technical problems of the previous program. As officials approach a new program, they will assert with great confidence that *this time* all important uncertainties have been anticipated. Yet the problems of the new program will differ in unexpected ways from the problems of the old program, and the cycle will repeat itself once again.

decisive in favor of the weapon-system concept.[60] Note again how the inflexibility of an elaborately planned development process results both in a restricted technical search for design options and in a minimal ability to balance performance requirements as development efforts yield new information. It is not clear that, simply because advanced performance is specified, this inflexible process produces the optimum combination of performance capabilities. A more flexible development organization, one better suited to make trade-offs among desired performance attributes in light of development results, would be better suited to push performance beyond existing technical frontiers.

If, as seems apparent, present acquisition practices are not the sole means available to achieve the general goals of the government's weapons acquisition enterprise, why have efforts to change these practices met with such limited success? A major reason, this study suggests, is that all reform necessarily has been implemented through established development organizations. New acquisition policies do not start with a clean slate; instead, they are fed into an intricate network of established organizations and suborganizations, formal regulations, traditional practices, mutual expectations, systems of reporting and review, and personnel procedures.[61] Over time, this network has formed relatively stable and routine processes for coordinating the immense variety of tasks that are traditionally involved in developing

[60] Alexander, *Weapons Acquisition*; Marschak, "The Role of Project Histories," pp. 90–126; Perry, *A Prototype Strategy*; Perry et al., *System Acquisition Strategies*, pp. 30–45; and U.S. Senate, Committee on Armed Services, *Weapon Systems Acquisition Process* (1972), pp. 1–43.

[61] Note, for example, that the Laird-Packard reforms of the early 1970s, which were designed to increase program flexibility, were stipulated as additions to the massive Armed Services Procurement Regulations, the "bible" of acquisition practices. See Packard's memoranda in U.S. House of Representatives, Committee on Government Operations, *Policy Changes in Weapon System Procurement*, pp. 313–326.

373

and procuring new weapon systems. These tasks are too extensive, too complicated to be displaced at a stroke through the mere stipulation of new policy measures. Change requires coordination with subordinate units of the development organization. These subordinate units will not swiftly embrace new policies. They share strong but objectively narrow beliefs in the conception of their task embodied in their routines. They see their task as being vitally important. Any attempt to modify their practices, or to reduce the importance of their participation, will be met with active opposition to (and subtle dilution of) the reforms. In short, new policies do not penetrate without friction the elaborate processes they are designed to change, but are adapted to them with little sustained alteration in the behavior or flexibility of development management.

Our analysis of the F-111 program suggests this pattern. The F-111 development effort routinely was conceived as a total weapon system, was scheduled concurrently according to traditional practice of the time, and was plugged into the whole variety of routine reporting and review channels (as well as some special channels to accommodate Navy involvement). The development process decomposed the design problem along dimensions that mirrored the contractor and Air Force development organizations. When unexpected problems arose, the usual response was a narrow search for marginal improvements in programmed components or subsystems (such as the engines and inlets, or the wing box) without much consideration of the possibility that an optional component or subsystem should be introduced.[62] To an outside observer, the problems and results of the program would suggest the inherent deficiencies of the total weapon system/concurrency approach to development. To the established Air Force development organization, however, the lessons of the program were far narrower and less disruptive: in subsequent programs, engine-inlet

[62] Perry notes this same pattern for the cruise-missile developments of the 1950s. See Perry, *System Development Strategies*, p. 122.

compatibility tests and fatigue tests were shifted to an earlier point in development, and the prototyping of a few subsystems was initiated, while development organization and procedures were otherwise unaffected.

The pattern is apparent again in the evolution of acquisition policy in the 1950s. The cruise-missile programs were recognized to provide technological challenges of a major order. But the aircraft-like cruise missiles fit the development organization's preconceived image of its task. Accordingly, while the "unsuitability of the standard organizational structure for tasks involving major uncertainties . . . was generally acknowledged," the modifications of organization and procedure for these programs was confined to "a very narrow path of functional rearrangement and reporting line changes."[63]

By contrast, the ballistic-missile programs generally were recognized to be "different." Combined with the high-level attention to and the urgency of these programs, this preconception of difference led to special arrangements for the ballistic-missile programs, arrangements providing for minimal disruption of established acquisition organization. Perry notes: "There is a good deal of inertial resistance to change in the broad; resistance to the creation of special status for one program tends to be massive. Thus, when exemption from existing rules becomes absolutely essential to the well being of one program, taking it away from the original sponsor is simpler than inducing that sponsor to give it the special consideration it may require."[64] A special organization was thus created to manage the ballistic-missile developments, with notable success.

However, even the favored ballistic-missile programs could not obtain complete *funding* independence from established organizations, especially for the production phase of the program (a phase at that time supervised by the Air Materiel Command, or AMC). This lack of independence for funding arrangements was ultimately decisive:

[63] Ibid., p. 126.   [64] Ibid., p. 129.

375

"It was around that item [funding control] more than any other that the monolithic program structure began to grow spongy. Anyone charged with any aspect of funding review could argue that he *had* to know the purpose of every expenditure. Knowing the purpose and having authority for funds approval, he was in a position to influence the program. . . . [As the missiles moved into production,] control of the financial documentation came more and more into the hands of an agency that denied any special advantages to product orientation, either theoretical or practical."[65] By the end of the ballistic-missile programs, their special status had faded, as the routines of established organizations increasingly penetrated program management. This evolution from special to normal status had occurred on a few other programs in the late 1940s and early 1950s (the B-47, the F-86D, and the F-84F). In response to severe development or production "crises," these programs acquired special reporting channels, funding procedures, and so on; but such an "exempt" status was transitory as matters reverted to normal once the pressing crisis had been resolved. This special response to crisis became less frequent in the 1950s. "Its potential seems neither to have been appreciated nor further explored, perhaps because such special arrangements thoroughly upset the regular order."[66]

Following the development success of the ballistic-missile programs, the Air Force moved to translate the elements of that success into future acquisition practice. Predictably, the translation was selective and minimally disruptive. The concurrent scheduling aspects of the programs, which had become normal practice in missile and aircraft developments anyway, received emphasis, while the organization preconditions for that scheduling—flexible, autonomous program management and multiple prototyping of subsystem options—did not.[67] Established organizations re-

---

[65] Ibid., pp. 72–73.   [66] Ibid., p. 52n.

[67] This translation effort actually misconstrued the ballistic-missile concurrency. The ballistic-missile programs were managed with ex-

sisted any broad proposals for reform. Because reform had
to be implemented through "the immutables of the Wright
Field environment," little actual change resulted, other
than the reinforcement of organizationally conservative
(and substantively incomplete) myths of success for concurrency and the weapon-system concept.[68]

Robert McNamara confronted a similar problem during
his tenure. His major procurement reforms involved changes
in planning procedures and changes in contract types. To
reduce duplication and "gold-plated" service requirements,
procedures were changed to require formalized project definition, with OSD review, for new weapon-system programs
(this, of course, within the larger program budgeting system
that was established). To control system costs, contracts
were changed from the "cost-plus" approach of the 1950s to
a "fixed-price" approach for new programs. The procedural
reforms apparently weeded out the most extreme cases of
unrealistic and duplicative programs, though at the cost
of further rigidifying the requirements process and generally reducing the number of projects committed to hardware development.[69] The contractual reforms were nearly

---

tensive testing, multiple prototyping, and continual revision of plans
as new information accumulated, before firm commitments were
made. But the Air Force extracted the lesson that developments
could be preplanned and could employ concurrent schedules. This
lesson did not disrupt established development organization. The
lesson of flexible, relatively autonomous program management would
have required "tearing apart" the Air Force development organization.

[68] Ibid., p. 130; Putnam, *Evolution*, pp. 13–22; and Interviews 5,
9, 10, 11, and 12.

[69] Art, *The TFX Decision*, pp, 89–99; Enthoven and Smith, *How
Much is Enough?*, pp. 31–72; and Kaufmann, *The McNamara Strategy*, pp. 194, 199. Perry et al. note (in *System Acquisition Strategies*,
p. 14) that the level of technical advance was generally lower in the
system developments of the 1960s, as compared to the developments
of the 1950s. This can be taken as evidence that the McNamara reforms did eliminate especially risky system developments that would
have been approved under the practices of the 1950s. However, an
alternative hypothesis that fits the observation of lower technical
advance in the 1960s is that the 1960s were a time when technology
had reached a natural plateau. By this latter interpretation, the 1960s

a complete failure, however. Instead of placing a fixed-price "ceiling" on costs and inducing changes in development behavior, these contracts induced a great expansion in the number of contract amendments (eliminating thereby the constraint of the fixed price) and left development behavior substantially unmodified. As had been the case in the past, contracts did not so much *control* as they did *reflect* the underlying behavior of acquisition organizations. The achievement of acquisition goals (cost, time, and performance) for programs of the 1960s was no better than it had been for comparable programs of the 1950s.[70] Once again,

---

are observed to have been a period of routine follow-ons to the path-breaking, necessarily risky developments of the 1950s, the latter of which included the first supersonic fighter planes, the first intercontinental ballistic missiles, the first submarine-launched ballistic missiles, and other, decidedly non-incremental ventures. The present study cannot resolve this conflict in interpretations.

[70] Irving N. Fisher, *A Reappraisal of Incentive Contracting Experience*, Rand Memorandum No. RM-5700-PR (July 1968); and Perry et al., *System Acquisition Strategies*, pp. 12–15. According to the latter report (p. 21n), other studies in progress confirm the same point: ". . . the differences in program outcomes that can be attributed to differences in contract types are for practical purposes undetectable." To understand why this might be so, note the following experience (from a fourth government report provided to the author): between 1962 and 1965, the "cost-plus" proportion of the business of a large West Coast defense contractor decreased from 75 percent to 25 percent, as fixed-price contracts replaced cost-plus contracts. Meanwhile, although the nature and volume of the contractor's business remained approximately the same, the number of contract changes *quadrupled*. To be sure, variations in contract type significantly influence the financial relations between contractors and the government. The argument is simply that, in spite of the variations in their financial effects, contract types cannot easily be manipulated to induce desirable changes or new "efficiencies" in acquisition behavior. For example, in the F-14 and C-5A programs, the prime contracts restricted the government's obligations to cover major cost growths for development *and* production. The government hoped that this contractual lid on costs would induce more efficient contractor behavior to minimize costs. Yet most observers agree that no particularly desirable changes in behavior were induced (indeed, inefficiencies may have resulted). In the absence of such improvements, the main effect of limiting the government's financial obligations was to drive the prime contractors (Grumman and Lockheed) to the verge of bankruptcy. In other words, even latent threats to corporate sur-

policy reforms had been adapted with minimal disruption to the routine processes of established organizations.

By the time the Nixon Administration entered office, the acquisition reforms of the McNamara era were widely considered a failure. While supporters of McNamara could point to the more orderly planning processes and innumerable administrative savings they had instituted in various operations of the Defense Department, they could not point to many major successes in weapons acquisition programs. Two especially controversial Air Force programs of the Mc-Namara years—the C-5A and the F-111 (the Navy version of which had just been cancelled)—epitomized to many the fundamental and serious problems that McNamara's reform efforts had failed to solve. The incoming Deputy Defense Secretary, David Packard, only echoed the conventional wisdom when he observed to a group of defense contractors, "Frankly, gentlemen, in Defense procurement, we have a real mess on our hands. . . ."[71] As befits a prominent, widely acknowledged "problem" in our political system, weapons acquisition became the subject of intense study in these years, by a Presidential panel, numerous committees of Congress, and others.[72]

---

vival—perhaps the most powerful summary incentive the government could ever impose, by contracts or other means—were not sufficient to break these programs out of the encumbrances of government management and established acquisition practices.

[71] See the text of Packard's speech before the Dinner of the Armed Forces Management Association, Los Angeles, California, August 20, 1970, reprinted in U.S. House of Representatives, Committee on Government Operations, *Policy Changes in Weapon System Procurement*, p. 323. An experienced defense contractor himself (a founder and chairman of the board of Hewlitt-Packard, a large electronics firm), Packard was appointed by Laird to assume primary responsibility for improving the conduct of weapons-acquisition programs.

[72] For example, see U.S. Defense Blue Ribbon Panel, *Report to The President*; U.S. Congress, Joint Economic Committee, Subcommittee on Economy in Government, *The Acquisition of Weapons Systems*, Hearings, 92d Cong., 1st Sess. (1971), Parts 1–7; and U.S. House of Representatives, Committee on Government Operations, *Policy Changes in Weapon System Procurement*.

In this context of developing consensus on the need for changes in acquisition practices, Secretaries Laird and Packard acted to remedy the perceived problems of the McNamara years. Specifically, they attempted to reduce the concurrency of major programs (a new policy labeled "fly before you buy"), to increase the autonomy of program management, to increase the flexibility of program contracts, and to increase the use of competitive prototyping in acquisition programs.[73] The success of these reforms has been mixed. Attempts have been made in the past to reduce concurrency—a Navy program to do so in the mid-1950s was dubbed "try before you buy"—but without notable success.[74] The initial production commitment for the showcase program of the Laird-Packard reforms, the F-15, occurred four months after the plane's first flight, precisely the same time lapse between first flight and production commitment as occurred on the F-111 program. First production deliveries of the F-15 to the operational command occurred 28 months after the plane's first flight, a five-month *shorter* testing period between first flight and initial production deliveries than was scheduled on the F-111A program.[75]

[73] See Packard's testimony in U.S. House of Representatives, Committee on Government Operations, *Policy Changes in Weapon System Procurement*, pp. 1–42.

[74] U.S. Senate, Committee on Armed Services, *Final Report on F3H Development and Procurement*, Report, 84th Cong., 2d Sess. (1956), p. 8.

[75] *TFX Hearings—Second Series*, Part 3, pp. 495, 514, 589, 633; U.S. Senate, Committee on Armed Services, *Fiscal Year 1973 Authorization for Military Procurement*, pp. 3598–3599, 3613; U.S. Senate, Committee on Armed Services, *Fiscal Year 1974 Authorization for Military Procurement*, p. 4427; and U.S. Senate, Committee on Armed Services, *Fiscal Year 1975 Authorization for Military Procurement*, p. 4249. The Air Force contended that the F-15 delivery rate—implicitly, the rate of production buildup—was very conservative. (If true, the fact noted in the text—that initial deliveries of the F-15 were made relatively soon after the first flight—would be of lesser consequence, since the rate at which planes were manufactured incorporating any unresolved defects would be low.) However, against the Air Force's claim of a conservative delivery rate, note the following representative comparison for the F-111 and F-15 programs. During the first 25 months of production deliveries in the F-

Attempts also have been made in the past to upgrade service procurement personnel. Indeed, this has been a staple recommendation of virtually every official study of acquisition reform over the past two decades and with little sustained success.[76] Attempts to increase contract flex-

---

15 program, a total of 167 F-15s were scheduled to be delivered. After 25 months of production deliveries in the F-111 program, 170 F-111s were actually delivered (this was before wing box and avionics problems reduced the rate of F-111 deliveries). Comparisons of this sort are very tricky. But this particular comparison makes a useful point: the planned rate of production for the F-15, the rate established under the "reforms" of the early 1970s, was not unambiguously more conservative than the actual rate which governed the F-111 program of the 1960s. By the mid-1970s, the pace of F-15 deliveries had been reduced, but not because of any DOD policy reforms. When defense budgets tightened in the mid-1970s, Congress cut Air Force requests for F-15 procurement. Some other features of the program, such as the prototyping of the F-15's radar and cannon, did represent steps toward conservatism, but overall the program was not a significant departure from acquisition practices of the 1960s.

[76] For example, the Robertson Report of 1956 (named after Deputy Defense Secretary Reuben Robertson, who headed this study on how to improve acquisition lead times on manned aircraft) recommended that senior officers be placed in charge of weapon system project offices, that the project offices be given control of all necessary resources, and that project offices be elevated within service command structures. However, the system-acquisition establishment proved "less than eager" to implement the recommendations of the Robertson Report: "The general Air Force reaction was to reiterate a faith in the existing functional organization and procedures and then gradually make tactical concessions to the [OSD] demand for reorientation [on specific programs]." (See Putnam, *Evolution*, pp. 9–10.) More recently, the Blue Ribbon Panel recommended, in a similar vein, that the services establish acquisition management as a career specialty, that they provide program managers with greater authority, and that they reduce the layers of authority between program managers and service officials. (See U.S. Defense Blue Ribbon Panel, *Report to the President*, pp. 79–81.) Through all these efforts, services oriented toward operational commands have proved resistant to elevating the status and duration of acquisition-management rotations. While the most recent efforts of Secretary Packard led to the appointment of high-ranking officers to a few project offices (the F-15 program director, for example, was a brigadier general), there is no firm evidence available to indicate a systematic upgrading of acquisition personnel and, at this early date, to indicate how durable the prominent personnel appointments will be.

ibility—through so-called milestone arrangements, which give the government unilateral decision options contingent on contractor performance at specified periods of the program—do offer a needed increase in the government's flexibility in the face of development problems. However, as suggested by the analysis of the F-111's engine-inlet compatibility problems, contracts can be fertile sources for self-deluding assumptions that provide high-level officials with the illusion of control over a vast development apparatus. So it may be with milestone arrangements. For example, when the F-15 failed one of its milestone tests, the test itself was modified to allow the program to continue as planned, as the pressures for schedule adherence once again proved larger than any contract provisions.[77]

Attempts to employ prototyping more extensively have met with somewhat greater success. In 1971, OSD initiated a number of relatively inexpensive competitive prototype programs as additions to the defense budget—the services successfully resisted attempts to impose prototyping arrangements on their own, mainline programs, such as the F-15.[78] Production plans were pointedly omitted from the specifications for these prototype programs. However, by 1974 under the pressure of tight acquisition budgets and high unit costs on its mainline programs, the Air Force yielded to OSD pressures for it to procure one of the prototypes (the Lightweight Fighter) in volume, to supplement

[77] See Clarence A. Robinson, Jr., "F100 Funding Shift May Alter DOD Policies," *Aviation Week and Space Technology*, Vol. 99 (December 17, 1973), p. 24; and U.S. Senate, Committee on Armed Services, *Fiscal Year 1975 Authorization for Military Procurement*, Hearings, 93rd Cong., 2d Sess. (1974), pp. 323–324.

[78] U.S. Senate, Committee on Armed Services, *Advanced Prototype*, Hearings, 92d Cong., 1st Sess. (1971), pp. 1–55, esp. p. 37. See also excerpts of a Packard speech, in "Packard's Hard Look," *Aviation Week and Space Technology*, Vol. 96 (March 6, 1972), p. 7; and U.S. Senate, Committee on Armed Services, *Fiscal Year 1975 Authorization for Military Procurement*, pp. 321–322, 324. For a further idea of the resistance of service development organizations to prototyping, see U.S. Senate, Committee on Armed Services, *Weapon Systems Acquisition Process* (1971), pp. 239–289, esp. pp. 275–280.

the more expensive F-15.[79] The Air Force will be procuring a "prototyped" fighter plane for the first time in roughly thirty years.

Although it is too soon to reach definitive judgment, the Laird-Packard reforms do seem to have introduced some needed flexibility and austerity into acquisition practices. While the changes have not been dramatic or extensive and the results in fact have been mixed, they do seem to represent an improvement. However, the likely duration of these changes is problematic. From the earliest years of military aviation in this country, the Air Force (and its antecedent, the Army Air Force) has gone through a repeated cycle: it adopts simplified management arrangements, only to move inexorably back to more complex arrangements, which, in turn, produce a crisis in acquisition results and generate pressures for the adoption of a new set of simpli-

[79] U.S. Senate, Committee on Appropriations, *Lightweight Fighter Aircraft Program*, Hearings, 94th Cong., 1st Sess. (1975), pp. 1–107. When the Air Force agreed to this procurement, the Lightweight Fighter program was renamed the Air Combat Fighter program. From the two prototypes competing for the award—General Dynamics' YF-16 and Northrop's YF-17—the Air Force selected the YF-16 (which was then relabeled the F-16). The Air Force initiated plans for a relatively rapid, 1960s-pace procurement program (nearly the same production pace is scheduled for the F-16 as was employed in the Air Force acquisition of the Navy's A-7 in the 1960s). Note that the Air Force's acquisition of the F-16 solved a political problem for the Defense Department—it provided General Dynamics with a major, long-term production program at a time when the company's Fort Worth facility barely was being sustained by the production of tail-end, F-111 procurements—and also provided a necessary impetus to the export prospects for the plane. Secretary Schlesinger and the Congress also attempted to force the Navy to procure the F-16, but the Navy eluded these pressures and opted instead to procure a thoroughly redesigned YF-17 (designated the F-18). This new, high-risk Navy program is an essentially standard effort fully reflecting the weapon system/concurrency norms of the past. For additional detail on the Navy's actions in the F-18 episode, see our earlier discussion in Chapter v, p. 253. See also "Navy to Get F-14s Planned for Marines," *Aviation Week and Space Technology*, Vol. 103 (August 11, 1975), p. 23; and "Washington Roundup: A-8, Mate," *Aviation Week and Space Technology*, Vol. 103 (July 28, 1975), p. 13.

fied arrangements. The cycle then repeats itself.[80] Sustained change has proved difficult to achieve. Transitional reforms have occurred in response to crises and, most recently, in response to the change of administrations in 1969, a fitting additional impetus in our political system. But basic patterns of behavior in the process have proved remarkably reassertive and resistant to any enduring change.[81]

Together with the view of the development process provided by our analysis of the F-111 program, this brief survey of reform efforts strongly suggests that the heart of the reform problem is an implementation problem. One can conceive acquisition strategies that would better manage

[80] Text of the speech given by Clarence L. "Kelly" Johnson, former head of the Lockheed "Skunkworks" and Vice-President of the corporation, "Prerequisites for a Successful Skunkworks," speech delivered before the Seminar on Prototyping, National Security Industrial Association, St. Louis, Missouri, February 23, 1972; and Perry, *The Role of Prototypes*, pp. 8–10. Cf. Steinbruner, *Cybernetic Theory*, pp. 84–85. Weidenbaum offers an apt description of this cyclical process of ineffective reform: "This process is so frequently repeated as to become trite, or at least predictable: it starts with public exposure of specific cases of inefficiency or worse. The General Accounting Office, a Congressional committee, an enterprising reporter or a new Administration calls attention to the tremendous waste of resources involved in the unsuccessful work on Aircraft X or the cancellation of Missile Y after the expenditure of several hundreds of millions of dollars. The next step . . . is to lambaste the current or just terminated procurement concepts and procedures as ineffective or archaic. The next, and often most highly touted, step is to announce a new procurement concept that will eliminate all of these shortcomings. . . . The final phase of the cycle, of course, is the growing public realization that the newfangled procurement system . . . has not performed much better than its predecessors." See Murray L. Weidenbaum, *The Economics of Peacetime Defense* (New York: Praeger, 1974), p. 65.

[81] For some perspective on this issue, see Danhof, *Government Contracting*; and Robert Schlaifer, *Development of Aircraft Engines* (Boston: Harvard Business School, 1950). Steinbruner postulates that, in a cybernetic process, the absence of outcome calculations and the lack of integration across separate dimensions of value should produce a gradually evolving crisis in the problem area. This postulate accords reasonably well with the cyclical evolution toward crisis that has occurred in the weapons acquisition process. See Steinbruner, *Cybernetic Theory*, pp. 84–85.

technical uncertainties, that would avoid firm commitments before hard information was available, that would expand the range of options available to decision makers (military as well as civilian), and that would still insure a healthy defense industry and a strong force posture. But these strategies cannot simply be willed into being. They literally would require tearing apart existing development organizations, reorganizing contractor operations, substantially modifying the Civil Service protection of thousands of civilian employees, and changing the organizationally (and, in poorly understood ways, culturally)[82] embedded view of the world shared by further thousands of service, development, and contractor officials. It is fair to say that so monumental a reform strains our capabilities to direct and sustain change through our political institutions.[83]

In sum, it is this difficulty to implement enduring change —not the inherent qualities of technology or the immutables of the enemy threat or the demonstrated superiority of present acquisition practices—that sustains the acquisition practices of this country. These practices exist in some substantial measure because they have existed, and the underlying structure of routines, incentives, and beliefs has

[82] Students of defense affairs have noted how the diffused authority and the elaborate regulation characteristic of American weapons programs reflect typically American cultural patterns of decision making, patterns as evident in the construction of county courthouses as they are in the acquisition of new fighter-bombers. The specific impediments these patterns present to acquisition reform are difficult to trace. In the terms of reference of the present study, these patterns would represent a portion of the shared structure of beliefs common to all participants in the acquisition process, a set of deeply rooted cultural "blinders" that selectively bias perceptions of what seems desirable or possible in acquisition practices. Obviously, neutralizing these impediments to reform would be extremely difficult. See Alexander, *Weapons Acquisition*, pp. 12–14; and Harvey M. Sapolsky, "The Military/Industrial State in Comparative Perspective," a paper prepared for the Conference on Comparative Defense Policy, United States Air Force Academy, Colorado Springs, Colorado, February 8–9, 1973.

[83] Sapolsky draws a similar conclusion from a different set of premises, in "The Military/Industrial State."

proved too powerful and complex to be manipulated readily by reform-minded officials.

What, then, can be done to achieve sustained improvement in the acquisition of major weapon systems? Perhaps very little by way of sustained improvement. To be sure, if Congress, defense officials, military professionals, working-level development officials, and defense contractors arrived at a consensus on major changes, the implementation problem would be eased considerably. But this vision obviously assumes away the heart of the reform problem. It presupposes a consensus for dramatic change that has been notably absent in the past and that would be, in our political system, difficult to create in the future. Note that, for all the controversies surrounding weapons acquisition over the years, the President and the Congress have continued to provide the funding necessary to sustain the more or less routine operation of acquisition organizations. While not necessarily requiring these routine operations, the general political environment clearly has provided wide latitude for them. Leaving aside the broader political environment, the expectation of consensus presupposes a unity of purpose and an explicit acknowledgment of "failure" that is unlikely among our established acquisition organizations. The services, defense contractors, and civilian defense officials resist the suggestion that their programs have failed. Development organizations resist acknowledging that their methods are inappropriate or unnecessary. They will have elaborate, reasonable-sounding arguments to support their resistance to change—the complexity and uncertainty of the problem insure that such arguments can be made. As long as the process at least produces planes that can fly and ships that can float, the *case* against present practices will never be unambiguous. Since allies in Congress will variously support this resistance to change, reform efforts bear a heavy, and what has been heretofore an insurmountable, burden of building consensus for broad and durable change.

If hopes for a system-wide consensus are likely to be disappointed, so, too, are hopes that consensus can be built on a smaller scale—that is, program by program, through the enterprising efforts of program managers skillful in the arts of bureaucratic politics. In his study of the Polaris system development, Sapolsky vividly demonstrates how a skillful program manager was able to thwart the intrusions of inflexible development practices into the management of the Polaris program.[84] Perry's study of the first ballistic-missile developments offers a similar insight.[85] Yet both studies offer revealing evidence of how the exceptional nature of these programs—their recognized uniqueness compared to prior weapons developments, the national urgency of the capability they offered, and the unusual technical challenges they presented—itself conferred substantial advantages on the program managers. The program managers made the most of these prior conditions, but we hardly can anticipate that the development of the next transport plane, fighter aircraft, or tank will offer similar opportunities for bureaucratic skills. Of necessity, most programs are "normal" programs, and they only confer normal bargaining advantages.

The most likely prospect for achieving and maintaining consensus on acquisition reform lies in the possibility of an extended period of disruptive financial shortages in the acquisition process, shortages that even those most wedded to existing acquisition practices will be forced to face. The military's sustained pursuit of maximum performance through an inflexible development process has resulted in a tenfold increase in unit acquisition costs every twenty years. Since acquisition budgets have not expanded similarly, the number of fixed-wing aircraft procured annually has suffered a dramatic decline. While in the Fiscal Year 1956 to 1965 period annual unit purchases averaged 1,800 aircraft, the Fiscal 1971 unit purchases were only 565 units and the

[84] Sapolsky, *Polaris*, chaps. 2, 3, and 8.
[85] Perry, *System Development Strategies*, pp. 54–73, 78–81, 122–131.

Fiscal 1973 purchases only 383 units.[86] If this trend continued, it would, by itself, severely disrupt acquisition organizations and operational commands. Sizeable cuts in operational forces might be required. The financial resources necessary to maintain the routine operation of existing development organizations might no longer be available. This prospect could make disruptive changes in acquisition practice an ironically conservative course of action, necessary to maintain force levels in an era of tight budgets. It could dislodge many of the organization myths and stereotypes underlying present methods of developing weapons. It could, in other words, impose the unity of purpose that has been missing (because it was so difficult to create) for past acquisition reforms.[87]

Although it might be comforting to place our hopes on this externally imposed consensus, we cannot be certain that it will occur or, if it does, what directions it will take.[88]

[86] "Harsh Procurement Choices Face DOD," *Aviation Week and Space Technology*, Vol. 97 (August 28, 1972), pp. 18–19; and "Washington Roundup: Defense Buying," *Aviation Week and Space Technology*, Vol. 97 (August 28, 1972), p. 11. The rise in acquisition costs is not, of course, the only reason for the decline in unit procurement. Other contributing factors have been the rise in defense manpower costs and the decline in the real level of defense spending.

[87] Alexander (*Design to Cost*, pp. 8–9) has noted the value of this kind of external coercion for inducing acquisition organizations to change.

[88] For a cautionary note on this issue, observe that similar predictions of the imminent necessity of changing design practices were being made in 1954: "If the trend toward the 10- to 15-ton, half-a-million-dollar fighter is not checked . . . fighter defense of the free world may go begging for want of the money and production manhours needed to buy it." (Goodyear, "The Lightweight Fighter," p. 388.) Within 15 years of this observation, fighters weighed 30 to 45 tons and cost 10 to 20 million dollars. Obviously, the imperative for change in 1954 was less coercive than was thought at the time.

So it may be today. In the face of current budget stringency, practices may be modified marginally—but with great publicity and symbolic emphasis—to eliminate only the most prominent excesses and to provide a ritualistic resolution of the many pressures for acquisition reform. Meanwhile, defense budgets in the long run may expand to subsidize what is effectively a continuation of standard practice. On this point, see Cecil Brownlow, "DOD Stresses 'Real

Any changes it induces could as easily be perverse as meliorative. Yet there are few immediate alternatives one can envision that really hold out the prospect of substantial improvement in our acquisition experience.

This conclusion does not mean that further acquisition studies and reform efforts will be of no value. A part of the problem with past reform efforts has been that they have attempted to change the behavior of organizations that were not very well understood. We do not know very much about *most* of the influential participants in the weapons acquisition process, even such major participants as the Air Force Systems Command, NASA, and the large defense contractors and subcontractors. It is folly to speak of reforming the acquisition process without understanding the influence and behavior of the many organizations to be changed, yet in fact reform efforts have been forced to proceed without much detailed understanding. Partially as a result, past reform efforts have concentrated on the manipulation of conspicuous summary features of the process, like contract types, which, our study and others suggest, are not likely to be fruitful avenues of reform. Successful reform will require a sensitivity to complex details of behavior in the acquisition process. Future studies can aid reform efforts by providing knowledge of these details.

But whatever the state of our knowledge, attempts at acquisition reform will continue, as indeed they must. While the prospects are problematic, we cannot be certain that there will never be an appropriate set of policy reforms and an appropriate confluence of contextual events to induce dramatic reform. Points of leverage may appear that we do not yet anticipate. For example, the prototyping

---

Growth' in Posture," *Aviation Week and Space Technology*, Vol. 102 (February 10, 1975), pp. 16–20. (See also footnote 80 of this chapter.) In any event, the changes that do occur may only reinforce existing rigidities. For example, fund scarcities may serve only to increase the burden on all programs to justify their resource needs and thus to expand the elaborate review, concurrence, and evaluation procedures that presently encumber system developments.

options fostered by former Deputy Defense Secretary David Packard appeared more attractive (to the Air Force at least) when tight acquisition budgets began forcing hard choices on the services. This may be a sign of future possibilities. Moreover, even if "successes" are only transitional—perhaps limited to single programs, only to fade away after the completion of those programs—positive results on a single program can be well worth the efforts required to achieve them, if for no other reasons than that the stakes in defense are high and the resource commitments are often exceedingly large.

Nonetheless, we probably will be deluding ourselves if we expect dramatic and sustained improvements from our continuing attempts at acquisition reform. Short of major changes within the Congress, the defense industry, and the Defense Department, changes in the separate and shared beliefs underlying present acquisition practices, attempts to implement enduring change are likely to fail. The frustrating dialectic between reform attempts and disappointing results will go on inconclusively. Future acquisition experience will continue to mirror an unsatisfactory past.

The material for this study has been drawn from four major sources. The first source is the publicly available material on the F-111 development in particular and the weapons acquisition process in general. Because of the unusual controversy of the F-111 program, the public record on the program is far more extensive than for most others. Hence, the argument in the text places a heavy reliance on sources available to the general reader. These sources are detailed in the Bibliography. (Note that the Bibliography does not list the annual authorization and appropriation hearings of the House and Senate armed services and appropriations committees. This study drew upon these hearings for Fiscal Years 1962 through 1976. However, only special Congressional hearings are listed in the Bibliography. The regular authorization and appropriation hearings easily can be obtained by the interested reader.) The second source is a set of approximately forty interviews with program participants. These interviews were important both for interpreting the public record on the program and for adding important additional information to it. A list of those interviewed precedes the Bibliography. The third source is the files of the Permanent Subcommittee on Investigations, Committee on Government Operations, United States Senate. The Subcommittee performed a detailed investigation of the origins and development of the F-111. The files of this investigation are a rich source of internal memoranda, test reports, and financial evaluations. The final source is four government reports provided privately to the author. These reports were invaluable for correcting omissions from the public record. Unfortunately, they cannot be specifically cited.

Our use of one specific source in this study deserves an additional comment. From mid-1966 through 1968, Secretary McNamara (followed by Secretary Clifford) held frequent high-level meetings on the F-111 program. These meetings were dubbed "Icarus" meetings, as described in the text. Apparently, no stenographic record was made for these meetings. An Air Force officer in attendance at the meetings did take unofficial notes; and these notes, in turn, were excerpted by McClellan Committee staff members (see *TFX Hearings—Second Series*, Part 3, pp. 540–574). However, because of the fragmentary and selective character of the Committee's excerpts, Icarus material has been cited or quoted only for illustrative purposes, or otherwise where the material could be corroborated by resort to other sources, such as interviews and memoranda.

In the footnotes, interviewees have been referred to by number. The key below gives the general institutional position of each interviewee at the time of the F-111 program.

1. Analyst, Office of the Secretary of Defense.
2. Analyst, Office of the Secretary of Defense.
3. Close student of the F-111 program.
4. Assistant Secretary for one of the services.
5. Member, Air Force Systems Command, with cost control responsibilities.
6. Contractor official.
7. Deputy to a high-level Air Force official.
8. Contractor official.
9. Navy officer and program official.
10. Congressional committee staff member.
11. Defense Research and Engineering official.
12. Air Force R&D official.
13. High-level Air Force official.
14. Air Force staff member with program responsibility.
15. Attorney, Air Force General Counsel's Office.
16. Information obtained from a visit to General Dynamics (this source included documents and multiple interviews).
17. High-level Navy official.
18. High-level Navy official.
19. Aeronautical engineer, Naval Air Systems Command.
20. Air Force officer and program official.
21. Analyst, government-sponsored research group.
22. Systems analyst, Office of the Secretary of Defense.
23. Government scientist.
24. Advisor to the Secretary of Defense.
25. Defense Research and Engineering official.
26. High-level Navy Officer.

"Aerospace in Perspective: Strategic Warfare," *Space/Aeronautics*, Vol. 51 (January 1969), pp. 84–95.

"Aerospace in Perspective: Tactical Warfare," *Space/Aeronautics*, Vol. 49 (January 1968), pp. 108–118.

"Aerospace in Perspective: Tactical Warfare," *Space/Aeronautics*, Vol. 51 (January 1969), pp. 96–105.

"Air Force Review Group Probes F100 Engine; Findings Imminent," *Aviation Week and Space Technology*, Vol. 102 (May 12, 1975), p. 18.

Alelyunas, Paul. "Air-to-Air Missiles," *Space/Aeronautics*, Vol. 44 (November 1965), pp. 68–75.

Alexander, Arthur. *Design to Price from the Perspective of the United States, France, and the Soviet Union.* Rand Memorandum No. P-4967, Santa Monica, February 1973.

———. *Weapons Acquisition in the Soviet Union, United States, and France.* Rand Memorandum No. P-4989, Santa Monica, March 1973.

Alexander, Thomas. "McNamara's Expensive Economy Plane," *Fortune*, Vol. 75 (April 1967), pp. 89–91, 184–187.

Allison, Graham T. *Essence of Decision: Explaining the Cuban Missile Crisis.* Boston: Little, Brown, 1971.

———, and Frederick A. Morris. "Armaments and Arms Control: Exploring the Determinants of Military Weapons," *Daedulus*, Vol. 104 (Summer 1975), pp. 99–130.

"An AFM Essay: The F-111B—White Hope or White Elephant?" *Armed Forces Magazine*, Vol. 13 (July 1967), pp. 28–29.

Anderson, Jack. "Civilian Control and the F-111B," *Washington Post*, October 8, 1972, p. D7.

Archer, Robert D. "The Soviet Bombers," *Space/Aeronautics*, Vol. 51 (April 1969), pp. 52–59.

———. "The Soviet Fighters," *Space/Aeronautics*, Vol. 50 (July 1968), pp. 64–72.

Armacost, Michael H. *The Politics of Weapons Innovation: The Thor-Jupiter Controversy.* New York: Columbia University Press, 1969.

Art, Robert J. "Restructuring the Military-Industrial Complex: Arms Control in Institutional Perspective," *Public Policy*, Vol. 22 (Fall 1974), pp. 423–459.

———. *The TFX Decision: McNamara and the Military.* Boston: Little, Brown, 1968.

Aspin, Les. "The View From The House (2): Games the Pentagon Plays," *Foreign Policy*, No. 11 (Summer 1973), pp. 80–92.

Baldwin, Hanson W. "The Navy at Ebb Tide," *The Reporter*, Vol. 30 (January 30, 1964), pp. 35–38.

Baumol, William J. *Welfare Economics and the Theory of the State.* London: Longmans, Green, 1952.

Booda, Larry. "New Delay Raises Doubts on TFX Future," *Aviation Week and Space Technology*, Vol. 77 (July 9, 1962), p. 49.

———. "Rift May Affect TFX Role, Configuration," *Aviation Week and Space Technology*, Vol. 79 (September 1963), p. 26.

———. "Soviet Gains Blunt U.S. Bomber Potential," *Aviation Week and Space Technology*, Vol. 75 (August 14, 1961), pp. 26–27.

———. "USAF and Navy Unable to Agree on Joint Tactical Fighter Project," *Aviation Week and Space Technology*, Vol. 75 (August 21, 1961), p. 27.

Borklund, C. W. *The Department of Defense.* New York: Praeger, 1968.

Brown, David A. "Accelerated Testing Set for F-14A," *Aviation Week and Space Technology*, Vol. 95 (December 20, 1971), pp. 49–53.

Brownlow, Cecil. "DOD Stresses 'Real Growth' in Posture," *Aviation Week and Space Technology*, Vol. 102 (February 10, 1975), pp. 16–20.

———. "Douglas Wins Contract for Missileer Design," *Aviation Week and Space Technology*, Vol. 73 (August 1, 1960), p. 33.

———. "F-111 Shows Bombing Support Strength in Indochina," *Aviation Week and Space Technology*, Vol. 98 (April 30, 1973), pp. 88–93.

———. "Mk. 2 Hits Severe Cost Problems," *Aviation Week and Space Technology*, Vol. 90 (March 3, 1969), pp. 16–17.

————. "Navy Plans Procurement of 463 VFXs," *Aviation Week and Space Technology*, Vol. 89 (December 23, 1968), pp. 18–19.

————. "Navy Stresses Simplicity, Reliability to Ease Budget Pinch," *Aviation Week and Space Technology*, Vol. 70 (March 9, 1959), pp. 78–80.

————. "New Engine Standards Raise F-15 Costs," *Aviation Week and Space Technology*, Vol. 98 (May 21, 1973), pp. 18–19.

————. "U.S. To Modernize Air Defense," *Aviation Week and Space Technology*, Vol. 97 (November 27, 1972), p. 12.

Bulban, Erwin J. "F-111 Lessons Applied to Other Projects," *Aviation Week and Space Technology*, Vol. 96 (June 26, 1972), pp. 123–125.

————. "General Dynamics Defends F-111 Program," *Aviation Week and Space Technology*, Vol. 87 (November 13, 1967), pp. 34–35.

Butz, J. S. "FB-111: Second Look at the Third Version," *Air Force and Space Digest*, Vol. 49 (February 1966), pp. 37–39.

Carson, Captain Donald D., USAF. "Dissimilar Aerial Combat Tactics—New Techniques in Battle Training," *Air Force Magazine*, Vol. 56 (March 1973), pp. 57–61.

"Case Studies in Military-Industrial Pressures," *Congressional Quarterly Weekly Report*, Vol. xxvi (May 24, 1968), pp. 1164–1178.

Celniker, Leo, and E. R. Schuberth. "Synthesizing Aircraft Design," *Space/Aeronautics*, Vol. 51 (April 1969), pp. 60–66.

Chayes, Abram. "An Inquiry Into the Workings of Arms Control Agreements," *Harvard Law Review*, Vol. 85 (March 1972), pp. 905–969.

Coles, H., ed. *Total War and Cold War*. Columbus: Ohio State University Press, 1962.

Conable, Barber B. "The View From the House (1): Our Limits Are Real," *Foreign Policy*, Number 11 (Summer 1973), pp. 73–80.

Crecine, John P. *Defense Budgeting: Organizational Adaptation to External Constraints*. Rand Memorandum No. RM-6121-PR, Santa Monica, March 1970.

————, and Gregory Fischer. *On Resource Allocation Processes in the U.S. Department of Defense*. Institute of Public Policy

Studies, University of Michigan, Discussion Paper No. 31, 1971.

Cyert, Richard M., and James G. March. *A Behavioral Theory of the Firm.* Englewood Cliffs: Prentice-Hall, 1963.

Danhof, Clarence H. *Government Contracting and Technological Change.* Washington: Brookings Institution, 1968.

Davis, Vincent. *The Admiral's Lobby.* Chapel Hill: University of North Carolina Press, 1967.

————. *The Politics of Innovation: Patterns in Navy Cases.* Denver: University of Denver Press, 1967.

Day, John S. *Subcontracting Policy in the Airframe Industry.* Boston: Harvard Business School, 1956.

Devanney, J. W., III. "The DX Competition," *U.S. Naval Institute: Proceedings,* Vol. 101 (August 1975), pp. 18–29.

"Defense Digest: F-111 Avionics Cost Sliced," *Armed Forces Management,* Vol. 16 (November 1969), p. 64.

"The Development of the McDonnell Phantom," *Interavia,* Vol. 21 (May 1966), pp. 737–741.

Dixon, Ford. "McNamara, General Dynamics, and the F-111: A Business and Political History." Unpublished Ph.D. dissertation, Texas Christian University, 1972.

Donnelly, Charles H. *United States Defense Policies in 1957.* House Document No. 436, 85th Cong., 2d Sess. (1958).

Dorfman, Robert, ed. *Measuring the Benefits of Government Investment.* Washington: The Brookings Institution, 1965.

Downs, Anthony. *Inside Bureaucracy.* Boston: Little, Brown, 1967.

Dulberger, Leon H. "Advanced Fighter-Attack Aircraft," *Space/Aeronautics,* Vol. 45 (April 1966), pp. 80–93.

————. "Advanced Interceptor Aircraft," *Space/Aeronautics,* Vol. 46 (November 1966), pp. 54–66.

————. "Advanced Strategic Bombers," *Space/Aeronautics,* Vol. 45 (June 1966), pp. 62–75.

Emme, Eugene, ed. *The History of Rocket Technology.* Detroit: Wayne State University Press, 1964.

Enthoven, Alain C., and Harry Rowen, eds. *Public Finances: Needs, Sources, Utilization.* Princeton: Princeton University Press, 1961.

————, and K. Wayne Smith. *How Much Is Enough? Shaping the Defense Program, 1961–1969.* New York: Harper and Row, 1971.

398

"F-14 Deficiencies," *Aviation Week and Space Technology*, Vol. 97 (July 24, 1972), p. 18.

"F-15 Durability Problems," *Aviation Week and Space Technology*, Vol. 98 (April 30, 1973), p. 93.

"F-15 Engine-Inlet Simulator Installed at USAF's AEDC," *Aviation Week and Space Technology*, Vol. 96 (February 28, 1972), pp. 44–45.

"F-111's Prove Worth in Southeast Asia," *Armed Forces Journal*, Vol. 110 (March 1973), pp. 22–23.

Fahey, James C. *The Ships and Aircraft of the U.S. Fleet.* Annapolis: U.S. Naval Institute, 1965.

Finney, John W. "C-5A Jet Repairs to Cost 1.5 Billion," *New York Times*, December 15, 1975, pp. 1, 21.

―――. "Pentagon Scored on Copter Costs," *New York Times*, May 22, 1972, p. 7.

―――. "Senate Unit Bars Navy F-111B Jets," *New York Times*, March 29, 1968, p. 13.

Fisher, Irving N. *A Reappraisal of Incentive Contracting Experience.* Rand Memorandum No. RM-5700-PR, Santa Monica, July 1968.

Fitzgerald, A. Ernest. *The High Priests of Waste.* New York: Norton, 1972.

Fox, J. Ronald. *Arming America: How the U.S. Buys Weapons.* Boston: Harvard Business School, 1974.

Francis, Captain John, Jr., USAF. "F-111: A Pilot's View," *Air Force Magazine*, Vol. 54 (April 1971), p. 36.

Fricker, John. "The People vs. the F-111," *Flying*, Vol. 84 (May 1969), pp. 64, S1-S11, 112, 117.

Gal, Harold. "Pentagon Halts Navy F-111 Work," *New York Times*, July 11, 1968, p. 17.

Getler, Michael. "Chaffee Pleased with 'Tomcat' Fighter," *Washington Post*, December 23, 1970, p. A4.

―――. "David Packard: Presiding Over a Revolution," *Armed Forces Magazine*, Vol. 16 (March 1970), p. 29.

―――. "The MIG and the Phantom," *Space/Aeronautics*, Vol. 51 (May 1969), p. 83.

―――. "Navy Drops Hotter Model of the F-14," *Washington Post*, July 28, 1971, p. A1.

―――. "TFX-Turned-Tomcat Has Navy by the Tail," *Washington Post*, December 16, 1973, pp. A1, A24.

Ginsburgh, Col. Robert N., USAF. "The Challenge to Military Professionalism," *Foreign Affairs*, Vol. 42 (January 1964), pp. 254–268.

Glines, C. V. "Will the First 'A' in NASA Be Given the Go-Signal?" *Armed Forces Management*, Vol. 16 (November 1969), pp. 34–35, 38.

Goodwin, Bert Z. "The TFX Hearings: A Study in Controversy Creation." Unpublished M.Sc. thesis, Massachusetts Institute of Technology, 1970.

Goodyear, Joseph. "The Lightweight Fighter," *Ordnance*, Vol. 39 (November-December 1954), pp. 388–392.

Grassett, Pierre. "Dogfighting Makes a Comeback," *Interavia*, Vol. 29 (December 1974), pp. 1188–1191.

Greathouse, William K. "Blending Propulsion With Airframe," *Space/Aeronautics*, Vol. 50 (November 1968), pp. 59–68.

Gunston, W. T. *Attack Aircraft of the West*. New York: Charles Scribner's Sons, 1974.

———. *Bombers of the West*. New York: Charles Scribner's Sons, 1973.

———. "TFX: A Next-Generation Military Aeroplane," *Flight International*, Vol. 81 (February 8, 1962), pp. 207–208.

Halperin, Morton H. *Bureaucratic Politics and Foreign Policy*. Washington: Brookings Institution, 1974.

———. *Defense Strategies for the Seventies*. Boston: Little, Brown, 1971.

———. *Limited War in the Nuclear Age*. New York: Wiley, 1963.

———, and Arnold Kanter, eds. *Readings in American Foreign Policy: The Bureaucratic Perspective*. Boston: Little, Brown, 1973.

Hammond, Paul Y. "A Functional Analysis of Defense Department Decision-Making in the McNamara Administration," *American Political Science Review*, Vol. 62 (March 1968), pp. 57–69.

———. *Organizing for Defense*. Princeton: Princeton University Press, 1961.

Harman, Alvin J. *Analysis of Aircraft Development*. Rand Memorandum No. P-4976, Santa Monica, March 1973.

———, assisted by Susan Henrichsen. *A Methodology for Cost Factor Comparison and Prediction*. Rand Memorandum No. RM-6269-ARPA, Santa Monica, August 1970.

"Harsh Procurement Choices Face DOD," *Aviation Week and Space Technology*, Vol. 97 (August 28, 1972), pp. 18–19.

Head, Richard G. "Decision-Making on the A-7 Attack Aircraft Program." Unpublished Ph.D. dissertation, Syracuse University, 1970.

————, and Erwin J. Rokke, eds. *American Defense Policy: Volume III*. Baltimore: Johns Hopkins University Press, 1973.

Hernandez, J. J. "Steps in Preliminary Evaluations," *Naval Aviation News*, November 1966, p. 37.

Hieronymous, William S. "Packard Urges Defense Decentralization," *Aviation Week and Space Technology*, Vol. 93 (August 31, 1970), pp. 15–16.

Hilsman, Roger. *To Move A Nation*. New York: Doubleday, 1967.

Hitch, Charles J. *Decision-Making for Defense*. Berkeley: University of California Press, 1965.

————, and Roland N. McKean. *The Economics of Defense in the Nuclear Age*. Cambridge: Harvard University Press, 1960.

Hotz, Robert. "Echoes from Domodedovo," *Aviation Week and Space Technology*, Vol. 87 (July 17, 1967), p. 21.

"House Unit Backs End to the F-111B: Action on Funds Viewed as Plane's Death Sentence," *New York Times*, July 3, 1968, p. 14.

Huntington, Samuel P., ed. *Changing Patterns of Military Politics*. Glencoe: The Free Press, 1961.

————. *The Common Defense: Strategic Programs in National Politics*. New York: Columbia University Press, 1961.

————. *The Soldier and the State: The Theory and Politics of Civil-Military Relations*. Cambridge: Harvard University Press, 1957.

Jane's All the World's Aircraft, 1961–62. New York: McGraw-Hill, 1961.

Jane's All the World's Aircraft, 1970–71. New York: McGraw-Hill, 1970.

Johnsen, Katherine. "DOD Funds Set at $75.7 Billion," *Aviation Week and Space Technology*, Vol. 97 (October 16, 1972), p. 14.

————. "New Budgeting Plan Shifts Rivalry from Services to Weapon Systems," *Aviation Week and Space Technology*, Vol. 75 (July 31, 1961), p. 24.

Johnsen, Katherine. "Senate Unit Slashes F-111B Funds," *Aviation Week and Space Technology*, Vol. 87 (August 14, 1967), p. 26.

Johnson, Clarence L. "Prerequisites for a Successful Skunkworks." Speech delivered before the Seminar on Prototyping, National Security Industrial Association, St. Louis, February 23, 1972.

Kanter, Arnold. "Congress and the Defense Budget: 1960–1970," *American Political Science Review*, Vol. 66 (March 1972) pp. 129–143.

————, and Stuart J. Thorson. *The Weapons Procurement Process: Choosing Among Competing Theories*. Institute of Public Policy Studies, University of Michigan, Discussion Paper No. 41, 1972.

Kaufmann, William H. *The McNamara Strategy*. New York: Harper and Row, 1964.

Kirchner, Englebert. "The Project Manager," *Space/Aeronautics*, Vol. 43 (February 1965), pp. 56–64.

Klein, Burton H. "A Radical Proposal for R&D," *Fortune*, Vol. 57 (May 1958), pp. 122ff.

————. "The Decision-Making Problem in Development," in Richard Nelson, ed., *The Rate and Direction of Inventive Activity: Economic and Social Factors*, Princeton: Princeton University Press, 1962, pp. 477–508.

————, T. K. Glennan, Jr., and G. H. Schubert. *The Role of Prototypes in Development*. Rand Memorandum No. RM-3467-PR, Santa Monica, 1963.

————, and William Meckling. "Applications of Operations Research to Development Decisions," *Operations Research*, Vol. 6 (May-June 1958), pp. 352–363.

————, W. H. Meckling, and E. G. Mesthene. *Military Research and Development Policies*. Rand Memorandum No. R-333-PR. Santa Monica, 1958.

Knorr, Klaus, and Oscar Morgenstern. *Science and Defense: Some Critical Thoughts on Military Research and Development*. Princeton: Center for International Studies, 1965.

Krasner, Stephen. "Are Bureaucracies Important? (or Allison Wonderland)," *Foreign Policy*, No. 7 (Summer 1972), p. 159–179.

Kuhn, Thomas S. *The Structure of Scientific Revolutions*. Chicago: University of Chicago Press, 1963.

Kurth, James. "A Widening Gyre: The Logic of American Weapons Procurement," *Public Policy*, Vol. 19 (Summer 1971), pp. 373–404.

———."Why We Buy the Weapons We Do," *Foreign Policy*, No. 11 (Summer 1973), pp. 33–56.

Levin, Stuart M. "F-15: The Teething of a Dogfighter," *Space/Aeronautics*, Vol. 52 (December 1969), pp. 36–47.

———."Why the Swing-Wing?" *Space/Aeronautics*, Vol. 50 (November 1968), pp. 69–75.

Liggett, Captain William R., USAF. "FB-111 Pilot Report," *Air Force Magazine*, Vol. 56 (March 1973), pp. 31–37.

"Lightweight Fighter Gets New Impetus," *Aviation Week and Space Technology*, Vol. 101 (July 15, 1974), p. 127.

Lindblom, Charles E. *The Intelligence of Democracy*. New York: The Free Press, 1965.

———. "The Science of 'Muddling Through,'" *Public Administration Review*, Vol. 19 (Spring 1959), pp. 79–88.

Livingston, Sterling J. "Decision-Making in Weapons Development," *Harvard Business Review*, Vol. 36 (January-February 1958), pp. 127–136.

London, Michael P. "B-1: The Last Bomber?" *Space/Aeronautics*, Vol. 53 (April 1970), pp. 26–33.

———. "Tactical Air Superiority," *Space/Aeronautics*, Vol. 49 (March 1968), pp. 62–71.

———. "VFX—The Navy's Choice," *Space/Aeronautics*, Vol. 50 (November 1968), pp. 50–57.

Lorette, Richard J. "The Relationship Between Pressures on the System Program Director and the Growth of Weapon System Cost Estimates." Unpublished D.B.A. dissertation, Harvard Business School, 1967.

Mansfield, Edwin, ed. *Defense, Science, and Public Policy*. New York: Norton, 1968.

March, James G., ed. *Handbook of Organizations*. Chicago: Rand McNally, 1965.

———, and Herbert A. Simon. *Organizations*. New York: Wiley, 1968.

Marschak, Thomas. "The Role of Project Histories in the Study of R&D," in Thomas Marschak, Thomas K. Glennan, Jr., and Robert Summers, *Strategy for R&D: Studies in the Microeconomics of Development*, New York: Springer-Verlag, 1967.

403

Marschak, Thomas, Thomas K. Glennan, Jr., and Robert Summers. *Strategy for R&D: Studies in the Microeconomics of Development*. New York: Springer-Verlag, 1967.

Marshall, A. W., and W. H. Meckling. "Predictability of the Costs, Time, and Success of Development," in Richard Nelson, ed., *The Rate and Direction of Incentive Activity*. Princeton: Princeton University Press, 1962.

McKean, Roland, ed. *Issues in Defense Economics*. New York: National Bureau of Economic Research, 1967.

McNamara, Robert S. *The Essence of Security: Reflections in Office*. New York: Harper and Row, 1968.

Mecklin, John. "The C-5: The Ordeal of the Plane Makers," Part II, *Fortune*, Vol. 72 (December 1965), pp. 158–159, 280ff.

Meehan, John D., and Thomas O. Millett. "Major Weapon System Acquisition: An Analysis of DOD Management Arrangements." Unpublished M.Sc. thesis, Air University, Wright-Patterson Air Force Base, Ohio, 1968.

Members of Congress for Peace Through Law, Committee on Military Spending. "Report on Military Spending," in U.S. Senate, Committee on Armed Services, *Fiscal Year 1970 Authorizations for Military Procurement*, Hearings, 91st Cong., 1st Sess. (1969), pp. 4228–4289.

Meyers, Harold. "For Lockheed, Everything's Coming Up Unk-Unks," *Fortune*, Vol. 80 (August 1, 1969), pp. 81, 131–134.

Momyer, Gen. William W., USAF. "The Evolution of Fighter Tactics in SEA," *Air Force Magazine*, Vol. 56 (July 1973), pp. 58–62.

Morris, Frederic A. "Perspectives on the Air Force Lightweight Fighter Program." Unpublished paper, Harvard University Program on Science and International Affairs, Cambridge, Mass., 1975.

"Navy Evaluates F-111B Substitutes," *Aviation Week and Space Technology*, Vol. 88 (January 29, 1968), pp. 22–23.

"Navy Facing Dilemma Over Decision on Fighter Plane," *Congressional Quarterly Weekly Report*, Vol. xxvi (February 16, 1968), pp. 284–286, 289.

"Navy's Reorganization Is Announced," *Naval Aviation News* (May 1966), pp. 10–12.

"Navy to Get F-14's Planned for Marines," *Aviation Week and Space Technology*, Vol. 103 (August 11, 1975), p. 23.

Nelson, Richard, ed. *The Rate and Direction of Inventive Activity*. Princeton: Princeton University Press, 1962.

————. "Uncertainty, Learning, and the Economics of Parallel Research and Development Efforts," *Review of Economics and Statistics*, Vol. 43 (November 1961), pp. 351–364.

————, Merton Peck, and Edward Kalachek. *Technology, Economic Growth, and Public Policy*. Washington: Brookings Institution, 1967.

Neustadt, Richard E. *Alliance Politics*. New York: Columbia University Press, 1970.

————. *Presidential Power*. New York: Wiley, 1960.

"New Muscle for Navy's Air Arm," *Business Week*, February 1, 1969, p. 58.

"New Plane Seen More Costly, Little Better Than F-111," *Congressional Quarterly Weekly Report*, Vol. xxvi (May 3, 1968), pp. 1007–1009 (reprinted, with Navy rebuttal, in U.S. Senate, Committee on Armed Services, Preparedness Investigating Subcommittee, *U.S. Tactical Air Power Program*, Hearings, 90th Cong., 2d Sess. [1968], pp. 27–31).

Nihart, Brooke. "Navy's F-14: Costly But Nothing Else Will Do the Job," *Armed Forces Journal*, Vol. 109 (December 1971), pp. 40–44.

Nossiter, Bernard. "Weapons Systems: A Story of Failure," *Washington Post*, January 26, 1969, p. A1, reprinted in U.S. Congress, Joint Economic Committee, Subcommittee on Economy in Government, *Military Budget and National Priorities*, Hearings, 91st Cong., 1st Sess. (1969), pp. 95–99.

Novick, David. "Decision-Making in the Department of Defense," in Edwin Mansfield, ed., *Defense, Science, and Public Policy*. New York: Norton, 1968, pp. 44–61.

"Packard's Hard Look," *Aviation Week and Space Technology*, Vol. 96 (March 6, 1972), p. 7.

Peck, Merton J., and Frederick M. Scherer. *The Weapons Acquisition Process: An Economic Analysis*. Boston: Harvard Business School, 1962.

"Pentagon Unimpressed By New Soviet Fighters," *Armed Forces Management*, Vol. 13 (August 1967), p. 13.

405

Perry, Robert L. "The Atlas, Thor, Titan, and Minuteman," in Eugene Emme, ed., *The History of Rocket Technology*. Detroit: Wayne State University Press, 1964.

――――. *A Dassault Dossier: Aircraft Acquisition in France*. Rand Memorandum No. R-1148-PR, Santa Monica, September 1973.

――――. *Innovation and Military Requirements: A Comparative Study*. Rand Memorandum No. RM-5182-PR, Santa Monica, August 1967.

――――. *A Prototype Strategy for Aircraft Development*. Rand Memorandum No. RM-5597-1-PR, Santa Monica, July 1972.

――――. *System Development Strategies: A Comparative Study of Doctrine, Technology, and Organization in the USAF Ballistic and Cruise Missile Programs, 1950–1960*. Rand Memorandum No. RM-4853-PR, Santa Monica, August 1966.

――――, et al. *System Acquisition Experience*. Rand Memorandum No. RM-6072-PR, Santa Monica, November 1969.

――――, et al. *System Acquisition Strategies*. Rand Memorandum No. R-733-PR/ARPA, Santa Monica, June 1971.

"Perspective: Navy Says It Wants the F-111B, Heavy or Not," *Space/Aeronautics*, Vol. 46 (November 1966), pp. 24, 29–30, 32, 34.

Pinkel, B., and J. R. Nelson. *A Critique of Turbine Engine Development Policy*. Rand Memorandum No. RM-6100/1-PR, Santa Monica, April 1970.

Plattner, C. M. "F-111 Shows Unique Interdiction Capability," *Aviation Week and Space Technology*, Vol. 90 (February 3, 1969), pp. 42–44, 49–51.

Powell, Craig. "FX: Designed to Control the Skies," *Armed Forces Management*, Vol. 15 (November 1968), pp. 38–40.

Pressman, Jeffrey L., and Aaron Wildavsky. *Implementation: How Great Expectations in Washington Are Dashed in Oakland*. Berkeley: University of California Press, 1973.

"Procurement Costs Continue Upward Spiral," *Aviation Week and Space Technology*, Vol. 103 (September 22, 1975), p. 15.

Putnam, W. D. *The Evolution of Air Force System Acquisition Management*. Rand Memorandum No. R-868-PR, Santa Monica, August 1972.

Quade, E. S., and W. I. Boucher. *Systems Analysis and Policy Planning: Applications in Defense.* New York: American Elsevier, 1968.

Ransom, Harry Howe. "The Politics of Air Power—A Comparative Analysis," *Yearbook of the School of Public Administration, Harvard University, 1958,* pp. 87–119.

Raymond, Jack. *Power at the Pentagon.* New York: Harper and Row, 1964.

Reece, James S. "The Effects of Contract Changes on the Control of a Major Defense Weapon System Program." Unpublished D.B.A. dissertation, Harvard Business School, 1970.

"Replacement Cost of C-5 Wing Set by USAF at $897 Million," *Aviation Week and Space Technology,* Vol. 102 (April 28, 1975), p. 30.

Ries, John C. *The Management of Defense: Organization and Control of the U.S. Armed Services.* Baltimore: Johns Hopkins University Press, 1964.

Robinson, Clarence A., Jr. "F100 Funding Shift May Alter DOD Policies," *Aviation Week and Space Technology,* Vol. 99 (December 17, 1973), p. 24.

Roherty, James M. *Decisions of Robert S. McNamara.* Coral Gables: University of Miami Press, 1970.

Ropelewski, Robert R. "C-5A Category 2 Test Finish Near," *Aviation Week and Space Technology,* Vol. 94 (May 3, 1971), pp. 36–44.

Russett, Bruce M. "Who Pays for Defense?" *American Political Science Review,* Vol. 63 (June 1969), pp. 412–426.

Sapolsky, Harvey M. "The Military/Industrial State in Comparative Perspective." Unpublished paper, Conference on Comparative Defense Policy, United States Air Force Academy, Colorado Springs, February 1973.

————. *The Polaris System Development: Bureaucratic and Programmatic Success in Government.* Cambridge: Harvard University Press, 1972.

Schemmer, Benjamin. "*How Much Is Enough?* Tells A Lot . . . But Not Enough," *Armed Forces Journal,* Vol. 108 (February 1, 1971), pp. 36–42.

Scherer, Frederick. *The Weapons Acquisition Process: Economic Incentives.* Boston: Harvard Business School, 1964.

407

Schilling, W. R. "The H-Bomb Decision: How To Decide Without Actually Choosing," *Political Science Quarterly*, Vol. 76 (March 1961), pp. 24–46.

———, Paul Y. Hammond, and Glenn H. Snyder. *Strategy, Politics, and Budgets*. New York: Columbia University Press, 1952.

Schlaifer, Robert. *Development of Aircraft Engines*. Boston: Harvard Business School, 1950.

Schlesinger, James R. *Defense Planning and Budgeting: The Issue of Centralized Control*. Rand Memorandum No. P-3813, Santa Monica, May 1968.

———. "Organizational Structures and Planning," in Roland McKean, ed., *Issues in Defense Economics*, New York: National Bureau of Economic Research, 1967.

Schultze, Charles, Edward R. Fried, Alice M. Rivlin, and Nancy H. Teeters. *Setting National Priorities: The 1973 Budget*. Washington: Brookings Institution, 1972.

Seamans, Robert C., Jr. "Tac Air: A Look at the Late '70s," *Air Force Magazine*, Vol. 56 (January 1973), pp. 32–36.

Shapero, Albert, "Life Styles of Engineering," *Space/Aeronautics*, Vol. 51 (March 1969), pp. 58–65.

Simon, Herbert A. *Administrative Behavior*. New York: Macmillan, 1947.

———. "The Architecture of Complexity," in Herbert A. Simon, *The Sciences of the Artificial*, Cambridge: MIT Press, 1968.

———. "A Behavioral Model of Rational Choice," in Herbert A. Simon, *Models of Man: Social and Rational*, New York: Wiley, 1957.

Smith, Richard Austin. "How A Great Corporation Got Out of Control," *Fortune*, Vol. 65, Part I (January 1962), pp. 64–69, 178–184; and Part II (February 1962), pp. 120–122, 178–188.

———. "The $7 Billion Contract That Changed the Rules," *Fortune*, Vol. 67, Part I (March 1963), pp. 96–101, 182–188; and Part II (April 1963), pp. 110–111, 191–200.

Snyder, Jack L. "Rationality at the Brink: Uncertainty and the Cognitive Dynamics of a Two-Value Game." Unpublished paper, Department of Political Science, Columbia University, 1974.

Sorenson, Theodore C. *Kennedy*. New York: Bantam, 1965.

Staff Report. "Inlets for Supersonic Aircraft," *Space/Aeronautics*, Vol. 47 (May 1967), pp. 92–100.

————. "TFX: Mission and Design," *Space/Aeronautics*, Vol. 29 (June 1963), pp. 72–83.

Stein, Harold, ed. *American Civil-Military Decisions: A Book of Case Studies*. New York: Twentieth Century Fund, 1963.

Steinbruner, John D. *The Cybernetic Theory of Decision: New Dimensions of Political Analysis*. Princeton: Princeton University Press, 1974.

————, and Barry E. Carter. "Organizational and Political Dimensions of the Force Posture: The Problems of Reform," *Daedulus*, Vol. 104 (Summer 1975), pp. 131–154.

Stockfisch, Jacob. *Plowshares Into Swords: Managing the American Defense Establishment*. New York: Mason & Lipscomb, 1973.

Stone, I. F. "In the Bowels of the Behemoth," *New York Review of Books*, Vol. xviii (March 11, 1971), pp. 29–37.

"Strategic Warfare," *Space/Aeronautics*, Vol. 53 (January 1970), pp. 59–69.

Stubbing, Richard A. "Improving the Acquisition Process for High-Risk Electronics Systems." *Congressional Record—Senate*, Vol. 115, 91st Cong., 1st Sess. (February 7, 1969), pp. 3171–3176.

Summers, Robert. *Cost Estimates as Predictors of Actual Weapons Costs: A Study of Major Hardware Articles*. Rand Memorandum No. RM-3061-PR, Santa Monica, 1965.

"Tactical Warfare," *Space/Aeronautics*, Vol. 53 (January 1970), pp. 71–79.

Tarr, David W. "Military Technology and the Policy Process," *Western Political Quarterly*, Vol. 17 (March 1965), pp. 135–148.

Taylor, Maxwell. *The Uncertain Trumpet*. New York: Harper and Row, 1959.

"The Test Pilots Report on New Developments: F-111 Flight Test Report," *Interavia*, Vol. 21 (January 1966), p. 52.

"The TFX Verdict," *Aviation Week and Space Technology*, Vol. 94 (January 4, 1971), p. 7.

Thomis, Wayne. "Whispering Death: The F-111 in SEA," *Air Force Magazine*, Vol. 56 (June 1973), pp. 22–27.

Tucker, Samuel A., ed. *A Modern Design for Defense Decision:*

A McNamara-Hitch-Enthoven Anthology. Washington: Industrial College of the Armed Forces, 1966.

"Two Wings in One: Variable Sweep Makes Headway," *Interavia,* Vol. 17 (May 1962), pp. 617–620.

Tybout, Richard A., ed. *Economics of Research and Development.* Columbia: Ohio State University Press, 1965.

Tyrell, C. Merton. *Pentagon Partners: The New Nobility.* New York: Grossman, 1970.

Ulsamer, Edgar. "TAC's Focus Is On Lean and Lethal," *Air Force Magazine,* Vol. 58 (March 1975), pp. 20–30.

U.S. Comptroller General. *Report to the Congress: Acquisition of Major Weapon Systems.* Washington: U.S. Government Printing Office, 1971.

U.S. Congress, Joint Economic Committee, Subcommittee on Economy in Government. *Economics of Military Procurement.* Hearings, 90th Cong., 2d Sess. (1968).

―――. *Military Budget and National Economic Priorities.* Hearings, 91st Cong., 1st Sess. (1969).

U.S. Defense Blue Ribbon Panel. *Report to the President and the Secretary of Defense on the Department of Defense.* Washington: U.S. Government Printing Office, 1970.

―――. *Report to the President and the Secretary of Defense on the Department of Defense, Appendix F: Staff Report on Operational Test and Evaluation.* Washington: U.S. Government Printing Office, 1970.

U.S. House of Representatives, Committee on Armed Services. *Review of Army Tank Program.* Hearings, 91st Cong., 1st Sess. (1969).

―――. *Department of Defense Decision to Reduce the Number and Types of Manned Bombers in the Strategic Air Command.* Hearings, 89th Cong., 2d Sess. (1966).

U.S. House of Representatives, Committee on Government Operations. *Eleventh Report: Organization and Management of Missile Programs.* 86th Cong., 1st Sess. (1959).

―――. *Policy Changes in Weapon System Procurement.* Hearings, 91st Cong., 2d Sess. (1970).

U.S. Senate, Committee on Appropriations. *Lightweight Fighter Aircraft Program.* Hearings, 94th Cong., 1st Sess. (1975).

U.S. Senate, Committee on Armed Services. *Advanced Prototype.* Hearings, 92d Cong., 1st Sess. (1971).

——. *Authorizing Appropriations for Military Procurement, Research and Development, Fiscal Year 1969, and Reserve Strength.* Report No. 1087, 90th Cong., 2d Sess. (April 10, 1968).

——. *The B-58 Program.* Committee print, 86th Cong., 2d Sess. (1960).

——. *The B-70 Program.* Committee print, 86th Cong., 2d Sess. (1960).

——. *Procurement Study.* Hearings, 86th Cong., 2d Sess. (1960).

——. *Supplemental Military Procurement and Construction Authorizations: Fiscal Year 1967.* Hearings, 90th Cong., 1st Sess. (1967).

——. *Weapon Systems Acquisition Process.* Hearings, 92d Cong., 1st Sess. (1971).

——. *Weapon Systems Acquisition Process.* Hearings, 92d Cong., 2d Sess. (1972).

——, Preparedness Investigating Subcommittee. *Award of X-22 (VTOL) Research and Development Contract.* Hearings, 88th Cong., 1st Sess. (1963).

——, Preparedness Investigating Subcommittee. *Eighth Report, Navy Aircraft Procurement Program: Final Report on F-3H Development and Producement.* 84th Cong., 2d Sess. (1956).

——, Preparedness Investigating Subcommittee. *Report on the U.S. Tactical Air Power Program.* 90th Cong., 2d Sess. (1968).

——, Preparedness Investigating Subcommittee. *Status of U.S. Strategic Power.* Hearings, 90th Cong., 2d Sess. (1968).

——, Preparedness Investigating Subcommittee. *U.S. Tactical Air Power Program.* Hearings, 90th Cong., 2d Sess. (1968).

——, Subcommittee on the Air Force. *Airpower.* Report, 85th Cong., 1st Sess. (1957).

U.S. Senate, Committee on Government Operations, Permanent Subcommittee on Investigations. *TFX Contract Investigation.* Report, 91st Cong., 2d Sess. (1970), (cited as *TFX Report*).

——, Permanent Subcommittee on Investigations. *TFX Contract Investigation.* Hearings, 88th Cong., 1st Sess. (1963), Parts 1–10 (cited as *TFX Hearings—First Series*).

411

U.S. Senate, Committee on Government Operations, Permanent Subcommittee on Investigations. *TFX Contract Investigation (Second Series).* Hearings, 91st Cong., 2d Sess. (1970), Parts 1–3 (cited as *TFX Hearings—Second Series*).

———, Subcommittee on National Security and International Operations. *Planning, Programming, Budgeting.* Hearings, 90th Cong., 1st Sess. (1967).

Waks, Norman. "Selective Competition in New Air Weapon Procurement." Unpublished D.B.A. dissertation, Harvard Business School, 1961.

"Washington Roundup: A-8, Mate," *Aviation Week and Space Technology*, Vol. 103 (July 28, 1975), p. 13.

"Washington Roundup: Defense Buying," *Aviation Week and Space Technology*, Vol. 97 (August 28, 1972), p. 11.

"Washington Roundup: F-111B Weight Loss," *Aviation Week and Space Technology*, Vol. 85 (July 25, 1966), p. 25.

Weegham, Richard B. "The F-111: A Pilot's Verdict," *Flying*, Vol. 84 (May 1969), pp. S12–S16, 85.

———. "The Great Defense Nose Dive," *Air Progress*, Vol. 32 (January 1973), pp. 46–48.

Weidenbaum, Murray L. *The Economics of Peacetime Defense.* New York: Praeger, 1974.

Weiner, Sanford Louis. "Resource Allocation and Organizational Design in Basic Research." Unpublished A.B. thesis, Harvard College, 1971.

Weiss, George. "The F-111: The Swing-Wing May Surprise You Yet," *Armed Forces Journal*, Vol. 108 (July 19, 1971), pp. 22–25.

Wetmore, Warren C. "Fuel Pallets Increase Range of F-15A," *Aviation Week and Space Technology*, Vol. 101 (September 9, 1974), p. 39.

"What's Ahead," *Aerospace Daily*, February 14, 1972, p. 249.

White, William D. *U.S. Tactical Air Power: Missions, Forces, Costs.* Washington: Brookings Institution, 1974.

"William R. Laidlaw: Defense's F-111 Expert," *Armed Forces Management*, Vol. 13 (December 1966), p. 29.

Wilson, George C. "AMSA Goal Limits F-111 Bomber Design," *Aviation Week and Space Technology*, Vol. 83 (December 20, 1965), pp. 21–22.

————. "McClellan to Resume F-111 Investigation," *Aviation Week and Space Technology*, Vol. 85 (August 22, 1966), p. 17.

————. "Variable-Geometry F-4 Proposed to Navy," *Aviation Week and Space Technology*, Vol. 85 (July 11, 1966), pp. 30–31.

Winston, Donald C. "Navy Studies F-111B Offensive Missions," *Aviation Week and Space Technology*, Vol. 87 (October 23, 1967), p. 29.

————. "$350 Million F-111B Request Facing Congressional Struggle," *Aviation Week and Space Technology*, Vol. 88 (February 5, 1968), p. 22.

————. "New Round Seen in F-111B Fight," *Aviation Week and Space Technology*, Vol. 88 (March 11, 1968), pp. 16–17.

Witkin, Richard. "Air Force Waste on Parts Charged," *New York Times*, February 22, 1972, pp. 1, 11.

————. "Why the Flak Around the F-111?" *New York Times Magazine*, April 2, 1967, pp. 34–49.

Witze, Claude. "FB-111: Answer to Our Strategic Needs?" *Air Force and Space Digest*, Vol. 49 (January 1966), pp. 18, 21–22.

————. "The F-111's Mark II Avionics System—Weapons Effectiveness or Electronic Gadget?" *Air Force and Space Digest*, Vol. 52 (August 1969), pp. 62–65.

Yarmolinsky, Adam. *The Military Establishment: Its Impacts on American Society.* New York: Harper and Row, 1971.

Zuckert, Eugene. "The Service Secretary: Has He A Useful Role?" *Foreign Affairs*, Vol. 44 (April 1966), pp. 458–479.

413

INDEX

ad hoc committees: role of,
191–192
Advisory Committee on D6AC
Steel, 195
Aerospace Defense Command,
see Air Force
afterburner: backpressure problem, 180; described, 123n;
importance for conventional
missions, 123n; and power
curve on turbo-fan
engine, 250n
aircraft:
A-3: proposal weight ad-
justment, 239n; take-off
weight, 243n; weight
growth, 272n
A-4: product improve-
ments, 371n; proposal weight
adjustment, 239n; weight
growth, 272n
A-5: proposal weight ad-
justment, 239n; RA-5 take-
off weight, 243n; weight
growth, 272n
A-6: landing approach
speed, 289n; proposal weight
adjustment, 239n; weight
growth, 272n
A-7: Air Force acquisi-
tion and commonality, 252;
contrast to F-111B and F-4
programs, 330, 332–334;
formally evaluated deficiencies of, 287n; gun, 252, 257;
as hard option, 164n; landing
approach speed, 289n; original VAX requirement, 265–
267; origins of, 43, 53, 100;
take-off weight, 243n; VAX
as TFX alternative, 274;
VAX separated from TFX
negotiations, 100, 145
A-10: as hard option, 164n;

volume of documentation,
154n
B-1: General Dynamics'
proposal, 201
B-29: exceptional development organization, 351n
B-47: design evolution,
351; special status, 376
B-52: design evolution,
350–351; and FB-111, 69
B-58: and Convair ex-
perience, 62; volume of documentation, 154; and weapon
system-concurrency concept,
209, 353
B-70: and weapon system-
concurrency concept, 353
C-5A: Air Force support
of, 251; and contract management, 362n, 378n; costs
of problem resolution, 218n;
and McNamara's reputation,
379
F-3H-1: and concurrency,
213
F-4: 44, 47, 51, 122n, 247,
302–303; Air Force acquisition
of, 49, 103, 105, 141, 311–312;
benchmark for F-111B per-
formance, 280–281, 282;
contrast to A-7 and F-111B
programs, 331; flawed analogy to F-111B, 366n; as hard
option, 107, 164n, 166; landing wind-over-deck, 285;
product improvements, 371n;
proposal weight adjustment,
239n; take-off weight, 243n;
variable-sweep version proposed, 296; versus MIG-21 in
Vietnam, 136n; weight growth,
272n; wind-over-deck, comparative, 248
F-6D: cancellation, 53, 142;

415

of fixes, 327; pattern of behavior on F-111B, 237, 315; program study in 1962, 59–60; and redesign decisions, 269–270, 318–324; and SWIP, 243; and weapons duplication, 46–47, 98, 140, 362

and mission problems: analytic behavior in early TFX decisions, 141–142; cybernetic behavior in early TFX decisions, 143–145; decision for joint program, 98–100; efforts to deemphasize nuclear weapons, 45–46, 98, 138, 140; F-105 and F-111 decisions' contrast, 84; F-105 modification and termination, 48–49; inferences drawn from the deficiencies clause, 218–231, 233–234; Massive Retaliation, 47–48, 98; menu of proven alternatives, 107, 166; neglect of doctrinal goals in joint requirement, 54, 100–102; normal improvement expectations, 218–231, 233–234; realization of conventional mission trade-off, 71, 121; receives narrow advice on TFX decisions, 104–110, 141; response to service requirements, 50–52; summary of mission decisions of, 161–162; uncritical acceptance of Air Force requirement, 103; and VAX, 100, 145, 266–267

McNaughton, John: death before assuming office, 301n

Medium-Range Ballistic Missiles (MRBM), *see* missiles

Meehan, John D., 208

Memorandum of September 1, *see* Specific Operational Requirement 183

military power, *see* aircraft engines: turbo-fan

Millett, Thomas O., 208

Minuteman, *see* missiles

Missileer, *see* aircraft: F-6D

missiles: Atlas, 209–210, 357–358; contrast of ICBM and cruise missile programs, 358–359; cruise missiles construed to be routine, 354–356, 375; Eagle, 44; financial arrangements for ICBM programs, 357; ICBM design flexibility, 376n; ICBM loss of unique status, 359–360; ICBM programs as policy reforms, 375–376; Jupiter, 47; Matador, 47, 355; Minuteman, 209–210, 357–358; MRBM's threaten aircraft role, 91–92; Navaho, 355–356; Nike-Hercules, 47; Phoenix (*see* Phoenix); Polaris, 360, 387; Regulus, 47, 355; Skybolt, 251; Snark, 47, 355–356; Thor, 47, 209–210, 357–358; Titan, 209–210, 357–358; unique organization of ICBM programs, 356–359

mock-up inspection, 115

National Advisory Committee on Aeronautics, *see* National Aeronautics and Space Administration

National Aeronautics and Space Administration (NASA): 39, 40, 42, 52, 112, 120, 389; curtailment of aeronautical research by, 191, 197–198; and drag problem, 66–67, 321–322; and F-102 redesign, 155; involvement in requirements process, 343–344; judgment on F-111 feasibility, 83; reactivation of aeronautical research, 201; variable-sweep work, 39–40, 198–199; warnings on supersonic dash, 94, 96

Navaho, *see* missiles

Naval Air Systems Command: leverage over bi-service programs, 253n, 258

Navy: attack and fighter pilots, 279–281; avoidance of F-16 procurement, 253, 383n; and bi-service programs (*see* bi-

427

Library of Congress Cataloging in Publication Data

Coulam, Robert F.   1948–
  Illusions of choice.

  Bibliography: p.
  1. F-111 (Fighter planes)   2. United States—
Armed Forces—Procurement.   3. McNamara, Robert S.,
1916–   I. Title
UG1242.F5C68   358.4'3   76-24292
ISBN 0-691-07583-2